The BAPTISTS in SCOTLAND

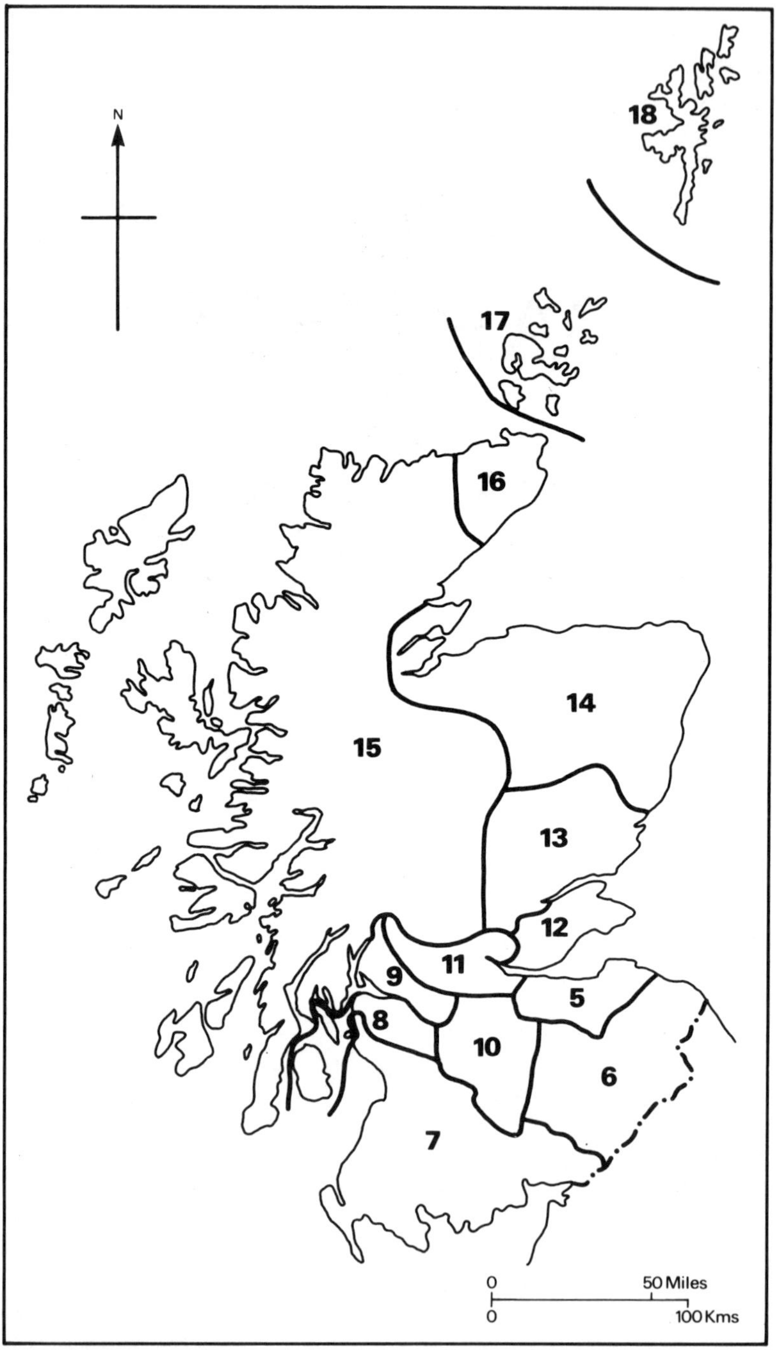

SCOTLAND: SHOWING AREAS COVERED BY CHAPTERS 5—18.

The Baptists in Scotland

A History

Edited by

D.W. Bebbington

Glasgow
The Baptist Union of Scotland
1988

Copies of this book are available from:

The Baptist Bookshop
12 Aytoun Road
Glasgow
G41 5RT
Scotland

British Library Cataloguing in Publication Data
The Baptists in Scotland.
1. Scotland. Baptist churches
I. Bebbington, D.W. (David William), 1949 –
II. Baptist Union of Scotland
286[1]. 1411

ISBN 0-901729-10-8

Printed by
Campsie Litho Ltd
51 French Street
Glasgow
G40 4EH

CONTENTS

CONTRIBUTORS

J.A. Andrew, M.A., A.R.I.C.S.
Chartered Surveyor
Member, Dumfries Baptist Church
Author of Chapter 7.

I.L.S. Balfour, M.A., LL.B., B.D., Ph.D., S.S.C., N.P.
Solicitor
Elder and Church Secretary, Charlotte Baptist Chapel, Edinburgh
Secretary, Scottish Baptist College
Law Agent and Member of Council, Baptist Union of Scotland
President of Baptist Union of Scotland, 1976-77
Author of Chapter 4.

J.R. Barclay, M.A., Dip. Ed., Dip. R.E., Dip. Acc., F.R.Met.S.
General Secretary, Edinburgh Medical Missionary Society
Church Secretary, Morningside Baptist Church, Edinburgh
Secretary, Scottish Baptist Men's Movement
Vice-Chairman of Council of Management, Atholl Baptist Centre, Pitlochry
Member of Council, Baptist Union of Scotland
Author of Chapter 5.

D.W. Bebbington, M.A., Ph.D., F.R.Hist.S.
Lecturer in History, University of Stirling
Deacon, Stirling Baptist Church
Secretary, Scottish Baptist History Project
Editor.

L.N. Cowan, M.A., C.Q.S.W.
Field Social Worker
Deacon, Larbert Baptist Church
Joint Author of Chapter 11.

G.R. Deyell
Crofter
Church Secretary, Sandsting Baptist Church
Author of Chapter 18.

J.S. Fisher, B.U. Dip.
Retired Civil Servant
Deacon, Inverness Baptist Church
Author of Chapter 14.

J.M. Gordon, M.A., Dip.Th.
Minister, Crown Terrace Baptist Church, Aberdeen
Chairman of Department of Church Life and Member of Executive, Baptist Union of Scotland
Author of Chapter 3.

Katherine M. Gordon
Housewife
Member (Minister's Wife), Kirkwall Baptist Church
Joint Author of Chapter 17.

S.D. Henry, M.A.
Principal Teacher of History, Lochgelly High School
Church Secretary, Leslie Baptist Church
Author of Chapter 12.

J.J. Johnston
Pastor, Wick Baptist Church
Member of Council, Baptist Union of Scotland
Author of Chapter 16.

K.W. McNeish, A.L.B.C.
Pastor, Hawick Baptist Church
Member of Council and of Doctrine and Inter-Church Relations Committee, Baptist Union of Scotland
Author of Chapter 6.

D.E. Meek, M.A., Ph.D., F.R.Hist.S.
Lecturer in Celtic, University of Edinburgh
Elder, Charlotte Baptist Chapel, Edinburgh
Joint Author of Chapter 2 and Author of Chapter 15.

D.B. Murray, M.A., B.D., Ph.D.
Chaplain, St. Columba's Hospice, Edinburgh
Formerly Minister of Dublin Street Baptist Church, Edinburgh
Lecturer and Member of Committee, Scottish Baptist College
Chairman, Scottish Baptist History Project
Author of Chapter 1 and Joint Author of Chapter 2.

J. Quinn, B.D.
Minister, Adelaide Place Baptist Church, Glasgow
Chaplain to Baptist Students, University of Strathclyde
Author of Chapter 13.

D.R. Reeves, M.A., M.Litt., Dip.Ed.
College Lecturer
Member, Johnstone Baptist Church
Author of Chapter 8.

J.W. Scott
Farmer
Secretary, Kirkwall Baptist Church
Joint Author of Chapter 17.

Margaret A. Scott
Schoolteacher
Member (Church Secretary's Wife), Westray Baptist Church
Joint Author of Chapter 17.

D.R. Watts, B.A., M.Phil., M.R.T.P.I.
Economic Development Officer
Member, Chawn Hill Evangelical Church, Stourbridge
Formerly Deacon, Bearsden Baptist Church
Formerly Chairman, Social Responsibility Core Group, Baptist Union of Scotland
Author of Chapters 9 and 10.

F.C. Wright
Missionary, Baptist Missionary Society
Formerly Minister, Denny Baptist Church
Formerly Member of Council, Baptist Union of Scotland
Joint Author of Chapter 11.

MAPS

MAP SYMBOLS

Maps 5.1, 5.2, 9.2 and 10 carry their own tables of symbols.

On the other maps, symbols are used with the following meanings:

● Churches now in existence

○ Churches now closed

◉ Fellowships not yet constituted as churches

◇ Temporary preaching stations

FIGURES

INTRODUCTION

In Glasgow on a fund-raising tour for the Baptist Missionary Society in 1802, Andrew Fuller, the society's first secretary, told the members of a church there that he had heard of 'the baptists in Scotland being negligent of free preaching to the unconverted'. Consequently he 'earnestly exhorted them to make it evidently appear that they were far more anxious that those around them should become Christians than that they should embrace our opinion as to baptism'.[1] Previously the socalled Scotch Baptists, the chief grouping in the land that accepted believer's baptism by immersion, had been so scrupulous in defining New Testament principles of church order that they had placed relatively little emphasis on spreading the gospel. From Fuller's time evangelism increasingly became the settled priority of Baptists in Scotland. It has remained so up to the late twentieth century. The Great Commission of Jesus to make disciples has rung in their ears. Baptists have stood in the Evangelical tradition.

They possess all the hallmarks of Evangelicalism. Firstly, they are conversionist. They believe that nobody is automatically a Christian. A person must have his life changed by receiving the gospel. Secondly, they are activist. They think it essential to spread the faith. One of only three statements in the Declaration of Principle of the Baptist Union of Scotland is 'That it is the duty of every disciple to bear witness to the Gospel of Jesus Christ, and to take part in the evangelization of the world'.[2] Thirdly, they are biblicist. They insist that the Bible is the authoritative source of the Christian message. Preaching and devotion alike are moulded by the scriptures. Fourthly, their teaching is crucicentric. The cross is their chief theological preoccupation. The primary content of the gospel, they hold, is that Christ died for our sins. Ever since the beginning of the nineteenth century, these four features have been as characteristic of Baptists as of other Evangelical Christians in Scotland and elsewhere.[3]

Yet within the Evangelical community Baptists have held certain distinctive convictions. Primary is their doctrine of the church. Only true believers, they claim, should be members of a Christian community. Before conversion, a person has no qualification for church membership. Hence Baptists enquire into the religious experience of applicants for admission to the church, receiving only those who can make a credible profession of Christian allegiance. This is the principle of the gathered church: believers are gathered into fellowships from the rest of society. Further, they practise congregational church government. Each church member has a share in determining the policy of the fellowship. Supreme authority for discerning the will of Jesus Christ is therefore vested in the church meeting, the assembly of all members for business purposes. While it is true that the role of the church meeting has sometimes been eclipsed by strong leaders, only rarely has the membership not in theory held ultimate responsibility for decision-making.

The other principle of church order cherished by Baptists is the independence of the local church. Each congregation, once constituted as a separate body, has liberty to interpret the will of Christ for itself. No external ecclesiastical body possesses authority over a local church. It is therefore inaccurate to speak of the denomination as 'the Baptist Church'. There are only Baptist Churches. Whether large, like Charlotte Chapel in Edinburgh with 908 members, or tiny, like Lunnasting in Shetland with three, each separate congregation is autonomous.[4] Yet Baptist Churches have normally enjoyed a formal connection with each other, whether through the Home Mission (until 1971), District Associations or (since 1869) the Baptist Union of Scotland. All three have played an important role in home evangelism, doing what individual churches would find it difficult to do alone.

The practice that gave Baptists their name is believer's baptism. The principles enumerated so far have equally been held by Congregationalists, but in their early days Baptists were unique in rejecting the baptism of infants. They did not claim that baptism was for adults alone, but for believers alone. They discovered in the New Testament that the act of baptism in all the clearly recorded cases takes place after the coming of faith. Thus they were prepared to baptize young people as well as adults if they showed evidence of conversion. Further, Baptists have normally insisted that immersion rather than sprinkling is the proper mode of baptism. This dramatic method of Christian initiation is at once a factor limiting the quantity of church growth and a factor encouraging its quality. The superficially committed hesitate before so public a demonstration of allegiance. The barrier of believer's baptism helps ensure a measure of real conviction among church members.

Baptist Churches have usually, since the later nineteenth century in Scotland, been served by professionally trained ministers. No task, however, has been restricted to ministers. Lay preaching and lay presidency at communion have been quite acceptable. Although formal recognition of full-time female ministry was rejected by the 1985 assembly of the Baptist Union, women preach in a number of churches and have held pastoral oversight in the past.[5] The minister or pastor —the terms are interchangeable — of a church has normally been assisted by a number of deacons, people chosen by the congregation for leadership. In Scotland, perhaps on the analogy of the Presbyterian practice of ordaining elders for life, Baptist deacons commonly hold office until death or resignation.

There have been variations among Baptists in both practice and doctrine. Originally they restricted communion to those baptized as believers, but gradually the Lord's Table came to be open in nearly all churches to any sincere Christian. Frequently the transition in the nineteenth century away from closed communion occasioned disputes. A number of churches took the further step of opening membership to those not baptized as believers, usually with safeguards about the views of the minister and deacons. Unlike in England, however, this pattern did not prevail, and recently founded churches have normally upheld closed membership.[6]

Baptists of all types in early nineteenth-century Scotland were Calvinists in doctrine. Although Scotch Baptists adopted certain distinctive views, their overall theological scheme was Calvinistic, stressing the sovereignty of God in salvation.[7] The Arminian theology of the General Baptists in England gained no more than a foothold.[8] The views of James Morison, founder of the Evangelical Union in Scotland, at once more liberal and more revivalist than Calvinism, made a greater impact.[9] Moody and Sankey encouraged a drift of opinion in the same direction.[10] In the twentieth century the denomination was firmly in the Conservative Evangelical camp. It generated its own Fundamentalist controversy in the 1940s along lines similar to those that divided many American Protestants in the 1920s and even more similar to the rift among the Southern Baptists of the USA in the 1980s.[11]

Baptists form a worldwide confessional body, most of them being linked through the Baptist World Alliance founded in 1905. What particular features have marked out Baptists in Scotland? No legacy has survived from the Baptists of the Commonwealth period in the mid-seventeenth century. The earliest Baptist Church to have continued to this day, the cause at Keiss in Caithness (1750), introduced a number of distinctive elements, but its geographical isolation prevented its example from being copied elsewhere.[12]

It is the so-called Scotch Baptists, and especially their theologian Archibald McLean, who made the influential innovations. The Scotch Baptists copied certain New Testament practices like footwashing and the love-feast. More significantly, they taught that each church must possess a plurality of elders. The elders functioned as a team of co-pastors. Like other distinctive features of the Scotch Baptists, multiple leadership was steadily eroded during the nineteenth century. No church in Scotland retains this form of church order, although it is still maintained by ten Welsh-speaking churches in North Wales and by Brierfield Baptist Church in Lancashire.[13] One legacy of the Scotch Baptists, however, does survive in the general custom of observing the Lord's Supper weekly. Another Baptist grouping, the followers of the Haldanes, did the same and Baptist preferences must have been reinforced by the practice of the Brethren. Yet the prevalence of weekly communion among Baptists in Scotland, which contrasts with its normal observance fortnightly south of the border, goes back to the foundation of McLean's first church in Edinburgh in 1765.

Recent research has established that religious Dissent has been much more powerful in Scotland than has often been supposed. In the 1790s, for instance, more than 70% of the adult population of Jedburgh worshipped outside the Established Church. Most Dissenters remained Presbyterians, attending either the Secession or the Relief Church. In the 1830s, before the Disruption created the Free Church of Scotland, 30% of worshippers in Edinburgh and 27% in Glasgow were Presbyterian Dissenters. Methodism was weak in Scotland, except in Shetland, but the Independents (also called Congregationalists) could claim 4% of Scottish churchgoers at the time of the government census of religion in 1851. It was in this atmosphere of vigorous religious pluralism that Baptists made their early advances. By 1851 they had gained the allegiance of about 1% of Scottish churchgoers.[14] Over a century later, in 1984, when there was a Bible Society census, Baptists attracted about 3% of adult church attenders.[15]

Previous work on the Baptists provides a foundation on which this volume rests. A history of the Scotch Baptists was published as early as 1844.[16] In the same year there also appeared a survey of the Baptist Churches in Scotland as part of the work of the short-lived Baptist Union of that period.[17] It included a small measure of historical information, as did the annual *Reports* and *Year Books* published by the Baptist Union after its firm establishment in 1869. The standard work has been the *History of the Baptists in Scotland*, issued by the Baptist Union in 1926. The volume was by many hands but welded together by George Yuille, the retired secretary of the Union. Especially in the entries on individual churches, which were submitted by the churches themselves, it contains a body of information and self-understanding that can never be superseded. In the following year James Scott, soon to become secretary of the Union, gained a doctorate with a dissertation on the history of Baptists in Scotland.[18] There, for a long time, matters rested.

The centenary of the Union in 1969 stimulated a renewed interest in the past. Derek Murray, a contributor to this volume, wrote a masterly summary of the history of the Union entitled *The First Hundred Years*.[19] He contributed an article to *The Baptist Quarterly* on Baptists in Scotland before 1869 and went on to study the Scotch Baptists against their background in a doctoral dissertation.[20] Fergus Little conducted a survey of records relating to Baptists in Scotland on which he reported in *The Baptist Quarterly*.[21] Dudley Reeves, another contributor to this book, included considerable material on the Baptists in a dissertation on relations between Scottish and English Evangelicals around 1800 and in a number of associated articles.[22] A short history of Baptists in Scotland from a Reformed and anti-ecumenical viewpoint was issued in 1983.[23] In the same year David Watts published a study of Baptist church growth in Glasgow in a collection of papers on *Baptists in the Twentieth Century*.[24] Two years later there appeared an essay on Scottish Baptists and the First World War by Sam Henry.[25] The last two were the firstfruits in print of the Scottish Baptist History Project, which since 1979 has held twice-yearly meetings under the chairmanship of Derek Murray. It is the Project that has produced this work.

Other writings on the Baptists in Scotland include a number of biographies, church histories and articles over the years in *The Scottish Baptist Magazine*. They will remain a quarry for the historian of this subject. Beyond them lie newspapers, which frequently carried reports of Baptist affairs, and church records, often remarkably full. Although some are kept by the Baptist Union or in public repositories, most remain in the possession of individual churches. Their extreme importance as a primary source makes it welcome to note that they are at present being professionally surveyed and listed under the auspices of the National Register of Archives (Scotland). From such material a great deal more waits to be learned.

The present book includes two types of chapter. The first four chapters analyze the major developments affecting Baptists in Scotland in specific periods. Against the background of broad socio-economic change, the writers have outlined the main trends in Baptist thought and practice. The remaining fourteen chapters concentrate on the various areas of Scotland depicted in the frontispiece. Each chapter considers why the churches in its area have grown or declined over the whole time of their existence. For Baptists this must be a central question. They believe in the importance of the individual congregation and in the priority of evangelism. Study of an area permits both consideration of the work of each church and comparison between churches in similar socio-economic settings. It is likely to be an illuminating approach for those who wish to understand the reasons for church growth.

What answers emerge? It is clear that economic growth favours church extension work among Baptists, both by creating concentrations of population sufficient to sustain a church and by supplying the finance that is needed, especially for land purchase and building maintenance.[26] When prosperity wanes, conversely, the departure of the people can seriously handicap church work.[27] In the early industrial period, repeatedly it was the independent artisans of the growing urban areas who formed the pool from which Baptists, like other Dissenters, were drawn in large numbers.[28] New centres of population, whether in New Towns or places of fresh industrial development, have provided some of the most fertile soil for Baptist growth since the Second World War.[29] Baptists have by no means been confined to the towns,[30] but with the increasing urbanization of Scotland their main strength has come to be concentrated there. The ability to identify areas of economic and demographic growth and to turn them into areas of church growth has been one of the chief reasons for Baptist success.

Repeatedly chapters identify a willingness to change as a condition of growth. A preparedness to abandon old ways and old buildings is isolated as the key reason for the relative effectiveness of urban mission in and around Glasgow.[31] Adaptability is often a consequence of able leadership, which several chapters recognize as a crucial factor in Christian work.[32] Individual ministries can make all the difference between a sharp increase and a steady ebb in membership.[33] Team leadership has sometimes served Baptists well.[34] A nucleus of committed members is also a virtual precondition for making an impact on a neighbourhood.[35] Their morale is important. Dissension normally weakens churches, though division may also lead, in favourable circumstances, to further growth.[36] To aim for consensus in change must be one of the chief goals in Baptist church life.

It is clear that without the strictly spiritual factors churches would not have grown. The wave of revivalism stemming from 1859 led to a significant increase in the number and strength of Baptist causes, just as it benefited the Brethren.[37] The Welsh Revival of 1904-5 likewise affected Baptists in Scotland.[38] More recently charismatic renewal has reinvigorated certain churches.[39] A dedication to prayer helped to prepare for some of the more spectacular outbursts of vitality.[40] There was also a persistence in evangelistic ventures, whether open-air rallies, gospel tea meetings, house-to-house visitation or Billy Graham Crusades.[41] Much of the evangelism was co-ordinated through the Home Mission, the associations or the Union. Only because of help from outside, especially with personnel, did many causes take root or blossom.[42] Conversely the lack of external assistance goes a long way towards explaining the blanks on the map of Baptist witness in Scotland past and present.[43] Mutual support, itself perhaps a spiritual factor among independent churches, was a significant element in growth.

As a result of all these factors, Baptists have established a presence in most parts of Scotland. The latest available figures, showing changes in membership between 1985 and 1986, are instructive about area strength. The three associations reporting a decreased membership over that year were Glasgow, Lanarkshire and the South-West. In the depressed industrial heartland of the west of Scotland (the South-West includes north Ayrshire), Baptists were not, overall, making advances. Another group of associations had increased their membership by no more than five: Argyllshire and the Isles, Dunbartonshire, Fife, Shetland and the non-association churches of Caithness and Orkney. This almost static group encompassed two counties in the central belt together with the remotest parts of the land. A third group had improved by no more than twenty-four: Angus and Perthshire, Borders, Central and Renfrewshire. These areas, mingling industrial and agricultural employment, were able to make some progress. The two outstanding associations for growth, however, were Edinburgh and Lothians, which reported 148 extra members, and Northern, with 63. The churches in and around the capital and the oil-rich north-east registered the greatest success. It was the year when, for the first time since records began, Edinburgh surpassed Glasgow in its Baptist strength.[44] That may be one of the most significant shifts in the history of the Baptists in Scotland.

It remains to thank all those who have helped in the preparation of this book. The contributors, often busy people, have responded cheerfully to suggestions from the editor. All were in membership of Baptist Churches in Scotland at the time of writing their chapters. Particular thanks go to Donald Meek and Derek Murray, who took over responsibility for chapter 2 at a late stage and contributed in many other invaluable ways. Miss Christine Lumsden gave major assistance in the collection of statistics and the Rev. and Mrs A.T. Peck dug out information for distant contributors from the records of the Baptist Union. Miss Margaret Hendry of the Department of History, University of Stirling, gave unstinting secretarial support. Mrs M.J. Lacey and Mrs Eileen Bebbington prepared the index and Mrs Rachel Meek was an expert proof reader. Mr Ray Harris of the Department of Geography, University of Edinburgh, prepared the maps, Mr Norman McNeish of Campsie Marketing eagerly undertook the printing and the Rev. Robert Armstrong, Publications Secretary of the Baptist Union, gave advice and support. The Rev. Peter Barber and Mr Ian Bremner, General Secretary and Treasurer of the Baptist Union respectively, endorsed the enterprise and recommended its publication to the executive and council of the Union. A loan from the Union has helped to make the book possible. Another loan from the Whitley Lectureship, also essential for publication, is gratefully acknowledged. Charlotte Baptist Chapel, Edinburgh, generously paid the cost of producing the maps. The Baptist Historical Society made a spontaneous contribution to expenses. It is hoped that the resulting volume will prove an instructive analysis of the Christian mission undertaken by Baptists in Scotland.

Notes

1. Fuller to Mrs Fuller, 25 Sept. 1802, in A.G. Fuller, 'Memoirs of the Rev. Andrew Fuller', *The Complete Works of the Rev. Andrew Fuller*, 5 vols (London 1831), I p cxvi.
2. *Scottish Baptist Year Book (SBYB)*, 1987, p 8.
3. See D.W. Bebbington, 'The Gospel in the Nineteenth Century', *Vox Evangelica*, 13 (1983), pp 19–28.
4. *SBYB*, 1987, pp 131, 143.
5. See cap 4, pp 85-6, cap 14, p 273, and cap 15, p 298.
6. See esp cap 4, p 85.

7. See cap 1, pp 21-2.
8. See cap 2, n 67, and cap 11, p 201.
9. See cap 2, pp 39-40, and cap 8, p 153.
10. See cap 3, pp 54-5.
11. See cap 4, p 74.
12. See cap 1, pp 15-16.
13. See D.W. Bebbington in *The Ministry Today* (Baptist Union of Scotland Viewpoint Booklet, Glasgow 1984), pp 30-4. *Brierfield Baptist Chapel: centenary, 1886-1986* (Brierfield 1986).
14. C.G. Brown, *The Social History of Religion in Scotland since 1730* (London 1987), p 61. I am grateful to Dr Brown for allowing me to read the text of his innovative book before publication. It should be noted, however, that the classification of Baptists in the book as Presbyterian Dissenters is misleading.
15. Peter Brierley and Fergus Macdonald, *Prospects for Scotland: report of the 1984 census of the churches* (Bromley, Kent, 1985), p 44.
16. Patrick Wilson, *The Origin and Progress of the Scots Baptist Churches from their Rise in 1765 to 1834* (Edinburgh 1844).
17. *First Yearly Report of the Baptist Union of Scotland* (Cupar 1844).
18. James Scott, 'The Baptists of Scotland: an historical survey' (Glasgow PhD 1927).
19. D.B. Murray, *The First Hundred Years: the Baptist Union of Scotland* (Glasgow 1969).
20. D.B. Murray, 'Baptists in Scotland before 1869', *Baptist Quarterly*, 23 (1970), pp 251-65. Murray, 'The Social and Religious Origins of Scottish Non-Presbyterian Dissent from 1730 to 1800' (St Andrews PhD 1977).
21. F.G. Little, 'Historical Registers of Scottish Baptists', *Baptist Quarterly*, 24 (1972), pp 229-32.
22. D.R. Reeves, 'The Interaction of Scottish and English Evangelicals, 1790-1810' (Glasgow MLitt 1973).
23. W.J. Seaton, *A Short History of Baptists in Scotland* (Dunstable, Beds, 1983).
24. David Watts, 'Baptists in Glasgow: the twentieth-century challenge of urban growth and decline', in K.W. Clements, ed, *Baptists in the Twentieth Century* (London 1983).
25. S.D. Henry, 'Scottish Baptists and the First World War', *Baptist Quarterly*, 31 (1985), pp 52-65.
26. See, e.g., cap 10, p 187-8, cap 16, p 315, cap 13, p 245.
27. See, e.g., cap 12, p 228-30, cap 15, p 291-2.
28. See cap 1, p 17-18. cf Brown, *Social History*, pp 148-50, 154-7.
29. See, e.g., cap 5, p 106, cap 10, pp 193-4, cap 18, p 333.
30. See, e.g., cap 13, p 240-1, cap 15, *passim*
31. See cap 9, p 183.
32. See, e.g., cap 8, pp 147-9, cap 13, pp 242-4, cap 18, pp 327-30.
33. See, e.g., cap 12, p 220.
34. See, e.g., cap 14, p 276, cap 17, p 319-20.
35. See, e.g., cap 7, p 142, cap 13, p 256.
36. See, e.g., cap 17, p 320-1, cap 8, p 153.
37. See, e.g., cap 6, p 120-1, cap 14, p 266-8. cf F.R. Coad, *A History of the Brethren Movement* (Exeter 1968), pp 172-3.
38. See, e.g., cap 11, p 207, cap 14, p 271.
39. See cap 4, pp 77-8, cap 5, p 109.
40. See, e.g., cap 5, p 103, cap 6, p 120.
41. See cap 3, pp 59-61, cap 4, pp 70-73.
42. See, e.g., cap 10, p 188-9, cap 12, p 224-5, cap 15, pp 285-6, 301.
43. See cap 7, pp 136-8.
44. *SBYB*, 1987, p 35.

D.W. Bebbington

Airthrey, near Stirling
June 1987.

1. THE SEVENTEENTH AND EIGHTEENTH CENTURIES

It has been truly remarked that Scottish Baptists lack the Great Tradition of their brothers and sisters in the faith south of the border. There is no memory of troubles and persecutions going back to the seventeenth century, no history of the slow acquisition of full rights of citizenship, no tradition of ejectment and suffering. The Covenanters, who may be said to correspond to Nonconformists in Scotland, were in no way friendly to Independency or to the Baptists. It was for pure Presbyterianism that they suffered. With the exception of a lone church in Caithness, the origin of the present denomination is to be found in the latter part of the eighteenth century, and these 'Scotch' Baptists left a tradition that has been overlaid by later developments.

To understand the Scottish dimension of Baptist history, and the late and slow growth of Baptist Churches on Scottish soil, we must begin by looking briefly at the course of the Reformation in the sixteenth century. In the middle of the century the Calvinist form of Protestantism propounded by John Knox and others displaced earlier Lutheran influence, and took firm root, especially in the towns and among the lesser nobility. The process of changing Scotland into a Reformed realm was long and complex. The pivotal date is 1560, when the Reformed Confession of Faith was accepted by Parliament. For more than a century there was tension between church and state, and between Presbyterianism and Episcopalianism, and in 1690, after many changes, a relatively moderate Presbyterianism became the faith of all but a few Scots, or at least of their ministers. The Revolution Settlement excluded only extreme Covenanters, the inhabitants of some Catholic areas in the north and west, and a remnant of Episcopalians, who remained unreconciled until their deaths.

During this period all the institutions and practices of the church were subjected to scrutiny, and the mass was replaced by the communion. Baptism was no longer seen as effecting salvation but as the sign and seal of the love and choosing of God. 'By baptism we are engrafted in Christ Jesus, to be made partakers of His justice, whereby our sins are covered and remitted.'[1] The Reformers did not confine the subjects of baptism to believers, and John Knox, alarmed by the bad name that continental Anabaptists had acquired, had written to his brethren in 1557 to warn them of their dangerous and horrible excesses. The Scots Confession of 1560 reads: 'We confess and acknowledge that Baptisme apperteineth alswell to the infants of the faithfull as to those who are of age and discretioun. And we dampne the errour of the anabaptistes who deny baptisme to apperteine to children befoir that thei have faith and understanding.'[2]

With a popular national church appealing to scripture, and with the gradual fusion of Scottishness with Presbyterianism, there was little room for Independency in Scotland, and Baptist principles were even less acceptable. In 1584 the English Independent Robert Brown landed at Dundee from Holland, possibly expecting sympathy from fellow opponents of Episcopacy. Although he was received kindly at first, he soon had to flee again, after he had the temerity to address the presbytery of Edinburgh on the over-severity of its discipline. Between 1588 and 1590 another Independent pioneer, Robert Penry, found shelter in Scotland, but there is no evidence that he was able to make converts.

In the early seventeenth century reports appear of conventicles. In 1624, in Edinburgh, there were 'divers sects, such as Brownists, Waderdowpers (or Watterdippers) and such like'.[3] There were similar reports from Stirling and Aberdeen. Works by Puritan theologians undoubtedly came into Scotland at this period, but Scottish divines were unreceptive to ideas from Independents.

The Commonwealth Period

On 3 September 1650 Cromwell's army defeated the Scots at Dunbar, and the cause of Charles II was at an end for ten years. During the next eighteen months the armies of the Commonwealth occupied the whole country, bringing it into a close union with England, and struggling with the obduracy and divisions of the Scottish church. Many of the soldiers and chaplains of Cromwell's armies were Independents and Baptists, and they brought their ideas and ways of worship with them. There was a false dawn of Baptist life which faded quite suddenly at the end of the decade, after the death of Oliver Cromwell, and which was quite extinguished with the return of the Stewart monarchy in 1660.

In the short time given to them, the Cromwellian Baptists did notable things. A Declaration of Toleration of those who were not Presbyterian, but 'behaved themselves peaceably and innoffensively', was promulgated at Dalkeith on 15 January 1652, and the ministers of the Kirk were quick to object. Stranger things were to follow. 'This yeir [1653] Anabaptistes daylie increst in this natioun, quhair nevir name was of befoir, at leist durst not evow thameselffis: bot now many made oppin professioun thairof and avowit the same; sa that thryse in the oulk, viz. on Monday, Weddinsday, and Fryday thair wer sum dippit at Bonyngtoun mylne betwixt Leith and Edinburgh, both men and women of guid rank. Sum dayis thair wald be sundried hundreth persones attending that actioun, and fyftene persones baptized in one day by the Anabaptistes.'[4] So wrote Nicoll in his diary for February 1653.

There are several references to Baptist mission in Scotland in the records of the church at Hexham. 'The twentieth day of the tenth month 1652, the church, with prayer, fasting and the imposition of hands of the minister, ordained brother Hickhorngill a minister and their messenger into Scotland.'[5] In the few letters preserved Hickhorngill writes of the differences of opinion concerning payment of ministers, and of his kind reception at Leith and Perth. He tells the church at Hexham of 'divers honest Scotch people that long to be gathered into the same gospel order with us, but they want a faithful pastor'.[6] By April 1653 Hickhorngill is referred to as 'our sometime precious, but now alas deluded brother' and Thomas Stackhouse has taken his place at Leith. The church in Leith republished a London Confession of Faith in 1653.[7]

Some parish ministers seem to have taken up a Baptist position, although it is not always easy to distinguish between Baptists and Independents. Nicoll records in May 1652, 'Lykewyse ane Mr Alexander Cornwell, minister at or beyonde Lynlithgow, quha did marry pepill privily . . . Also ane callet Thomas Charteris, minister at Stanehous, maintaining Anabaptisme, wald not baptise infants.'[8] This Charteris is mentioned as the minister of East Kilbride in the *Fasti*.[9] He was admitted from Stanehouse around 1653, when he ministered to a congregation of Independents or Anabaptists. He is said to have occupied much of his time in the business of horse-trading.

At Cupar in Fife, another garrison town of the Cromwellian army, Baptist teaching gave the presbytery some trouble, and in its records we have a glimpse of a genuine native community of believers. In July 1656 the presbytery met at 'Sires' (Ceres): 'This day a reference from the Sessioun of Cupar is presented to the Presbyterie, craveing advice what shall be done with these women that ar dipped.'[10] In November those women were summoned to appear before the presbytery. They were named as Elspeth, Isobel and Christian Miller, and they duly appeared on 1 January 1657. 'The moderator Questioned them, if they did owne ther baptisme in ther infancie? Answered that they did not owne it. 2 They maintained that Christ died for all intentionally. 3 That the soul sleeps with the body till the Resurrection. 4 that saints and true believers may fall away from true saving grace. 5 that the doctrine of election is not absolute. They grant that the Spirit of God is irresistible; which tenents were contradictorie.'[11] After due process, pleading and reasoning, in July 1658, 'The Presbytery having considered the whole process concerning C.M., who hath rejected and made defection from the doctrine, worship, discipline and government of the Kirk of Scotland, and hath not only turned to the Anabaptisticall way, but hath also drunk therewith all the Arminian errors . . . will excommunicate her.'[12] Arminian doctrine, focusing on the belief that Christ died for all, made these Baptists especially unwelcome. Their treatment was drastic, and it is not surprising that another Anabaptist couple, William Thomson and his wife Isobel Webster, submitted to have their four-year-old child baptized publicly, having repented their Anabaptism.

Army chaplains were much involved in debates with ministers in these stirring times, and records of several disputations of James Brown, a chaplain in Fairfax's regiment, have survived. In 1652 he debated with James Wood in Cupar Kirk on the doctrines of original sin, infant baptism and limited atonement. 'Mr Wood had the far best of both dayes, bot Browne wold not be conuinced', wrote a contemporary diarist.[13] Brown baptized several of his regiment in the River Eden during that month. James Guthrie was a noted minister of the Protester or extreme Presbyterian faction, and Brown chose him for his next encounter. There were several debates at Stirling in 1652, when the subjects were original sin, free will, toleration and, especially, limited atonement. To Brown, the infant was born without sin, and could choose evil or good, while Guthrie held that there is a seed of evil in each child. 'Mr James Guthrie in a public disputation in the Church at Stirling did to the conviction of all overthrow one of the chief ringleaders of the Anabaptistes,' wrote a contemporary.[14] But Brown was not content to accept such a verdict and returned to the fray later in the year. In January 1653 he was recalled to England.

The Baptists for the most part brought what seemed an alien creed as well as an alien practice to Scotland. They finally left during political trouble. In January 1654 they were alleged to be involved in a plot against the city of Edinburgh, and to vindicate their loyalty submitted to government a document described as 'The Humble Address of the Baptized Churches, consisting of officers, soldiers and others, walking in gospell order at Leith, Edinburgh, and St Johnstoune'.[15] Reports were sent to England about the activities of the Anabaptists and Quakers of Leith, and in the general atmosphere of unrest and suspicion, the causes dwindled. Some Baptists were involved with the 'Fifth Monarchy' movement and perhaps some were truly subversive. General Monk, effectively the governor of Scotland, lumped them all together and in 1658 they were purged from the army and from public office in Scotland. The brief episode had ended, toleration was withdrawn, and in 1672 the law that every child must be presented for baptism within thirty days of birth received the royal assent.

We have one little picture of what might have been. Lady Craigie is said to have been amongst those baptized at Bonnington, and we meet her in old age living with her son at Gradoun near Berwick. In the diary of Andrew Hay of Craignethan she appears as 'ane anabaptiste and a great entertainer of Quakers and is like to be a snare to these young folk, if God prevent it not'.[16] On his next visit to Gradoun he writes, 'Ther I met the Lady Craigie, whom I find very sharp, but exceeding perverse in her opinion of anabaptisme.'[17] Lady Craigie died in November 1663, 'in the assurance of mercy and faith thro' Christ Jesus'.[18] Perhaps there were others like her, who have disappeared from history. There is no doubting the zeal of the Cromwellian soldiers and their chaplains, and the small progress the Baptist cause made can be attributed to the strong position of the national church, to distaste for a conqueror's religion and to the firm opposition shown to Anabaptism by Scottish divines from John Knox onwards.

The Origins of Non-Presbyterian Protestant Dissent

When Baptists reappear in Scotland in the middle of the eighteenth century they may be regarded as part of a native religious movement, which, although it saw itself as indebted to English Independency, nevertheless had a history and theology of its own. After the Revolution Settlement of 1690, when the Established Church finally adopted Presbyterianism, there was a gradual turning away from the rigours of the Covenanting period. Scotland, especially after its Parliament was united with that of England in 1707, grew in economic strength, and in contact with the common heritage of European culture. The 'Moderate' ministers strove to become men of polite learning and good manners, and the rough edges of church discipline and doctrinal preaching were smoothed away. Although the edifice of Calvinism remained intact, much more emphasis was placed on morality and good behaviour. In 1712 the right of laymen, as patrons of the parishes, to appoint ministers was reintroduced, and this gave rise to many unpopular settlements and local discontents.

The story of the eighteenth-century secessions from the Church of Scotland has often been told in all its intriguing detail. The first Secession in the 1730s, associated with the Erskine brothers, drew off much of the zeal for old-fashioned piety and discipline into self-supporting and sometimes easily-divided congregations. In 1751 Gillespie of Carnock was deposed for objecting to forced settlements, and soon the Relief Presbytery was formed. These alternative churches, together with the remnants of the extreme Covenanters, now organized as the Reformed Presbyterian Church, provided places of worship and devotion within the Presbyterian framework.

The earliest Scottish Independency can be traced to another small secession, that of the followers of John Glas of Tealing. From them came the Scotch Baptists, who drew from their former associates many of the unusual tenets and features of church life that characterized them. Glas was born in the manse at Auchtermuchty in 1695, and was destined to be the fifth in an unbroken line of ministers in his family. After his studies, he was settled in Tealing, near Dundee, in 1719. The parish was disturbed by arguments about the Covenants, and Glas was forced to examine his views of Christ's kingdom. Gradually and reluctantly he came to the conclusion that the kingdom of Christ is purely spiritual, and as such is independent of state control, sanction and support. At the same time he became convinced that the church is a body composed of true believers who possess a real knowledge of saving grace, separated from the world. He gathered at Tealing some seventy folk who walked together in brotherly love and submitted themselves to Glas's discipline.

In 1725 the most influential of his many works, *The Testimony of the King of Martyrs*, was published. To practise Independency did not by itself lead to expulsion from the Church of Scotland, for Henry Davidson of Galashiels and Gabriel Wilson of Maxton met with like-minded folk on sabbath evenings in Maxton in the 1730s, and were expressly allowed to do this by the presbytery. But John Glas, combative, and gathering support, was more of a threat. After a tortuous and widely discussed series of cases in church courts he was deposed in 1730 by the Commission of Assembly. Only one other minister, Francis Archibald of Guthrie, was deposed with him, but he had some support in the church at large.

Glas moved to Dundee and there ministered to a small group of supporters, some of whom had come with him from Tealing. Soon there was a church in Arbroath, and then in 1733 in Perth, where the Sandeman family began their long association with the church. Robert Sandeman married Glas's daughter, and became the chief writer and publicist of the movement, which spread to various towns in Scotland, and to England and New England.

The Glasite Church developed from the study of the scriptures a number of interesting practices and beliefs which were to influence Scotch Baptists. Both in the adoption of weekly communion and in the use made of 'unlearned preachers', Glas pointed the way to later movements. Elders might not be learned, but they were an essential part of the church, and for the due ordering of the congregation there must be more than one. The Scotch Baptists were to follow this practice, and also learnt from the Glasites that the scriptures enjoined the washing of feet and the kiss of charity at appropriate times. For members coming a distance a meal between services was useful, and in the Glasite tradition it became obligatory as a time of intimate fellowship among the members. Strict abstention from the eating of blood and things strangled was enforced, and the principle of unanimity in all decisions led to many disfellowshippings.

In theology Glas was a Calvinist, firmly convinced of the doctrines of election and of saving grace. His view of faith was, however, unusual, for he held that there was a danger of confusing faith with its effects. He and his followers defined faith as a bare belief in the facts of the gospel, and excluded feelings and fruits. This intellectualist idea of faith must have appealed to those who were tired of looking for signs and motions of the heart, and who had been the victims of over-emotional preaching of the gospel. Glas and Sandeman offered a simple, unfussy view of gospel truth, and a church life regulated in all its details. As the years went by, Glas led his churches further into isolation from other Christians, and their exclusiveness and reluctance to evangelize make their survival to the present day the more remarkable.[19]

John Glas died in 1773.[20] In the decade before his death there was renewed interest in his writings, and two new movements arose that were influenced by him. In Fife, in 1768 James Smith of Newburn and Robert Ferrier of Largo resigned their parishes, influenced by reading Sandeman's *Letters on Theron and Aspasio*. They began to hold meetings at Balchrystie, on the border between their former parishes, and they published their reasons for secession in *The Case of James Smith and Robert Ferrier truly represented and defended*.[21] At the same time in Glasgow the remarkable industrialist David Dale had with others left the parish church and set up a chapel of ease which in 1769 became an independent church with Dale as an elder. He corresponded with the church at Balchrystie, and the two groups became known as Old Scots Independents. Never a large body, they shared Glasite ideas of church order and doctrine, but without the exclusive spirit of the parent body. Dale was active in all co-operative good works in the west of Scotland.[22]

The other group which emerged in the 1760s was the Scotch Baptist connexion. Archibald McLean and Robert Carmichael, the founding fathers, were both much influenced by Glas and Sandeman, and had been for a time members of the Glasgow Glasite Church. They saw the scriptures as presenting a model of church life for all time, and sought to restore primitive Christianity as it existed before the corrupting influence of the world distorted it. They were not, however, the first Baptists in eighteenth-century Scotland. That honour belongs to Sir William Sinclair of Dunbeath in Caithness, whose story has often been told but of whom not very much is certainly known.

Sir William was a member of the widespread Sinclair family which owned many estates in Caithness. The Caithness lairds were famous for their litigation and debts, and Sir William's father, whom he succeeded in 1742, left debts and lawsuits which eventually ruined his son. He had to sell the Dunbeath estate in 1752, and the rest of his patrimony in 1765, when he left the north and retreated to Edinburgh. Despite his background, Sir William had turned from the ways of his class and become a sincere Christian. Somewhere, perhaps in England, he had been baptized, and on his return to his estate he gathered a small group who were dissatisfied with the local minister and formed them into a church at Keiss on New Year's Day 1750. It is reported that the Keiss Church observed the passover before communion, which was celebrated weekly, and footwashing.[23] Sir William drew up a hymn book for his flock containing his own paraphrases of scripture.[24] The Glasites had published their first song book in 1749, but Sir William was something of a pioneer in congregational praise. He had a reputation for eccentricity, but he laid a firm foundation and the church continues. When he had to move to Edinburgh he wrote to his people exhorting them to faithfulness, and telling them that he was looking for a sympathetic fellowship in the truth. A letter to him from Robert Sandeman indicates where such was found: 'As to your chusing to attend on our public doctrine for some weeks consequently no title to enquire after your reasons [sc. is given to us].'[25] So we are left to speculate on relationships. Mysteries continue to surround the life of Sir William but his pioneering place is secure. He died in 1768, having made no contact with the followers of McLean. Indeed McLean did not discover the existence of the Keiss Church until much later.

1765 is the year that saw the beginning of Baptist witness in Edinburgh, when McLean and Carmichael had reached a settled point in their doctrines. McLean was born in East Kilbride in 1733, heard Whitefield, was apprenticed to a printer in Glasgow, and acquired an impressive store of learning, studying the scriptures in their original languages.[26] He was a member of the Established Church until he read Glas's *Testimony*, and in 1762 he joined the Glasgow Glasite Church, leaving during the next year over a disputed case of discipline. In 1767 he went to seek his fortune in London, but he soon returned to Edinburgh, where he became overseer in a printing works. In 1764 he had reached Baptist conclusions from his study of the scriptures and in 1768 he became an elder in the new Baptist society. In later years he was the chief teacher and guide to the connexion and was set free from the need to earn his living by the church.

Robert Carmichael, perhaps because he was not a writer, and because he died young, has not received so much recognition. He had been an early student for the ministry of the Anti-Burgher Secession Church, had kept a school in Edinburgh, and had preached to a congregation of exiles in London, whence reports of rash teaching had emanated in 1751. He was, however, accepted and settled as minister of the congregation of Anti-Burghers in Coupar Angus. There he read Sandeman's *Letters on Theron and Aspasio*: 'he was reckoned a dry legal preacher . . . Palaemon's [Sandeman's] letters fell into his hands and he read them — he studied them — he laid aside his former way and preached the faith and cross of Christ — became popular — was admired and followed — and now he is suspected of heresy, having lost his zeal for the standards.'[27] So wrote James Cant of Perth to Robert

Sandeman on 8 March 1761. By the beginning of the next year Carmichael was in trouble with the presbytery on points of doctrine which show he was deeply influenced by Glasite teaching, and he was in close contact with Glas and Sandeman. After a very short time as elder in the Glasgow Church, he moved to an Independent Church in Edinburgh in 1764, and while there reached Baptist views. In 1765 he travelled to London and was baptized by John Gill in the Barbican baptistry. On his return to Edinburgh he baptized seven members of the Independent Church in the Water of Leith at Canonmills.[28] Soon afterwards McLean came from Glasgow and was baptized. The names of the first Baptists were: Dr and Mrs Robert Walker, Joseph Strachan, Elizabeth Brown, John Harlaw, Margaret Harley and Joseph Wainwright. In 1769 Carmichael went as elder to Dundee, but in 1774, shortly before his death, he returned to Edinburgh.

Scotland in the Later Eighteenth Century

We have outlined the origins of the first continuing Baptist Church in Edinburgh, and it would be useful to set the growth of the Baptist Churches against the social and religious development of Scotland in the later eighteenth century. The population of Scotland grew from about one million in 1707 to an estimated 1,265,000 in 1755, and to 1,608,000 in 1801.[29] By the end of the century Scotch Baptists, along with Old Scots Independents and Glasites, numbered perhaps one thousand full members, plus some families of members and numbers of hearers, say only four thousand folk in all. Yet they were a growing body, and soon, with the evangelism of the Haldanes and their helpers, the numbers in the Independent Churches would increase quite dramatically.

Scotland was also changing economically. Outside the rapidly growing towns health was improving with better diet and the spread of some knowledge of hygiene. The use of the land was much improved; there were new farming methods, and landlords were taking an interest in the best use of their farmland and in better housing for their tenants. After the Union of 1707 Scotland was gradually shedding its image as a very poor country, and it began to share in the general British prosperity.

Trade with America prospered and this was the age of the Glasgow tobacco barons. It was also the age of pioneer industrialists, men like David Dale, whose mills at New Lanark set new standards for production and for care of the workforce. The handloom weavers, who worked to a master, but in their own homes and at their own pace, gave an impression of relaxed prosperity, if not of flamboyance, and they had leisure for radical politics and new ideas about religion. In all the weaving centres theology was much discussed. Paisley, Dunfermline, Dundee (the capital of Dissent), Kirkcaldy, Newburgh,

Largo, Perth — all places with Scotch Baptist congregations by the end of the century — were centres of handloom weaving and allied trades.

By the 1760s the Moderate Party seemed supreme in the courts of the Church of Scotland. Its members stood for the acceptance of due law in the church, since she was not a voluntary society, but one founded by the commands of Christ. Order, they held, is essential to a civilized society, and the rules and decisions of the General Assembly must be obeyed, or chaos will result. At the same time a learned, urbane, and civilized clergy was sought for the Kirk, so that ministers would be at home with the lairds, and church and state would live in harmony. The Moderates have often had a bad press, and been seen as lazy, worldly latitudinarians. While this is undoubtedly true of some, the ideals of the age are not to be despised. The combination in such men as Alexander Carlyle of Inveresk of robust faith, pastoral concern, tolerance and an undisguised liking for the pleasures of this world was not all bad.[30]

Opposed to the Moderates in the Assembly and the lower courts of the church was the so-called Popular Party, strong for the rights of parishioners, and noisy in denunciation of the polite establishment. It is too simple to equate this group with Evangelicalism, which was to be found in the Secession Churches, according to one interpretation, or was not yet born and would appear only in the Haldane era, according to another. All held to the Westminster Confession and a credal Calvinism. Only later in the century were questions raised about subscription to the standards, and some ministers, praised by Robert Burns, accused of Arianism or Socinianism. Seceders were vigorous, not yet behind the times as the Auld Lichts among them were to become in the next century. They were strong in the cities and towns, especially among the emerging middle classes. In the second half of the century Irish immigrants began to restore the depleted ranks of Roman Catholics, and the Episcopalians began to emerge from the penal limitations put on them in 1690.

New currents of thought were flowing. Archibald McLean lived at the same time as the sceptical philosopher David Hume and the national poet Robert Burns. Miracles and the uniqueness of revelation were not so widely accepted as they had been in earlier times. Scotland was entering the Age of Enlightenment in all the arts, from architecture to philosophy, and church life was necessarily affected. James Boswell, in his travels, his changes of religion, his struggles with his conscience, his acquaintance with the literary world of his day, seems far away from the austere world of the Independent Churches, yet a cousin, Robert Boswell, WS, was a prominent member of the Edinburgh Glasite Church. Scotland was still a small society, and even the Scotch Baptists were exposed to the winds of the intellect blowing across

Europe and into their land.

The Early Scotch Baptists

We are fortunate in knowing quite a lot about the composition of some of the churches. The Glasites have kept every scrap of information from their early days, and we are able, on the basis of church lists, to build up a picture of the churches in Dundee and Perth, and we can assume, on less evidence, that the other Independent and Baptist communities were reasonably similar. By 1792 every sort of Dissent had taken root in Dundee, and, according to the First Statistical Account there were, out of 23,500 inhabitants, 1,160 Glasites. The Glasite membership list of 1782 names 206 people, so we must assume that the rest were members of families and hearers.[31] This thriving community has left a picture of itself in the annotated lists. In 1774 there were four elders, one a former minister, one a writer (lawyer), one a bleacher and one a thread manufacturer. There were seven deacons, all connected with the textile industry. The male members included three merchants, thirty weavers, five tailors and ten threadmakers. There were ninety women, to whose names no description was added. In Perth, at the same period, there were many textile workers, and some in the learned professions.

It is less easy to be precise about the first Scotch Baptists. Of the group baptized in Edinburgh in 1765 we have further details only of the Walkers. Robert Walker was a surgeon whose wife, Charlotte, was the daughter of Sir John Jardine of Applegirth, a member of a well-known Annandale family.[32] In 1778 Charles Stuart of Dunearn, who had been minister of the Cramond parish near Edinburgh, joined the Edinburgh Church. Later he qualified as a physician, and became known as a writer and the editor of Christian and missionary magazines. His library is now part of the New College collection. William Braidwood, who had been an elder in the Independent Church, became a Baptist in 1778. Later in life he was the first manager of the Caledonian Insurance Company, and, like Charles Stuart, was affluent enough to own a house in George Square. Henry David Inglis was the other distinguished member of the Edinburgh Church in its early days. He was the grandson of Colonel Gardiner, known now for his part in the battle of Prestonpans, but in earlier times renowned for the story of his conversion, related in a pamphlet by Philip Doddridge. Inglis joined McLean's church in 1777, was elected an elder in 1784 and found a special ministry preaching in the villages around Edinburgh. In 1794 he qualified as an advocate, and felt drawn to a ministry to prisoners under sentence of death. We know little of the status of the ordinary members of the church in Edinburgh, although by the thirties of the next century the original church was described as being 'largely poor and working class in composition'.[33]

In Glasgow Neil Stuart, a wright, was appointed elder in 1769. His colleague was George Begg, a weaver of some substance, who was admitted Burgess and Guild Brother of the city in 1757.[34] In 1777 the church of David Dale was divided on the question of baptism, and in that and the following year sixteen members seceded to the Baptists, including an elder, Robert Moncrieff, brother of the Rev. Sir Henry Moncrieff, minister of the West Kirk in Edinburgh. Robert Moncrieff became Burgess and Guild Brother as a druggist in 1778.[35] He was a powerful preacher and an asset to the Glasgow Church, which was weakened by his comparatively early death in 1788. His fellow elder was James Duncan (1738-1811), who had been a Glasite as late as 1771. He was a bookseller in the city and became Burgess and Guild Brother in 1782.[36] His eldest son was printer to the university and also an elder of the church. James Watt, who had studied for the Anti-Burgher ministry, joined the Glasgow Church in 1794. He had wide interests, became a physician and possessed a gift for evangelism. From 1797 to 1802 he ministered in Aberdeenshire, forming a link between Scotch Baptists and the Haldane movement.

John Goodsir, described as a surgeon, was an elder of the Largo Church and shared office with Thomas Patterson, a weaver. The founders of the Kirkcaldy Church were merchants and manufacturers, like Ninian Lockhart, whose family is still represented in the Baptist Churches. When the church in Paisley was set in order in 1795, the elders were Thomas Watson, a 'foreman', and William Marshall, a shoemaker. Most of the trustees in a list of 1798 were men connected with the textile trades.[37]

Some of the early Scotch Baptists were learned men, many were in business, and we can assume that most of the members were independent thinkers, willing to find the will of God in the scriptures, and attracted to the close and careful fellowship of this rather exclusive body of Christians. At first, when believers from outside Edinburgh were convinced, they were baptized in the capital and became members of the mother church. The first Glasgow converts were baptized in Edinburgh in 1769, and not long afterwards McLean went to Glasgow to ordain elders and set the church in order. A baptism took place in the Clyde at the Herd's House on Glasgow Green in the presence of large numbers of curious onlookers.[38] In late 1770 a group of believers in Montrose, who had been Glasites, embraced Baptist principles. Both McLean and Carmichael went to set them in order and to baptize them. The *Scots Magazine* for 1770 reported this: 'Montrose, Sept. 11. On Sunday last Mr McLean, an Anabaptist Preacher, baptized seven men and two women in the water of Esk, by plunging them backwards in deep water. In the afternoon, Mr Carmichael, another of their preachers, preached in favour of their mode of baptism.'[39] Converts came from many places around Edinburgh. Three men from Galashiels were baptized in 1782, but it was not until 1804 that a church with elders was set in order there. Until then the believers were dependent on visiting members from Edinburgh for the 'order and administration of the Ordinances'.[40]

At the end of the century centres of Baptist witness were to be found as follows: Edinburgh (1765); Dundee (1769); Montrose (1770); Glasgow (1770); Largo (baptisms 1778, church 1791); Dunfermline (1780); Galashiels (branch of Edinburgh 1782, church 1804); Newburgh, Fife (branch of Edinburgh 1782, church 1804); Perth (baptisms 1784); Paisley (1795); Kirkcaldy (branch of Edinburgh 1795, church 1798). In all these places Glasite Churches had previously been formed, and in most of them there were also Old Scots Independents. They were places with a tendency to dissent!

The Thought and Practice of the Scotch Baptists

Archibald McLean was the most considerable writer among the Scotch Baptists. His works had influence in England, where Scotch Baptist Churches were founded in Newcastle, Nottingham, Beverley, Hull, Whitehaven, Liverpool, Chester and London. In North Wales the advocacy of McLean's ideas by J.R. Jones of Ramoth led to splits in the Baptist Churches and the birth of a Scotch Baptist Welsh-speaking fellowship which still has ten chapels today.[41] The subjects on which McLean wrote indicate the important theological matters for the movement. His main work is *The Commission given by Jesus Christ to His Apostles Illustrated*. This was first published in 1785 and frequently reprinted. In it he outlines the contents of the apostolic gospel and has a lengthy section on baptism and on the ordinances of a scripturally ordered church. He also wrote controversially on baptism and published many sermons together with a detailed commentary on Hebrews. Like Glas, McLean held that the scriptures contain not only a complete system of all the doctrines necessary for salvation but also a perfect set of laws and an infallible code of behaviour for all ages and all circumstances. The independency of the local church was argued for by Glas and taken for granted by McLean. Church and state are to be separate. Indeed, to Henry David Inglis the panoply of state visible at the time of the General Assembly of the Church of Scotland is a sign of Antichrist.[42]

McLean and his churches also shared the Glasite view of faith. He insisted on the simplicity of the gospel offer: 'much has been said and written on the nature of that faith to which the promise of salvation is made, and various have been the definitions given of it, many of which served no other end than to perplex the subject. Everybody knows that faith or belief, in the ordinary sense of the word, is that CREDIT which we give to the truth of anything which is made known to us by report or testimony . . . The word pistis, faith or belief, is evidently used by the inspired writers in the same sense in which it is commonly used or understood.'[43] Faith is straightforward, and the belief of Christians is reasonable and logical, given acceptance of the scriptures. The resurrection of Jesus is the foundation principle, and it is true irrespective of men's believing.

This devotion to the words of scripture, and the search for clarity, led McLean into theological difficulties over the doctrine of the eternal generation of the Son. He took issue with the Westminster Confession on this point, fearing that the concept of eternal generation, which he could not find explicitly in scripture, might lead to Arianism. Therefore Scotch Baptists were taught that Christ is the Son of the Eternal God, not the Eternal Son of God. This led to dissension in the Edinburgh Church. Dr Walker championed the orthodox view and was excluded from the church, thus depriving it of its only wealthy member. In Glasgow the dispute went the other way, and Neil Stuart moved to Sabellianism, and thence to Arianism, and he embroiled the infant Dundee and Montrose Churches in his heresies. Stuart and his followers were excommunicated in 1776.[44]

McLean saw the history of the church in the light of prophecy, and considered the conversion of Constantine as a disaster for the 'primitive purity and simplicity of the Christian faith'.[45] He is not precise about the course of the future, but holds to a form of post-millennialism according to which the rule of the saints will be characterized by a pure and primitive church order. Unlike Glas, who was suspicious of all direct missionary measures, preferring to leave these to the sovereignty of God, McLean was a keen evangelist. He believed that the commission of Matthew 28 had been given to the successors of the apostles, that is to the duly ordained elders of the church, and he encouraged the churches to send out evangelists. Dr Watt went to Aberdeenshire, others went to the Highlands towards the end of the century and there must have been many other journeys. In 1838 the Edinburgh Church sent out a circular letter detailing some evangelistic efforts in the south-west. 'Our brother preached twice at Blairganach, seven miles from Sanquhar, to shepherds tending their flocks. The person who first professed scriptural views of baptism in Sanquhar is a shepherd here . . . He was baptised by Dr Watt about forty years ago.'[46]

McLean also supported with great zeal the newly formed Baptist Missionary Society, and was quite willing to co-operate with Fuller and other English Baptists, despite important differences. In 1795 he preached and published a sermon on *The Duty of using Means for the Universal Spread of the Gospel of Christ*, and he arranged collections in all the churches of the connexion. He insisted also on the need for the translation of the scriptures into the oriental languages, and raised money for that object.[47]

It was in the internal life of the church and its discipline that the Scotch Baptists were most at variance with Baptists of the present day. The conviction, inherited from the Glasite writers, that God had laid down in scripture a perfect church order, led to an intense desire to conform to it, and also to a tendency for churches to split on apparently minor matters. In each church it was essential for good order to have elders, and only if the church was remote could a single elder be tolerated. These men were solemnly set aside, with the agreement and participation of the other churches, after examination of their life and doctrine. We have seen that some of them were learned men, but Scotch Baptists repudiated the idea of a trained ministry. McLean was relieved by his folk of the need to work, and was enabled to give his whole time to writing and to strengthening the churches, but this was exceptional. Only when missionaries were sent out was this precedent followed. The great controversies which severely weakened the churches were over the status of elders. In early days a brother from Newburgh insisted that the church could observe the Lord's Supper even if elders were absent.[48] McLean would not accept this, and those who, like Charles Stuart of Dunearn, took a more liberal line, left the church. In 1810 the churches split on the issue. The connexion lined up behind the conservative or liberal churches, and despite attempts to heal the dispute, it recurred in 1834, and was never resolved.

Deacons were also appointed to care for the poor, for the Independent Churches were proud not to accept help from the parish. They also prepared and distributed the elements at communion. The Lord's Supper was observed each Sunday, and at it the fellowship offering was received from members only. In 1746 Glas had written in defence of infant baptism, presumably with English Baptists in mind, and in 1766 McLean composed a series of *Letters Addressed to Mr John Glas on the Subject of Baptism*, claiming that it was the first treatise setting out the Baptist position to be published in Scotland. It was the practice of believer's baptism that most marked out the followers of McLean in the eyes of the world and most caught the public attention.

The Scotch Baptist Churches were subject, as part of their very being, to strict discipline, based by McLean on Matthew 18 verses 15-20, and we have in the records of the Clyde Street Church in Edinburgh some examples of how elders investigated cases of wrongdoing within the fellowship and of how carefully procedures laid down by McLean were followed. Reconciliation was sought, discretion enjoined and the final decisions taken by the whole church led by the elders.[49] Such discipline both required and maintained purity of church fellowship, but it led, unfortunately, to many sad departures from the churches.

The worship of the church included much scripture, the singing of psalms and hymns, exhortations by the brethren, a sermon by an elder and prayers led by several of the brethren. The communion followed the afternoon service. Between the services there was a meal called the 'love-feast', which was enjoined on the church as a sign of brotherly love. At it matters of fellowship business and care of the sick and poor were discussed in confidence. The salutation, or kiss of charity, was observed 'on certain occasions' and footwashing was commended 'when it is really serviceable'.[50] In the course of time plain meeting houses were erected for the churches, with a room for worship, one for the love-feast and other apartments. There was an elders' desk, a precentor's seat and a deacons' or table seat, which served also as the Lord's Table.[51] The Glasite Meeting House in Barony Street, Edinburgh, still gives some idea of what a Scotch Baptist Church looked like.

Archibald McLean died in 1812. His church in Edinburgh continued to flourish, as did several others, but the Scotch Baptist movement was about to be overtaken by events. The rise of aggressive evangelism by other types of Baptists, changes in society and inherent weaknesses led to a slow decline of the Scotch Baptist order. It can be said positively that the churches pioneered Baptist principles with assiduity and bravery in a largely Presbyterian Scotland. By giving laymen the chance to exercise gifts of preaching and leadership, by introducing congregational hymn-singing, by efforts of evangelism largely unrecorded, by fidelity to scripture and by disseminating their principles in print, a few men and women played a great part in preparing for the revivals of the nineteenth century. On the other hand the very principles of the movement limited its expansion and led to the exclusion of many talented men who disagreed over one point or another. The sad divisions of 1810 and 1834 were the outcome of over-rigorous discipline. From these disputes the movement never recovered.

Notes

1. *The Works of John Knox*, ed D. Laing, 6 vols (Wodrow Society, Edinburgh 1846-64), 2 p 114.
2. ibid, p 117.
3. Gordon Donaldson, 'The Emergence of Schism in Seventeenth-Century Scotland', *Scottish Church History* (Edinburgh 1985), p 209.
4. *Nicoll's Diary, 1650-1657*, ed D. Laing (Bannatyne Club, Edinburgh 1836), p 106.
5. *Records of the Churches of Christ gathered at Fenstanton, Warboys and Hexham, 1644-1720*, ed E.B. Underhill (Hanserd Knollys Society, London 1854), p 291.
6. ibid, p 328.
7. George Yuille, ed, *History of the Baptists in Scotland* (Glasgow 1926), p 31.
8. *Nicoll's Diary*, p 94.
9. *Fasti Ecclesiae Scoticanae*, ed Hew Scott, 7 vols (Edinburgh 1915-28), 3 p 267.
10. *Ecclesiastical Records of the Presbyteries of St Andrews and Cupar, 1641-1698*, ed G.R. Kinloch (Abbotsford Club, Edinburgh 1837), p 176.
11. ibid, pp 177-8.
12. ibid, pp 181-2.

13. *The Diary of Mr John Lamont of Newton, 1649-1671*, ed G.R. Kinloch (Maitland Club, Edinburgh 1830), p 48, quoted by W.I. Hoy, 'The Entry of Sects into Scotland', in *Reformation and Revolution*, ed Duncan Shaw (Edinburgh 1967), p 188.
14. Hoy, 'Entry of Sects', p 195.
15. Clarke MSS 27 fol 133, Worcester College, Oxford, in W.T. Whitley, *A Baptist Bibliography*, 2 vols (London 1916), 1 p 57. For the Baptist presence in the north-east during the Commonwealth, see cap 14, pp 258-9.
16. *Andrew Hay of Craignethan's Diary, 1659-1660*, ed A.G. Reid (Scottish History Society, Edinburgh 1901), p 181 (5 Nov. 1659).
17. ibid, p 183.
18. *Memoirs of Walter Pringle of Greenknow*, 2nd edn (Edinburgh 1751), p 35.
19. D.B. Murray, 'The Social and Religious Origins of Scottish Non-Presbyterian Protestant Dissent from 1730 to 1830' (St Andrews PhD 1977).
20. J.T. Hornsby, 'Later Career of John Glas', *Records of the Scottish Church History Society*, 7 (1934), pp 94-115.
21. *The Case of James Smith and Robert Ferrier Truly Represented and Defended* (Edinburgh 1768).
22. Harry Escott, *A History of Scottish Congregationalism* (Glasgow 1960), pp 24-36.
23. Yuille, ed, *Baptists in Scotland*, p 41.
24. *Collection of Hymns and Spiritual Songs* [1751], 2nd edn (Edinburgh 1847). cf *Julian's Dictionary of Hymnology* (London 1892), p 1030.
25. J.T. Hornsby, 'John Glas and his Movement' (Edinburgh PhD 1936), p 205, citing autograph letter.
26. William Jones, 'Memoir of the Author', *The Works of Mr. Archibald McLean*, 6 vols (London 1823), 6 pp x–xiv.
27. *Supplementary Volume of the Letters of J. Glas, etc.*, ed W. Morrison (Perth 1865), p 14.
28. *Scots Magazine* (1765), p 614.
29. T.C. Smout, *A History of the Scottish People, 1560-1830* (London 1969), p 259.
30. A.L. Drummond and James Bulloch, *The Scottish Church, 1688-1834* (Edinburgh 1973), p 70.
31. Sir John Sinclair, ed, *The Statistical Account of Scotland, 1791-1799 : Angus* (East Ardsley, Wakefield 1976), p 180, and list of Glasite members in private hands in Edinburgh.
32. *Edinburgh Marriage Registers, 1757-1800*, ed F.J. Grant (Scottish Record Society, Edinburgh 1922), p 810.
33. *Report of the Commission of Enquiry into the opportunities of public religious worship, and means of religious instruction, and the pastoral superintendence afforded to the people of Scotland*, 6 vols (Edinburgh 1837-8), 3.
34. *The Burgesses and Guild Brethren of Glasgow, 1573-1750*, ed J.R. Anderson, 2 vols (Scottish Record Society, Edinburgh 1925), 2 p 196.
35. ibid, p 111. 36. ibid, p 128.
37. *The Thomas Coats Memorial Baptist Church, Paisley, Jubilee Book, 1944* (Paisley 1945), p 29.
38. Yuille, ed, *Baptists in Scotland*, p 47.
39. *Scots Magazine* (1770), p 517.
40. Patrick Wilson, *The Origin and Progress of the Scots Baptist Churches from their Rise in 1765 to 1834* (Edinburgh 1844), p 20.
41. [T. Witton Davies], 'The McLeanist (Scotch) and Campbellite Baptists of Wales', *Transactions of the Baptist Historical Society*, 7 (1921), pp 147-81.
42. H.D. Inglis, *Letters, Sermons and Tracts* (Edinburgh 1812), p 191.
43. McLean, 'Commission', Works, 1 pp 74-7.
44. Wilson, *Origin and Progress*, p 13.
45. McLean, 'Commission', *Works*, 1 pp 314-15.
46. *From the Baptist Church Meeting in Bristo Street, Edinburgh* (Edinburgh 1838), p 2 (Circular letter).
47. Jones, 'Memoir', *Works of McLean*, 6, pp lxxiii–lxxv.
48. Wilson, *Origin and Progress*, p 23.
49. Waugh Papers, Baptist Union of Scotland Records.
50. McLean in *Rippon's Register* (London 1794-97), 3 p 365.
51. J. Williamson, *Reminiscences of the Old Baptist Church, Pleasance* (Edinburgh 1901), frontispiece.

D.B. Murray

2. THE EARLY NINETEENTH CENTURY

Baptist witness in Scotland was significantly diversified and strengthened in the first half of the nineteenth century. Two movements in particular stimulated its development. The first of these was led by Robert and James Haldane, who are often regarded (incorrectly) as the founders of the Baptist denomination in Scotland. The second movement (which owed much to the first) was characterized by the emergence of 'English' Baptist Churches in Scotland. These churches differed from the Scotch Baptist Churches in the nature of their leadership, since they were led by a single pastor rather than a plurality of elders. As the nineteenth century progressed, the 'English' Baptist pattern came to dominate the Scottish Baptist tradition.

The key to Baptist growth in Scotland in this period lies largely in a new enthusiasm for missionary activity which began to appear in the late eighteenth century. The Haldane movement was concerned essentially with home mission, but this interest was shared by the 'English' Baptist Churches and even by the rather inward-looking Scotch Baptists. The changes occurring in Scottish society after 1790 afforded many opportunities for missionary enterprise in both rural and urban areas.

The Eighteenth-Century Background

The activities of British Evangelicals in the eighteenth century, and especially in the period 1780-1800, helped to determine events in Scotland. A major spiritual movement, the Evangelical Revival, was under way in England and Wales by 1750. Associated primarily with George Whitefield and John Wesley, both clergymen of the Church of England, the revival stimulated the growth of Evangelical Anglicanism, and eventually produced the Methodist denominations.[1] It also affected the older English Dissenting bodies, including Particular Baptists, among whom some held a high Calvinistic theology that left little scope for evangelistic endeavour. In 1785 Andrew Fuller, a Particular Baptist pastor at Kettering, Northamptonshire, published a book entitled *The Gospel Worthy of All Acceptation*, in which he expressed doubts about the validity of hyper-Calvinism, and argued that true Calvinism is essentially a missionary theology.[2]

In Scotland the Evangelical Revival had less powerful and less immediate effects. Nevertheless, noteworthy links are detectable. In 1742 George Whitefield preached at Cambuslang during a major revival which had already begun before he arrived,[3] and John Wesley visited Scotland regularly. Neither Whitefield nor Wesley was warmly received in Scotland by the Protestant denominations. By associating with the Established Church,

Whitefield irritated the Seceders who had invited him north, and Wesley's Arminian theology was unacceptable to many Scots.[4]

Yet Scotland was not devoid of important spiritual movements. The impact of the revival at Cambuslang was felt further afield, stimulating revivals elsewhere in the Lowlands and in the Highlands too. These movements were, however, far from assuming a national cohesiveness, and even though they commonly occurred within the Established Church, that church also included Moderate clergymen, whose preaching tended to emphasize decent moral rectitude rather than personal salvation.[5] By the 1790s, therefore, Scotland still offered much scope for revivalist preaching. Indeed, its more northerly parts could readily be seen as a mission-field by those with missionary interests. From 1709 the Society in Scotland for the Propagation of Christian Knowledge (SSPCK), a strongly Presbyterian body, was trying to 'civilize' the Highlands, and the Jacobite Rebellion of 1745 had drawn fresh attention to their allegedly unruly Gaelic-speaking population. The Secession Churches and the Relief Church were also active in evangelism, and the latter had first sent missionaries to the Highlands about 1784.[6]

Involvement by non-Presbyterians in missionary outreach to the Highlands and other parts of Scotland was the direct result of the enthusiasm for foreign missionary endeavour which was generated by the Evangelical Revival. By the 1790s this enthusiasm was apparent in the formation of missionary societies and in the departure of British missionaries for foreign fields. In 1793 William Carey, a Baptist from Northamptonshire, set sail for India as the first missionary of the newly founded Baptist Missionary Society (BMS).[7] Carey's example caught the attention of the public, not least because of the assiduous fund-raising efforts of Andrew Fuller, who became the first secretary of the BMS. Fuller visited Scotland on five occasions, travelling as far north as Aberdeen and Dingwall. Fuller's advocacy of the Indian mission drew considerable Scottish support, and it encouraged some Scots to contemplate missionary service at a time when the attitude of the Established Church to foreign missions was distinctly lukewarm. Fuller's presence in Scotland helped to strengthen the handful of small 'English' Baptist Churches which were emerging in the land, and he corresponded regularly with some of the most influential Baptist pastors.[8]

The foreign missionary movement was not, however, restricted to Baptists; it was promoted by several other Evangelical bodies, and it often led to co-operation among Evangelical believers from different denominations, including Anglicans such as Charles Simeon.[9] It also stimulated home mission in Britain itself. The BMS, indeed, supported two missionaries, William Steadman and John Saffery, in Cornwall. Itinerant preaching by Baptists and other Dissenters was becoming common in the villages and rural areas of England from the 1780s.[10] The value of employing itinerant preachers in Scotland was appreciated from the 1790s, and itinerancy assumed increasing importance among Scottish Baptists after 1800. In Scotland, as in England, the desire to promote the gospel by means of itinerant evangelists was in tune with the increasingly mobile nature of society.

Scottish Life and Society

By 1800 Scotland stood on the threshold of momentous social change which produced circumstances conducive to the growth of the Baptists. This was largely the consequence of industrialization. The arrival of steam-driven machinery heralded the demise of traditional, usually home-based, methods of industry. There was created a body of entrepreneurs upon whom large labour-forces gradually became economically dependent. The keynotes of the period are the fracturing of time-honoured social structures, particularly in the rural areas, and the creation of new, unsettled relationships between the owners of industry and their employees. A radical political consciousness was also developing, especially after the French Revolution, and it was not uncommon for the opponents of Evangelical activism to regard it as politically subversive. While this charge was often overstated, it was not without some foundation, and it is at least significant that Baptist principles took root in those parts of the Lowlands and Highlands in which social change was most noticeable.[11]

In the Lowlands, the cotton, linen and woollen industries expanded markedly in this period. The advent of machinery led to the establishment of mills and factories for the production of textiles. Initially such mills, like that established by David Dale at New Lanark, were often situated where there was a convenient source of water power, but the harnessing of steam allowed much greater freedom of location. Later mills were located mainly in towns and cities, which began to grow at the expense of the countryside. In Paisley the cotton industry assumed a particular importance, while in Dundee the production of linen was a staple employment.[12] In both towns Baptists are well attested in the early nineteenth century, and appear to have drawn support among the handloom weavers, whose circumstances became increasingly precarious as machinery ousted muscle. In the Borders the woollen industry grew vigorously, and towns like Galashiels, where there was a Baptist Church by 1804, achieved a lasting reputation for their products, although Aberdeen, at the other end of Scotland, was able to maintain a firm place as a producer and exporter of woollen goods. Not only were workers in the textile industries sometimes identified with the Baptist cause, but occasionally so too were their employers. In Paisley, the Coats family developed its particular speciality in cotton manufacture which made the firm of J. & P. Coats a household name. Successive members of this family contributed generously to Baptist causes throughout Scotland. In Perth, the Pullars were involved in the production of dyestuffs, and they also became patrons of Baptist evangelistic enterprise.[13]

Heavy industry was similarly developing in Scotland in this period, and it was usually situated where raw materials were readily available. The well-known Carron Iron Company was established as early as 1759, but the introduction of blast-furnaces greatly increased production in the years before 1850. This encouraged the concentration of heavy industry in the Lowland south, where the population grew markedly. Glasgow trebled its population within a generation, and several of its most influential Baptist Churches emerged in the period 1820-50.[14] At the same time, coalfields expanded rapidly to meet the need for fuel.

Much of the labour-force required in the developing industries was supplied by workers from the rural areas of Scotland, including the Highlands. Before 1800 Highlanders had often obtained seasonal employment on Lowland farms, especially at harvest time, but by the 1820s substantial numbers were coming south to the industrial heartlands.[15] In the Highlands, the population was growing rapidly in the north and west after 1800, mainly because of vaccination, the adoption of the potato as a main food crop, and the demand for kelp ash during and immediately after the Napoleonic Wars. A labour-intensive industry based on the harvesting of kelp from the shorelines was encouraged by several Highland landlords, who provided their labourers with units of land known as 'crofts'. The decline of the kelp industry in the 1820s was followed by the potato failures of 1836 and 1846, with the result that many Highlanders migrated or emigrated, mainly to Canada or Australia. This intensified a process of social change and population displacement, commonly known as the 'Highland Clearances', which had been taking effect from the second half of the previous century, when landlords began to exploit more thoroughly the commercial potential of their estates.[16] In such areas as mainland Argyll and Perthshire, which did not benefit from the kelp boom, migration and emigration were under way well before 1820. The establishment of Independent and Baptist Churches in the Highlands tended to occur shortly before periods of social upheaval and population displacement, beginning in Perthshire and moving gradually westwards. This was not conducive to the long-term stability of the churches, and many congregations were severely disturbed by emigration.[17] Events in the Highlands graphically illustrate the vulnerability of Baptist Churches to the effects of economic change, and even in the more prosperous Lowlands, Baptist Churches were often affected by industrial recession and emigration.[18]

As the coalfields grew and the cities received a progressive influx of labourers from the rural areas and the Highlands, a concern for the salvation of the industrial labour-force became evident in certain circles. This coincided with the increasing interest in foreign mission which was becoming evident in Scotland in the late 1790s. The various impulses which combined to produce a home missionary conscience are represented in the person of John Campbell, an Edinburgh ironmonger whose immediate family connections were with Killin, Perthshire. Campbell had a Relief Church background, but he moved towards Independency. Active in the production and distribution of tracts, the establishing of Sunday Schools and the evangelizing of industrial workers, Campbell preached regularly to the coalminers of Gilmerton Colliery, Midlothian.[19] It was at Gilmerton, with the encouragement of Campbell, that James Alexander Haldane was given his first preaching opportunity.[20]

The Haldane Movement

James Haldane and his older brother, Robert, were remarkable individuals whose commitment to itinerant evangelism from 1797 contrasts sharply with their earlier careers. Descended from the prestigious Haldane family of Gleneagles, they both embarked initially on naval service, Robert in the Royal Navy, and James in the East India Company, where he rose to the rank of captain. Leaving the navy in 1783, Robert resumed his earlier studies at Edinburgh University, and for some ten years he lived as a country gentleman on his estate at Airthrey, near Stirling. The events of the French Revolution moved him deeply, and for a time he hoped that its principles would be extended. Robert's desire to champion a revolutionary cause was satisfied shortly afterwards when he experienced evangelical conversion. By 1794 James too had made a similar commitment, and had also retired from his secular career.[21]

As the Haldanes had wide experience of foreign lands, it is not surprising that, after their conversion, they should have planned to participate in some aspect of overseas mission. In 1795 Robert read the first number of the periodical accounts of the Baptist Mission in India, and he immediately determined to use his time and property in missionary service. His hope of going to Benares with a band of men was shared by James, but their plan was foiled by the East India Company. Thereafter their thoughts turned to home missionary activity, partly through the influence of Charles Simeon, who toured Perthshire with James Haldane in 1796, but largely through the encouragement of John Campbell, whom James accompanied on a tour of the west of Scotland in the spring of 1797, when they established a number of Sunday Schools. After discovering his preaching talents at Gilmerton, James Haldane embarked in July 1797 on a major expedition to the northern counties and the Orkney Islands. He was accompanied by two like-minded men who had also preached at Gilmerton, Joseph Rate, a student from David Bogue's Independent Church in Gosport, and John Aikman, a retired merchant. Further tours of this kind were undertaken, including a tour to southern Scotland in 1798 and another to Shetland in 1799. By 1800 James Haldane and John Campbell had reached Cumbrae, Bute, Arran and Kintyre. In most places Haldane's preaching drew crowds and often attracted opposition, which he sometimes turned to advantage.[22]

Following the summer tour of 1797, the Haldanes and their associates established a home missionary society on the model of the Hampshire Association for itinerant evangelism, which had been founded by their friend David Bogue. The Society for Propagating the Gospel at Home (SPGH) began its work early in 1798, and employed itinerant preachers.[23] In 1798 also, Robert Haldane sold a large part of his Airthrey estate, and devoted the proceeds to home evangelism.[24] His liberality was evident not only in the provision of training classes for SPGH students, but in the purchase and erection of preaching centres. The first of these was the Circus (a former variety theatre) in Little King Street, Edinburgh, which was opened by the English evangelist, Rowland Hill. The Circus congregation moved in 1801 to the new Tabernacle erected at the head of Leith Walk. The designation 'Tabernacle' reflected the influence of Whitefield, mediated to the Haldanes through John Campbell. Further Tabernacles were established in Glasgow, Dundee, Wick and other places, including Campbeltown in Kintyre, where the Haldanes' influence was strong.[25] The Edinburgh Circus and Tabernacle were of great importance in giving a platform to influential English preachers, all of them Evangelicals of different denominations, and most of them committed to the principles of home and foreign missions.

Until 1799 the Haldanes developed their impressive programme of home evangelism as members of the Established Church. Their activity did, however, arouse major opposition, not least because they were laymen intruding into the sacrosanct territory of ordained ministers. Matters were not helped by their initial denigration of Established Church clergymen. By late 1798, with the advice of Greville Ewing, the former minister of Lady Glenorchy's Chapel, Edinburgh, who had now joined them, the Haldanes were moving towards Congregational Independency, and in February 1799 James was ordained as pastor of the Circus Church. The breach with the Established Church was underlined later that year when the General Assembly issued its Pastoral Admonition, which effectively branded the SPGH as a vehicle of religious and political anarchy.[26]

Although the Haldanes were opposed from without, they had to face difficulties within their own ranks, and these were the more destructive in the long term. While they were expeditious organizers, they entered Evangelical circles without a firm theological foot-hold. Their understanding of the scriptures, and especially of the New Testament, developed as they proceeded, and points of interpretation regarding the practices of the New Testament church caused irritation, particularly when they tried to reproduce them in their own congregation. The teachings of Glas and Sandeman gained favour with the Haldanes after 1803, and plurality of elders and mutual exhortation became topics of disagreement.[27] Even more contentious was the Haldanes' move from paedobaptism to believer's baptism by immersion. From 1804 James Haldane had doubts about the validity of paedobaptism, but only in 1808 did he move decisively to believer's baptism, when he was baptized by immersion. Robert followed soon afterwards.[28]

The Haldanes had made a decision with unfortunate consequences. Division emerged in the Edinburgh Tabernacle and in Haldane-supported churches elsewhere. Bitterness and rancour resulted when Robert Haldane turned Independents out of their buildings and called in his debts. Greville Ewing was left to direct the course of Independency in Scotland, and the SPGH disintegrated. It was a sad conclusion to an important, formative chapter in Scottish Evangelical history, but for the development of the Baptist movement in Scotland, it was undoubtedly a major stimulus. Numerous Baptist Churches split from existing Independent Churches, and the issue of believer's baptism was brought forcibly to public attention. The result is apparent in the dates of foundation of Baptist Churches in Scotland in the period 1800-10. Of the forty-one churches in existence by 1810, no fewer than twenty-three dated their origins to the years 1808-10, and most of these were the product of the debate which had been given prominence by the Haldanes.[29]

Barclay, Anderson and the 'English' Baptists

The Haldanes' adoption of believer's baptism was doubtless encouraged by the small but significant number of former students who had attended their classes with a view to employment in the SPGH, but who were later baptized by immersion. These men were instrumental in founding several Baptist Churches in Scotland by 1805. Their churches were located in the north (at Thurso) and in the Gaelic-speaking West Highlands (at Bellanoch, near Lochgilphead), as well as in the Lowlands. When Andrew Fuller visited Scotland in 1805 to promote the BMS, he found one such church and pastor at Saltcoats:

> At Saltcoats, I met with one of the baptist ministers from the Tabernacle connection, of whom there are nine or ten, who have lately been baptized. They have formed churches, which are the only ones in Scotland with whom either myself or any other English baptist would be admitted to

communion . . . many have come off from the old connection [i.e. Scotch Baptists] to join them.[30]

On Sunday 27 July Fuller went to Kilwinning, 'and heard preaching in the morning at the baptist place of worship, which consisted of an upper room, and was much crowded'.[31] The pastor of the Kilwinning Church was George Barclay, who similarly belonged to 'the Tabernacle connection'. A native of Kilwinning with an Established Church background, Barclay had studied at Haldane classes in Dundee and Glasgow from 1799 to 1802, and had begun to work as an Independent preacher in Kilwinning in that year. As the result of a friend's enquiry, he began to search the scriptures for guidance on baptism, and in October 1803 he was baptized in Edinburgh by Dr Charles Stuart, a Scotch Baptist. Several people who were converted through his ministry were baptized by him, and a Baptist Church was constituted in Kilwinning on 12 December 1803. At the time of its constitution, the Kilwinning Church had no connection with any other Baptist Church in Scotland and no known links with Baptists in England. Yet its order, with a pastor and deacons, was designated 'English' since it differed from the Scotch Baptist custom and corresponded to that normally found in Baptist Churches in England.[32] In reality, however, the Kilwinning Church was a development of the Haldane congregational model.

To find fellowship with like-minded Baptists, George Barclay did not need to travel south of the Border. In Glasgow and Edinburgh attempts were being made to establish 'English' Baptist Churches from about 1801. An 'English' Baptist Church was constituted in Glasgow in November 1801 with James Lister as its pastor, but it was not a stable fellowship, and it ceased in 1806.[33] The origin of the Glasgow Church is obscure hitherto. It is said to have had links with the earlier Pen (or Pend) Church in Paisley,[34] but this was probably not the parent foundation; the instability of the church and the date of its demise tend to suggest that it was an off-shoot from the Haldane movement, since such off-shoots were liable to be disturbed by the disputes which afflicted the Haldanes' Tabernacle.

In Edinburgh the beginnings of 'English' Baptist fellowships are more clearly documented, and owe much to the direct influence of Baptist students who had come north to study at Edinburgh University, since Scottish universities, unlike their English counterparts, were not effectively closed to Dissenters. The first such fellowship in Edinburgh met at Cordiners' Hall, and drew much support from former members of the Haldanes' Circus Church who had been dismissed when they submitted themselves to believer's baptism by immersion. George Barclay of Kilwinning formed close links with the fellowship at Cordiners' Hall, and in 1805 he conducted two baptisms there. The Cordiners' Hall fellowship was, however, beset by the disputes which engaged the Haldanes (principally mutual exhortation), and it eventually withered, the few remaining members rejoining the Haldanes' Tabernacle in 1808.[35] Early 'English' Baptist Churches in the cities thus appear to have been less stable than their sister churches in the smaller towns, perhaps because they were closer to the Haldane epicentre, and therefore more likely to be disturbed by disputes. Mature leaders like George Barclay were scarce at the outset, and strong leadership was essential for the growth of the infant churches.

The establishing of a stable, outward-looking 'English' Baptist Church in Edinburgh did not take place until 1808. This was the work of Christopher Anderson, a broad-minded pastor who tried to avoid the contentions which had racked the earlier 'English' Baptist Churches and the Haldane movement. A native of Edinburgh, Anderson was deeply influenced by the aims and ministry of the Haldanes, and following his conversion he became a member of their Circus Church. Through contact with Baptist students from England, he rejected paedobaptism and was baptized by immersion in 1801, with the result that he lost his membership of the Haldanes' church. Nevertheless, he regularly attended the new Tabernacle, although he now associated with the fellowship in Cordiners' Hall and with the 'English' Baptist Church in Glasgow. Anderson was also strongly influenced by the foreign missionary movement, and particularly by the Carey mission to India, which he first heard described by Andrew Fuller in 1799. He was accepted as a missionary by the BMS, and trained at John Sutcliff's Academy in Olney and Bristol Baptist College in 1805-6. However, his poor health compelled him to remain at home, and on returning to Edinburgh in 1806, he purchased the Scotch Baptist meeting-house in Richmond Court.[36] His congregation grew slowly, and in 1808 he was ordained as pastor of the Richmond Court Church (now, in a later setting, Charlotte Baptist Chapel).

Through his link with Cordiners' Hall, Christopher Anderson established a close friendship with George Barclay. Together they maintained a strong interest in the work of William Carey, to which they contributed both finance and manpower. In the difficult years of estrangement between Carey and the BMS, Anderson and Barclay gathered substantial sums of money to sustain the mission, and Anderson acted as its secretary and as trustee for its property.[37] The Kilwinning and Edinburgh Churches also sent several missionaries to India. Anderson's church sent out John Mack, who was professor of natural philosophy at Serampore from 1822 to 1845, and Thomas Swan, who was a divinity tutor at Serampore between 1827 and 1829. Like Anderson, both men trained at Bristol Baptist College.[38] From the Kilwinning Church went George Barclay's son, William Carey Barclay, who became a printer and translator at Serampore.[39] Other Baptist Churches in Scotland also supported the Serampore mission, and it helped to provide a focus for the various streams in Baptist life.

Besides their contribution to foreign missionary activity, Anderson and Barclay were leaders in home missionary enterprise. In 1807-8 they established an itinerant society for home mission, in which Anderson had a very prominent role. Anderson in particular had a remarkable capacity for hard, practical work, demonstrated saliently by his foundational role in the interdenominational Edinbugh Gaelic School Society (1810), his part in establishing the Edinburgh Bible Society (1809), his itinerant labours in the Highlands and his periodic visits to Ireland.[40]

While the 'English' Baptist model of church government appealed to men like Barclay and Anderson who were influenced by the Haldanes, one-man pastorates were also reproduced naturally by ministers of the Established and other Churches who came to accept believer's baptism and joined the Baptist movement. Some of these developments were idiosyncratic or anomalous. In the late eighteenth century Frederic Macfarlane, a former Anti-Burgher minister in Montrose, formed a Baptist Church in Skinners' Hall, Edinburgh, which maintained a single pastor and was noted for its exclusivism and 'monastic style'. In 1823 William Shirreff, who had been an Established Church minister for twenty-five years, became the sole pastor of the Scotch Baptist Church meeting in Albion Street, Glasgow.[41]

In the 1820s two more 'English' Baptist Churches were formed in Glasgow (those latterly located in South Portland Street and Adelaide Place), and one in Aberdeen (the precursor of Crown Terrace). Thus the 'English' Baptist Churches gradually gained ground, evidently for a variety of reasons. The single-pastor model probably suited the desire which some may have felt for a Baptist counterpart to the Presbyterian tradition. It was also labour-efficient and relatively easy to establish in the context of home missionary activity. Virtually all the Baptist Churches in the Gaelic-speaking Highlands, whether off-shoots from Independency or original Baptist foundations, were of the 'English' type. Only in Aberdeenshire, where Scotch Baptist missionaries were active, are there significant traces of the earlier polity being followed in rural churches.[42]

Home Missionary Societies

The distinctively Baptist contribution to home mission in Scotland was small in terms of the number of missionaries active before 1808, and much depended on individual preachers and churches. The Scotch Baptists nevertheless established a fund to support home mission, and in 1797 Dr James Watt, who became a pastor of the John Street Scotch Baptist Church in

Glasgow, was active in itinerant evangelism around Edinburgh and in the north-east.[43]

The main impetus in itinerant evangelism was provided by ex-Haldane preachers and the struggling 'English' Baptist Churches. The earliest Baptist arrangement for Highland mission was established about 1805 with the support of the 'English' Baptist Church in Glasgow, which had an active Highland interest from its inception. After the demise of the Glasgow Church, this interest was maintained by George Barclay and Christopher Anderson, who established the Scotch Itinerant Society in 1807-8.[44] A concern to fill the vacuum created by the collapse of the Haldanes' SPGH was one of the factors which prompted their action. In scope and resources, however, their society was scarcely comparable with the SPGH. It was no more than a shoestring organization which was supported by the Kilwinning and Richmond Court Churches in Scotland, and by a small body of subscribers in England, including Andrew Fuller's church in Kettering. Yet, were it not for the personal generosity of Anderson, who regularly made up the annual deficit, the society would not have survived as it did until 1824. Anderson, who in effect sustained the society, attempted to provide itinerant evangelism in large tracts of rural Scotland and in some of the towns by means of a small, but immensely diligent, body of men — Alexander McLeod in Perthshire, Dugald Sinclair in Mid-Argyll and the Hebrides, David Gibson in Kirkcudbrightshire, and (latterly) John Gilmore in Aberdeen and David Douglas in Falkirk.[45]

When the Haldanes adopted Baptist principles in 1808, they did not attempt to form a Baptist organization which would match the SPGH. For some years after 1808, the Haldanes conducted their home missionary activities in a less conspicuous manner from their Leith Walk Church.[46] By 1820 they supported a substantial body of itinerant missionaries, mainly in the Highlands, but in the years between 1808 and 1830 they maintained a relatively low profile. In Perthshire, where the work of the SPGH was particularly vigorous, former Haldane missionaries who became Baptists had to maintain themselves until 1816, when the Baptist Highland Mission was formed through the efforts of William Tulloch of Blair Atholl. In founding the Mission, Tulloch obtained the support of three Scotch Baptist leaders in Glasgow (James Watt, James Buchan and David McLaren) and of Baptists in Perth (including Robert Pullar).[47] When James Haldane returned to prominence in 1830, becoming a secretary of the Baptist Home Missionary Society for Scotland, he was heavily dependent on William Tulloch for advice regarding the support and placement of Highland preachers.[48]

By 1820 Baptist home missionary activity in Scotland embraced two societies and one church-based source, but there was an increasing awareness that a corporate effort was required. Anderson's society had accumulated a substantial deficit, and by 1824 it had merged with the Haldanes' work to form the Home Missionary Society for Scotland, with George Barclay as its secretary.[49] The Baptist Highland Mission joined this body in 1827, and the Baptist Home Missionary Society for Scotland (BHMS) thus came into existence.[50] The BHMS therefore combined the expertise and continuing activities of the chief promoters of Baptist home mission in Scotland, and it became a major means of Baptist growth. The financial difficulties of home mission were greatly eased by the appointment of the first travelling agent, Lachlan Mackintosh of Grantown-on-Spey, who operated full-time in this capacity from 1831. Mackintosh travelled throughout Britain and visited Ireland, and he was able to raise very substantial funding for the society among sympathizers in England.[51] The number of preachers maintained by the society grew gradually from twenty-one in 1829 to twenty-eight in 1844,[52] and while its main concern was the Highlands and Islands, including Orkney and Shetland, it supported several preachers in Lowland stations. Sometimes it sent preachers to areas of industrial development in the Lowlands. In 1829, for example, it stationed Daniel Dunbar at Grahamston, in the immediate vicinity of the Carron Iron Works.[53]

The formation of the BHMS was an important milestone in the development of Baptist witness in Scotland. Uniting Baptist leaders and preachers of different backgrounds, its cohesive power was doubtless of importance in implanting the concept of wider denominational union in the minds of Baptist leaders in 1827 and again in the 1830s.

The Scotch Baptists: Decline and Disruption

At the beginning of the new century, the Scotch Baptist Churches were still in a relatively flourishing condition. They were multiplying at the rate of two per annum during the first twenty years, some of the churches arising spontaneously, and others being the fruit of such missionary endeavours as those of Dr James Watt in Aberdeenshire. Churches at Stirling, Dunfermline and Perth were founded between 1805 and 1808. The Edinburgh Church in particular was served by notable elders. Archibald McLean lived and worked until 1812. Henry David Inglis died in 1805, but the other outstanding leader and writer, William Braidwood, lived until 1830.[54]

Several factors contributed to this continued prosperity. The people who formed these churches combined a warm zeal with a liking for controversial divinity, and were nourished by the writings of McLean and Braidwood, and by Dr Watt's book on believer's baptism, for which he had been expelled by the Secession. The revival of Evangelical religion associated with the Haldanes drew some people from the old-fashioned Scotch Churches, but it also stimulated some growth. In about 1808 an Independent Church in Glasgow, with a membership of 200, under the pastoral care of Messrs McLaren and Buchan, joined the Scotch Baptist Church of forty members, making a strong body.[55] These Scotch Churches, although not united in any formal way, were kept in touch by annual letters and by a series of correspondences, originally conducted by Archibald McLean, in which news is mingled with exhortation and teaching, so that the connexion could be kept in total agreement on all points.

Not surprisingly in such an argumentative body, unanimity proved impossible. Already in 1784, at the instigation of members of the Newburgh group, the question of the necessity of eldership for the proper constitution of the church in a locality was raised. In particular the discussion was about the propriety of holding the Lord's Supper without at least one elder. In 1784, although some valued members were lost to the churches, peace was restored. The presence of an elder, it was agreed, was essential for the proper observance of the Lord's Supper. In 1810, perhaps because of the growth of the churches, this was not so. When argument over the same issue reached its climax, the churches in Glasgow, Dundee and Aberdeen divided. In Glasgow Dr Watt was the leader of the liberal group, holding that no elder was needed, and seceded with 160 members to form a separate church.[56] The Edinburgh Church stood firmly by the conservative position. The other churches lined themselves up with one side or the other, Paisley, Dunfermline and Liverpool taking the liberal side. In 1821 a list of orthodox churches, that is those in connexion with Edinburgh, was drawn up. It reports 991 members in seventeen churches, and there is the revealing comment, 'the prospect is by no means cheering'.[57]

The Edinburgh Church continued to grow and prosper until in 1834 the same old controversy broke out again. Attempts had been made at reunion, and there was a deep feeling that the 1810 division should not be allowed to continue indefinitely, but when two churches in Aberdeen did unite, the Edinburgh Church was forced to decide whether it could recognize this body. It divided in the process, with great bitterness. James Williamson tells of his own experience as a child of the church:

> At length she [his mother] came home in great distress, sobbing and crying bitterly, and told us that the church was rent in twain. This unhappy division divided families as well as the church. My youngest sister and I remained with the advanced or liberal party, while my mother and sister hived off with the sterling, true-blue, orthodox party.[58]

The liberal party soon recovered and built the Bristo Place Church. The conservative party, which had most of the office-bearers with it, withdrew to

Argyle Square. Eventually, in 1874, it was to reunite with Bristo. Both churches sent out circulars justifying themselves, and more division followed. The more liberal churches were now on the way to becoming akin to the other Baptists of the Haldane and 'English' foundations, while the most rigorous continued to decline gradually until the last in Scotland, in Lower Largo, closed in 1927. Soon paid pastors were being appointed to supplement the elders, and the peculiar practices and doctrines of the McLeanite churches were gradually forgotten. Some churches, such as that in Auchtermuchty, under the leadership of the Dron brothers, found a home with the Campbellites, or Churches of Christ, who preserved certain of the features of the older tradition, such as a plural eldership.[59]

New Currents in Evangelical Thinking

To the several strains of theology among Baptists in Scotland, there was soon to be added another which contributed largely to the formation of the Union and the college, and gave Baptists a strengthened impetus to evangelism. In the 1830s there were powerful new influences abroad in Scotland. The troubles over patronage were pointing towards the Disruption of 1843, while the challenges of Edward Irving, John McLeod Campbell and others were forcing a renewed look at Calvinist orthodoxy and at the work of the Holy Spirit.

Most Baptist Churches were relatively untouched by these alarms, but there was another alleged heretic who was to have a much greater effect. In the spring of 1839 James Morison, a Seceder probationer, was sent north to preach in the Cabrach, and on the way he read Finney's *Revivals of Religion*. When he reached his destination, he laid aside his manuscript and preached from the heart. Next year he was ordained in Kilmarnock, and taught the universal scope of the atonement. He was subjected to a long and searching process before the church courts, and in 1841 was deposed. Along with his father, a Secession minister in Bathgate, and a few others, he founded the Evangelical Union in May 1843, and proclaimed the 'three universals', the universal love of God, the universality of the atonement and the universality of the work of the Holy Spirit.[60]

Amongst those attracted by this broadening of Calvinism was young William Landels from Eyemouth, who studied with Morison, and soon was pastor of an EU church in Ayrshire. With help from the Berwick Baptist minister, A. Kirkwood, he was led to accept believer's baptism, and soon came (in 1846) to a rather apprehensive Cupar Church. Kirkwood, a Baptist of the old school, vouched for his orthodoxy, and the Cupar Church flourished. Landels, whose subsequent career led him to the highest offices, links the old world and the prosperous Victorian heyday of Nonconformity. He was an effective preacher of evangelistic gift, a writer, journalist, controversialist, and a man of his time, or ahead of it. He was all this in his early Cupar days, and he helped to lead the Scottish Baptists into a new era.[61]

Another man who was inspired by the Morisonian theology and who had more influence among Scottish Baptists was Francis Johnstone. He came from an Edinburgh family connected with Rose Street and the Tabernacle. After study at Edinburgh University, he went to Bradford College, and in 1835 began his ministry at Boroughbridge in Yorkshire. In 1842 he came to Cupar in Fife, and was caught up in the excitement surrounding the impending Disruption, and in the ferment caused by Morison's trial. For Johnstone, the new views grew naturally out of what he had learnt in his early days at Haldane's Tabernacle. He was in no way a theological liberal in a later sense. Yet he preached and wrote about a wider application of the gospel that was attractive to many, and gained for him the opprobrium of his seniors. His aggressive methods and suspect theology did not commend him to the older leaders, and their reaction to him, while perhaps understandable, does not do them much credit. Their prejudices became particularly evident when Johnstone allied himself with an attempt to unite the work of the churches.[62]

Attempts at United Work and Witness

There were many types of Baptists in Scotland by 1820, and there can be no doubt that they expended great energy on promoting their own principles. Some of their leaders, however, were acutely conscious of their failure to work together, and there were at least two attempts to promote united action in this period. The first of these was in the 1820s, and is known only because of the survival of the papers of Archibald Smith, pastor of the Scotch Baptist Church meeting in Clyde Street, Edinburgh. At the monthly prayer meeting of the church on 18 March 1827, an anonymous circular was read. The writer addressed the Baptist Churches of Scotland in sorrow at their disunity, and the consequent failure of witness. He announced that a number of individuals had resolved to meet in Edinburgh at half past seven every Wednesday evening to spend an hour in prayer about such matters. He asserted that Baptists were basically united about the doctrines of the word of God, and that they were all agreed on the independency of the local church. The main differences concerned the number of pastors and the practice of exhortation. He appealed for forbearance. In April 1827 several pastors and members of various churches met to consider the propriety of forming a Union of the Baptist Churches in Scotland, and this was approved unanimously. This meeting was held in Elder Street Chapel, and participants included Alexander McLeod, a pastor from Glasgow and formerly an itinerant evangelist in Perthshire, Jonathan Watson of Cupar, later to become the first president of the Union formed in 1869, and John Gilmore, pastor of an 'English' Church in Aberdeen. In June a further meeting was held in Elder Street Chapel. Delegates from twelve churches were present, and letters were read from twenty churches, which were, with the exception of six, favourable to union. Here the records fail, and it seems that this brave attempt at united work foundered on the continuing doctrinal prickliness that would characterize the Scottish Baptists for a long time, and on the extreme independency of the local church, which made stronger churches withhold their support.[63]

The next attempt to form a Union was more successful for a time, even though it was soon associated with the name of Francis Johnstone. A Scottish Baptist Association, consisting mostly of Home Mission churches, was formed at Tullymet in 1835. James Haldane preached at the inauguration, and the churches set out to fulfil four objectives:

a. to increase brotherly love and friendly intercourse among the churches, such as agree in holding the sentiments generally called evangelical;
b. to promote united exertion in the cause of Christ in general and Baptist sentiments in particular;
c. to obtain accurate statistical information;
d. to address to the churches an annual letter and progress report.

The founding churches were Tullymet, Blair Atholl, Grantown, Lawers, Killin, Perth, Cupar, Millport, Greenock and Campbeltown.[64] Although such leaders as James Paterson of Glasgow and William Innes of Edinburgh were willing to preach at annual gatherings, they would not give greater support, and when Johnstone arrived in Cupar in 1842, he found a small body indeed. Almost at once he was appointed joint secretary with Robert Thomson of Perth, and changed the name of the body to the Baptist Union of Scotland, with seventeen churches associated.

The first meeting of the new organization was held in Cupar in 1843. Johnstone was a keen collector of statistics, and laid before the churches a list of towns of considerable size where there was no Baptist witness. There were large aims for fellowship, education and evangelism. James Blair and T.P. Henderson were appointed as full-time evangelists, and new churches were formed, sometimes near older, staider Baptist bodies, as in Dunfermline and Galashiels. Approaches were made for union with the BHMS, which did not at this time take place.[65] It seems that the Union felt the responsibility for larger towns, and the Home Mission for the thinly populated parts of the country, but the real reason may have been connected with theological differences, and an unfortunate wrangle over an article in the *Free Church Magazine.*

In 1845 the *Free Church Magazine* took exception to a tract circulated by the Union. It was published by the London Baptist Tract Society, and its title, *The Origins, Claims and Antiquity of the Baptists*, suggests that it was a hard-hitting booklet. In the next number of the *Magazine*, there was a letter signed by Haldane, Innes, H.D. Dickie, Anderson, Watson and other leading Baptists of the older schools, disclaiming all knowledge of it, and making very disparaging comments on the 'small section ... merely a fragment claiming a lofty name' that had lately arisen. The Union asked some pertinent questions in its reply, and defended its right to be considered a force among Scottish churches. Johnstone and Landels from this time ceased to be invited to the committee of the BHMS, the one long-standing area of united Baptist work in Scotland.[66] Gradually the Union dwindled, and on Johnstone's removal to England in 1856, it dissolved.

Against such odds the new evangelism made great progress, and with the work of the Union in evangelism, training and the gathering of facts, Baptist life takes on a more modern look. The statistics contained in the first annual report of the Union, for 1844, show that some thirty-two new churches had been formed in the period 1820-44, with twenty-five of these belonging to the years 1831-44. Some of these churches were of considerable significance, including James Paterson's church in Hope Street, Glasgow (which later moved to Adelaide Place).[67] Soon, in 1846, another important church, meeting latterly at Marshall Street, Edinburgh, was formed by Francis Johnstone himself.[68] The fruit of the ongoing labours of the Home Mission was also apparent in the constituting of several new churches in Orkney and Shetland, and in the Inner Hebrides. The 1844 report lists a total of ninety-one churches, with approximately 5,500 members, of whom some 1,000 were Gaelic-speaking.

In 1837-8 the results of a government survey of church accommodation in Scotland were published. Every congregation in the country was asked a variety of questions concerning seating accommodation, stipend, means of finance and services provided. Baptist Churches took part, sometimes under protest, and we have an interesting picture of their state. In general it is evident that congregations far outnumbered membership, that most pastors were very poorly paid and that the majority of members were designated 'poor and working class'. In Edinburgh the exceptions were the strict party of Scotch Baptists, who were largely engaged in business, and the Elder Street Church (later Dublin Street). In this church, where members were admitted without necessarily being baptized, less than half of them were poor and working-class. A list of membership with occupations for this church in 1841 shows that many different trades and professions were represented. The minister was paid as much as £200 per annum, a distinction which he shared with James Paterson of Hope Street, Glasgow.[69]

Ministry and Theology

The desire to promote home mission by means of itinerant evangelists was an important factor in encouraging formal ministerial education among Baptists. The classes held by the Haldanes and their associates in Glasgow, Edinburgh and Dundee prepared some men who later became Baptists,[70] but men of original Baptist persuasion usually had to seek training in England in the early nineteenth century. Bradford Baptist Academy under William Steadman received several men from Scotland. They later returned to Scotland as itinerant evangelists and pastors, or else served in England or Ireland.[71] Bristol Baptist College prepared several Scottish Baptists for missionary service in India, and most Scots who went to Bristol would have had a foreign missionary interest. One distinguished Scottish missionary who served at Serampore, Dr John Leechman, attended Glasgow University and Bristol Baptist College.[72]

Although there was something of a prejudice against a trained ministry in Scotland, especially among Scotch Baptists, several Baptist pastors who had links with Independency or with the 'English' Baptist tradition held classes of their own. Lachlan Mackintosh of Grantown-on-Spey had such a class which he maintained in the 1820s with the support of Robert Haldane.[73] Francis Johnstone also attempted to provide training for students. He began in Cupar with four men whom he boarded and taught, and transferred his academy to Edinburgh in 1846. Among his students were James Culross, Oliver Flett and Finlay Forbes, men of repute in later years.[74]

Baptist leaders applied their learning well, and several wrote books. The most prolific writers of this era were the Haldane brothers, who produced many theological and polemical pamphlets. Robert Haldane, who engaged in evangelistic work in Switzerland and France in 1816-19, composed a well-known commentary on the Epistle to the Romans, based on lectures given at Geneva, and first published in French in 1819.[75] He also wrote *Evidences and Authority of Divine Revelation*, published in 1816. This was the first work to deduce from a high doctrine of inspiration the infallibility of the scriptures, and it is the source of the modern Evangelical belief in verbal inspiration.[76] Robert Haldane later took a stand against the inclusion of the Apocrypha in the Bibles published by the British and Foreign Bible Society.[77] James Haldane's *View of Social Worship* of 1805 showed something of the influence of Sandeman and the Glasite tradition, and advocated a close following of scripture in worship.[78]

William Innes wrote several works, mainly of a didactic nature, and was himself in the book trade. Francis Johnstone, besides promoting a number of monthly magazines, published a theological exposition called *The Gospel*

Roll, while George Barclay of Irvine wrote on baptism and prophetic subjects, and also controverted John McLeod Campbell.[79] Christopher Anderson produced a scholarly work on the *Annals of the English Bible* and some devotional books, as well as numerous reports and memorials.[80]

It cannot be said that there was much conscious study of liturgy. Yet Baptist writers defined themselves incidentally, often against the Sandemanian position, and by practice the worship and order of the churches began to approximate to something at least recognizable today.

Wider Relations

Baptists were, in general, inclined politically to conservatism, at least until Johnstone's time, although the Haldanes had been suspected of sedition in the nervous years following the French Revolution. After 1815, when cautious political views were safe to hold, the only political activities in which Baptists participated were the establishing of the right to burgh franchise in the 1830s, and a slight excitement over the Reform Bills.[81] At the end of the period, when the churches contained some leading businessmen, support was expressed for the emancipation of American negro slaves, and emissaries were kindly received.[82] Baptists were on the way to their Victorian support of the Liberal Party.

The Disruption of 1843 does not appear to have caused much unrest among Baptists. In Perthshire and the northern Highlands, as well as in Kirkcudbrightshire, home missionaries noted the contentious nature of the debate, and in some places Baptist work suffered as congregations were temporarily distracted.[83] Although the Free Church might have been expected to be more sympathetic to Baptists than the Established Church, it continued to hold to the principle of the State Establishment of the faith. Relationships with the Independents were poisoned by the financial and personal squabbles after the Haldanes became Baptists, and, although Baptist leaders sought and obtained ecclesiastical respectability, the churches remained small and insignificant compared with the large Presbyterian bodies. Early Evangelical Presbyterian support for the BMS dwindled as Scotland created its own missionary societies, and it was only in such bodies as the Bible Society that there was real co-operation.

Conclusion

When Francis Johnstone wrote his 'Summary and Remarks' at the end of the first report of the Baptist Union, he attempted a brief review of the progress of Baptist life in Scotland. According to Archibald McLean, there were about 380 Baptists in Scotland in 1795; by 1844 there were about 5,500.

'In half a century,' wrote Johnstone, 'considering the increase of population etc., alas! how little progress have we made! Had we been doing our duty, instead of 5,000 we might at least have been 50,000.' According to Johnstone's statistics, the average membership of a Baptist Church was sixty-one, and thirty-nine churches had thirty or fewer members. The largest churches were those at Hanover Street (soon to merge in John Street) and Hope Street, Glasgow, with approximately 300 and 400 members each, and those at Bristo Street and Elder Street, Edinburgh, with 260 and 280 members respectively.[84]

Yet, while Baptists had not increased their numbers as substantially as Johnstone would have wished, much was achieved in the period 1800-50. The number of churches in Scotland had grown noticeably, and this provided the foundation for further advance. There was also the prospect of bringing together the diverse strands of Baptist life, and, despite its fragility, the Union which had been supported so strongly by Johnstone pointed to the possibility of a new era of united effort.

Notes

1. A. Skevington Wood, *The Inextinguishable Blaze: spiritual renewal and advance in the eighteenth century* (Exeter 1967).
2. Raymond Brown, *The English Baptists of the Eighteenth Century* (London 1986), pp 71-82, 115-41.
3. Arthur Fawcett, *The Cambuslang Revival: the Scottish Evangelical Revival of the eighteenth century* (Edinburgh 1971).
4. D. Butler, *John Wesley and George Whitefield in Scotland* (Edinburgh 1898).
5. See, in general, A.L. Drummond and James Bulloch, *The Scottish Church, 1688-1843* (Edinburgh 1973). See also Friedhelm Voges, 'Moderate and Evangelical Thinking in the later Eighteenth Century: differences and shared attitudes', *Records of the Scottish Church History Society*, 22 (1985), pp 141-57.
6. John MacInnes, *The Evangelical Movement in the Highlands of Scotland* (Aberdeen 1951). D.E. Meek, 'Evangelical Missionaries in the Early Nineteenth-Century Highlands', *Scottish Studies*, 28 (1987), pp 1-34.
7. Brown, *English Baptists*, pp 119-21.
8. D.R. Reeves, 'The Interaction of Scottish and English Evangelicals, 1790-1810' (Glasgow M Litt 1973), pp 23-43. Hugh Anderson, *The Life and Letters of Christopher Anderson* (Edinburgh 1854), pp 19-21. J.W. Morris, *Memoirs of the Life and Writings of the Rev. Andrew Fuller* (London 1816).
9. Wood, *Inextinguishable Blaze*, p 219. Reeves, 'Interaction of Scottish and English Evangelicals'.
10. D.W. Lovegrove, 'Particular Baptist Itinerant Preachers during the late 18th and early 19th Centuries', *Baptist Quarterly*, 28 (1979), pp 127-41. Brown, *English Baptists*, pp 123-4.
11. See, in general, T.C. Smout, *A History of the Scottish People, 1560-1830* (London 1981 edn), pp 366-420; Bruce Lenman, *An Economic History of Modern Scotland, 1660-1976* (London 1977), pp 101-55; T.C. Smout, *A Century of the Scottish People, 1830-1950* (London 1986), pp 7-31.
12. On the textile industries, see the works cited in n. 11, and also A.J. Durie, *The Linen Industry in the Eighteenth Century* (Edinburgh 1978), and the summary account of the 'Textile Industries' by the same author in *A Companion to Scottish Culture*, ed David Daiches (London 1981), pp 371-2.
13. For the Coats family, see *The Thomas Coats Memorial Baptist Church, Paisley, Jubilee Book, 1944* (Paisley 1945). The Pullars have not yet been studied in detail.
14. Smout, *History of the Scottish People*, p 367. See cap 9, pp 162-7.
15. C.W. Withers, *Gaelic in Scotland 1698-1981: the geographical history of a language* (Edinburgh 1984), pp 182-208.
16. See, in general, James Hunter, *The Making of the Crofting Community* (Edinburgh 1976), and Eric Richards, *A History of the Highland Clearances*, 2 vols (London 1982-5).
17. See further cap 15, pp 291-2.

18. See further caps 9, pp 175-81, and 10, 190-6.
19. Dudley Reeves, 'John Campbell in Scotland', *Banner of Truth*, 126 (1974), pp 12-17.
20. Dudley Reeves, 'James Haldane: the making of an evangelist', *Banner of Truth*, 103 (1972), pp 24-30.
21. The main source for the lives and work of the Haldanes is Alexander Haldane, *Memoirs of the Lives of Robert Haldane of Airthrey and of his Brother, James Alexander Haldane* (London 1852). For a good summary account, see also Harry Escott, *A History of Scottish Congregationalism* (Glasgow 1960), pp 45-85.
22. A specific instance involved the apprehension of James Haldane and John Campbell when they were preaching in Argyll. See Haldane, *Haldane Lives*, pp 283-5.
23. ibid, pp 191-3.
24. ibid, pp 207-8.
25. ibid, p 231.
26. For the text of this admonition, see James Ross, *A History of Congregational Independency in Scotland* (Glasgow 1900), pp 278-82.
27. 'Mutual exhortation' involved the exhortation of one another by members of the church in the course of worship. In the Glasite tradition, exhortations consisted of 'scriptural phrases connected together by a theme, concluding without any application'. See D.B. Murray, 'The Influence of John Glas', *Records of the Scottish Church History Society*, 22 (1984), pp 50, 53-4, and also L.A. McMillon, *Restoration Roots* (Dallas 1983), pp 75-6.
28. Haldane, *Haldane Lives*, pp 357-8.
29. Escott, *Scottish Congregationalism*, pp 82-5. *The First Yearly Report of the Baptist Union of Scotland* (Cupar 1844).
30. Morris, *Fuller*, pp 146-7.
31. ibid, p 151.
32. For an account of George Barclay's life and work, see A.B. Thomson, 'Some Baptist Pioneers in Scotland during the Eighteenth Century and the Early Years of the Nineteenth: George Barclay', *Scottish Baptist Year Book (SBYB)*, 1902, pp 24-31.
33. George Yuille, ed, *History of the Baptists in Scotland* (Glasgow 1926), pp 60-1.
34. David Gilmour, *Reminiscences of the 'Pen' Folk* (Edinburgh 1873 edn).
35. Anderson, *Anderson*, pp 9-10, 68-9. Thomson, 'Baptist Pioneers: Christopher Anderson', *SBYB*, 1907, p 155.
36. Anderson, *Anderson*, pp 1-98.
37. ibid, pp 254-336.
38. ibid, p 257. List of Scottish students trained at Bristol Baptist College (by courtesy of the Rev. Sidney Hall).
39. Thomson, 'George Barclay', p 30.
40. Anderson, *Anderson*, pp 99-156.
41. ibid, p 65. Yuille, ed, *Baptists in Scotland*, pp 62-4.
42. ibid. See cap 14, p 276.
43. See cap 1, pp 22, and cap 14, p 262.
44. See cap 15, p 284.
45. Anderson, *Anderson*, pp 99-102, 117-19. For the early balance sheets of the society, see Dugald Sinclair, *Journal of Itinerating Exertions in some of the more destitute parts of Scotland*, 6 vols (Edinburgh 1814-17).
46. Yuille, ed, *Baptists in Scotland*, pp 72-3.
47. William Tulloch, 'Memoir of the late Mr Wm. Tulloch', *BHMS Report*, 1861, pp 20-1. See further cap 15, p 286.
48. This is clear in the surviving letters of Haldane to Tulloch, now preserved among the Waugh Papers, Baptist Union of Scotland Records, bundle 2.
49. See notes 45-6.
50. *Address by the Committee of the Baptist Home Missionary Society for Scotland* (Edinburgh 1827).
51. *BHMS Reports*, 1831, pp 13-14; 1833, p 25; 1843, p 22.
52. ibid, 1829, 1844.
53. ibid, 1829, p 58.
54. See cap 1, pp 16, 19, and cap 5, p 95.
55. James Scott, 'The Baptists of Scotland: an historical survey' (Glasgow PhD 1927), p 47.

56. ibid, p 81.
57. T. Witton Davies, 'A Scotch Baptist Circular', *Transactions of the Baptist Historical Society*, 6 (1919), pp 253, 257.
58. J. Williamson, *Reminiscences of the Old Baptist Church, Pleasance* (Edinburgh 1901), p 18.
59. A.C. Watters, *History of the British Churches of Christ* (Indianapolis, Ind., 1948), p 16. D.M. Thompson, *Let Sects and Parties Fall: a short history of the Association of Churches of Christ in Great Britain and Ireland* (Birmingham 1980), pp 13-32, 38-9.
60. Escott, *Scottish Congregationalism*, pp 116-17.
61. T.D. Landels, *William Landels, D.D.* (London 1900), pp 31-5.
62. For Johnstone, see the *Jubilee Handbook of Marshall Street Baptist Church* (Edinburgh 1896). cf Johnstone, *The Work of God and the Work of Man in Conversion* (Edinburgh 1848).
63. Waugh Papers, bundle 8. For some further discussion of this Union, see D.B. Murray, 'Baptists in Scotland before 1869', *Baptist Quarterly*, 23 (1970), pp 251-65 (esp pp 261-2).
64. Scott, 'Baptists of Scotland', p 89 (quoting the Minutes of the Scottish Baptist Association).
65. ibid, p 91.
66. See further Murray, 'Baptists in Scotland before 1869', p 264.
67. *First Yearly Report.* In Yuille, ed, *Baptists in Scotland*, p 169, Paterson is said to have espoused the principles of the 'General Baptists', at the same time as 'holding strongly to the practice of the English Baptist Churches'. If the use of the term 'General Baptists' is accurate, it would imply that Paterson and his church adhered to an Arminian theology, rather than the Calvinism of the other 'English' Baptist Churches.
68. See cap 5, p 99.
69. *Report of the Commission of Enquiry into the opportunities of public religious worship, and means of religious instruction, and the pastoral superintendence afforded to the people of Scotland*, 6 vols (Edinburgh 1837-8). For the composition of Elder Street, see further cap 5, p 99.
70. Haldane, *Haldane Lives*, pp 329-32. cf R.F. Calder, 'Robert Haldane's Theological Seminary', *Transactions of the Congregational Historical Society*, 13 (1937).
71. Besides Francis Johnstone, Scottish pastors who trained at Bradford before 1850 included Dugald Sinclair, John MacMillan (briefly at Inveraray), John Gilmore and David Douglas. *Annual Reports of the Northern Education Society*, 1804-25, Manchester Congregational College. We owe this reference to Dr Deryck Lovegrove.
72. List of Scottish students at Bristol Baptist College. Yuille, ed, *Baptists in Scotland*, p 251.
73. ibid. Haldane, *Haldane Lives*, p 331.
74. Yuille, ed, *Baptists in Scotland*, p 253.
75. Haldane, *Haldane Lives*, pp 402-71.
76. cf A.L. Drummond and James Bulloch, *The Church in Victorian Scotland, 1843-74* (Edinburgh 1975), p 251.
77. Haldane, *Haldane Lives*, pp 489-523.
78. Murray, 'Influence of John Glas', pp 53-4.
79. G.M. Tuttle, *So Rich a Soil: John McLeod Campbell on Christian Atonement* (Edinburgh 1986), p 37.
80. For a check-list of writings by Baptists, see Yuille, ed, *Baptists in Scotland*, pp 296-307.
81. Waugh Papers, Baptist Union of Scotland Records.
82. C.D. Rice, *The Scots Abolitionists, 1833-61* (Baton Rouge, La, 1981), p 207.
83. Angus MacNaughton, the Baptist pastor in Islay, noted that 'a great stumbling-block is cast in the people's way by the contention of different parties', and Duncan Cameron of the Lawers station claimed that 'many are much occupied with the agitation about the Free Church'; Peter Grant of Grantown-on-Spey wrote, 'Our greatest difficulty is to draw the minds of the people from this fearful struggle to the concerns of their precious souls'. Yet several Baptist Churches in the Highlands experienced revivals at this time. See *BHMS Reports*, 1844, pp 14-15, 21; 1845, pp 13-14; and also cap 15.
84. *First Yearly Report.*

D.E. Meek
D.B. Murray

3. THE LATER NINETEENTH CENTURY

In 1882 William Tulloch, president of the Baptist Union of Scotland, recalled the precarious beginnings of the Baptist Union. 'The thin straggled line of the little Baptist regiment contrasted most disadvantageously with the serried ranks and well disciplined troops of the Presbyterian corps.'[1] In mid-nineteenth-century Scotland Baptists suffered from lack of organization, congregations were few and limited in numbers, and many of them held independent views that kept them jealously apart.

Social and Economic Background

Baptist development between 1850 and 1914 must be understood in relation to a number of major changes which altered the structure and character of Scottish society. The continuing forces of industrial development, political conflict and social transformation presented the Church with immense problems and new opportunities. While it is true that within this broad context Baptists were a relatively small and uninfluential group, nevertheless by the end of the century they had become a vigorous and respected denomination.

The industrial growth of the period was accompanied by an acceleration of the movement of people from the countryside into the cities. In the fifty years from 1851 to 1901 the number of male workers employed in farming dropped by half.[2] Rural areas, particularly the Highlands and Islands, were seriously affected by migration to the cities and towns, and by emigration to the dominions of Canada, Australia and New Zealand. Between 1861 and 1911 there was a net loss of 737,036 by emigration, while in the same period the growing industrial county of Lanarkshire increased its population by 63,957.[3] Reports of the Baptist Home Mission constantly refer to the work being diminished by emigration. The 1855 report makes a brave attempt at seeing blessing in the export of godly people to wider fields of service.[4] In 1913 the annual report of the Baptist Union finds a little comfort in the loss of 401 members by emigration as compared with the previous year's loss of 546.[5] In small fellowships such losses were a serious problem.

The economic boom fuelled industrial development on an unprecedented scale, fostering the growth of areas like Clydeside, Lanarkshire and Dundee. Clydeside generated a concentration of heavy industry, shipbuilding and engineering, so that by the end of the century it is estimated that 70% of employment in the Glasgow area was skilled work.[6] With the expansion of the iron and steel industry came an insatiable demand for coal, and the mining areas of Lanarkshire, Ayrshire and Fife became close-knit communities. This was also the age when the textile trade was at its peak, and huge factories were built in Paisley. In these and other industrial areas like Dundee, Kirkcaldy and parts of the Borders, Baptist Churches grew strong. There were unprecedented booms, but there were also slumps. The effects of these developments on church life are highlighted in the 1878 report as the churches were forced to adjust to changing economic conditions. 'The churches have been passing through severe trials, especially in the mining and manufacturing districts, from the long depression of trade and the removal of many in search of employment.'[7]

Industrial development was not without its cost. Mass employment led inevitably to areas of dense population while the laissez-faire economy opened up an economic chasm between the labouring masses and the owner-employers. Crowded industrial towns and cities inevitably produced degrading living conditions and working-class ghettoes. A census in 1861 revealed that 34% of all Scottish houses had only one room and 37% had two rooms. Fifty years later half of the total population still inhabited two-room or single-room houses.[8]

Agitation for political reform culminated in a widened franchise after 1867 and political life became progressively more inclusive and representative. Congregational church government and freedom from state connection were principles well in tune with the spirit of the time. Scottish Baptists, like their English counterparts, supported the Liberal Party since it was most likely to promote the various Nonconformist concerns. For example, in 1913 pressure from the temperance lobby forced the concession of the Scottish Local Veto Bill.[9] As the century wore on, elections began to be a forum for the aspirations of the working classes. One effect of this in the new century was the increasing attraction of the Labour Party, especially for those who were alienated from the churches.

In education the major development in the second half of the century was the passing of overall control from the Kirk to the state in 1872. Earlier, educational opportunities had been significantly increased by denominational rivalry in providing schooling. One crucial effect of introducing compulsory education was the relieving of the churches of their general educational responsibilities. Almost immediately Sunday Schools began to move from hired halls to church premises, thus becoming part of the denominational congregation. Within a short time Sunday Schools had changed from being educational establishments to more rigorously religious institutions.[10] The longer-term effect, important before the end of the century, was the creation of a working class of thinking and often radical workmen who were no longer in awe of the educated middle classes.

The plight of the poor, many believed, was due to culpable negligence, laziness and immorality. It was by no means obvious to the powers that be that poverty was the result of an unjust economic system. There was a failure by the rich to understand the scale and horror of the industrial ghettoes. The alienation felt by the poor and the uncomprehending revulsion of the well-off found physical expression in the co-existence of suburban affluence and tenement squalor. In the churches class distinctions came to play an increasing part. Pew rents existed in some Baptist Churches and were actually commended in a presidential address as a way of helping to maintain the ministry.[11] As society's divisions invaded church life, the poor began to feel themselves marginal members, receivers of charity.

Alongside the undeniable poverty of working people, a new mentality of self-respect and fierce independence began to assert itself. The churchgoing working man's lifestyle offered stability for family life within a framework of hard work, self-discipline, literacy and financial independence.[12] This self-respect and basic decency is all the more significant since there were frequent complaints about drunkenness, immorality and vice, usually with reference to the working class.[13] Undoubtedly there was much moral laxity, and it was by no means confined to the working classes or the industrial centres. The Baptist Assembly of 1885 passed a resolution which deplored 'the widespread vice and immorality which the recent terrible revelations made known', and urged churches of the Union to 'encourage a higher and nobler life and character among young people'.[14]

Social developments created a situation favourable for Baptist church growth. For example, Partick and Govan grew by almost three and four times respectively in forty years, and Glasgow's population soared from 275,000 in 1841 to 784,000 in 1911.[15] In densely populated areas where there was no parish church, a small gathered fellowship was often attractive to an initially migrant population searching for identity to replace the older community patterns. However, this was not always the case. At a public conference in 1873 the subject discussed was the low state of the churches. Amongst several reported comments it was stated that there was a 'lack of social intercourse'. William Grant of Edinburgh told of one person's experience in a Baptist Church. 'He left that meeting without anyone taking the slightest notice of him . . . he left quite freezed.'[16]

The rise of an artisan class, improvements in education and political reform created a large group who were attracted to the congregational principle and the freedom that underlay it, and who valued the framework of ethical support to be found in an Evangelical church. On the debit side, however, the alienated mass of the poor, and the obvious inequalities of an increasingly affluent society, created resentments that would ultimately rebound. Political progress, increased education and the intellectual revolution caused by science and biblical criticism combined to create a hard secular core disillusioned with the ecclesiastical world.

The Religious Climate and Social Action

The church context within which Scottish Baptists did their work was complex and unsettled. The aftermath of the Disruption was a legacy of denominational rivalry which, amongst other things, weakened the primacy of the Church of Scotland. There were long legal battles over property division, and a general preoccupation with a whole network of concerns crucial to Presbyterianism but of little relevance to other churches. The overwhelming dominance of Presbyterianism, however, was not broken by the Disruption. By the middle of the century there were approximately one million Presbyterian communicants; Baptists numbered perhaps six thousand.[17]

The Free Church of Scotland, which was solidly Evangelical, faced a post-Disruption Kirk determined to re-group and fulfil its obligations. During the major revivals of the period and in support of evangelistic agencies, Baptists found themselves co-operating with other Evangelicals. In the later part of the century, when there were divergent views of the church's role in social action, the Church of Scotland sought to remove the root causes of social decay, such as poverty, bad housing and poor sanitation. The more Evangelical approach, which attempted to change society by the conversion of the individual, was also increasingly represented in the Church of Scotland.

The tension between social action and evangelism came to a head after the First World War, but already Baptists were wrestling with the ethical implications of the gospel they preached. 'Think of the unblest poverty that is growing side by side with enormous wealth . . . crushing the spirit in ways that comfortable people cannot understand. Think of the haunts of vice . . . the drunkenness . . . the little children. Christ's churches cannot fold their hands and say 'we knew it not'. You are not your brother's keeper; you are your brother's brother . . . you are bound to care for him.'[18] In 1888 William Landels commended the work of the Salvation Army as preparing the way for evangelism. 'Although we can scarcely regard it as a genuinely evangelistic movement, it is a valuable pioneering agency . . . which has broken habits which stood in the way of the reception of the gospel.'[19] The weightiest contribution to Baptist thinking came from J.T. Forbes in his address to the Baptist Union of Scotland Assembly in 1904, and in a later address to the Baptist Union of Great Britain and Ireland at a meeting in Glasgow. He told Scottish Baptists, 'Social salvation is the body of which spiritual individual salvation is the soul.' 'Debt, dirt, drink and the devil, seem literally to rule in the slums.' He referred to the inconsistency between the Church's teaching and prevailing forms of economic oppression and corruption, and he called for 'a sanctifying of political speech and agitation to God. We ought to make new conditions to foster the new life the gospel makes.'[20]

In fact, by the time Forbes spoke, Baptist laymen were becoming increasingly involved in politics at local and national levels. Sir Hugh Gilzean Reid, distinguished journalist and founder of *The Buchan Observer*, became Liberal Member of Parliament for Aston Manor in 1885-6. In 1854 he had been baptized and joined John Street Baptist Church in Aberdeen, moving from there to Peterhead and Edinburgh. He created the Edinburgh Co-operative Building Society, enabling thousands of working men to rent or buy decent housing, and went on to own *The North Eastern Daily Gazette* based in Middlesbrough.[21] William Adamson, a third generation miner, was heavily involved in miners' welfare and local politics. He served as Labour Member of Parliament for Fife West from 1910 to 1931 and acted as leader of the party from 1917 to 1921. He was a member, deacon, secretary and Sunday School Superintendent in the Dunfermline West Baptist Church. Sir Thomas Glen-Coats, thread manufacturer and an honorary Colonel of the 2nd Battalion, Argyll and Sutherland Highlanders, was Liberal MP for Renfrewshire West from 1906 to January 1910. Other Baptist MPs were Sir John Mills McCallum, soap manufacturer in Paisley and a member and deacon of Thomas Coats Memorial Church, and Sir Robert Pullar, a proprietor of a dye works and a solicitor in Perth.[22]

There were other clear instances of Baptists becoming involved in social action. In 1878 eight new church buildings were opened and the annual report justifies them as 'centres whence flow forth the most beneficent influences for the amelioration and regeneration of the race'. [23] In 1896 Baptists were involved in twelve mission extensions in which there were sewing classes, Bands of Hope and Sunday Schools ranging from twelve scholars in Lochgilphead to over five hundred in Frederick Street, Glasgow.[24] Christian businessmen like Thomas Coats of Paisley and the Pullar family in Perth gave financial help to many social and denominational projects.

The presence of mission churches and mission Sunday Schools exposed the desperate plight of many poorer families. Social welfare was disorganized and any public assistance was usually low and always tainted with the stigma of poor relief. The large number of desperately poor children exercised many churches and inspired the work of William Quarrier. In Glasgow in the 1860s Quarrier launched the Industrial Brigade. Street urchins were organized into the 'Shoeblack Brigade', the 'News Brigade' and the 'Parcel Brigade', and by doing such small tasks they were able to earn enough money to live above destitution. In 1872 a refuge and mission centre was set up which gave lodging to 2,137 homeless children in its first ten months.[25] In 1878 the first phase of the Bridge of Weir Orphan Homes was completed and the major work of Quarrier began. The 1892 figures are a remarkable tribute to Quarrier's vision. There were 731 children at Bridge of Weir; 454 new children were admitted from the City Home in Glasgow; and 669 'homeless, friendless wanderers' had been given a night's shelter in model lodging houses.[26]

The key to social reform, according to most Baptists, was temperance. Whether drunkenness was understood as a flight from the misery of poverty, or its cause, it was regarded as a major obstacle standing between the churches and those they sought to reach. 'The cursed traffic [in alcohol] ruins more souls in a week than the preaching of the gospel rescues in a year.'[27] J.W. Hansley, a prison chaplain, described crime as condensed alcohol.[28] A calculation of average income amongst poorer families, compared with amounts of alcohol consumed, reveals a gap in income which could be bridged only by crime. 'Intemperance is stalking abroad, cursing our land, devastating our homes, entering our churches and emptying our pews . . . .'[29] Temperance societies had been in existence in Scotland since the 1830s, but it was the middle of the century before the churches adopted temperance as a major preoccupation. Temperance committees were formed in the Free Church in 1847 and in the Church of Scotland in 1848. It was 1881 before Baptists had an organization which expressed the denomination's concern. In 1857 three Baptist pastors registered for a conference 'On the Suppression of the Liquor Traffic' held in Manchester.[30] After 1870 temperance strategy focused on the young and many Bands of Hope were formed. In 1896 there were sixty-one Bands of Hope in Baptist Churches.[31] In 1876 the assembly passed a resolution deploring the continuing prevalence of drunkenness; there was a public conference at the 1879 assembly dealing with intemperance; and in 1881 the Scottish Baptist Total Abstinence Society (SBTAS) was formed.[32] Baptists were involved in wider temperance agencies too. Francis Spite, provost of Clydebank, was a tea dealer and health food specialist who became director of the Scottish Temperance League and chairman of the Band of Hope Board. He was secretary of the SBTAS from 1891.[33] In 1913 Miss Henderson, a deaconess at Stirling, led several missions to Shetland and the north-east. At the high season there was a large influx of fisher girls (Fraserburgh and Peterhead had an increase of over 8,000 workers). A number of these missions were run in conjunction with the SBTAS, illustrating the connection in Baptist strategy between temperance and evangelism.[34]

Public concern about drunkenness was also reflected in improved legislation with the Forbes Mackenzie Act of 1853, and the Publicans' Certificate (Scotland) Act of 1876. In 1894 the Liberal Government introduced a Local Option Bill which was defeated before the second reading passed. Seventy Baptist Churches presented petitions.[35] The widely attested benefits of temperance in harmonious families, together with a measure of comfort and financial independence, are positive evidence (as the extent of drunkenness and its consequences are negative evidence) that the churches' persistent opposition was fully justified. On the other hand mass drunkenness on Sundays suggests that a large section of the poorer population was hostile to temperance. The churches' unequivocal stance against the drink trade served to drive a wedge further between temperate churchgoers and the non-churchgoing sections of the working classes.

Theological Developments

Changes in society coincided with fundamental changes in theology and church life. The three main Presbyterian Churches officially minuted their gratitude to God for the revivals of 1859-61.[36] Various factors combined to make the 1850s an age of religious susceptibility. The revivals associated with Charles Finney in the large cities of the United States demonstrated the effectiveness of new evangelistic techniques. The 1851 religious census highlighted the churches' failure to reach the working population. Already in Scotland the dominant theological system of Calvinism was being modified under the influence of James Morison,[37] and it was soon to be further affected by the ministry of Moody and Sankey.

The theology and practice of evangelism were particularly influenced by the uncompromisingly Arminian tone of much revivalist preaching and method, and by the pragmatic argument that it was effective in bringing large numbers to Christ. The attempt to create a spiritually receptive atmosphere and the universal offer of the gospel followed by a call to decision cut across the bows of orthodox Calvinism. The Moody and Sankey campaigns of 1873-4 introduced a new type of sacred song which displayed emotional warmth and eschewed doctrinal precision in favour of evangelical experience. Underlying Moody's preaching was a theology of the cross that was warm and moving. 'The Gospel which he preached was therefore one of change, not in the mind of God, Who was eternal and unchanging love, but in the mind of man, who can be delivered from guilt and fear and reconciled to God once he knew God's love in Christ.'[38]

The mid-century revivals in America and Ulster were well publicized, fuelling interest and curiosity. In Scotland there were prayer meetings in which the gospel was freely offered to all. The 1859-61 revivals began in Galloway and then affected Glasgow, spreading out to reach all Perthshire and the north-east from the Moray Firth to the Firth of Tay. Presbyterian gains in Scotland were substantial, one estimate being 33%.[39] Further, instead 'of debate and discussions, as in days of yore, on church laws and reform, ministers and elders cheerfully devoted most of the time in conference on the best means of saving souls and promoting the interests of Christ's kingdom'.[40] The effect was most dramatic for the Brethren. Their numbers were greatly increased in Ayrshire, Lanarkshire, Glasgow and the north-east, while at the same time their scattered and spontaneously started congregations became an identifiable and more organized Christian presence.[41] Baptists were also affected, though in less immediately obvious ways. Existing congregations were strengthened and a new impetus to evangelism and co-operative effort was given. Later, in 1877, a Loan Fund was proposed at the Baptist Assembly because 'due to the revival of religion there has been a great increase in building operations'.[42] Curiously enough, there were very few new Baptist Churches founded in the aftermath of the 1859-61 revivals. In general the revivals and evangelistic campaigns left their mark on worship, with the increasing use of hymns, and on evangelism, as new stimulus was given. Evangelism became a force capable of melting frigid sectarianism between denominations, and in particular isolationism amongst Baptists. In Perth, on 22 August 1860, a crowd of about 4,000 people was addressed by Church of Scotland, Church of England, United Presbyterian, Congregationalist and Baptist ministers. The sponsors claimed they had 'buried sectarianism in the South Inch of Perth that day and saw no Christian weep over its grave'.[43] An increasing concern for social reform can be traced to the need of revived churches and zealous Christians to find a practical outlet for their faith, usually in missions and social projects in working-class areas.

In Glasgow the city's United Evangelistic Association came into being. It maintained a dozen agencies of evangelism and social relief including the work of the Tent Hall.[44] The Glasgow Bible Training Institute was formed. Baptists gave wholehearted support to the new forms of evangelism and learned many lessons that influenced their own approach. The concept of having a week of mission, the growing use of hymn books and the increased urgency of evangelistic services were lasting features of Baptist life that owed much to revival influence.

The second half of the century saw the emergence of a new religious scepticism. Developments in natural science, a growing dissatisfaction with the dogmatic basis of Christianity, the increase in educational opportunity and literacy, with their attendant results in more critical and independent thought, all combined to create a new mistrust of biblical faith. Yet it was not the assured results of scientific discovery so much as its gradual effect on popular opinion that contributed to the nascent scepticism of the late nineteenth century. The belief that science provided evidence of the inaccuracy of the Bible was a conclusion attractive to those already alienated from the Church. The book of Genesis became the field for an intellectual tug of war between a vigorous young scepticism armed with scientific evidence, and the Church, initially tolerant, but gradually drawn into the debate in an attempt to reverse the growing suspicion that science had disproved the Bible. New techniques of biblical study, originating from Germany, contributed further to the theological restlessness of the age. Higher criticism concerned itself with the date, structure and sources of biblical books, and lower criticism occupied itself with trying to establish the textual accuracy of a document. In response chairs of biblical criticism were founded in four Scottish universities.[45] In the Free Church of Scotland Christian apologetics was predominantly conservative and reasserted the doctrine of 'the plenary, verbal inspiration of the Word of God'. The defensive conservatism of the Free Church led in 1881 to the removal of William Robertson Smith from the chair of oriental languages and Old Testament exegesis at the Free Church College, Aberdeen. His espousal of German biblical criticism, particularly that of Wellhausen, was criticized as undermining belief in the full inspiration of the Bible.[46]

Baptists were greatly preoccupied with the work of evangelism and church extension at this time. Their numbers were still relatively small and many of their members did not move in the social circles in which matters of science and criticism were debated. Yet there are hints of some awareness of contemporary trends. In 1877 P.W. Grant of Perth Baptist Church published a work entitled *The Bible Record of Genesis True*. John Urquhart of Glasgow produced *The Inspiration and Accuracy of Holy Scripture* and a useful volume called *The New Biblical Guide*. In 1869 a warning was sounded by James Culross from Stirling. 'Many anticipate a battle with infidelity, skilled, cultured, scientific ... the points of attack are different, the weapons are new.' In giving this warning he was pleading for an informed Christian apologetic, 'an argument, a defence ... This readiness to give an answer is the next thing in importance to the experimental knowledge of the gospel.'[47] P.W. Grant included in his presidential address, delivered in 1891, a stout defence of the Bible as 'such a divine and complete and all-sufficient revelation as to supply every real want, and to sustain all needful faith'. He admits the possibility of the biblical record being inconsistent with scientific or historical evidence, but refuses to see such facts as fatal to biblical authority. The perfect sufficiency of scripture is not that it is 'unerring as to every detail of the human record' but 'unerring as to the divine revelation of all needful moral, spiritual, eternal, redemptive truth'. He closes with the reassuring observation that whatever the learned may conclude, and whatever the most extravagant criticism will allow, 'all Christians may be perfectly assured that all the alterations thus made would fail to affect one single doctrine of any essential consequence'.[48] Baptists were aware of the questions posed, but they tended to be too preoccupied with evangelism and propagating Baptist principles to be greatly affected by the more intellectual concerns of science and theology.

Baptist worship was less clerical and less formally structured than that of the Presbyterian Churches. Nevertheless there were broad trends in worship patterns which left a permanent impress on Baptist practice. The experience of the revivals and the influence of revival theology had created a dissatisfaction with the doctrinal limitations of the psalms as vehicles for expressing Christian theology. While they were replete with mentions of providence, God's goodness and the law of God, and while they contained many beautiful expressions of devotion, they were devoid of references to the atonement, salvation by grace through faith, life in Christ and the promise of eternal life. After the awakenings it became more and more important in worship to express the emotional and experimental dimension of Christian faith. The introduction of organs, the use of hymn books, the commencement of church choirs and the regular use of evangelistic services were amongst the lasting changes in Baptist worship. In 1877 there is a reference to the need to compile a new hymn book.[49] Some larger churches like Thomas Coats Memorial in Paisley, Adelaide Place in Glasgow and Dublin Street in Edinburgh had their own hymn books. In 1894, on the initiative of the Young People's Christian Endeavour Society and after considerable discussion, the congregation of Crown Terrace, Aberdeen, decided 'that an organ should be used in the services of the church'. Two hundred and seventy-six circulars were issued, and of these 165 were returned saying 'yes', fifty-three answered 'no', one paper was spoilt and fifty-seven papers were not returned. These figures reveal considerable opposition, but an organ was purchased the following year for approximately £100, the bulk of the sum being raised by the Christian Endeavour Society.[50]

In summary, industrial growth, political reform, population movement, urbanization and the related problems of poverty, intemperance and decay form the social background of Baptist development during the period. The post-Disruption re-alignment of Presbyterianism, the relation of the gospel to social problems, the fight against alcohol abuse, the erosion of Calvinism, the influence of revival and the beginnings of the conflict with science and criticism provide the more immediate context within which the Baptist denominational consciousness was formed.

The Formation of the Baptist Union of Scotland

Until the creation of the Baptist Union of Scotland in 1869, the Baptist Home Missionary Society (BHMS) was the main body concerned with advancing the denomination through evangelism. Its sphere of operations was mainly the Highlands and Islands, although at least thirteen Lowland churches benefited from its support. The BHMS worked through a number of itinerant evangelists and pastors. They were clearly men of immense dedication who accepted extreme poverty for the sake of the gospel. There are many expressions of concern about the health of missioners in the society's reports. Small churches supported by the Home Mission were severely hampered by population movement, as can be illustrated by the example of the Colonsay Church, which lost nine members in 1852.[51]

After 1869 the relationship between the society and the Union became one of co-operation, and in fact they continued in parallel until 1931. The number of agents reached as high as thirty. In 1910 it was reported there were still fifty-six mission stations attached in some way to the denomination.[52] In the later part of the century an increasing amount of financial support came from larger city churches, and there was substantial financial help from English Baptists. Union sensitivity to the needs of the Home Mission is clearly evident in the 1878 report. Expressing gratitude for the £64,000 spent on twenty-four new churches in the nine years of the Union's life, the secretary commented that all this had been raised 'without diminishing the resources of the Home Mission, but the reverse; for besides the considerable sum which the Union has saved the Mission, its ordinary income has been doubled since the operations of the Union commenced'.[53] The figures for the BHMS report for 1909 show that £450 came from Union subscriptions, £612 was from mission churches, and £500 from English Baptists.[54]

Assessment of the work of the Home Mission must be in terms of the ongoing life of mission churches still in existence, but must also recognize the widespread influence of converts who emigrated and disseminated Baptist witness and principles. Less tangible is the lingering memory in the small congregations of the indomitable men of God who led them. Duncan Ferguson who served the Ross of Mull for forty years, for instance, was still remembered sixty years later.[55]

The first Baptist Union lasted only from 1843 till 1856. Francis Johnstone was the main driving force and the one man capable of arguing the case for co-operation. Failure was due to possible rivalry with the Home Mission, lack of support by key figures and the Morisonian views of Johnstone.[56] In 1856 Dr James Paterson of Adelaide Place in Glasgow formed an association of individual Baptists which evolved into the present Baptist Union in 1869. At its annual conferences in 1865 and 1866 members of the association discussed the possibility of forming a Union of churches. Negotiations culminated in a meeting in January 1869 at which the following resolution was unanimously approved. 'That a Union of Evangelical Baptist Churches of Scotland is desirable and practicable, and that its objects should be to promote Evangelical religion in connection with the Baptist Denomination in Scotland, to cultivate brotherly affection and to secure co-operation in everything related to the interests of the Associated churches.'[57] At the inaugural meeting in October of the same year William Tulloch commented: 'the courting and wooing are all over, and the banns have been publicly proclaimed, in due order, none objecting, and none forbidding, and nothing now remains but the happy consummation of the too-long deferred Union'.[58] In his presidential address of 1882, Tulloch recalled the excitement and the vulnerability of the new Union. At the birth of the Union fifty-one churches consisting of 3,700 members covenanted together in a co-operative fellowship with agreed aims.[59] By 1914 it had become a significant denomination of 137 churches with over 20,000 members.[60]

Evangelism and Extension

From the outset the Union was committed to a vigorous programme of evangelism. Evangelistic deputations of ministers, in the beginning sent in pairs, became a continuous policy, as the denomination's resources of evangelists were organized and put to fuller use. In 1909, seventy-six ministers were listed as being available for evangelistic missions.[61] Early reports speak with excitement about the results. 'The kind of people gathered was just what we wished, the rough and apparently non-churchgoing . . . one of the most pleasing aspects was that men and children in their ordinary working clothes . . . there were open airs with two to three hundred present and well attended enquirers' meetings afterwards. Many who listened had not been in a place of worship for years.'[62] The conclusion was that congregations had been heartened by the sympathy and co-operation of sister churches. The opinion of the press was also favourable. 'The interest excited by this effort has been such as to lead to the hope that the Baptist Union of Scotland will persevere in and still more extend such operations and it may well encourage the Church Courts of other denominations in organizing similar efforts for carrying the gospel to the masses in our cities.'[63] Reports from aided churches in 1913 reveal new and imaginative approaches to evangelism. In Irvine the members had been 'visiting homes with gospel papers'; in Kilmarnock there were encouraging attendances at 'kitchen meetings'; in Larbert there were 'Saturday night open-air meetings'; at Largo a successful series of 'children's sand services'; the Shettleston Church had distributed 300 copies per month of its own gospel magazine, *The Shettleston Home Messenger.* All of this activity elicited the comment from one hard-pressed church member at Vale of Leven: 'Our pastor is fearless, hardworking and gives us plenty to do.'[64]

Despite this, as Tulloch pointed out in 1882, the churches failed to reach the highly educated and cultured on the one hand and the mass of toiling poor on the other. He warned: 'Unless we break over the stereotyped forms and habits of modern church life we cannot touch the one or the other'.[65] As early as 1873 at the public conference of the Baptist Union a layman from Cupar complained that 'we look too much to the pulpit and too little to evangelistic labour' and he suggested teams of evangelists should be formed to work alongside the ministers.[66]

Together with evangelistic effort there was church extension work. Every year new churches were being established or buildings opened. Of course some causes were short-lived and some were tiny, but the overall impression of the period is one of extension and consolidation. From the returns made to the Union in 1879 two consecutive comments show the contrasting fortunes of some churches. 'The cause never looked so well or hopefully.' 'The chapel was sold, and the church has ceased to exist.'[67] Nevertheless during the period over eighty churches joined the Baptist Union, helped in many cases with aid in ministry, in building loans and in other ways.

A study of the churches added during the period can reveal what was probably the primary factor in the formation of each. Twenty-five churches came into being in places where there had been local church-sponsored extension. Over thirty new churches were established due in part to the personal initiative of one individual. The Union and Home Missionary Society took direct initiatives in at least ten churches, while District Associations were directly responsible for six and heavily involved in supporting several others. Local missions and local revivals featured in the starting of six others, and in at least seven cases there seems to have been a discovery of Baptist principles through Bible study or Baptist propaganda. Four churches developed from house fellowships, and, perhaps less happily, nine churches were the result of secession from existing causes.

William Landels argued in 1888 for a fund to finance strategic church extension. Concerned about the investing of scarce resources in small, short-lived churches, or churches that would always be too small to support their own ministers, he argued for a reasoned, planned approach. He suggested some guiding principles. The Union should guarantee support for two or three years to an efficient minister to form a church in large towns where there was a reasonable chance of it becoming self-supporting in a short time. Where there was an existing fellowship, help should be given to procure a building in which the church could consolidate its work. In some cases the Union should initiate a movement without local help, while in other cases the Union should support the efforts of those who had already started.

In the same address, Landels takes issue with those Baptists who oppose extension work into areas where there is an existing Evangelical witness. Conceding the principle that sinners becoming Christians is more important than Christians becoming Baptists, he insisted on the obligation 'to teach them all things' that Christ commanded.[68] Such Baptist militancy is characteristic of the period, and more than one president took the opportunity to spell out Baptist principles. Insisting on Baptist distinctives in

1880, William Grant declared, 'The love of charity and the dread charge of bigotry, must not be allowed to emasculate our denominational life.'[69] While Baptists were in harmony with other Evangelicals in their beliefs about saving truth, four principles justified separate existence. Membership of a Christian Church should consist only of those who are believers; believers alone should be baptized; each individual church has independence of government; Baptists do not recognize creeds or confessions of faith. 'Against all Creeds, Confessions, Traditions whatsoever - Catholic or Protestant - Baptists place the open Scriptures.'[70]

Internal Concerns and Wider Involvement

During the first twenty-five years the Union wrestled with the question of ministerial training. Traditional resistance to the idea of full-time ministry came from the Scotch Baptists, one of whom had argued that the idea was unwise, unspiritual and unscriptural.[71] By the end of the century improved living standards made the payment of a pastor's stipend more attainable. In addition the need for more consistent pastoral care, the attraction of an educated minister's preaching, the influence of the English pattern of full-time trained ministry and the example of men trained in English colleges, particularly Spurgeon's, all conspired to make a full-time trained ministry more acceptable to those emerging from a Scotch Baptist background.[72]

For the rest of the denomination there had never been a question as to the value of training for ministry. The Haldanes' approval, Spurgeon's example and the traditional Scottish respect for education made trained ministry a priority in the aims of the Union. Before 1850 attempts at ministerial training had been limited, local and short-lived. Francis Johnstone had been involved from 1845 to 1856 in offering a thirty-six-month course covering five theological subjects and six arts subjects. Since Johnstone carried on the work alone it came to an end when he moved to Cambridge in 1856.[73] After this training became the concern of the newly formed Baptist Association and then Dr James Paterson. Both ventures were short and failed to win general support, but they trained men whose leadership and drive would have a lasting effect on Scottish Baptist life.

The formation of the Baptist Union of Scotland in 1869 ought to have resolved the question, but a series of accidents compounded by underlying tensions frustrated each attempt to form a denominational college. Much depended on the availability of the right people. In 1869 Dr James Culross was appointed sole tutor. Culross was minister at Stirling and greatly respected for his godliness and scholarship. He wrote many books of biblical exposition which were widely read and are fine examples of Victorian devotional writing.[74] Culross, however, moved south soon after his appointment. His successor, Hugh Anderson of Bratton, appointed in 1871, died unexpectedly in 1872, and Paterson took over once again for three years.

In an address at the inaugural meeting of the Union in 1869, Culross laid to rest the idea that learning was culture minus evangelical experience. 'In training, young men should be brought into contact with, and under the influence of, the fullest knowledge, the clearest spiritual insight, the ripest experience, the highest guiding wisdom, the loftiest and most intense enthusiasm existing among us.' As to sound education, 'we are all alive to this and perfectly at one in respecting it'. Good training should 'kindle everything in them that will catch fire'.[75] It is noteworthy that in 1880 churches clearly approved of college-trained men since all six leaving students received unanimous calls to Scottish pastorates.[76]

In long discussions from that year onwards there were three options: to appoint one tutor to conduct the whole course; to send students to existing colleges in the south; or to form a denominational college, fully equipped and adequately endowed. In 1880 the third plan was just in operation, but in 1882 a motion was passed at the assembly to revert to the first alternative. From this point the whole enterprise was in disarray and the Union finally relinquished responsibility in 1893. In 1894 the Baptist Theological College of Scotland was established with Dr Joseph Coats, professor of pathology in the University of Glasgow, as president, and with a staff of three part-time lecturers.[77] By 1909 students received for training since the formation of the Union numbered seventy-six.[78]

Meanwhile the life of the churches continued to develop. Sunday School work was passing through a boom period. In 1869 there were 2,467 scholars; in 1889 there were 10,220; by 1914 the total was 19,522. The ratio of teachers to pupils overall was approximately one to eight.[79] There was deep concern in 1876 at the low state of many churches, and in the report of that year various reasons are given. The one positive note struck is a reference to Sunday School work. 'The increased interest felt in the godly up-bringing of the young, as evinced by the increased attendance at Sabbath Schools . . . augurs well for the future.'[80] Yet the 1891 statistics reveal that only 1,096 scholars were over fifteen years of age, and in the preceding year only ninety-eight had become church members. In the same report eighty-three churches report ninety-eight schools.[81] The Sabbath School Association of Scotland was well aware of the strategic importance of Sunday Schools. 'We can readily see that a Sabbath School can often be formed where a church cannot, and the school become the germ and prophecy of a church.'[82] The 1909 Sunday School Committee report gives an idea of the range of activities. A children's day was held, various teachers' conferences were arranged, scholars' booklets on various Christian heroes were published and over 18,000 distributed as free literature. An ambitious Sunday School Examination Scheme was well established and there were fifty-six libraries with a total of 11,472 volumes.[83]

Other organizations supplemented the work of Sunday School among the young. In 1896 apart from over sixty Bands of Hope, there were fifteen sewing classes, five of them in mission areas, almost seventy Christian Endeavour Societies and various other activities such as singing classes, swimming clubs, penny savings banks and a Band of Mercy.[84] The third Boys' Brigade Company was founded in 1885 at Adelaide Place's St Clair Street Mission Hall, but discontinued because the deacons disapproved 'anything that tends to foster a warlike spirit in boys'.[85] In 1887 the 76th Company of the BB was founded in Partick Baptist Mission, and there is praise for the work of the Boys' Brigade in the 1891 Sunday School report.[86]

By 1876 the churches were beginning to discover the benefits of joint action at the more local level of associations. The report for that year indicates the emergence of the Northern and Glasgow Associations, and the formation of an association of ministers in the shires of Perth, Stirling and Fife.[87] Aware of the strategic importance of local initiative and pooled resources in church planting, the Baptist Union encouraged association development. George Yuille, part-time secretary of the Baptist Union from 1880 to 1919, encouraged the formation of the Stirlingshire and Clackmannanshire Association in the area around the scene of his own distinguished ministry at Stirling.[88] The potential resources of an association of local churches, both in terms of finance and practical support, are well illustrated by the Fife Association between 1900 and 1910. During this period it played a major part in the establishing of at least five new churches within the county.[89]

Scottish Baptists had an interest and involvement in foreign mission at a variety of levels. Support for the Baptist Missionary Society became organized and more regular. In 1909 giving to BMS from Scotland amounted to £5,015.[90] Local auxiliaries were formed in Ayr in 1869 and Glasgow in 1881.[91] The Missionary Committee of the Union was appointed in 1898 'to carry out the strengthening and extension of missionary operations'.[92] Since Hindu women were largely confined to the zenana (the kitchen quarters), only other women could reach them with the gospel. In consequence the denominational Zenana Mission, served by women only, was formed in London in 1867. Miss Kirkland of Dunoon and Miss Eekhout of Hillhead were sent out as the first Scottish Zenana missionaries in 1893.[93] The Baptist Industrial Mission was a separate Scottish enterprise. Formed in 1895, it commenced its work near Lake Nyasa very much along the lines that had been advocated by David Livingstone. The mission aimed to spread the gospel in Central Africa by creating work in agriculture and manufacture and using the proceeds for missionary enterprise. Scottish Baptists also had missionary links with Italy, Germany and Bohemia, and provided missionaries for a great variety of interdenominational societies.[94] BMS work was mainly concentrated in Congo, China and India. During the period 1880-1914 over thirty missionaries from Scottish churches served with BMS and at least twelve with the China Inland Mission.[95] Some laid down their lives. William McCurrach and his wife, from Crown Terrace, Aberdeen, were martyred during the Boxer Uprising in China in August 1900 while serving with the BMS.[96] In 1894 David Charteris of Adelaide Place, Glasgow, went missing while attached to an interdenominational Industrial Mission.[97] Other individuals shared almost equally in the costliness of mission. Together their story is part of the larger tradition of sacrifice for the sake of the gospel.

Conclusion

From 1844 to 1914 Baptists had grown from 91 to 137 churches, and from some 5,500 to 21,053 members.[98] They were no longer a thin straggling line but a denominational structure of Union, associations, subsidiary societies and numerous committees. Baptist evangelistic activity was energetic, imaginative and persistent. Baptist Churches had developed busy programmes of auxiliary organizations, especially amongst children. The denomination had made significant contributions to the temperance movement, to meeting the problems of poverty and social decay, and to the emergence of a warmer theology of mission. It possessed its own theological college, several Baptists had made significant contributions to theological and devotional literature and missionary work had benefited both in finance and supply of candidates.

Nevertheless in 1914 a note of caution was sounded. 'The total membership of the Union has been virtually stationary during the past five years though there are indications of abounding activity among the churches ... we cannot be content with this. How shall we change it that the tide of the Spirit may flow again?'[99] The coming century would reveal whether or not the tide did turn.

Notes

1. *Report of the Baptist Union of Scotland (RBUS)*, 1882, p 43.
2. T.C. Smout, *A Century of the Scottish People, 1830-1950* (Glasgow 1986), p 58.
3. A.L. Drummond and J. Bulloch, *The Church in Late Victorian Scotland, 1874-1900* (Edinburgh 1978), p 195.
4. *Baptist Home Missionary Society Report*, 1855, pp 7, 9.
5. *Scottish Baptist Year Book (SBYB)*, 1913, p 68.
6. Smout, *Scottish People*, p 87.
7. *RBUS*, 1878, p 13.
8. Smout, *Scottish People*, pp 33, 119-20.
9. George Yuille, ed, *History of the Baptists in Scotland* (Glasgow 1926), p 247.

10. C.G. Brown, 'Religion and the Development of an Urban Society: Glasgow, 1780-1914' (Glasgow PhD 1981). Vol 2 offers detailed information on Sunday School development in Glasgow.
11. *RBUS*, 1872, p 23.
12. Hugh McLeod, *Religion and the Working Class in Nineteenth-Century Britain* (London 1984), cap 3.
13. See D.J. Withrington, 'The Churches in Scotland, c 1870-1900 : towards a new social conscience', *Records of the Scottish Church History Society*, 29 (1977), pp 155-68.
14. *RBUS*, 1885, p 15.
15. Smout, *Scottish People*, p 41.
16. *RBUS*, 1873, p 34. cf McLeod, *Religion and the Working Class*, p 23.
17. *RBUS*, 1890, p 23. The Baptist figure given is under 4,000, but by 1844 there were already some 5,500 church members. See below, n 98.
18. *RBUS*, 1870, pp 26-7.
19. *RBUS*, 1888, p 58. For Landels, see cap 2, pp 39-40.
20. *SBYB*, 1905, pp 25-30.
21. Adam Mackay, *Distinguished Sons of Cruden* (Peterhead 1922), pp 135-89. D.W. Bebbington, 'Baptist M.P.s in the Nineteenth Century', *Baptist Quarterly*, 29 (1981), pp 13-14.
22. ibid, pp 263, 266-7, 270, 271.
23. *RBUS*, 1878, p 12.
24. *RBUS*, 1896, pp 45-6.
25. James Ross, *The Power I Pledge* (Glasgow 1971), pp 35-40.
26. ibid, p 53. See also cap 8, p 150-1.
27. *SBYB*, 1909, p 270.
28. ibid.
29. Smout, *Scottish People*, p 138. *RBUS*, 1885, p 49.
30. Brown, 'Development of an Urban Society', 1 pp 105-6.
31. *RBUS*, 1896, pp 45-6.
32. *RBUS*, 1876, p 7; 1879, p 7. Yuille, ed, *Baptists in Scotland*, p 246.
33. N. D. Logan, 'Drink and Society in Scotland, 1870-1914' (Glasgow PhD 1984), p 448.
34. *SBYB*, 1913, pp 150-1.
35. Yuille, ed, *Baptists in Scotland*, p 247.
36. J. Edwin Orr, *The Light of the Nations* (Exeter 1965), pp 132-4.
37. See cap 2, p 39.
38. Drummond and Bulloch, *Church in Late Victorian Scotland*, p 12. cf S.N. Gundry, *Love Them In: the life and theology of D.L. Moody* (Grand Rapids, Mich., 1982 edn), esp cap 4.
39. Orr, *Light of the Nations*, p 139. See R. Currie, *et al.*, *Churches and Churchgoers: patterns of church growth in the British Isles since 1700* (London 1977), pp 39-45, 172 for actual figures.
40. *RBUS*, 1882, p 43.
41. F.R. Coad, *A History of the Brethren Movement* (Exeter 1968), pp 171-3.
42. *RBUS*, 1878, p 13.
43. Orr, *Light of the Nations*, p 136.
44. *A Book of Remembrance: the jubilee souvenir of the Glasgow United Evangelistic Association's evangelical and ameliorative schemes, 1874-1924* (Glasgow 1924).
45. A.L. Drummond and James Bulloch, *The Church in Victorian Scotland* (Edinburgh 1975), pp 248-9.
46. ibid, pp 251-3.
47. *RBUS*, 1869, p 14.
48. *RBUS*, 1891, pp 84-6.
49. *RBUS*, 1877, p 7.
50. Crown Terrace Baptist Church Minute Book, 1870-1906, 12 Sept. 1844; 12 Dec. 1894; 13 Feb. 1895.
51. Yuille, ed, *Baptists in Scotland*, p 116.
52. *SBYB*, 1910, pp 49, 51.
53. *RBUS*, 1878, p 10.
54. *SBYB*, 1909, pp 16-17.
55. Yuille, ed, *Baptists in Scotland*, p 115.
56. See cap 2, pp 41-2.
57. *RBUS*, 1869, p 6.
58. *RBUS*, 1869, p 7.
59. *RBUS*, 1890, p 23; *RBUS*, 1876, p 9.

60. *SBYB*, 1915, p 73.
61. *SBYB*, 1909, p 65.
62. *RBUS*, 1871, pp 14-17.
63. *RBUS*, 1870, p 12.
64. *SBYB*, 1913, pp 61-6.
65. *RBUS*, 1882, pp 46-7.
66. *RBUS*, 1873, pp 33.
67. *RBUS*, 1879, p 11.
68. *RBUS*, 1888, pp 51-8.
69. *RBUS*, 1880, p 35.
70. *SBYB*, 1909, p viii.
71. Yuille, ed, *Baptists in Scotland*, p 250.
72. See D.W. Bebbington in *The Ministry Today* (Baptist Union of Scotland Viewpoint Booklet, Glasgow 1984) pp 30-4.
73. Yuille, ed, *Baptists in Scotland*, p 253.
74. e.g. *Behold I Stand at the Door and Knock* (London 1874); *Man of Sorrows* (Stirling 1896); *Christ's Joy* (London 1899).
75. *RBUS*, 1869, pp 12-13.
76. *RBUS*, 1880, pp 20-1.
77. Yuille, ed, *Baptists in Scotland*, p 256. For Dunoon Baptist College, see cap 15, p 292.
78. *SBYB*, 1909, pp 77-8.
79. *RBUS*, 1890, p 23; *SBYB*, 1914, p 56.
80. *RBUS*, 1876, p 12.
81. *RBUS*, 1891, pp 44-6.
82. *RBUS*, 1886, p 29.
83. *SBYB*, 1909, pp 94-5.
84. *RBUS*, 1896, pp 45-6.
85. John Springhall *et al*., *Sure and Steadfast: a history of the Boys' Brigade* (London 1983), p 41.
86. Yuille, ed, *Baptists in Scotland*, p 177; *RBUS*, 1891, p 47.
87. *RBUS*, 1876, p 9.
88. Yuille, ed, *Baptists in Scotland*, p 230, for fuller details of the contribution of George and Jessie Yuille in and beyond the Baptist Union.
89. ibid, p 242. See also cap 12, pp 224-5.
90. *SBYB*, 1909, p 18.
91. D.B. Murray, *The First Hundred Years: the Baptist Union of Scotland* (Glasgow 1969), p 76.
92. ibid, p 76.
93. Yuille, ed, *Baptists in Scotland*, pp 266-7.
94. ibid, pp 267-8.
95. ibid, pp 290-5.
96. ibid, p 293. H.R. Williamson, *British Baptists in China, 1845-1952* (London 1957), pp 51, 67.
97. Murray, *First Hundred Years*, p 77.
98. *The First Yearly Report of the Baptist Union of Scotland* (Cupar 1844), p 23. *SBYB*. 1915, p 73.
99. *SBYB*, 1914, p 64.

J.M. Gordon

4. THE TWENTIETH CENTURY SINCE 1914

In 1984 the state of the churches in Scotland was investigated by a Bible Society census. The Baptists were found to be 'the only denomination to have advanced in membership over the last four years . . . [with] by far the highest rate of church attendance per membership . . . The number who attend church twice on Sunday is high . . . and the large proportion of children, young people and the middle-aged is significant.' The Baptists were faring well. 'Inevitably', went on the summary report, 'such statistics must raise the question, why are the Baptists in this exceptional situation?'[1] That is a question we must address by examining their history during the twentieth century.

Economic Trends, War and Baptist Responses

The First World War (1914-18) had profound consequences for Scottish Baptists, then numbering 21,053 church members, with as many again in Sunday School, in 137 churches. While deploring its evils, they had no doubt about the rightness of the cause.[2] Over 5,000 volunteered for the colours within the first two years,[3] and many others, including women, were relocated in support of the war effort. One church was reduced to one-eighth of its roll, with every Sunday School leader and most of the deacons away from home.[4]

The war had even more profound consequences for the Scottish economy. The East Coast fishing industry collapsed through loss of export markets;[5] steel-making, ship-building and coal-mining prospered during the war only to slump, along with textiles, in the trade depression of the 1920s.[6] Unemployment reached 27% and 400,000 Scots emigrated between 1921 and 1931 — the highest figure for any European nation.[7] Only seven of the seventy-seven steel furnaces were in blast in 1931[8] and, even when re-armament began to stimulate the economy from 1933 onward, prosperity came slowly and patchily.

However, neither the dreadful loss of nearly 1,000 young Baptists in the war[9] nor the economic problems which followed it discouraged Scottish Baptists from building churches in the new housing estates of Rosyth (1923), Cathcart (1923), Mosspark (1924), Knightswood (1929), Stenhouse, Edinburgh (1932), and King's Park (1934), nor from planting another six new churches in existing communities.[10] Halls were erected with the intention (seldom realized) of building a 'traditional' church at a later date. The Union gifted four-fifths of the cost, reputedly higher than any comparable organization in the world, but generally did not support a full-time ministry until the church could guarantee a proportion of the stipend.[11]

As well as starting new causes,[12] Scottish Baptists were active in upgrading existing churches, halls and manses. Even in years of serious depression, between 1929 and 1932, better church buildings were erected at Bo'ness, Inverness, Johnstone, Shettleston, Whiteinch and Uddingston, new halls added at Cambuslang, Knightswood, Harper Memorial and Wishaw, and new manses acquired at Denny, Peterhead and George Street, Paisley.[13] The 1935 total membership, 23,310, was the highest ever achieved, despite an alarming loss of younger people to find work in new areas.[14]

Along with church building went a concern for reasonable stipends. The first-ever Sustentation Fund, launched enthusiastically in 1914 with a target of £30,000, closed in 1920 at the staggering total (for those days) of £52,000, boosting the minimum stipend to £120 a year for a single man, £150 for a married man. To qualify for aid, churches had to federate under the scheme, contribute the first £70 of stipend, and call a man 'recognized' by the Union — a sore point with some, who raised it year after year, as interference with the freedom of the local church.[15] Generally, however, the fund 'carried on a noble ministry, and had it not been for the timely grant, many a minister would have suffered severe strain'.[16] A separate scheme provided a small pension for retired ministers or their widows.

The Second World War (1939-45) also affected Scotland in many ways. Loss of attenders through conscription, requisitioned buildings and transfers to work in England were not compensated for by gains through evacuation from the air-raids and V-bombs in the south.[17] Many non-munition factories closed forever, leaving Scotland over-dependent on her traditional heavy industries.[18] She lost 34,000 men killed in action and a similar number of young women took permanent jobs in England or married Allied soldiers.[19] Centralized control of life, introduced for the war, temporarily held back emigration, but every year from 1946 to 1964 some 25,000 left Scotland for good, more going overseas than just 'drifting south'.[20] On the other hand, Labour's 1945 return to government, and the whirlwind nationalization which followed, kept unemployment under 4% for all those years and more.

Church life was disrupted by the war — with blackout, evacuation, requisition of halls, rationing, travel restrictions and over 3,000 young Baptists serving in the forces.[21] Mercifully, not so many died as in the Kaiser's War but fourteen Baptist civilians were killed in the Clyde air-raids and six churches damaged.[22] There was not the same universal approval for war on this occasion — thirteen assembly delegates dissented from a public resolution in favour of the country's 'heroic stand against Nazism'.[23]

Nevertheless, the denomination came through the war and the austerity of the post-war years in good heart,[24] responding generously to an appeal for '30,000 Guineas' to keep stipends in line with inflation.[25] The greatest economic challenge in its history — to create thirty-four new churches in as many years from 1952 onwards — was yet to come but the importance of a building for growth of a new church had already been demonstrated time and again.[26]

In 1946 one-seventh of Scotland's population was crammed into three square miles of central Glasgow.[27] Government response was the unimaginative sprawling housing estates of Drumchapel, Easterhouse and Castlemilk in Glasgow, Craigmillar and Wester Hailes in Edinburgh, together with the New Towns of East Kilbride, Glenrothes, Cumbernauld and Livingston. In every one of these, and in many more, new Baptist Churches were established. Policy differed from the inter-war period in three ways. First, with an awareness that many pre-war extension churches had still not added a sanctuary to their hall, the Union architect, Robert Rankin, erected multi-purpose church/halls from Alness to Bourtreehill, from Glenrothes to Erskine — with baptistry, pulpit and flexible hall accommodation.[28] Secondly, before there was even the nucleus of a church, the Union appointed and supported 'pioneer ministries' or 'initial pastorates' so that when a new church was constituted its first act was to call as pastor the man who had, until then, been employed and directed by the Union.[29]

The third change was not from choice. The Union's gift had to be cut from four-fifths to two-thirds and then to one-half of the total cost — although the balance was still lent.[30] Church extension appeals for capital were poorly supported both by individuals and by the denomination at large[31] but, as national earnings rose (Prime Minister Macmillan's remark, 'You've never had it so good', became a national slogan), the Union was able to allocate £5,000 a year from income toward new buildings.[32] Older churches were sold or relocated by local authorities — the John Street Church in Glasgow became the new work in Castlemilk;[33] the Cumbernauld Church was paid for by the Women's Auxiliary Jubilee Fund of 1959;[34] new churches repaid their 'loans' in advance of target, releasing funds for elsewhere;[35] other denominations, facing closures, made over buildings on favourable terms.[36] Consequently, despite falling membership, an indifferent economic background and the terminal decline of Scottish heavy industry from the late 1950s, Scottish Baptists funded their thirty-four new buildings. Then, as other calls were made on resources, a new policy was tried — single appeals for the specific churches at Dedridge (opened 1984) and Bridge of Don (opened 1987).[37] That done, and with no one cause urgently requiring help, the 1986 assembly reverted to its General Extension Fund.[38]

Union initiative did not, of course, deter other churches from independent action. Bishopbriggs, the International Church (Aberdeen), Cornton (Stirling), Collydean (Glenrothes) and Oxgangs (Edinburgh) were acquired or built with full Union approval but with largely local support.[39] Furthermore, with the aim of greater social involvement, the post-war years saw much adaptation of existing properties, while some churches, like St Andrews, Kirkintilloch and Irvine, took over adjoining property for halls, bookshops and general community service.

Scottish industry, relatively successful in the later 1960s, was boosted, especially in the north-east, by the discovery of oil and natural gas in the early 1970s; but Scotland's export-based economy fared badly as escalating oil prices cut back international trade from 1974. Inflation of 17%, 23%, 15% and 17% in 1974/5/6/7 and 22% in 1980 set individual churches a challenge which led to the widespread adoption of two aids to stewardship — 'covenants', by which treasurers recovered the tax element of giving over seven years (later four),[40] and 'budgeting', not just for 'survival' but for 'growth'.[41] There was little to cheer in the Scottish economy of the 1980s. With continued national recession and 14% unemployment, the churches had to struggle even to maintain stipends, let alone to fund new outreach. By 1986, 40% were no longer able to support a full-time ministry.[42] Careful housekeeping continued to be an imperative of church life in largely adverse economic conditions.

Evangelism

'The dissemination of the Gospel of Christ in Scotland', the third object of the Union, has been pursued at denominational, church, personal and interdenominational levels. One of the chief denominational agencies was the Home Mission. In 1914 it employed twenty-one missionaries for twenty-five churches and three times that number of out-stations.[43] It was largely the fear that integration might diminish evangelistic zeal for these areas which delayed formal amalgamation with the Union until 1931.[44] In fact, amalgamation gave the opportunity for almost continuous evangelistic enterprise, as one national initiative led into another. A campaign in 1933 involved over a hundred churches. Irvine reported 150 converts, including several grown-up families, and Wishaw 110, half over eighteen.[45] In 1936, many adopted the Scottish Churches' Council plan for simultaneous national evangelism consisting of dedication, visitation, campaigning and shepherding.[46]

The Baptist World Congress of 1939 recommended, and Scottish Baptists adopted, a five-year programme, entitled 'Every Member an Evangelist' — one year of preparation, a second for deepening spiritual life, a third for mission to youth, a fourth for mission to the community, and, finally, mission to the world.[47] Well supported at first, it ran into difficulties later in the war,[48] but led into the Baptist Advance Campaign of 1951[49] which, in turn, merged with church extension. One hundred and twenty churches then joined in the three-year Crusade of Visitation Evangelism (1956-9),[50] which was so successful that it was repeated in 1960-2.[51] The late 1950s were also the era of the Youth Rally, particularly on Saturday evenings. Denominational initiative here started in Stirling, then extended to the Assembly Hall in Edinburgh, the objective being evangelism as well as fellowship, inspiration and teaching.

1963 brought the Call to Mission (the new word for evangelism)[52] and in the late 1960s three national efforts were running simultaneously: Evangelism in Depth, Think Again, and One Step Forward, with 1,000 Baptists from 115 churches attending a conference on evangelism in 1968.[53] The centenary of the Union (1969) was marked by a hundred churches working together for three years of Simultaneous Evangelism — preparation, proclamation, preservation[54] — leading to several hundred conversions and a new sense of unity among Scottish Baptists[55] but also leading one president to question whether programmes might not obscure the real needs of human beings.[56] In 1977 the assembly voted to join other Scottish churches in the National Initiative in Evangelism[57] but a far greater impact was made by its own Scotreach during the years 1984 to 1986, when 144 churches participated in three years of preparation, mobilization and consolidation.[58]

There is an objective assessment of all this activity in the report on the Bible Society census of Scottish churches taken in 1984: 'the membership growth recorded by the Baptist Union reflects the energy with which they have called their churches over recent years to the concerns of Church Growth'.[59] It was, of course, wider than that: from 1937 the Evangelistic Committee encouraged summer seaside missions, offering financial assistance. Missions in Ayr, Dunoon, Leven, Kinghorn and Portobello[60] continued for many summers — one during an air raid![61] — and up to six a summer are still held, with Anstruther, Girvan and Crieff being particular post-war favourites.[62]

At church level, Sunday Schools were the main evangelistic agency, supplemented by Bands of Hope, Young Worshippers' Leagues, Ropeholders (the Baptist Missionary Society youth organization) and Christian Endeavour Societies, all bearing fruit in conversions and dedicated lives.[63] The Union Sunday School Committee held teacher training conferences, issued lesson booklets, conducted Bible examinations and honour shield competitions;[64] they hired out lantern slides (up to seventy-five in a set) on a variety of biblical and historical subjects, with over 200 sets issued in a typical winter.[65] As films became popular, a 16mm cine projector was donated in 1939 by J. Arthur Rank, a dedicated Methodist, for the same purpose, although wartime transport restricted its use.[66] The magazines *Pioneer*, later *The Venture*, *The Fiery Cross* and *Comment* linked the various youth groups.[67] Then the foundations laid by the full-time Director of Christian Education[68] were consolidated from 1978 by the Department of Church Life, whose literature, conferences, missions, Sports Day and Youth Choir[69] trained and encouraged new generations to take their place in Scottish Baptist life.

In connection with these various national plans for mission, local churches organized their own 'outreaches', usually for a week and usually with a visiting evangelist. In addition, at least one of the regular Sunday services was normally evangelistic, supplemented at one time by Saturday gospel meetings, and later by youth rallies, gospel rhythm concerts and outreach cafés. The emphasis at all times was on gathering people in to hear the preaching of the word. Caution against too rosy a picture is given by an association report of a six-week outreach in 1929: 'Notwithstanding a very large distribution of attractive leaflets, not many, apart from our own people, attended the meetings.'[70] Much the same was said, nearly sixty years later, about the Commonwealth Games Outreach conducted by Charlotte Chapel in 1986.[71]

At the personal level Sunday School teachers and youth leaders instilled into successive generations the importance of individual commitment to Christ. The First World War gave many opportunities for personal witness, especially at the Front, as letters testify, and also at home.[72] A Committee of Enquiry of 1927-9 viewing the many problems facing Scottish Baptists stressed the need for personal conversion, consecration and the importance of 'soul-winning'.[73] On the outbreak of the Second World War, a residential canteen was opened in Hamilton Barracks, Glasgow, in which many spiritual conversations took place.[74] National bodies may plan, but it is individual Christians who make contact with people, and so, between 1972 and 1982, much effort went into the WIN (Witness Involvement Now)[75] and WOW (Win our World)[76] Schools designed to train church members in personal evangelism.

At interdenominational level, Scotland took up the Archbishop of Canterbury's 'Recall to Religion' in 1937, and Baptists co-operated gladly with other denominations, preaching the gospel in cinemas, trade union meetings, public parks and tenements.[77] The Evangelical outlook of Presbyterian leaders like D.P. Thomson and Tom Allan encouraged Baptist involvement in interdenominational missions after the Second War — Christian Commandos (1947/50),[78] Tell Scotland (1952),[79] the All-Scotland Crusade with Billy Graham (1955),[80] the Jesus Movement of Arthur Blessitt (1972),[81] Luis Palau and Dick Saunders (the 1980s).[82] Baptists were active in organization and counselling, prayer and practical support. The secretary of the Baptist Union referred to the All-Scotland Crusade as 'a demonstration of the saving power of the Spirit comparable only with New Testament times',[83] and there was a 'spectacular upsurge' in membership figures that year.[84]

These 'spectacular' events must, however, be seen against a general 'Retreat from Religion'. The armistice presidential address (1919) drew a sombre picture of a world losing interest in God.[85] Subsequent comments by Baptist leaders tell a similar story. In 1935 there was criticism of the drift from organized religion, changed attitudes towards Sunday, and the cult of the open road.[86] In 1965 it was said there had been no period in history when the church had been subjected to more pointed criticism or when the Christian way of life had been more insidiously attacked.[87] By 1984 it was established that only 17% of the population of Scotland attended church on an average Sunday.[88]

So serious was the decline of Christian belief and practice that Baptists were prepared from an early date to see Scotland treated as part of a mission-field by churches overseas. The Foreign Mission Board of the Southern Baptist Convention of the USA was prepared, from 1959 onward, to evangelize in Scotland. In that year fifteen Americans were welcomed for a month.[89] Southern Baptist literature formed the basis of a largely unsuccessful attempt to launch All-Age Christian Education on American principles.[90] From 1975 to 1979 the Union Secretary, Andrew MacRae, forged new links leading to pulpit exchanges,[91] ministries in Brechin[92] and Aberdeen,[93] a stream of 'Mission Service Corps' personnel,[94] and the site for the Bridge of Don Church in Aberdeen.[95] In 1983 there were ten Southern Baptists working in Scotland,[96] including a full-time ministry in Wigtown.[97] For Scottish Baptists with their independent traditions to work harmoniously with visiting American teams[98] illustrates how attitudes can change. Some other movements of thought are examined next.

Movements of Thought

A combination of their commitment to the Evangelical faith and their relative geographical isolation spared Scottish Baptists from being drawn into many of the twentieth century's more divisive theological issues. Between the wars, the assembly had to adjudicate only once on a doctrinal question — when the pastor of the Grantown-on-Spey church, E.J. Roberts, was removed from the list of accredited ministers in 1933 for liberal views (his phrase) about the deity of Christ. One of the distinctive principles of Baptists, as published in the *Year Book*, is not to require adherence to any creed or confession of faith, but to test belief against scripture alone.[99] Roberts invoked that liberty, but his views were judged to be 'Unitarian' and so to fail the test.[100] Since then there have been four widespread discussions in the denomination — over 'Modernism' in 1944, ecumenical involvement from 1948 to 1968, the charismatic movement from 1968 onward, and (currently) whether there should be women in the ministry.[101]

The Modernist debate arose from concern expressed in 1941 that thirty-five men had left the ministry in the previous thirty years. An existing commission of enquiry was asked to investigate the whole state of the denomination. Its report was discussed in detail at the 1943 assembly,[102] remitted to the churches for comment, and brought back to the 1944 assembly for decision.[103] It was attacked by an ex-president of the Union, John Shearer, as 'sheer evasion of facts'. He claimed the real cause of denominational malaise was 'Modernism' in the Baptist Theological College of Scotland.[104]

What was variously described as 'Modernism', 'Liberalism' or 'Rationalism' came fairly late to Scotland. American Protestantism had been riven by the Fundamentalist/Modernist controversy in the 1920s.[105] Modernism was seen to undermine the authority of scripture, to deny the fall of man, the deity of Christ, the necessity of atonement, the second coming and much more. Any deviation from orthodoxy in the preaching or conversation of younger ministers in Scotland was traced to 'Modernist teaching' at the college. The issue came to a head in the jubilee year of the college, which did not lack for support from among its 109 former students.

There were in fact two debates scheduled for the same morning at the 1944 assembly, with the press excluded. For the first, on the report of the commission, the assembly simply thanked the commission and disbanded it. The attack on the teaching policy of the college was therefore switched to the second scheduled debate, on the relationship of the college to the Union.[106] It had been recommended that the college should come under the direct control of the Union; its critics took the opportunity of moving that the Union should dissociate itself from its allegedly wayward college. In the debate, not only the teaching policy of the college but also the orthodoxy of individual staff members was attacked.[107]

The outcome was a request (which the college declined) to amalgamate with the Union. A booklet criticizing the college by John Shearer, *The Downgrade of Modernism*, was publicly condemned by the council of the Union and debated at the following assembly.[108] Having failed to persuade the denomination to sever its links with its theological college, the Evangelical Baptist Fellowship sponsored its own Bible College (the contrast in name was not accidental), with ten students, most of whom went to pastorates abroad because the Union did not then recognize such men. In 1949 it acquired premises in Queen's Drive, Glasgow, for residential students, but it lasted for only a few years. As passions cooled, both its former secretary and its former treasurer were elected presidents of the Union, in 1959 and 1965 respectively.[109]

The Modernist issue was succeeded by a more protracted controversy over ecumenical involvement. Until 1948 Scottish Baptists worked happily but informally with a wide range of Protestant organizations. In 1910 they gave hospitality for the Edinburgh World Missionary Conference from which the modern ecumenical movement dates; they were represented from the beginning (1923) on the Scottish Churches' Council;[110] they worked for common interests in evangelism and moral issues through a variety of interdenominational bodies. When representatives of sixty communions from fifty countries met in Edinburgh for the Faith and Order Conference of 1938, the Union was strongly represented. Although it circulated a report to the churches, the Union council decided not to affiliate at that stage to the World Council of Churches (WCC) which the conference proposed.[111]

When the WCC came into being after the war, at a conference in Amsterdam in 1948, the Scottish Baptist representative recommended the Union to affiliate both to the WCC and to its local expression, the British Council of Churches.[112] In a full assembly debate that year, the leadership pressed, despite strong opposition, for immediate affiliation. Following a tied vote, a careful recount was taken and the Union affiliated by 81 votes to 80. That affiliation began a lengthy and divisive debate which occupied the assembly, off and on, for the next twenty years. Some were convinced the ecumenical movement was a creation of God's Spirit and so felt keenly the criticisms levelled at it. Others challenged its whole basis, claiming the aims of the WCC were too wide; Evangelicals were discriminated against; mission was affected; and the importance of the Bible was undermined.[113]

A call for immediate withdrawal, defeated at the 1951 assembly by 218 votes to 113,[114] was to be renewed at the 1953 assembly in Dundee. After private consultation with the office-bearers of the Union, the proposers dropped their motion in exchange for a formal committee of enquiry into the workings of the WCC.[115] Its majority report to the 1955 assembly, occupying sixteen pages of the *Year Book*, recommended continued affiliation for a seven-year period. A dissenting minority, two elders of Charlotte Chapel, wished immediate withdrawal. They circularized every Scottish Baptist Church with a detailed critique of the WCC, and notified the assembly that Charlotte Chapel would withdraw from the Union.[116] This was a potent factor in the decision, taken by a majority of 197 to 176, to 'withdraw affiliation for 7 years in the hope that the basis of the WCC be brought nearer our own Faith and Order'. When Charlotte Chapel then called for the Union for disaffiliate also from the British Council of Churches (BCC) and its Scottish equivalent, the Union declined, and Charlotte Chapel, the largest and best known church in the Union, withdrew from membership. It was the only church to do so at the time. When the seven years from 1955 ended, the Union examined the question afresh. The 1963 assembly accepted by a majority of 316 to 59 that nothing significant had changed.[117] The Union remains outside the WCC and Charlotte Chapel outside the Union.

When the 1964 Faith and Order Conference of the BCC called for organic unity of the churches by 1980, the Union responded with a statesmanlike document presented to the 1967 assembly, pointing out the importance of spiritual (as opposed to organic) unity.[118] Its call for charity and involvement but no organic link was accepted and then implemented in the happiest possible way — Donald McCallum, Derek Murray and Andrew MacRae as individuals accepted invitations to chair the Scottish Churches' Council (SCC) committees on evangelism, Christian Aid and mission respectively.[119] Over the years other well known Baptists have held influential posts in both the Scottish and the British Councils.

Apart from such personal involvement, Scottish Baptists have generally been on the fringe of the ecumenical movement, but that did not prevent the debate about affiliation to the SCC and BCC continuing; one by one, five other churches left the Union in protest.[120] The concern stemmed partly from the anti-Catholicism which is bred into whole communities in Scotland, particularly in Glasgow and Lanarkshire. Repeated assurances had to be given, by those in favour of dialogue, that if the Roman Catholic Church were ever granted more than observer status in consultations, Baptists would withdraw.[121] The assembly tolerated, not easily but without suspending the talks, a team of three Baptists meeting three Roman Catholics for a frank exchange of theological views.[122] Between 1965 and 1985 the assembly would not approve of Baptists being other than observers at the multilateral conversations aiming for the unification of the Scottish churches.[123] At the same time as the multilateral discussion reported, no fewer than three other significant ecumenical documents were issued, *Baptism, Eucharist and Ministry* (WCC), *Not Strangers but Pilgrims* (BCC) and *Baptists and Reformed in Dialogue* (Church of Scotland). The leadership made an active response to all four, but its participation in the St Andrews Conference of the ecumenical Inter-Church Process drew strong protest from some.[124]

There have of course been many local joint activities throughout Scotland, but these have depended on the attitude of individual churches and sometimes of individual members within the churches. When other Protestant denominations joined to set up an 'ecumenical church' in the new town of Livingston, Baptists felt justified in establishing a separate church as well. From time to time, Baptists have not received a fair allocation of school, hospital and university chaplaincies, nor accommodation in the development areas, but when administering believer's baptism to Church of Scotland members became an acute issue in 1976, mutually acceptable guidelines were quickly agreed.[125] Largely harmonious relationships with other churches have depended chiefly on personality and personal contact.

Scholarly and devotional writings by Scottish Baptists have commended the denomination to others as well — the best known authors in our period being W. Graham Scroggie, minister of Charlotte Chapel, Andrew G.W. MacBeath, latterly principal of the Bible Training Institute, Glasgow, Reginald E.O. White, latterly principal of the Baptist Theological College of Scotland, and John W. Drane, currently lecturer in the University of Stirling. The number and the quality of academic degrees awarded to Baptist laymen in higher education in the last two decades is another indication of the influence which Scottish Baptists have in the wider world.

The Keswick Convention for the deepening of spiritual life, held annually in July under the banner 'All One in Christ Jesus' was, together with various 'Local Keswick Conventions', well supported by Scottish Baptists both between the wars and after the Second World War. Proclamation of the premillennial return of Christ was often heard on its platforms. The theme found a ready echo in much preaching among Scottish Baptists. 'Pre-Millennialism', wrote Graham Scroggie, 'is an energising hope.'[127] Keswick teaching and the advent hope created an empathy with like-minded Evangelicals of every Protestant denomination.

The greatest single influence on doctrine, practice and behaviour in Scottish Baptist Churches over the last decade or so, however, has been the charismatic renewal movement, particularly in its impact on public worship. Until the early 1970s, worship followed a fairly standard pattern, but charismatic song books, together with congregational participation and music-and-movement, have changed not only the content of many services, but also their length! Renewal has in some instances tended to diminish the place given to the church meeting, and the apparently authoritarian style of leadership sometimes associated with the movement has caused concern to those who believe that all church members should participate in decision-making. For both reasons, the charismatic influence has been widely discussed at denominational level,[128] but most of the charismatic Baptist leaders have wished to stay within the Baptist fold. Those who have formed their own fellowships have neither wished to stay within the Union nor to call themselves Baptists.

Scottish Baptists in general have taken different attitudes to the charismatic movement as it has itself evolved in character.[129] Its earlier emphasis on 'tongues' has given way to a new emphasis on 'prophecy', 'tongues' being used now more for personal devotions. Along with 'prophecy' there came a greater interest in 'healing', and a dedication to resisting the occult.

From the beginning the movement has been trans-denominational, the Scottish Churches Renewal and other agencies breaking down traditional barriers, not least between Protestants and Roman Catholics.[130] Sometimes, however, new barriers have been erected within fellowships — between those who are invited to extra-church activities, like praise and prayer meetings in homes, and those who are not; or between those who attend large-scale holiday conferences like Green Belt, Spring Harvest and the Dales and those who do not. The influence of the charismatic movement is by no means confined to those churches which have consciously taken a particular stance — its vitality has benefited congregations which would not describe themselves as such. Balancing receptivity with discrimination has exercised the minds of many, and helpful guidelines were offered at the 1986 assembly.[131] We stand too near to the renewal movement to form any historical evaluation of it, but when its history comes to be written, it is likely to be said that the impact on Scotland was far greater, and lasted far longer, than earlier observers expected.

Social Attitudes and Involvement

'As a Christian do you see the necessity of dissociating yourself from all such practices and pleasures as might be considered questionable or of a 'worldly' nature?' This question, appearing on membership applications until the mid-1970s,[132] illustrates the bulwarks which Baptists built against the increasing secularization of the twentieth century. Cinemas, gambling, card playing, smoking and (when it first arrived) television, were 'worldly'. External behaviour (where one went, how one dressed and whose company one kept) became the test of spirituality. This way of defining worldliness, encouraged by Baptist leaders with roots in the Brethren, isolated churches from the community around. It was not until the 1960s that Scottish Baptists, generally, acquired enough confidence in themselves to go out and influence 'the world'.

There was a second reason for lack of involvement in the community. Along with the barriers against secular society went barriers to guard 'the truth'. 'Churchianity' was disparagingly contrasted with 'Christianity', and 'nominal Christians' with 'believing Christians'. Since these 'liberal Christians' advocated social work and preached a 'social gospel', Baptists stressed that real evangelism was through the pulpit, not through community service. It was an over-reaction, and led the Social Service Committee to complain that churches and associations simply would not include social concerns in their programmes.[133] The 1944 commission of enquiry accepted the criticism that 'we have laid the emphasis too exclusively on personal salvation, to the neglect of the social implications of the Gospel'.[134] The present General Secretary, reflecting on those days, wrote, 'I too was brought up in a pious evangelicalism which seemed detached from real life . . . the Fellowship I attended was remote from the real issues of the society around it'.[135]

The Social Service Committee, having no resources to do anything other than to educate opinion,[136] drew attention to slum clearance, religious education, censorship of films (or the lack of it), betting, hygiene, Sunday trading, unemployment, disarmament, juvenile delinquency and re-marriage of divorced persons. Where appropriate, and in accordance with the fashion of the day, the assembly sent strongly worded public resolutions expressing the Baptist view to the government and any other body involved. Affiliation to the various Councils of Churches from 1948 widened the areas of concern to include world poverty, immigration, South Africa and atomic weapons,[137] but even the Christian Citizenship Committee (thus renamed in 1959)[138] could do little more than offer advice on current issues — Sunday observance, divorce, abortion, race relations, temperance, gambling, broadcasting standards, birth control, euthanasia, artificial insemination by donor, pornographic literature, horror comics, Premium Bonds, penal reform, the occult, drug abuse. The president of 1972 asked whether the resources of a small denomination were being spread too thinly.[139]

When Baptist consciences were stirred to greater social action, it was initially in concern for their fellow-Baptists — the Robertson Rest Home near Dundee for members of the Rattray Street Church (1947), Beulah Eventide Home for members of Charlotte Chapel (1958), Arbroath Youth Centre (1965) and the Tor Eventide Home primarily for members of Edinburgh Baptist Churches (1971). Then, using ground at the back of the Pitlochry Church, its pastor, Watson Moyes, and his wife Kathleen, a teacher of hearing-impaired children, pioneered the Atholl Baptist Centre from 1971, offering Christian training to the churches, especially to young people.[140] A distinctive feature has been the training of young Christians through sharing holidays and courses with the disabled and disadvantaged, to the enrichment of all.

The next opportunity for wider service motivated by Christian love was the Glasgow City Centre ministry, initiated by the Adelaide Place Church[141] and developed in three ways — a pioneer ministry (which lasted from 1975 to 1978) to the streets of central Glasgow,[142] a hostel (Elpis Centre) for homeless girls, and three flats for alcoholics. In 1978, the Union appointed a 'community minister' with a social work qualification who served for seven years.[143] The flats had to be discontinued,[144] but the Elpis Centre moved to larger accommodation in Hillhead Street, and continues, funded by Urban Aid Grants. In 1977 the Morningside Church in Edinburgh started community homes for the mentally handicapped (the Ark Housing Association),[145] and since 1983 Alan Berry, minister of the South Leith Church, Edinburgh, has seen his vision realised for the 'Bethany Christian

Centre' for up to twenty-two homeless people of either sex and without limit of age.

As these new concerns developed, support has dwindled for the temperance movement. The Scottish Baptist Total Abstinence Society (founded 1881) had two aims: to promote abstinence among Baptists and to further the temperance cause generally. In the former it achieved such success that when the society became the Temperance Committee of the Union in 1923,[146] no Baptist Church had a licence-holder in membership, every minister was an abstainer and the churches all used unfermented wine. Lists in the *Year Book* helped to ensure that no one broke rank![147] On the wider crusade, Scottish Baptists bombarded the government with resolutions, particularly in wartime.[148] They demonstrated their concern by employing an evangelist to travel the length of Scotland taking pledges, campaigning for 'dry areas' and preaching the gospel as the only effective answer to addiction.[149] Their greatest hope, that Scotland would follow the United States and Norway with prohibition,[150] was never realized, but they had their successes in securing some dry areas, in excluding drink from the Empire Exhibition in Glasgow in 1938 and from the stadium for the first Commonwealth Games in Edinburgh in 1970. A 'Statement on Total Abstinence', distributed with the approval of the Union council in 1981, was well received.[151]

Institutions

The churches continue to be bound together as a denomination by the Baptist Union of Scotland. Its appointment of a field secretary in 1906, fourteen years before a full-time secretary, illustrates its desire to be the servant, not the headquarters, of the churches. Scottish Baptists have generally been suspicious of any central control, but, recognizing the increasing role which the Union could play in many areas of church life, the assembly of 1920 appointed Thomas Stewart as full-time secretary.[152] Recognizing also that neither Union nor college could develop without premises of its own, the denomination purchased 'Baptist Church House and College' at 113 West Regent Street, Glasgow, in 1925.[153] Owned four-fifths by the Union and one-fifth by the college, its Council Chamber, Secretary's Room (used also by committees), College Library/Lecture Room and Ladies' Room were the focal point of denominational life for the next forty-five years — except for one week every October.

The annual assembly has been held in the month of October, usually from Monday to Thursday, in Glasgow, Edinburgh or such other place as issues an invitation. It is a deliberative assembly consisting of ministers and lay delegates from all subscribing churches. More business sessions were added in 1961 to allow even greater time for participation.[154] A vice-president, alternating between minister and layman, is elected and assumes the presidency at the next assembly. The president's address, reproduced in the *Year Book*, expresses whatever lies on his heart, and, together with his visits to the churches, sets the theme for the year.

Between assemblies the work was carried forward until 1978 by a council and committees. In 1914, there were a modest half dozen of these — Sunday School, Evangelistic, Church Extension, Loan and Building, Provident (i.e. retirement) and Foreign Mission. That structure served its day, but by 1977 the increasing complexity of the work, carried out by no less than sixteen committees and all on an honorary basis, led Andrew MacRae to propose professional leadership, under three departments, Mission, Church Life and Publications. Each department draws expertise from throughout the denomination.[155] For every pound sterling given in a typical year, 35p goes to support ministry, 27p to church extension, 25p to administration, 5p to education, 4p for assembly and committees, and 4p for affiliations.[156]

By 1970, both Union and college urgently required more accommodation. The Union moved to a detached villa at 14 Aytoun Road, Pollokshields, providing a spacious Council Room, lounge, office accommodation, cafeteria and a panelled Oak Room where (appropriately) the enormous oak table, the secretary's desk in West Regent Street, continues to be the focal point for committee decisions. The Union has benefited from so much devoted service, both before and after the move, that it would be invidious even to begin to mention names — appropriate recognition is given in the *Year Book*.

Prior to 1966 the secretary of the Union was also the 'Superintendent of the Sustentation Fund', a task that involved little beyond distributing moneys to aided churches. From 1966, Andrew MacRae began to offer an active superintendency, extending it to non-aided churches also. This soon attracted more than any 'Secretary and Superintendent' could manage. Shortly after Peter Barber was appointed General Secretary in 1980, he recommended the appointment of a superintendent, along the lines of the English pattern, offering help to candidates for the ministry, probationers, ministers and their families, and available to advise churches about vacancies and any other pastor-church relationships.[157] The early reports of Eric Watson, the superintendent appointed in 1983, show how much the service was needed.[158]

The District Associations, by contrast, have assumed a lesser role in Scottish Baptist life over recent years. Their detailed reports, in the *Year Book* until paper shortage in 1943 excluded them, show fellowship and support at local level, particularly in the foundation of new causes,[159] exchange of pulpits and up to five conferences per year, mostly of a devotional nature. However, with declining membership, better communications and a Union increasingly equipped to serve the churches, there was less need for the traditional activities of associations. Furthermore, a greater ecumenical spirit, fostered partly by the charismatic movement, led Baptists to meet with other groups, and so to undercut the place for traditional association gatherings.

The Women's Auxiliary (WA), founded in 1909 with the motto 'By Love Serve One Another', has 'organised the womanhood of the Churches'[160] as an independent body. When the Sustentation Fund was launched in 1914, the WA raised one quarter of the £30,000. It sent two motor ambulances to the First World War, staffed canteens, packed parcels and provided garments. WA District Unions, formed in 1921, encouraged local branches, and an Annual Rally and Thanksgiving was inaugurated in 1926, by which time there were seventy-two branches.[161] From 1930, the first Sunday in October was designated 'Women's Day'. Successive *Year Books* note the energy given to visiting the sick, the lonely and absentees from church, sewing and knitting to help church funds and missions, arranging gospel meetings for women, holding times of prayer and generally enlisting every woman in the church into some form of Christian service. When the Church Extension Appeal was launched in 1951, only the WA reached its allotted target.[162] In the 1980s its members gave over £8,000 to the Dedridge building.[163]

The Lay Preachers' Association, formed in 1926, has helped to co-ordinate pulpit supply. The Scottish Baptist Men's Movement has been active since 1947, not only in holding conferences and missionary meetings, but also its library project benefited equally the college and pastors overseas.[164] The latest auxiliary, the Scottish Baptist Housing Association, has been unable to gain government recognition and so has no access to public funds for developments, but it could be activated if opportunity were to arise.

At the outbreak of the First World War, the Baptist Theological College of Scotland, with twenty students, was still meeting in an upper room of the Adelaide Place Church, Glasgow. Through a splendid gift, a full-time principal Dr Jervis Coats and a fourth part-time lecturer had just been appointed. In 1925 the college, jointly with the Union, moved to 113 West Regent Street, Glasgow. It aimed to produce a graduate ministry, with students taking a Scottish arts degree and learning theology concurrently in the ten weeks of the university summer vacation. If applicants were not ready for university, they were accepted as probationers and coached for the university's preliminary examination.[165] From 1930, a full term in the college was possible after graduation, then two. While a degree remained the ideal until 1965, there were always non-graduate entrants to the Scottish Baptist ministry through colleges in the south or through the Union examinations.[166]

The college has at all times maintained its academic independence but, from 1935, agreed that a minority of its committee should be elected by the Union. These men and women have been put to excellent use by the college, and have served on its two sub-committees, the Board of Studies and the Business Committee.

In post-war years, the rising age of students, some with less formal education, together with the introduction of a primary BD[167] in the University of Glasgow, led to the college introducing in 1965 its own non-graduating course of three years — general arts subjects were not excluded, but they were combined with theology and spiritual equipment for the ministry. The resulting college diploma confers ministerial recognition at probationer level throughout Great Britain.[168] Many, however, have gained an external qualification at the same time, from 1956 to 1983 the external BD of the University of London or the certificate or diploma of the University of Cambridge. Now, after an assignment for two years to the International Baptist Seminary in Rüschlikon in Switzerland, a BD may be granted from there.

The college, believing that geographical proximity to the University of Glasgow would foster closer links, used its one-fifth share of the sale of 113 West Regent Street in 1970 to purchase a terraced villa at 31 Oakfield Avenue.[169] The liaison with the university did not, however, materialize, and when a children's home next door to Baptist Church House closed in 1980, college and Union acquired the site as equal owners.[170] Rapid social change in the 1960s led to more tuition in practical skills, such as counselling, which the grant-making bodies recognized by funding the new Diploma of Practical Theology that followed academic studies.[171] From 1978 candidates have been selected by a Joint Board of college and Union, which now deals with all applications for the ministry and designs courses — collegiate or non-collegiate — appropriate to every man.[172] Recognizing the importance of lay people in Christian leadership, the Scottish Baptist College (as it had become in 1981) introduced a Christian Service Certificate for non-ministerial candidates in 1986.[173] Throughout the period it combined flexibility with an insistence on the centrality for ministry of a theological training.

Support for the Baptist Missionary Society (BMS) was strengthened by the appointment in 1937 of a full-time society representative in Scotland[174] who toured extensively among the churches, as the convener of the Union's Foreign Mission Committee had done before him. The representative had office accommodation in Church House, both when first appointed and when the Union moved to Pollokshields. Information was also shared through the annual missionary deputation to the churches, by literature (particularly the monthly *Missionary Herald*), by study circles, mobile exhibitions and the assembly missionary rally. The churches responded well, both in finance and in a regular stream of nurses, teachers, doctors, administrators and ministers as missionary candidates. The Baptist Zenana Mission, designed to reach the women's quarters of Hindu houses, had become the more general Women's Missionary Auxiliary.[175] The Medical Mission Auxiliary of the BMS, actively supported in Scotland since 1904, promoted medical involvement in many parts of the world.[176]

The church overseas was deeply influenced by the independence movements which followed the Second World War. Paternalism was gradually replaced by partnership. Visits to Britain by overseas church leaders helped to emphasize the change. The church overseas itself influenced home thinking. The Church of North India, inaugurated in 1970, was the first ecclesiastical union in which, through the BMS, British Baptists were directly involved.

While most churches still support the BMS, interest has diversified in recent decades in two particular ways. First, many non-denominational societies ('Faith Missions') have attracted finance and personnel from the Scottish Baptist constituency. They have provoked interest in areas where BMS does not work. Second, as medicine, education and agriculture have made the love of God credible in practical ways, numerous new agencies have sprung up to alleviate physical need. Christian Aid and The Evangelical Alliance Relief (TEAR) Fund have both gained strong backing.

Scottish Baptists are represented also on the Baptist Union of Great Britain and Ireland (though it chiefly serves churches in England and Wales), the European Baptist Federation and the Baptist World Alliance. The last two General Secretaries have had a particularly active and significant role in international Baptist life. Scottish Baptists have regularly sent delegates to interdenominational bodies including the Scottish Churches' Council, the British Council of Churches, the Church and Industry Committee, the David Livingstone Trust and the National Bible Society of Scotland.

Church Life

Between the wars there was virtual uniformity of services, not only throughout the country but also over the years. Sunday services were at 11 a.m. and 6.30 p.m., with an emphasis in the morning on teaching (using the *Baptist Church Hymnal*) and in the evening on gospel preaching (with *Redemption Songs* or Sankey's *Sacred Hymns and Solos*). The morning service opened with a psalm or paraphrase. Services (except in the Highlands) were assisted by an organ and included an offering. The Lord's

Prayer was usually sung or said, the Authorised Version of the Bible was universally used in public, and communion was normally held weekly,[177] some churches still using the common cup. Sermons averaged half an hour, and the evening service was often supplemented by musical items. Ladies wore hats, and children did not leave part-way through the service. The evening service was usually the better attended in those days.

There was little change until the 1960s. Innovations of the last twenty years have been attributed to the influence of secular 'pop culture', the charismatic movement, new translations of scripture and the numerous collections of worship choruses. Ministers have contributed to the informality by abandoning distinctive forms of dress such as the clerical collar. In 1922 five churches, all in the islands, kept the communion table closed to those not baptized as believers.[178] Fifty years later a number of churches still maintained this practice, but the great majority invited all Christians to participate. At the same time only one church in thirteen in Scotland permitted those not baptized as believers to enter church membership.[179]

Women have played a leading and honourable role in Baptist church life since its beginning, and, when lay preachers were 'recognized' in 1927, women were listed on the same terms as men. The last thirty years, however, have seen the greatest involvement of women, not because there are fewer men available, but because changing attitudes have allowed them to be appointed in their own right. A survey of 72 Baptist Churches in 1984 disclosed that women taught in Sunday Schools (all 72), held office as deacons (37), served communion (33), preached (28) and acted as secretaries and treasurers (9). The ratio of women in membership to men varied between 6 to 1 and 1.3 to 1, the average being 2 to 1.[180]

In 1982 the first female application to the Ministerial Recognition Committee was received. The full Union council resolved to recommend acceptance only if two-thirds of its members voted in favour. When only a simple majority was obtained,[181] the committee report was sent to churches, one of which brought the matter to the 1985 assembly. Discussion lasted most of a morning, after which 231 voted in favour, 235 against, narrowly short of a simple majority and 80 short of the two-thirds that had been stipulated for this forum also. The whole matter was remitted back to the committees for further thought.[182]

The college has taken, and will continue to take, non-ministerial lady students, training them (for example) for missionary service. Although free to accept any person, the college resolved that out of deference to the policy of the Union, it would not take ladies who had ministry in mind. Consequently they went to England. A church which is not dependent on Union aid is free to call any person it chooses to the pastorate, but in recent years no Scottish Church has called a lady minister. That event will no doubt be the starting point of the next history of Baptists in Scotland.

It would, however, be wrong to end on a debatable point, because such success as Scottish Baptists have enjoyed is without doubt grounded in the priority which they have given to prayer. Ninety-eight per cent of churches have a mid-week meeting for prayer and Bible Study.[183] The monthly *Scottish Baptist Magazine* invites weekly prayer for particular churches. Likewise the *Fellowship of Prayer,* a leaflet sent out every month since 1967,[184] encourages the prayers of people throughout the country for the well-being of others and the honour of the name of the Saviour.

In 1986 Baptists claimed 16,632 members in 173 churches.[185] Although the membership figure represents only approximately 0.5% of the total adult population of Scotland,[186] it is a significant proportion in a secularizing society. Their Bible-based spirituality and their strong doctrinal convictions, even if sometimes the cause of internal disagreement, have stood the Baptists in good stead. Their evangelistic priority, at certain stages embraced to the exclusion of a broader understanding of mission, has spurred them to a constant quest for converts. The combination of central services provided by a growing Union with great scope for local initiative guaranteed by congregational independency has permitted a strategy that, despite failures, has translated the theory of evangelism into effective church growth. It is hard to resist the conclusion that Baptists in Scotland have remained relatively strong because of their wholehearted identification with Evangelical Christianity.

Notes

1. Peter Barber in Peter Brierley and Fergus Macdonald, *Prospects for Scotland: report of the 1984 census of the churches* (Bromley, Kent, 1985), p 45.
2. One lone objection is noted by S.D. Henry, 'Scottish Baptists and the First World War', *Baptist Quarterly,* 31 (1985), p 61. For support see *Scottish Baptist Magazine (SBM)*, 1914, p 137; 1915, p 186; 1917, p 33; 1918, p 17; *Scottish Baptist Year Book (SBYB),* 1915, p 27; 1916, p 21, Home Mission p 6; 1917, p 18; 1918, p 26; and W.A. Mursell, *The Bruising of Belgium and Other Sermons During Wartime* (Paisley 1915), p 24.
3. 5,000 estimated at October 1916: *SBYB*, 1917, p 47.
4. *SBYB,* 1916, p 36.
5. Christopher Harvie, *No Gods and Precious Few Heroes* (London 1981), p 14. *SBM*, 1915, p 142. *SBYB*, 1915, p 22.
6. R.H. Campbell, *Scotland since 1707: the rise of an industrial society* (2nd edn, Edinburgh 1985), pp 186-202.
7. W.M. Marwick, *Scotland in Modern Times* (London 1964), p 167. *Scotland's Changing Population* (London, n.d.), p 11.
8. Marwick, *Scotland*, p 157.
9. Henry, 'Scottish Baptists and the First World War', p 63.
10. Larkhall (1919), Hermon, Glasgow (1920), Girvan (1921), Musselburgh (1933), Cleland (1935), Montrose (1937).

11. e.g. *SBYB*, 1940, p 131: Stenhouse, Edinburgh.
12. Places where outreach did not take root include (references to *SBYB*): West Calder, 1924, p 88; Kilbirnie, 1928, p 141; Auchtermuchty, 1937, p 167; Falkland, 1939, pp 115, 131; Blairgowrie, 1939, p 131; West Pilton, Edinburgh, 1939, pp 133-4; Kelty, 1942, p 127; Uphall, 1942, pp 126-8. Cronberry, Ayrshire: D.B. Murray, *The First Hundred Years: the Baptist Union of Scotland* (Glasgow 1969), p 98.
13. *SBYB*, 1930, p 135; 1931, p 145; 1932, p 147.
14. *SBYB*, 1936, p 79.
15. Murray, *First Hundred Years*, pp 92-3. *SBYB*, 1915, p 28; 1916, p 23; 1942, pp 145-6. For comparative figures in other churches, see John Highet, 'The Churches' in A.K. Cairncross, ed, *The Scottish Economy* (Cambridge 1954), pp 312-13.
16. *SBYB*, 1936, p 165.
17. *Scotland's Changing Population*, p 16.
18. Harvie, *No Gods*, pp 52-4.
19. *Scotland's Changing Population*, p 12.
20. *The Scottish Economy 1965 to 1970: a plan for expansion* (London 1966), pp 1-3.
21. John Stewart, *Adelaide Place Baptist Church during World War II* (n.p. 1983), pp 3-4. *SBYB*, 1941, pp 148, 184-5; 1942, p 172; 1943, p 42; 1945, pp 46, 66; 1946, p 70.
22. *SBYB*, 1941, p 123; 1942, pp 124, 172.
23. *SBYB*, 1940, p 160; 1973, p 152.
24. *SBYB*, 1943, p 67; 1944, p 66; 1946, p 89.
25. *SBYB*, 1944, p 49; 1946, p 59; 1947, p 79; 1948, pp 140-1.
26. *SBYB*, 1941, pp 124-5; 1943, p 70.
27. Joy Tivy, 'Population Distribution and Change', in *The Glasgow Region: a general survey*, ed Ronald Miller and Joy Tivy (Glasgow 1958), p 250.
28. *SBYB*, 1962, pp 118, 138, 165; 1977, p 73. Between 1962 and 1982 Rankin designed and supervised 22 churches.
29. *SBYB*, 1965, p 167; 1972, pp 33, 62; 1976, pp 13, 57 (Erskine); 1978, p 49 (Castlemilk).
30. *SBYB*, 1974, p 55; 1981, p 54; 1985, p 91.
31. *SBYB*, 1953, p 121; 1954, p 117; 1955, p 120; 1956, p 124; 1957, p 122; 1977, p 62; 1980, p 17; 1981, p 33 Nevertheless the Centenary Fund exceeded its target of £50,000 (*SBYB*, 1971, p 52; 1973, p 20).
32. *SBYB*, 1962, p 121; 1966, p 129; 1969, p 20; 1975, p 18.
33. *SBYB*, 1971, p 15.
34. Murray, *First Hundred Years*, p 125.
35. e.g. *SBYB*, 1968, p 177; 1976, p 16; 1977, p 43; 1978, p 49; 1982, p 83.
36. South Church of Scotland, Kirkintilloch: *SBYB*, 1952, p 182. East Kilbride Church of Scotland: *SBYB*, 1957, p 116. Parish Church in Cupar: *SBYB*, 1973, p 62. UF Church in Craigmillar: *SBYB*, 1974, p 41. UP Church in Brechin: *SBYB*, 1977, pp 18, 36.
37. *SBYB*, 1983, pp 28, 50, 81, 84, 91; 1984, p 60; 1985, pp 28, 49; 1986, pp 88, 94.
38. *SBYB*, 1987, p 83.
39. *SBYB*, 1975, pp 41, 59; 1978, p 50; 1982, pp 54, 83, 50.
40. *SBYB*, 1977, pp 38, 39, 171; 1978, p 43.
41. *SBYB*, 1973, p 61; 1977, pp 17, 38.
42. *SBYB*, 1987, p 60.
43. *SBYB*, 1914, Home Mission, p 7.
44 Murray, *First Hundred Years*, pp 84-5. *SBYB*, 1932, pp 178-9.
45. *SBYB*, 1934, pp 93, 112.
46. *SBYB*, 1937, pp 119, 171.
47 *SBYB*, 1941, p 149; 1943, p 70; 1944, p 70.
48. *SBYB*, 1944, p 70; 1945, p 70.
49. *SBYB*, 1952, p 147.
50. *SBYB*, 1959, p 160; 1960, p 159. John Highet, *The Scottish Churches: a review of their state 400 years after the Reformation* (London 1960), pp 85-6.
51. *SBYB*, 1961, p 162; 1963, p 166.
52. *SBYB*, 1964, p 136.
53. *SBYB*, 1969, p 36.
54. *SBYB*, 1969, p 58; 1970, p 16.
55. *SBYB*, 1971, p 15.
56. *SBYB*, 1973, pp 6-12.
57. *SBYB*, 1978, p 46; 1979, pp 22, 47, 103-4.

58. *SBYB*, 1983, pp 28, 49, 94; 1984, pp 65-7; 1985, pp 55-6; 1987, pp 58-9.
59. Peter Bisset in Brierley and Macdonald, *Prospects for Scotland*, p 21.
60. *SBYB*, 1938, pp 138-9; 1939, pp 143-4.
61. *SBYB*, 1941, p 174.
62. e.g. *SBYB*, 1971, p 31; 1972, p 30; 1982, p 86; 1983, p 45; 1984, p 57.
63. George Yuille, ed, *History of the Baptists in Scotland* (Glasgow 1926), pp 240-1. *SBYB*, 1946, p 80.
64. *SBYB* reported annually until 1978 — e.g., 1927, p 137; 1943, p 76; 1961, p 129.
65. *SBYB*, 1943, p 78; 1953, p 162.
66. *SBYB*, 1941, p 123; 1943, p 70; 1944, p 70; 1945, p 71; 1946, p 77.
67. *SBYB*, 1951, p 149; 1952, p 158. Murray, *First Hundred Years*, p 130.
68. *SBYB*, 1963, pp 120-4, 136; 1964, pp 121, 134; 1965, p 125; 1971, p 31.
69. *SBYB*, 1980, pp 70, 90; 1982, p 50; 1983, p 45; 1984, p 57.
70. *SBYB*, 1930, p 87.
71. *SBM*, Oct. 1986, p 3, is an optimistic view: the attendance of outsiders was minimal.
72. Letters of testimony to evangelistic opportunities in the *Charlotte Chapel Record* from November 1914 and in the Home Mission reports in *SBYB*.
73. *SBYB*, 1930, Committee Report, p 5.
74. *SBYB*, 1943, p 69; 1945, p 69; 1946, p 73.
75. *SBYB*, 1975, pp 14, 40; 1976, p 40; 1977, p 42; 1979, p 49; 1981, p 54; 1983, p 49.
76. *SBYB*, 1979, pp 21, 49; 1980, p 54; 1981, p 54.
77. *SBYB*, 1938, p 168; 1939, p 184; 1940, p 182; 1941, p 174.
78. *SBYB*, 1951, p 136. John Highet, *The Scottish Churches Today* (Glasgow 1950), pp 90-3. Highet, *Scottish Churches* (1960), pp 82-4.
79. Highet, *Scottish Churches* (1960), pp 86-7.
80. ibid, pp 87-123.
81. *SBYB*, 1973, p 37.
82. *SBYB*, 1982, pp 54, 85, 97; 1983, p 87.
83. *SBYB*, 1956, p 129.
84. From 19,263 to 20,133 in 1955, and 177 more in 1956: *SBYB*, 1956, pp 87, 129; 1957, p 127.
85. *SBYB*, 1920, pp 26-7.
86. *SBYB*, 1937, p 166.
87. *SBYB*, 1966, p 140.
88. Brierley and Macdonald, *Prospects for Scotland*, p 5.
89. *SBYB*, 1959, p 161; 1960, p 159.
90. *SBYB*, 1964, pp 122, 170. cf *SBYB*, 1963, p 135; 1964, p 120; 1965, p 165; 1966, p 160; 1968, p 175; 1970, p 31; 1974, p 35; 1979, pp 42-3; 1981, p 48.
91. *SBYB*, 1978, p 19; 1979, p 19; 1982, p 79; 1984, p 92.
92. *SBYB*, 1976, pp 49, 69; 1977, p 44.
93. *SBYB*, 1978, pp 18, 50; 1979, pp 19, 51.
94. *SBYB*, 1978, pp 19, 67; 1979, p 19; 1980, pp 16, 19, 69, 91; 1984, p 39.
95. *SBYB*, 1980, p 69.
96. *SBYB*, 1984, p 39.
97 *SBYB*, 1983, p 27; 1984, pp 39, 60.
98. *SBYB*, 1987, p 53.
99 e.g. *SBYB*, 1914, p vii.
100. Murray, *First Hundred Years*, pp 102-3.
101. The last topic is discussed near the end of this chapter, pp 85-6.
102. Murray, *First Hundred Years*, pp 112-13.
103. *SBYB*, 1945, pp 47-8.
104. *Charlotte Chapel Record*, June 1944, p 79.
105. G.M. Marsden, *Fundamentalism and American Culture: the shaping of twentieth-century Evangelicalism, 1870–1925* (New York 1980), pt 3.
106. *SBYB*, 1945, p 48.
107. Murray, *First Hundred Years*, pp 110-11.
108. *SBYB*, 1946, pp 53, 58-9.
109. D.S.K. Macleay and J.D. Taylor.
110. *SBYB*, 1924, p 86.
111. *SBYB*, 1938, pp 126-7; 1940, p 124.
112. *SBYB*, 1949, p 115.

113. cf *Liberty in the Lord* (Baptist Revival Fellowship, London 1964), pp 34-7. *Ecumenism Examined* (Baptist Union of Ireland, Belfast 1966).
114. *SBYB*, 1952, pp 121-2.
115. *SBYB*, 1956, p 116.
116. *Charlotte Chapel Record*, Nov. 1955, pp 166-79.
117. Murray, *First Hundred Years*, pp 117-18.
118. *SBYB*, 1968, pp 148-51.
119. *SBYB*, 1971, pp 30, 59; 1972, p 36; 1973, pp 35, 43; 1975, p 14; 1976, pp 38, 58; 1982, p 69; 1985, p 98; 1986, p 72.
120. Harper Memorial: *SBYB*, 1967, pp 126-8. Inverness: *SBYB*, 1970, p 59. Hermon, Glasgow: *SBYB*, 1971, p 49. Old Cumnock: *SBYB*, 1971, p 36. New Cumnock: *SBYB*, 1971, p 51.
121. *SBYB*, 1968, p 150.
122. *SBYB*, 1977, pp 80, 85-6; 1978, p 85.
123. *SBYB*, 1979, pp 71, 76; 1981, p 56; 1982, p 56. The Union was briefly a member, not just an observer, but when it became clear in 1982 that the aim remained unification of church life in Scotland, the Union reverted to observer status: *SBYB*, 1983, pp 52, 86.
124. *SBM*, 1987, readers' letters, Apr., p 2; May, pp 2–3.
125. *SBYB*, 1977, pp 64, 67, 72; 1978, p 47; 1979, p 67.
126. J.C. Pollock, *The Keswick Story: the authorized history of the Keswick Convention* (London 1964).
127. W.G. Scroggie, *The Lord's Return* (London n.d.), p 122.
128. *SBYB*, 1974, p 93; 1976, p 55; 1979, pp 99-102; 1982, p 32; 1984, p 63. *Scottish Baptists and the Charismatic Renewal Movement* (Baptist Union of Scotland Viewpoint Booklet, Glasgow n.d.).
129. For the earliest stages, see Peter Hocken, *Streams of Renewal: the origins and early development of the charismatic movement in Great Britain* (Exeter 1986); and for the subsequent development of the British mainstream, Edward England, *The Spirit of Renewal* (Eastbourne 1982).
130. *Crusade*, Mar. 1980, pp 28-30.
131. *SBYB*, 1987, p 32.
132. This question was revised by Charlotte Chapel when the interviewing elders found it increasingly difficult to understand, let alone explain what it meant!
133. *SBYB*, 1926, p 177.
134. *SBYB*, 1945, Commission of Enquiry Report, p 3.
135. Peter Barber in *SBM*, Aug. 1986, p 10.
136. *SBYB*, 1926, p 137.
137. *SBYB*, 1957, p 115.
138. Murray, *First Hundred Years*, p 130.
139. *SBYB*, 1973, p 10.
140. *SBYB*, 1968, p 132; 1969, p 56; 1978, pp 86, 89; 1984, p 70. See also cap 13, pp 254-5.
141. *SBYB*, 1975, p 59; 1978, pp 41, 50.
142. *SBYB*, 1976, p 13; 1979, p 68.
143. *SBYB*, 1982, pp 29, 85.
144. *SBYB*, 1983, p 50; 1984, p 96.
145. *SBYB*, 1982, pp 55, 95. *SBM*, May 1987, p 1. *Scottish Baptist News*, Apr. 1987, p 5.
146. *SBYB*, 1925, pp 100, 160-1.
147. Yuille, ed, *Baptists in Scotland*, p 246.
148. *SBYB*, 1915, p 27; 1916, p 23; 1917, Abstinence Report, p 7; 1918, p 24; 1919, p 23; 1940, p 160; 1941, pp 151-2; 1942, p 153; 1943, p 54; 1944, p 55.
149. *SBYB*, 1914, Abstinence Report, pp 6, 8-11; 1967, pp 125, 136. Yuille, ed, *Baptists in Scotland*, p 246.
150. *SBYB*, 1920, Abstinence Report, p 3.
151. *SBYB*, 1982, p 18; 1983, p 50.
152. Murray, *First Hundred Years*, p 97.
153. *SBYB*, 1926, pp 96, 102.
154 *SBYB*, 1962, p 131.
155. *SBYB*, 1979, pp 15-18, 93-9.
156. *SBYB*, 1974, p 66.
157. *SBYB*, 1983, p 72; 1984, p 37.
158. *SBYB*, 1984, pp 68-9; 1985, pp 57-8; 1986, p 56.
159. Yuille, ed, *Baptists in Scotland*, p 242.
160. WA Constitution.

161. Yuille, ed, *Baptists in Scotland*, p 245.
162. *SBYB*, 1957, p 125.
163. *SBYB*, 1985, p 98.
164. Murray, *First Hundred Years*, pp 126-7.
165. Yuille, ed, *Baptists in Scotland*, p 258.
166. *SBYB*, 1947, p 61.
167. *SBYB*, 1972, p 167.
168. *SBYB*, 1974, pp 43, 70, 85, 87.
169. *SBYB*, 1969, p 34; 1970, p 33.
170. *SBYB*, 1982, pp 80, 82, 91.
171. *SBYB*, 1981, p 151.
172. *SBYB*, 1978, pp 19, 45; 1979, p 46.
173. *SBYB*, 1986, p 173.
174. Murray, *First Hundred Years*, pp 125-6.
175. Yuille, ed, *Baptists in Scotland*, p 265.
176. ibid, p 266.
177. *SBYB*, 1945, Commission of Enquiry, pp 16-17.
178. Murray, *First Hundred Years*, p 141.
179. *SBYB*, 1977, p 41.
180. *The Role of Women in the Church* (A Report prepared for the Executive of the Baptist Union of Scotland) (Glasgow 1986), p III.
181. *SBYB*, 1984, p 93.
182. *SBYB*, 1986, pp 102-6.
183. Brierley and Macdonald, *Prospects for Scotland*, p 44.
184. *SBYB*, 1968, p 153.
185. *SBYB*, 1987, p 35.
186. Brierley and Macdonald, *Prospects for Scotland*, p 44.

I.L.S. Balfour

5. EDINBURGH AND LOTHIAN

The region called Lothian covers the former counties of East, Mid and West Lothian and the city of Edinburgh. Edinburgh, the capital city of Scotland, was a city of 57,195 people in 1755.[1] Although the city lost its independent Scottish Parliament at the Union in 1707, it retains to the present day the status and some of the attributes of a capital. The Established Church, the Church of Scotland, and the Scottish legal system, which has a number of features distinguishing it from the English system, are based in Edinburgh. The founding of the Bank of Scotland in 1695 and subsequent developments in banking, insurance and finance have made Edinburgh one of the financial centres of the world. The University of Edinburgh, although it was the youngest of the four older Scottish Universities, being founded in 1583, attracted not only local people but also many from England, where, until 1828, there were only two universities, at Oxford and Cambridge. As these two universities were effectively open only to those in the Church of England, Edinburgh and the other Scottish universities attracted able scholars from the English Dissenting tradition, some of whom remained to work and to contribute to Scottish life. These developments have given Edinburgh a very strong professional element in the city. In addition there is industrial activity in electronics and electrical engineering, brewing and aspects of food production.

East Lothian is a rich agricultural area with inland centres like Haddington and Gifford, and is fringed by some small fishing ports like Dunbar, Cockenzie and Port Seton. In the west, part of the Midlothian coalfield extends into East Lothian. Midlothian includes much hill land for sheep grazing in the Pentland and Moorfoot Hills. The main farming land is in the Esk valley, where the older towns of Dalkeith, Lasswade and Penicuik are situated. Musselburgh at the mouth of the Esk is the largest town and includes the harbour at Fisherrow and a number of industrial premises. Other towns such as Gorebridge, Loanhead and Roslin were influenced by the development of the coalfield, where there are now only two working mines, Bilston Glen and Monktonhall.

West Lothian was mainly associated with mining. The coalfield, which is now virtually exhausted, is the eastern extension of the central coalfield of Scotland. The mining of oil shale, which was important in the industrial development of the district, ceased in 1962.[2] In fact some of the earliest developments in oil refining were made in West Lothian by men such as James Young, who is known as 'Paraffin Young'. The decline in mining led to various attempts to provide alternative employment. One attempt was to build commercial vehicles at Bathgate, but after about twenty years this

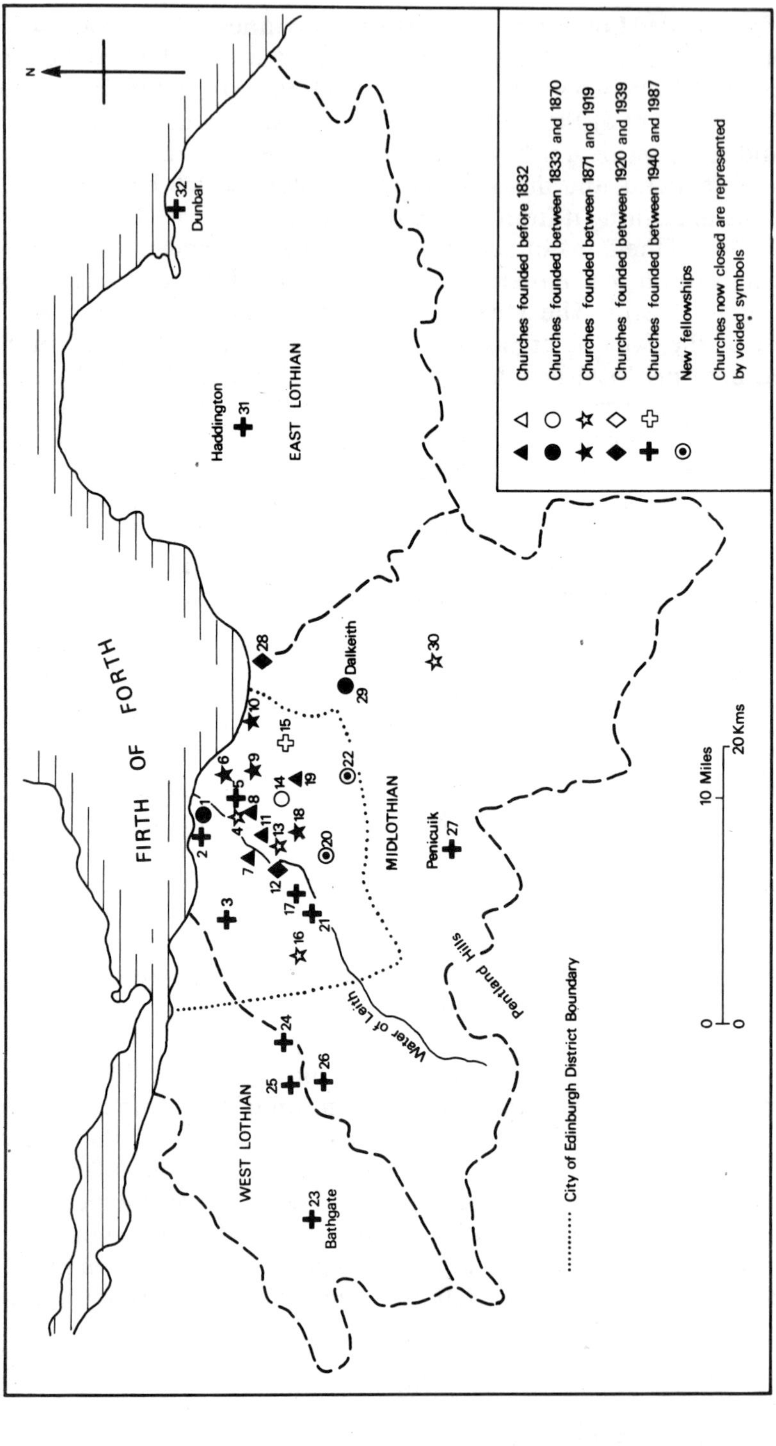

MAP 5.1 : EDINBURGH AND LOTHIAN BAPTIST CHURCHES.

Key to Map 5.1

1. Leith
2. Granton
3. Barnton
4. Stockbridge
5. Bellevue
6. South Leith
7. Bristo
8. Dublin Street
9. Abbeyhill
10. Portobello
11. Charlotte Chapel
12. Stenhouse
13. Gorgie
14. Marshall Street
15. Craigmillar
16. Ratho
17. Wester Hailes
18. Morningside
19. Duncan Street
20. Colinton Mains
21. Currie
22. Burdiehouse
23. Bathgate
24. Broxburn
25. Ladywell
26. Dedridge
27. Penicuik
28. Musselburgh
29. Dalkeith
30. Stobhill
31. Haddington
32. Dunbar

industry was hit by the trade recession in the United Kingdom in the late 1970s. A more successful attempt has been the establishment of the New Town of Livingston, which is now the largest town in the district with a population of over 60,000.

An Abortive Start

After the Reformation in 1560 there was little sign of any Baptist witness until the mid-seventeenth century. It is possible that Baptist opinions were professed in Edinburgh conventicles during the 1620s, but the charge may have been levelled at dissidents simply as a form of slur.[3] With the coming to Scotland of the Commonwealth army there also came toleration of religious groups which worshipped in different ways. In addition to putting troops in garrison towns, Cromwell established four citadels, one of which was in Leith, the port for Edinburgh. A Baptist Church was formed there about 1652. By 1653 the church was meeting on alternate Sundays in Leith and Edinburgh. While the soldiers stationed in Leith formed part of the membership of the church there were local people who accepted the truth of believer's baptism and joined the church. The first baptisms took place in the Water of Leith at Bonnington Mill. After the Commonwealth period the church declined and it appears to have ceased soon after.[4]

Renaissance, 1750-1832

After the failure of the Jacobite Rebellion of 1745-6 had brought peace to Edinburgh, a new era of prosperity arose. The city doubled its population from about 25,000 in 1700 to 57,195 in 1755.[5] This population was still confined within the walls of the city, resulting in gross overcrowding. Prosperity brought plans to improve the city. Development took place to the

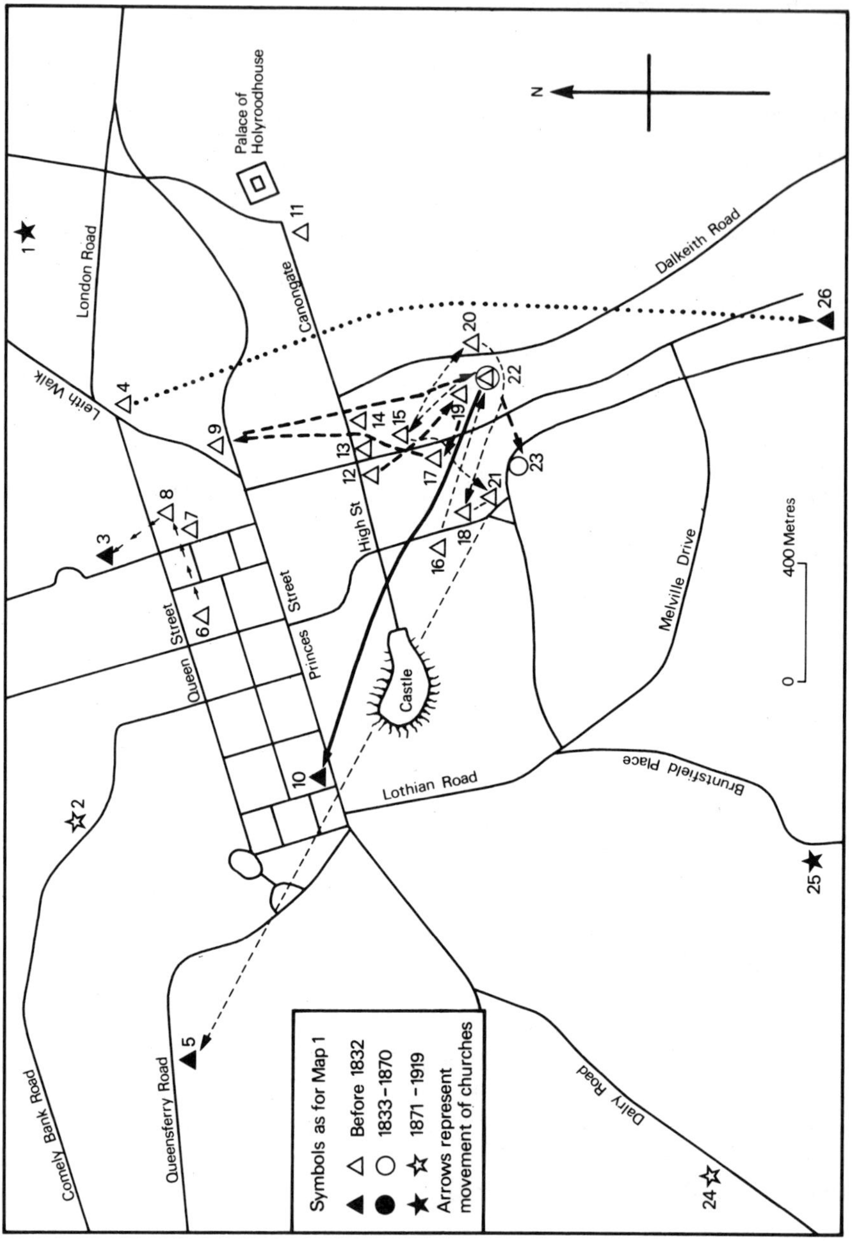

MAP 5.2 : EDINBURGH CITY CENTRE BAPTIST CHURCHES.

Key to Map 5.2

1. Abbeyhill	10. Charlotte Chapel	19. Roxburgh Terrace
2. Stockbridge	11. Cordiners' Hall	20. Pleasance
3. Dublin Street	12. Hunter Square	21. Bristo Placc
4. The Tabernacle	13. Skinners' Hall	22. Richmond Court
5. Bristo	14. Masons' Hall	23. Marshall Street
6. East Thistle Street	15. St. Cecilia's Hall	24. Gorgie
7. Clyde Street	16. Magdalen Chapel	25. Morningside
8. Elder Street	17. Adam Square	26.Duncan Street
9. Waterloo Rooms	18. Argyle Square	

south of the walls with the building of a number of squares including Argyle Square and George Square.[6]

On the fringe of the Old Town in the Cowgate the first Baptist Church in Edinburgh met in a pre-Reformation building, the Magdalen Chapel. After Robert Carmichael had been baptized in London on 9 October 1765 he returned to Edinburgh to baptize seven in the Water of Leith, near Canonmills. With Carmichael as pastor, this group constituted the first enduring Baptist Church in Edinburgh in November 1765. Archibald McLean, who was working in Glasgow, soon followed in baptism in the Water of Leith, moved to Edinburgh and became co-pastor with Carmichael in 1768. The following year Robert Walker was chosen co-pastor with McLean on the removal of Carmichael to Dundee.[7] The church favoured a plurality of pastors and was opposed to a 'one-man ministry'. It was the pioneer of these principles which were to become known as 'Scotch Baptist'. It was not long before the Edinburgh Church had problems. Division was caused over the interpretation of the pastoral office. Some believed that the presence of a presiding elder was necessary to lead at communion and to baptize believers. Others believed that the right to administer the ordinances was not confined to elders. Another division took place in 1774 when there was a difference between McLean and Walker over a matter of discipline. As much of the cost of renting the Magdalen Chapel was borne by Walker, the church had to leave and met for two years in McLean's home. Soon after this division, in 1777, McLean published his book *Defence of Believer's Baptism*. This led to growth in the church and particularly in the quality of those from other churches who were convinced of believer's baptism. Two of them soon became leaders. In 1778 William Braidwood, who wrote a number of books, was chosen co-pastor with McLean, who had served for two years as sole pastor. In 1784 Henry Inglis, later an advocate, was selected to join McLean and Braidwood.[8]

After meeting for some time in McLean's home, the congregation moved in 1787 to the first place of worship designed for a Baptist Church in Scotland, a building erected in Richmond Court, the area of growth to the south of the Old Town. It was later to be occupied by two other Edinburgh Baptist Churches, those that became Charlotte Chapel and Marshall Street.[9]

At the time the Edinburgh Church was developing, Lord Provost George Drummond was keen to have a bridge built across the partly drained Nor' Loch to link the Old Town to the ridge to the north where it was hoped to build an extension to the city. This eventually led to the building of what is still called the New Town, centred on George Street. While the New Town was being built, permission was received to construct a bridge from the Tron Church across the Cowgate to the south. At the southern end on the Kirk o' Field site, what is now the Old Building of the University of Edinburgh was erected in 1789. Many older houses were demolished and replaced by new buildings.[10] As the Edinburgh Church grew it worshipped in a number of buildings in this area. In 1802 it had purchased St Cecilia's Hall in Niddry Street. In a few years a larger building was required for the growing membership, and so one was erected in the Pleasance. This was opened in 1811.[11]

This period saw the establishment of other churches which were based on the so-called 'English' Baptist model. The major influences in these developments were connected with the Haldane revival. Three continuing churches in the city owe a debt to the Haldanes and particularly to the ministry of James Haldane at the Tabernacle. In addition, perhaps five more short-lived causes drew strength from Haldane's congregation. One was meeting in Cordiners' Hall, Horse Wynd, as early as 1801, but drew only small numbers before its rump returned to Haldane's ministry in 1808 or shortly afterwards. Another fellowship assembled briefly in Masons' Hall, Blackfriars Wynd, in 1801-2. A third, originally gathered by Frederic Macfarlane, a former Anti-Burgher minister, and worshipping in Skinners' Hall, was described in 1806 as 'an off-set from the Tabernacle'. Another group, probably ephemeral, split off from Macfarlane's fellowship.[12] A fifth body that separated from the Tabernacle in 1824 turned into a Scotch Baptist Church which worshipped in Clyde Street and in the 1830s drew a congregation of 120. It eventually seems to have united with the original Scotch Baptist Church.[13]

Prior to acceptance of believer's baptism by the Haldanes in 1808, Christopher Anderson, whose father attended the Independent Church in Candlemaker Row, began attending the Scotch Baptist Church in Richmond Court. Then Anderson was attracted by the preaching of James Haldane, who at that time remained an Independent. As three of Anderson's brothers had been baptized in the Scotch Baptist Church, he was influenced by them. He was also swayed by students from England at the University of Edinburgh who were Baptists. Anderson was persuaded by them of believer's baptism and was immersed in March 1801. After studying at the University of Edinburgh, Bristol Baptist College and Olney, he was convinced that he should minister in Edinburgh. Believing that the Scotch Baptist order was unscriptural, he was determined to found a new cause on the lines of the 'English' Baptist Churches. As the Scotch Baptists were moving from Richmond Court, their premises were purchased in 1806 and a new church formally constituted in January 1808. Thus the church which is now Charlotte Chapel began in the same area of Edinburgh as the first Baptist Church.[14]

Since the New Town had been developed to cater for the well-to-do, the character of the Old Town changed. There were left behind in the Old Town the tradesmen, shopkeepers and the poor. It was one of Anderson's aims to invite the poor as well as the others to hear the gospel. Within the New Town there were many who were by no means prosperous. These were the servants of the well-to-do, working in the houses as domestics or in the mews to provide transport. Further building soon took place west and north of the New Town core. In the thirty years between the first census of 1801 and that of 1831 the population of the old county of Edinburgh grew from 122,597 to 219,345, a 78% increase.[15] A growth in Baptist work was to be expected.

The first of the Baptist Churches in the area was on the fringe of the New Town, the Tabernacle at the top of Leith Walk. This church became Baptist when the Haldanes adopted the practice of believer's baptism in 1808. The members who were not convinced of believer's baptism left to form an Independent Church in Bernard's Rooms, West Thistle Street, one of the service roads of the New Town, in 1809. This church called Dr William Innes, formerly in the Church of Scotland, as minister. He himself became convinced of believer's baptism a year later, resigned the pastorate of the Independent Church, and along with seventeen others founded a Baptist Church in East Thistle Street, which moved in 1813 to Elder Street.[16] Meantime at the Richmond Court Chapel, with Christopher Anderson as pastor, the increase in attendance led to the need for larger premises. In 1818 Anderson purchased Charlotte Chapel in Rose Street, the other service road in the New Town, from the Scottish Episcopalians, who moved to their new church building at the west end of Princes Street.[17]

By the end of the third decade of the nineteenth century there was one Scotch Baptist Church in the Pleasance, another in Clyde Street and three churches in or near the New Town. In the rest of Lothian there were churches at Dalkeith, formed in 1820, Musselburgh, formed about the same year, and

Stobhill, near Gorebridge, formed in 1808. By 1844 Dalkeith and Musselburgh had disappeared, though Dalkeith was to be reconstituted in 1852. In 1844 Stobhill, which did not survive much longer, had fifteen members.[18]

Second Stage of Growth, 1832–1870

By 1832 the Scotch Baptist Church had over three hundred members meeting in its premises in the Pleasance. Under the leadership of its three pastors and seven deacons there were a number of able men in business and the arts in membership. But the growth and development of the church was interrupted by a division over the observance of the Lord's Supper in 1834. After a schism earlier over the matter of whether or not it was necessary to have an elder present at communion, the problem arose again. The issue was whether churches should remain in fellowship with congregations taking the more liberal view that elders were not essential. Another split in the church took place. The more rigid party seceded to form another Baptist Church, the Minto House Church, Argyle Square, where Chambers Street now is. This church lasted until 1874, when the members rejoined the original church. In 1844 the Minto House Church had about 130 members while the original church had 260.[19]

After occupying the building in the Pleasance for twenty-four years, the Scotch Baptist Church returned to St Cecilia's Hall for a short period while the new building in Bristo Place was being built. The building was opened in 1835 and was used until 1935. It was located on the margins of poorer housing in the older part of the city and better housing to the south. The cost of the building was met by the generosity of several men who were pioneers in the insurance industry, one of the continuing important financial activities of the city.[20]

The mid-century period that witnessed the creation of vigorous congregations of the Free Church of Scotland also saw developments among Baptists. Two of the new causes were short-lived. One was in Dunbar, which probably lasted only five years (1842-7). It appears to have been the only Baptist witness in the town over the years except for an attempt by a Reformed Baptist group in the 1960s and 1970s. The other short-lived church was in Roxburgh Terrace, Edinburgh, which lasted from about 1850 to 1860.[21]

The port of Leith was expanded in the nineteenth century with the opening of the Victoria Dock in 1851, with the construction of piers and with the creation of the Albert Dock in 1869. In 1838 the first railway line was built to the docks to carry coal for export from the Midlothian coalfield. Pit-props, along with timber, were imported from the Baltic countries. With the improvement of rail and road links Leith became a port for the import of goods, such as tea (Melrose's) and grain. Shipbuilding was important at Leith until 1983, when the last yard closed. 'Sirius', the first steamship to cross the Atlantic, was built at Leith.[22]

The evangelist of the Baptist Union, James Blair, held meetings in Leith in September 1845. This marks the beginning of Leith Baptist Church, which was formally founded in 1849. After various meeting places were used, the present site in Madeira Street was acquired in 1875 and the present building opened in 1885. One of those who helped in the founding of the Leith Church was Francis Johnstone, who came from Cupar to establish a new church in Edinburgh. Using the Merchants' Hall in Hunter Square, close to the Tron Church, a new Baptist cause was formed in 1846 with twenty-one members. Within a few months the move was made to a hall in Roxburgh Terrace; then in 1847 another was made to the School of Arts in Adam Square, where the church grew rapidly. This was almost in the centre of the very densely populated Old Town with its newer southern extension. A further move was made just over a year later to the Waterloo Rooms. Progress was arrested from 1852 onwards by dissension which resulted in Johnstone's departure for Cambridge in 1856. The church acquired the chapel in Richmond Court which Bristo and Charlotte Chapel had used in their earlier days. Difficulties, however, continued until Johnstone returned in 1860 with a view to having a new building on what was considered to be a more suitable site. This was eventually found in Marshall Street, where the new building was opened in 1877.[23]

The Elder Street Church grew in membership from 150 in 1841 to 286 in 1846. In this period 232 members were received in while ninety-six, including those who died, ceased to be members. This growth meant that larger premises were required. In 1858 the church moved to Dublin Street. The communicant roll of the 1840s shows that the members were engaged in various types of employment. Amongst the men there were over twenty shopkeepers selling a variety of goods. Again over twenty of the male members were in manual occupations, including shoemakers, brushmakers, slaters, boatbuilders, cabinetmakers, upholsterers and six engaged in the printing trade. The professions were represented by sixteen members, including physicians, teachers, a stockbroker, an accountant, an artist and an Inspector of Prisons. Eighty-eight of the women on the roll had no vocational designation after their names, while sixty-seven were recorded as wives and usually specified by their husband's jobs (e.g. draper's wife). Thirty-one members are recorded as daughters, but only six as sons. There were fifty-seven women listed as servants. The latter might be a reflection of the location of Elder Street in the New Town where many servants were required to staff the homes of the well-to-do. Of the total of 382 names on the roll, 243 were women and 139 men.[24] In 1985, for comparison's sake, Morningside had 318 members, of whom 207 were women and 111 men.[25] Thus it is not necessarily a new phenomenon for a church to have more women in membership than men. The Morningside members' roll for 1985 does not list occupations, but within the membership there were about a dozen doctors and twenty nurses. There were fifteen actively involved in education at various levels while there were a number of wives and retired people who had been teachers. The financial and legal professions were well represented, especially accountants. The emphasis on the service occupations in Morningside is a reflection of the nature of employment in the city in the 1980s.

James Haldane sustained his strong evangelistic ministry at the Tabernacle up to his death in 1851. The building was capable of holding over three thousand people. Although in 1844 its membership was only 174,[26] congregations were much larger. After Haldane's death, however, the Tabernacle Church declined. It was clear to William Tulloch, who was called to the pastorate in 1855, that the Tabernacle was no longer a useful building for the church. In 1864 it moved to Duncan Street in Newington on the south side of Edinburgh. The building there had previously been a Baptist Church for a short time but had been sold to the United Presbyterian Church.[27] At the time the building had first been erected it was virtually out in the country. Even by 1864 most of the nearby Grange district was farm land, but during the remainder of the nineteenth century the area was built up with a mixture of types of dwelling ranging from large detached houses to tenement blocks of flats.

Thus with the establishment of new churches and dissension in existing congregations, there were in the 1850s, within less than a mile of each other near the Old Town, four Baptist Churches: Bristo Place, Argyle Square, Richmond Court and Roxburgh Terrace. Less than a century later there were none. For a period of nearly fifty years there were no new churches founded. There were relocations such as the movement of Richmond Court Church to Marshall Street and the Tabernacle to Duncan Street, but at a time of extensive church provision there seemed to be sufficient Baptist causes in the city.

Further Expansion, 1870–1919

Great evangelistic missions were held by Moody and Sankey in the city in 1874 and 1881, but their impact appears to have been greater on Presbyterian Churches than on Baptist Churches.[28] The membership figures for the churches, other than the Scotch Baptist Church, were as follows: 1871, 958; 1876, 890; 1881, 980; and 1886, 1050.[29] There was clearly no rapid advance in these years.

Bristo appointed William Grant, previously one of its co-pastors, as its first full-time pastor in 1870. During his ministry, up to 1902, the membership increased from about 200 to over 600.[30] For much of this period the Charlotte Chapel membership was about 200. There was a peak in 1880 of 305 members, but this was cut to 232 in 1881 when there was a roll revision.[31]

The great growth in church membership came in the period 1891 to 1900, when membership of the Edinburgh and Lothian churches grew from 1,167 to 2,280, an increase of 95%. This expansion was much greater than the population increase, which was a mere 4%.[32] The upsurge probably reflects earlier neglect. The population had previously been increasing in Edinburgh and West Lothian more rapidly than the growth in membership since the middle of the century. It appears there was a slow response to development of new areas in Edinburgh and to the expansion of the coal and shale mining towns in West Lothian. Growth of population in East Lothian, more of an agricultural area, was much less.

In the 1860s and 1870s several slum clearance schemes were begun to improve the conditions in the Old Town and neighbouring areas. In addition, with the increase of industry and further development of railways, including the opening of the Forth Bridge in 1894, more housing was required. This led to the expansion of the city to include Dalry, Gorgie, Merchiston, Morningside, Prestonfield and Willowbrae. Leith, a separate burgh until 1920, was also expanding, so that along Leith Walk, Leith and Edinburgh joined together. Similarly, Portobello, separate until 1896, was growing as a seaside resort and residential suburb. Movement within the area was being made easier through the development of cheaper transport by means of horse buses and tramcars.[33]

Apart from the village of Ratho, eight miles west of Edinburgh, the churches established in the 1890s were in the areas of growth in Edinburgh, Leith and Portobello. Ratho Church was formed in 1892 following two missions in 1891. After meetings had been held in hired premises, a building was erected through a loan from the Baptist Building Fund and opened in 1896. In 1912 a number of members left to join a Brethren meeting. Ratho Church never really recovered from this loss.[34]

South Leith Church was founded in 1891. After meeting in hired halls for two years, the church occupied the present building in Casselbank Street (formerly Hope Street). It served the south of Leith, while the Leith Church in Madeira Street catered for the northern part of the town.[35]

In the 1880s missions were held by Baptists at Portobello, and there was great interest in baptisms in the Firth of Forth, but the formation of a church was slow to come about. After John Wallace had retired from the pastorate of the Dalkeith Church, he lived in Portobello and helped the nucleus, who eventually formed a Baptist Church in 1897. The old Town Hall was purchased in 1919 and the church installed above shops that subsequently included a public house run by a former world boxing champion. The growth of the cause was slow until the end of the First World War. In fact the church owed quite a lot to the support of the Edinburgh churches, especially Bristo Place and Marshall Street.[36]

The minister of the Leith Church, J. Cumming Brown, saw that the Morningside Free Church in Morningside Road was advertized for sale in 1894. Presbyterian Churches had moved into the growing areas of Bruntsfield and Morningside much more quickly than the Baptists. The last quarter of the century had seen rapid growth of tenements, terraced houses and large detached villas in the area. The Free Church had outgrown its building and was moving a short distance away. At a Baptist ministers' fraternal meeting, Cumming Brown suggested buying the premises, but no one could say how the price could be raised. As members of the Free Church were concerned that the property might 'fall into the hands of the Romanists', they were prepared to ask a lower price of £3,000 from the Baptists.[37] While financial encouragement was not available from either the local Baptist Churches or the Baptist Union, Brown established a church with twenty members, including himself, at a meeting in Torrance's Tearooms near Morningside Station on 3 October 1894. The congregation moved into the church building before the end of the year.[38]

With the closure of the Tabernacle in 1864 there was no Baptist Church near the mainly tenement housing between Leith Walk and Easter Road. Services were started by George Macdonald in October 1895 and a church constituted in December. This was the origin of Abbeyhill Baptist Church. Like other churches, it used at first a variety of halls and rooms. The present building in Brunswick Road was opened on 30 November 1902.[39]

The growth of tenements to the south-west of Haymarket close to industrial development and railway yards led to tentative measures to establish a Baptist Church in the Gorgie-Dalry area. After attempts in the 1890s which failed, the Edinburgh Association of Baptist Churches in 1904 was concerned for 'Extension Work in Edinburgh'. Eventually a Reformed Presbyterian Church was purchased in Gorgie. A Baptist Church of fifty members was established on 9 December 1907.[40] A similar attempt to establish a cause in a working-class district at Stockbridge was short-lived. Although a church was begun in 1897, it lasted only until 1905.[41]

While there were new churches being established, one church, Charlotte

Chapel, nearly closed. At the turn of the century the membership was 200, but the life of the church was at a low ebb. At roll revision the membership was cut to 108, with a really active group of only about thirty.[42] The down-town nature of Rose Street with its many public houses contrasted with the rest of the New Town. As there was no public transport on Sundays, people had to walk to church. As well as competition from the growth of churches in the areas of new housing, the unattractiveness of Rose Street affected attendance. But there were those who were given the vision of revival and who prayed for it. The turning point in the life of the Chapel came with the calling to the pastorate of Joseph Kemp, who began his ministry in February 1902 with a congregation of thirty-five. Revival came and the membership grew to over 800 by the end of Kemp's ministry in 1915. The reconstructed chapel building to cater for the growing congregation was opened in 1912.[43]

By 1914 Edinburgh and Leith had a spread of churches which meant that no densely populated area was far from a Baptist Church. The needs of growing areas had been seen by either individuals or by the churches acting together through the Edinburgh Association.

Inter-War Development, 1919–1945

The population of Edinburgh continued to grow slowly, rising from 420,264 in 1921 to about 440,000 in 1939. The boundaries of the city were extended to include Leith and the parishes of Liberton, Colinton, Corstorphine and Cramond. This period was also a time of slum clearance when new council estates were build at Niddrie, Craigmillar, Granton and Pilton. Other schemes were laid out in Stenhouse and Sighthill. Private estates, particularly of bungalows and semi-detached houses, were built in Duddingston, Greenbank, Blackhall, Davidson's Mains, Barnton and Corstorphine. There was a major expansion of the built-up area of the city, helped by the development of the electric tram and motor bus system.[44] Cheap transport was now available on a Sunday, although there were Christians, including some Baptists such as Charles Howden, secretary of Morningside, who refused to use it on the grounds that they were making people work on the sabbath. Howden even had a struggle with his conscience about being given a lift in a car on a Sunday in his old age in the 1940s.[45] As yet few owned cars.

During these years the membership of the Baptist Churches in the area grew from 3,155 (1921) to 3,662 (1939).[46] Most of the growth was in the existing churches, especially in Charlotte Chapel, where the membership reached 1,129 in 1939.[47] The Edinburgh Baptist Association was active in these years considering extension work, but was hesitant. 'The suburban districts are growing rapidly', it was reported in 1929, 'and the matter may have to be faced, but building costs are high and any scheme would require to be backed by much earnest endeavour and even sacrifice on the part of the churches.'[48] Central churches, that is to say, would lose members. This proved an effective deterrent. In 1926 Baptists living in Corstorphine began evening services in a hall, but this did not develop.[49] Sixty years on there was still no Baptist Church in the area, despite further house building after the Second World War. In the early 1980s, however, another attempt was made to start a cause.[50]

New churches were successfully planted. The Portobello Church and its minister, D. Merrick Walker, began evening services at 8 p.m. in the Pavilion Cinema in Musselburgh in 1931. A good start was made, but numbers fell off, and so after a three-month trial period the services ceased. Two years later services were again held, leading to the formation of the church in Musselburgh. Soon a hall was purchased. Support was given in the early years by the Portobello Church and by a missionary attached to Bristo Church.[51]

At the same time consideration was given to starting a church in the Stenhouse area, one of the new estates which was predominantly council housing. This was a venture supported by the Baptist Union and the Edinburgh Baptist Association (EBA), which included Charlotte Chapel. The Chapel provided help, particularly with personnel. The church was established in 1933. Although it is in the middle of a residential area, the membership has not grown as had been hoped. While these developments were taking place, consideration was given to starting a church in Niddrie Mains, a council estate east of Craigmillar. The idea was dropped as there was a lack of support from the churches.[52] In addition the EBA was looking at the Granton-Pilton area, where there were now 24,000 people, mostly as a result of slum clearance from the older parts of the city. The city authorities reserved a site for a Baptist Church in 1938. A start was made with meetings in 1939. A hall was opened on 9 July 1940 and the church had a membership of nineteen.[53]

Not all the developments in this period were concerned with new churches. Abbeyhill purchased halls adjacent to the church in the mid-thirties. The two neighbouring churches of Bristo Place and Marshall Street had had close links since William Grant's pastorate as they had united for services in August and September. This led in 1920 to a proposal from Marshall Street to Bristo Place that they should unite. The motion was defeated, and so the two churches continued separately. Inner-city depopulation eventually led to the closure of Marshall Street in 1942.[54]

Bristo Place, however, was prepared to change with the times. In 1919 it abandoned closed communion. The plurality of elders was ended in 1923 with the resignation of Percival Waugh, who was not replaced. Following this change, in 1927, the church, previously known as the Scotch Baptist Church, became officially Bristo Place Baptist Church. It was also considering moving away from Bristo Place. Members were transferring to the suburbs and there was no scope for development as the building adjoined two other churches. After considering sites near Bristo Place, which were deemed unsuitable, the church purchased one in 1932 at the west end of Buckingham Terrace, Queensferry Road, and the present striking building was opened in 1935. The selling of the Bristo Place building to the Roman Catholics was not approved by some. Again, some felt that a site further out towards the growing suburbs of Blackhall, Davidson's Mains and Barnton would have been better.[55] The removal of Bristo and the closure of Marshall Street left a gap in Baptist witness in an area where there were still a number of people and which was close to the University of Edinburgh and Heriot-Watt College, later to become Heriot-Watt University.

West Lothian remained a weak area for Baptists. The Ratho Church, never large, declined in numbers until it closed during the Second World War. Apart from Bo'ness, a cause in the Stirlingshire Association,[56] there was no Baptist Church in Lothian west of Edinburgh. Before the war and as a continuing part of the extension work of the EBA, the nucleus of a fellowship was gathered in Uphall and Broxburn. This led to the formation of the Broxburn Church in 1940.[57]

Developing Witness, 1945 to Present

After the war as life returned to normal, changes began to take place in popular attitudes to the churches. The practice of attending church regularly declined. It was also a period, for at least fifteen years, of the 'post-war bulge' when there were many more children born than in the thirties. This meant that in areas where there were many young couples, such as the council estates which were being built in Drylaw, Muirhouse, Wester Hailes and to the east and south of Liberton, children were numerous. This provided opportunities for children's and young people's work.

The population of the region increased from 706,000 in 1951 to 750,000 in 1981. Most of the expansion was in East and West Lothian while the population of Edinburgh remained almost constant at about 475,000. The rise in West Lothian was the result of the establishment of Livingston, while the building of estates for commuters to Edinburgh at places like North Berwick, Haddington and Longniddry increased the East Lothian population.

The first development of the period was the establishment of the Bathgate

Church in 1951, which grew until there were 108 members by 1957. Since then the town has had problems caused by the decline in coal and shale mining and the rise and fall of motor vehicle assembly. In addition the town has been affected by the development of the New Town, Livingston, close by. This has been reflected in the membership of the church, which has fallen to forty-three in 1986.[58]

One of the results of the Welfare State was an attempt to improve housing. This meant that many people had to be moved out of the tenement slums of the major cities, especially Glasgow. New Towns to accommodate them were built, including Livingston, fifteen miles west of Edinburgh, which was started in 1962. In the first parts of the town to be built, it was decided by some churches to work together in ecumenical experiment. The Baptists, as well as some others, decided to act independently.[59] This led to Livingston Baptist Church being formed in 1968 in the Ladywell district on the north side. With the growth of the town towards a target of 80,000 to 100,000 by the mid-eighties, there was soon a need for the church at Ladywell to start meetings in the southern part of the town at Dedridge. After worship had been held in school premises, a building was erected with the support of the Baptist Union in Dedridge. A separate church has now been formed. Membership has grown at both Ladywell and Dedridge, with 166 and 147 members respectively in 1986.[60]

In the post-war period in Edinburgh the establishment of new churches was slow. In the immediate post-war years, Sunday Schools were run in Longstone in the west (with over 300 children), Muirhouse (over 100) and Drylaw (over 100) near Granton in the north and Moredun (over 80) in the south-east.[61] Much of the support for Longstone came from Charlotte Chapel. This work eventually led, in 1973, to the establishment of Wester Hailes Church on the edge of the Wester Hailes council estate, and close to the private estate of Baberton. With the growth of the membership to 198 in 1986, the buildings have been extended.[62] Charlotte Chapel has also taken the lead in establishing a Baptist Church in Barnton in 1987.

As the churches in the Lothians became linked with those in Edinburgh, the local association name was changed in 1952 to the Edinburgh and Lothians Baptist Association (ELBA).[63] This body hoped that the Sunday School at Moredun would lead to the formation of a church. The staff for the Sunday School were drawn from the city Baptist Churches, and mostly travelled from other areas. After about ten years it became clear that no church would be established, and with staffing problems for the Sunday School, the Baptists withdrew from Moredun, passing the work on to the Brethren.[64]

The large council estate in Craigmillar continued to interest Baptists. This area is one of the most deprived in Western Europe. In the summer of 1985 male adult unemployment was over 40%. The United Free Church of Scotland started a mission in the area in 1940. After encouraging early years, by 1970 the work had declined to the stage where its future viability was questioned. As the mission was being served by Baptist lay preachers and retired ministers, notably John McKendrick, it was suggested to the Baptist Union that an Evangelical witness should be maintained. The Union took over responsibility from January 1974. There were problems right from the beginning in providing a suitable ministry from lay preachers who could communicate effectively with the local people. As the area had a name for teenage gang violence, it was difficult to find a minister willing to live in the area with his family. Harry Sprange, who had experience of work with young people in the Clapham area of London, became superintendent of the Craigmillar Baptist Centre with freedom to develop the work as he felt best. There was a sustained effort to grapple with the difficulties of the situation, especially the lack of mature Christians to live and work in the area and the lack of really active support from the local churches. After twelve years the Craigmillar enterprise ceased.[65] It is possible that another council estate area, Burdiehouse to the south of Edinburgh, will soon see the start of a mission under the oversight of Morningside.[66]

While these developments on council estates were taking place, the Gorgie Church was finding it difficult to maintain its witness. The area for a while had suffered from decline but many tenement blocks had been rehabilitated. While attempts were made to encourage others to attend, resources were limited, with an ageing membership and with a number living outwith the immediate area. One of the Gorgie families living on the pre-war Colinton Mains estate had started a house meeting which influenced some neighbours. Out of this grew the Colinton Mains Fellowship which was founded in 1983, and which purchased the halls of St Hilda's Episcopal Church. Meantime the Gorgie building was sold to the Episcopal Church and the members linked with Stenhouse to form the Stenhouse-Gorgie Church.[67]

In 1973 Morningside Church was badly burned by fire. After considering a move to a redundant Presbyterian Church, the members decided to rebuild and improve the facilities. After the reconstruction, giving an attractive tiered church, the membership has grown to 315 in 1986. This growth has been linked with an active Christian education programme, outreach in various forms and care for the handicapped.[68]

Dalkeith, a town about seven miles south-east of Edinburgh, and its neighbourhood have grown in the last thirty years. The rise in car ownership has enabled people to live outside Edinburgh where housing is a little cheaper, and to travel into the city to work. From 1945 to 1960 the membership of the Dalkeith Baptist Church was in the forties. In 1961 the membership was fifty-four and in 1986 it was 144.[69] During these twenty-five years the guidance of a succession of able ministers helped to take advantage of the situation.

During this period, depite the establishing of new churches and various evangelistic campaigns, the total membership of the ELBA churches decreased from 3,340 in 1945 to 2,697 in 1975. There has, however, been an increase to 3,137 in 1986.[70] These figures hide that fact that some of the older city churches have decreased in membership. The Dublin Street Church, for example, declined, and, though continuing, in 1987 sold its building, which had become unsafe. The growth has come in newer churches like Livingston and Wester Hailes, although some of the older churches like Dalkeith and Morningside have also grown. Charlotte Chapel, with its powerful pulpit ministry in central Edinburgh, has consistently contributed between a quarter and a third of the total membership of ELBA.

In addition to the churches which are members of the Edinburgh and Lothians Baptist Association, there are a number of churches in the region which use the name Baptist. Most of these churches adopt a more Calvinistic and fundamentalist position. A number are influenced very strongly by similar groups from the USA. There are such churches in the Bellevue district of Edinburgh, Currie, a south-western suburb, and in the town of Penicuik. In addition there have been attempts to form similar Baptist Churches in places such as Dunbar and Haddington. These latter groups have been small in size, often meeting in the pastor's home, and lasting a few years. While most of them have little to do with Baptist Union churches, the Currie Church has linked with other Edinburgh churches in the 'There is Hope' evangelistic mission since 1985.

Inter-Relationships

As each Baptist Church is an independent body which may — or may not — voluntarily link with other churches, there have sometimes been tensions in relationships. Charlotte Chapel resigned from the Baptist Union in 1955 in protest against its ecumenical affiliations, but retained nominal membership of ELBA.[71] The Wester Hailes Church, established from the outreach work of Charlotte Chapel, has not become a member of the Baptist Union. Relations with Roman Catholics and ecumenical bodies continue to pose difficulties. Although some local Councils of Churches, like the Morningside Council, include representatives of both a Baptist Church and the Roman Catholic Church, problems are raised when joint services of worship are arranged. Musselburgh Baptist Church is questioning whether representatives of the

Baptist Union should have taken part in the 1987 talks called 'Not Strangers but Pilgrims'.[72]

Bonds across denominational boundaries with other Christians, including Roman Catholics, however, have been formed through the influence of charismatic renewal. Co-operation in large-scale celebration and teaching meetings has been a hallmark of the movement. Yet renewal has also created tensions within Baptist Churches, especially over the conduct of worship, and between churches of the denomination. Leith Baptist Church (Madeira Street) has been particularly influenced by this movement. After its membership had declined to thirty-six in 1983, there was a sharp rise to 102 in 1986.[73] Some of this increase has come from attracting people, especially younger people, to the church. A number of the younger ones have been drawn from other congregations, while others have come from non-church backgrounds.[74]

Co-operation with other denominations has been common in the capital. From the beginnings of Charlotte Chapel its minister, Christopher Anderson, was involved in working with others. He joined in founding the Gaelic School Society and the Itinerant Society for preaching the gospel in the Highlands. Anderson was a founder member of the Edinburgh Bible Society and was one of its first three joint secretaries. The Edinburgh Bible Society was later merged with the Glasgow Bible Society to become the National Bible Society of Scotland.[75] Local Baptists have continued to serve on various committees of the Bible Society. One such at present is Sandy Robertson, one-time treasurer of Morningside, who is on the Finance Committee. Dr Donald Meek, an elder of Charlotte Chapel, has been completing the revision of the text of the Gaelic Bible for the Bible Society.

Many Baptists have been involved in mission in the city. Some of this involvement has been through mission halls established by the Baptist Churches; the rest has been through non-denominational missions. The Scotch Baptist Church had for a number of years two missions, one in the Pleasance, the other in Potterrow and then in Lothian Street, both not far from Bristo Place. With the changes in the area caused partly by the clearance of sub-standard housing and partly by redevelopment for the expansion of the University of Edinburgh, the Lothian Street Mission closed in 1954.[76] Dublin Street has maintained a mission at Canonmills, used in recent years as the Boys' Brigade Hall, in an area of poorer housing on the north side of the New Town. In 1913 Charlotte Chapel took over the High Street Mission until people were moved out of the area. In addition Charlotte Chapel ran a mission in Jamaica Street, on the north-western edge of the New Town, for about forty years until after the Second World War, and also one in the Cowgate which was linked to the work of the Livingstone dispensary of the

Edinburgh Medical Missionary Society.[77] These missions were primarily for the spread of the gospel amongst the poorer people of the city, most of whom were not likely to enter a church building. Much of the work was amongst children in Sunday School and mid-week meetings such as Band of Hope, Boys' and Girls' Brigades and Christian Endeavour. Another aspect of the work was the provision of meals, clothing and money for beds in lodging houses.

Non-denominational missions were providing a similar service in the poorer areas of the city. Carrubbers Close Mission (now Carrubbers Christian Centre), founded in 1858, in a close off the High Street, served the densely populated area of the Old Town. W.T. Oldrieve, president of the mission from 1917 to 1923, was a member of Morningside and president of the Baptist Union in 1915-16. Others who served on its committees included Gerald Griffiths, minister of Charlotte Chapel, and J.S. Rattray, an elder in Morningside.[78] The Edinburgh City Mission also had Baptists among its directors. They included Dr W. Graham Scroggie (minister of Charlotte Chapel), Robert Aitken (Charlotte Chapel) and C.W. Howden (secretary of Morningside) as directors in its centenary year in 1932.[79]

Baptists have also taken an active part in interdenominational organizations in the city. The Faith Mission, which trains men and women for evangelistic work, has its college in Edinburgh. Joseph Kemp lectured to the students when he was at Charlotte Chapel.[80] The present principal, Colin Peckham, is a Baptist.[81] The Edinburgh Medical Missionary Society, founded in 1841, is the oldest medical missionary society in Western Europe. The society has trained over twenty doctors for the Baptist Missionary Society, including William Carey, grandson of William Carey of Serampore College.[82] Several Baptists have served as directors and officers of the society.

Social Service and Outreach

In addition to preaching the gospel, Baptists have been involved in social work. Charlotte Chapel opened a home known as The White House in Fettes Row in the New Town for young women prostitutes in 1908. A midnight meeting had been held for the women in the chapel on Fridays when supper was served and the gospel proclaimed. Some of them were cared for by Joseph Kemp and his wife in their manse. The need for a home for those who could be induced to give up prostitution was met by the gift of The White House by J.C. Ross of Portobello Baptist Church.[83] In 1955 Beulah Home in Newhaven Road was purchased as an Eventide Home by Charlotte Chapel.[84] The Edinburgh and Lothians Baptist Association has also been responsible for an Eventide Home, the Tor. Situated in Corstorphine Road, it opened in 1971 with the support of all the churches.[85] In 1983 South Leith Baptist Church under Alan Berry opened a house, called Bethany, opposite the church for the care of homeless young people.

In 1977 Peter Bowes, together with certain members of his church at Morningside, was concerned for the care of the mentally handicapped adults who did not need to enter mental hospitals. This led to the founding of the Ark Housing Association, with its first house in Dalhousie Terrace, about a mile from Morningside Church. Ark now has thirteen houses in the east of Scotland where the mentally handicapped are cared for and integrated into the community. This interest, along with its proximity to the Royal Edinburgh Hospital, has led Morningside to care for the mentally handicapped and mentally disturbed, including a Bible Class especially for them.

One of the characteristics of the Baptist Churches has been their attempt to take the gospel to those who do not normally have the chance of hearing it. Both Charlotte Chapel and Morningside held open-air services on Bruntsfield Links. Christopher Anderson spoke there when it was on the outskirts of the city and F.M. Hirst and Campbell Dovey, ministers of Morningside, preached there before and after the Second World War. Charlotte Chapel also made use of the corner of Charlotte Street and Princes Street until traffic conditions made it impossible to hold such meetings. Dr James Scott, assistant to Joseph Kemp from 1906 to 1912 and leader of the open-air meeting, tells of over 850 conversions by this means. In the ministry of J. Sidlaw Baxter, Charlotte Chapel made use of the Usher Hall, Edinburgh's main concert hall, beginning in the winter months of 1938-9, and attracted congregations of between two and three thousand for three months. These evangelistic meetings were resumed in 1946 and continued during the rest of Baxter's ministry. After the war, in the summer, until 1986 services were held on Sunday afternoons at the Ross Memorial Bandstand in Princes Street Gardens.[86] House-to-house visitation has been carried out by churches in connection with national Baptist missions such as Scotreach (1983-6) and alongside other denominations in 'There is Hope' in 1985, 1986 and 1987. This continues the tradition of house-to-house distribution of tracts begun by Charlotte Chapel in 1886 and still maintained today.[87]

Contributions to City and Denominational Life

While it would be difficult to identify every Baptist, apart from ministers, who has contributed to the life of the city and region, there are some who were well known. Although he was not a member of a local church, the Right Hon. Ernest Brown was MP for Leith, as a Liberal (1927-31) and then as a Liberal National (1931-45). Amongst his ministerial posts was a short spell as Secretary of State for Scotland in 1940-1.[88] Tom Curr of Dublin Street was well known as a City Councillor and Justice of the Peace in the 1930s and 1940s. He made a major contribution to the Boys' Brigade in Edinburgh. His artistic skills were featured in cartoons in the evening newspapers and also in illustrated talks at Sunday School anniversaries and other meetings.[89]

Baptists have played a part in the professional life of the city. Dr Maxwell Williamson, an elder in Charlotte Chapel, was Medical Officer of Health for Edinburgh before the First World War, and Dr Harold J. Fraser of Bristo was Medical Officer of Health for Midlothian after the Second War. Dr Fraser was president of the Baptist Union in 1951-2 and was lay pastor of Broxburn for a few years. Amongst the staff of the Edinburgh Medical School, which has enjoyed an international reputation for many years, there are Professor Jim Farquhar of Morningside, a son of Adam Farquhar, president of the Baptist Union in 1939-40, and Dr William Cutting, again of Morningside. Dr Cutting is on the medical committee of the Baptist Missionary Society.[90] As the centre of the Scots legal system, Edinburgh has likewise seen several members of the legal profession as members of the Baptist Churches. Andrew Urquhart was secretary of Charlotte Chapel when Joseph Kemp became minister. He has been followed as secretary by two other lawyers, W. McDuff Urquhart and Ian Balfour. Lord Gibson, president of the Land Court from 1941 to 1965, was a deacon of Dublin Street and Labour MP for Greenock from 1936 to 1941.[91]

Baptists have also provided a number of leaders in education, trade, industry and commerce. Prof. Norman Hunt, former vice-principal of the University of Edinburgh, is an honorary elder of Charlotte Chapel. Andrew Clark, a prominent fruit merchant, was senior elder of the same church for many years until the late 1960s.[92] Robert Aitken of Charlotte Chapel was a partner in a well-known clothes shop in George Street (Aitken and Niven).[93] In the 1860s and 1870s, Hugh Rose, a paint manufacturer whose firm still exists, was a generous benefactor to denominational funds. He was a member of Dublin Street Church.[94] Since Edinburgh is the centre of national government for Scotland, the civil service is an important employer. W.T. Oldrieve of Morningside was principal architect for Scotland under the Office of Works.[95] Alexander McKinlay, who was secretary of Morningside in the 1940s, was Assistant Registrar General (Births, Marriages and Deaths) for Scotland.[96] Rose, Oldrieve and McKinlay were presidents of the Baptist Union in 1875-6, 1915-16 and 1945-6 respectively.

Although in 1986 the number of Baptists in Edinburgh and Lothian was about a sixth of the total for Scotland (3,137 out of 16,632), it appears that churches in the area have given a higher proportion of presidents of the Baptist Union than would be expected on the basis of the bare statistics. Out of 118 presidents, thirty held office when associated with a church in the area.

This could be a reflection of the calibre of the ministers and laymen in the capital city. It is noticeable from the lists that there were periods when presidents from Edinburgh were relatively frequent. There were, for instance, nine in the period 1869-89 and eleven in 1937-68. One of the only two in the period 1968-87 was Ian Balfour (1976-7), secretary of Charlotte Chapel, a church not in membership of the Union. Ian Balfour continues to serve the Baptist Union as Law Agent.

Of the eight secretaries of the Baptist Union, six, though not necessarily brought up in the area, had connections with it. William Tulloch (1869-80), W.B. Nicolson (1919-20) and Thomas Stewart (1920-30) were ministers of Edinburgh Churches. Dr James Scott (1930-49) had been assistant at Charlotte Chapel to Joseph Kemp from 1906 to 1912. Dr Andrew MacRae (1966-80) and Peter Barber (1980 - present) were brought up in Charlotte Chapel. This number might indicate the kind of men called to, and brought up within, the churches of the capital city.

Church Organizations

In addition to providing Sunday worship, the churches have had many organizations associated with them. Movements like Boys' Brigade, Girls' Brigade, Boy Scouts and Girl Guides have been represented in some of the churches. As Baptist Churches are Evangelical in outlook, it is perhaps surprising that in Edinburgh there are not more Boys' and Girls' Brigade companies, whose basis is more closely linked to the church than that of the Scouts or Guides. Is it a reflection of the social perceptions of the churches that the Brigades were often linked with missions, as in those run by Dublin Street and Bristo, while Scouts and Guides were formed in the church itself?

Christian education for the young was mainly through Sunday School and Bible Class, Christian Endeavour and Band of Hope, while for adults it was through the sermon, weekly Bible Study and regular reading of the scriptures at home. With declining attendances in many afternoon Sunday Schools after the Second World War, a number of churches moved the Sunday School to overlap with the morning service. Families were able to join together in worship. Others like Abbeyhill, Granton and Morningside used the idea from the USA of All-Age Christian Education. The whole age range attended classes for about an hour. This was followed by a period of worship. Morningside has developed since the mid-1970s a twice-a-year six-week Christian Education series held after a shortened evening service, resulting in some increase in attendance. A century earlier, in 1877, the Scotch Baptist Church had re-started a Mutual Improvement Association. This association was unusual, especially for a Scotch Baptist Church, in that no religious subject could be discussed. R.M. Pringle said that it was 'sometimes looked on askance' for this reason. At first it was open to men but women were admitted after the First World War. The Association ceased when the Second World War started.[97]

On the whole the work amongst men has not been as strong as that amongst women. There are men's meetings in the area such as the Edinburgh branch of the Scottish Baptist Men's Movement, and meetings in Portobello and Charlotte Chapel. Other churches like Bristo, Dublin Street and Morningside have had meetings in the past. A lot depends on the enthusiasm of one or two men for the running of these bodies. Women's meetings have taken a number of forms, including devotional gatherings and work parties for missionary support. These organizations have often given an opportunity for women to take a leadership role in an aspect of church life. In a number of churches women now have the opportunity to serve as deacons (e.g. Dublin Street 1955, Bristo 1956, Morningside 1974), although some churches still debar women from the diaconate.

Conclusion

The major purpose of the Baptist Churches has been to proclaim the gospel with the aim of extending the kingdom of God. Their preaching and teaching ministries, and also their social work, have been structured to achieve this. At times the effectiveness of the work of the churches appears to have been weak, especially when there has been dissension. At other times the results of revival have led to increases in membership, like that at Charlotte Chapel in Kemp's ministry between 1902 and 1915. Another characteristic is the way in which the churches have adapted to changing conditions, especially where the membership is alive to the opportunities of the fresh circumstances. This has led to growth in new settings like Livingston, but the inner-city areas, especially the poorer parts, have continued to be very difficult places for Baptist Churches to survive. Despite the general decline in Christian witness and church attendance of the twentieth century, the Baptist Churches have not suffered as much as some other denominations. Their members look forward to the future in the words of the motto of the City of Edinburgh, *Nisi Dominus Frustra*, taken from Psalm 127 verse 1: 'Unless the Lord builds the house, its builders labour in vain.'

Notes

1. David Keir, ed, *The Third Statistical Account of Scotland: The City of Edinburgh* (Glasgow 1966), p 98.
2. I.G. McIntosh and C.B. Marshall, *The Face of Scotland* (Oxford 1970), p 80.
3. Gordon Donaldson, 'The Emergence of Schism in Seventeenth-Century Scotland', *Scottish Church History* (Edinburgh 1985), p 209.
4. George Yuille, ed, *History of the Baptists in Scotland* (Glasgow 1926), pp 24-35. See also cap 1, pp 10-13.

5. Keir, ed, *Third Statistical Account*, p 98.
6. J.B. Barclay, *Edinburgh* (London 1965), p 58.
7. *Bristo Baptist Church Bicentenary, 1965* (Edinburgh 1965), p 9. See also cap 1, pp 16-17.
8. *Bristo Baptist Church*, p 10.
9. Yuille, ed, *Baptists in Scotland*, p 50.
10. Barclay, *Edinburgh*, p 59.
11. *Bristo Baptist Church*, p 11.
12. Hugh Anderson, *The Life and Letters of Christopher Anderson* (Edinburgh 1854), pp 28, 68-9, 12-14, 65. Yuille, ed, *Baptists in Scotland*, p 63. For the Cordiners' Hall Church, see also cap 2, pp 33-4.
13. D.B. Murray, 'Baptists in Scotland before 1869', *Baptist Quarterly*, 23 (1970), p 259.
14. William Whyte, *Revival in Rose Street* (Edinburgh n.d.), pp 7-17.
15. Keir, ed, *Third Statistical Account*, p 99.
16. Yuille, ed, *Baptists in Scotland*, p 123.
17. Whyte, *Rose Street*, p 18.
18. Yuille, ed, *Baptists in Scotland*, pp 278, 286. *The First Yearly Report of the Baptist Union of Scotland* (Cupar 1844), p 19. Yuille (p 289) is mistaken in supposing that Stobhill closed in 1842 because it is listed in the *First Yearly Report*.
19. *First Yearly Report*, p 19.
20. *Bristo Baptist Church*, p 19.
21. Yuille, ed, *Baptists in Scotland*, pp 278, 280.
22. J.S. Marshall, *The Life and Times of Leith* (Edinburgh 1986), pp 16-49.
23. Yuille, ed, *Baptists in Scotland*, pp 130-1.
24. Elder Street Communicants' Roll Book, 1841-6.
25. *Morningside Baptist Church Directory*, 1986.
26. *First Yearly Report*, p 19.
27. Yuille, ed, *Baptists in Scotland*, p 125.
28. Whyte, *Rose Street*, p 26.
29. *Scottish Baptist Year Book (SBYB)*, 1871, p 29; 1876, p 35; 1881, p 44; 1886, p 54.
30. *Bristo Baptist Church*, p 19.
31. *Charlotte Chapel Centenary Souvenir, 1808-1908* (Edinburgh 1908), p 14.
32. Keir, ed, *Third Statistical Account*, p 99.
33. Barclay, *Edinburgh*, p 82.
34. Yuille, ed, *Baptists in Scotland*, p 127.
35. ibid, p 133.
36. *Portobello Baptist Church Jubilee Souvenir Brochure, 1897-1947* (Edinburgh 1947), p 9.
37. Morningside Baptist Church Minute Book, 1894-1905, p 2.
38. ibid, p 5.
39. Yuille, ed, *Baptists in Scotland*, p 120.
40. ibid, p 128.
41. ibid, p 280.
42. Whyte, *Rose Street*, p 30.
43. Winnie Kemp, *Joseph W. Kemp: the record of a Spirit-filled life* (London n.d.), caps 4-9.
44. Barclay, *Edinburgh*, pp 93-4.
45. Personal knowledge.
46. *SBYB*, 1922, pp 53-4; 1940, p 112.
47. *SBYB*, 1940, p 112.
48. *SBYB*, 1929, p 87.
49. *SBYB*, 1927, p 85.
50. *SBYB*, 1983, p 50.
51. *SBYB*, 1932, pp 93-4; 1934, p 97.
52. *SBYB*, 1934, p 96.
53. *SBYB*, 1941, p 113.
54. *Bristo Baptist Church*, p 25.
55. Information from older members of Bristo Baptist Church.
56. For Bo'ness, see cap 11, pp 204, 211.
57. *SBYB*, 1941, p 113.
58. *SBYB*, 1958, p 84; 1987, p 125.
59. *Livingston: the first ten years, 1962-72* (Livingston 1972).
60. *SBYB*, 1987, p 141.
61. *SBYB*, 1953, pp 84-5; 1956, pp 84-5; 1958, pp 86-7.

62. *SBYB*, 1987, p 133.
63. Edinburgh and Lothians Baptist Association Minute Book, 26 Apr. 1960.
64. Information from the Rev. A.F. Duncan.
65. Report by the Rev. Harry Sprange to the Baptist Union, 1986.
66. Personal knowledge.
67. ibid.
68. ibid.
69. *SBYB*, 1962 p 86; 1987, p 127.
70. *SBYB*, 1946, p 51; 1975, p 112; 1987, p 35.
71. See cap 4, pp 75-6.
72. *Scottish Baptist Magazine*, Mar. 1987, p 2.
73. *SBYB*, 1984, p 129; 1987, p 131.
74. Personal knowledge.
75. Whyte, *Rose Street*, pp 15-16.
76. *Bristo Baptist Church*, p 31.
77. Whyte, *Rose Street*, p 41.
78. *Carrubbers Close Mission: centenary review, 1858-1958* (Edinburgh 1958), pp 10, 23.
79. *Edinburgh City Mission: a hundred years of work, 1832-1932* (Edinburgh 1932), p 32.
80. Whyte, *Rose Street*, p 37.
81. *SBYB*, 1987, p 154.
82. Edinburgh Medical Missionary Society List of Former Students.
83. Whyte, *Rose Street*, p 41.
84. ibid, p 68.
85. Information from the matron of the Tor.
86. Whyte, *Rose Street*, pp 42, 61, 64.
87. ibid, p 41.
88. D.W. Bebbington, 'Baptist Members of Parliament in the Twentieth Century', *Baptist Quarterly*, 31 (1986), pp 260-1, 264-5.
89. Personal knowledge.
90. ibid.
91. *Dublin Street Baptist Church Manual*, 1937, p 5. Michael Stenton and Stephen Lees, ed, *Who's Who of British Members of Parliament*, 4 vols (Hassocks and Brighton 1976-81), 3 p 127.
92. Information from Ian Balfour.
93. Personal knowledge.
94. D.B. Murray, *The First Hundred Years: the Baptist Union of Scotland* (Glasgow 1969), p 41.
95. Yuille, ed, *Baptists in Scotland*, p 132.
96. Information from Mr Kenneth McKinlay, grandson of Alexander.
97. *Bristo Baptist Church*, p 21.

J.R. Barclay

6. THE BORDERS

The Borders form a distinctive area of Scotland consisting of the land between the Pentland, Moorfoot and Lammermuir Hills to the north and the Cheviots to the south. On the west the boundary is the watershed of the source of the Tweed, Ettrick Water and Megget Water, while to the east the coast is met at Eyemouth and St Abb's Head. Berwick-upon-Tweed and the southern bank of the Tweed down river from near Coldstream are in England. For centuries the rich farmland of the lower Tweed was served by the market towns of Berwick and Kelso, whereas Jedburgh became a royal residence and centre of justice. Galashiels, Hawick, Peebles and Selkirk were small market townships, but with the advent of the making of tweed and woollen goods these towns vastly expanded.

The first woollen factory in Scotland came to Galashiels in 1788. The Manufacturers' Corporation of that town was founded with ten members in 1777, and by 1788 had reached twenty-three members.[1] Hawick followed this trend, and by 1817 about 500 of Scotland's estimated 1,450 frames were located in Hawick and the surrounding neighbourhood.[2] The development of manufacturing was possible both because of a natural increase in population and because people began to move into these towns. The population of Hawick rose from 2,928 in 1791 to 5,998 by 1838.

The Church has been in the Borders from early times and the great Border abbeys bear witness to its presence. The monopoly of the Established Church broke down during the eighteenth century. Both Burgher and Anti-Burgher Seceder churches sprang up in the region. The possibility of Dissent, together with the growing population, prepared the way for the beginnings of the Baptist Churches. Their origin resulted from questions being asked about baptism and church government and the impact of the Haldanes. Galashiels possessed a Glasite Church in Darnock from 1772 and in the town itself from 1775. The first evidence of the adoption of full Baptist principles comes from 1782. Archibald Cochrane, Henry Watson and William Johnstone of Galashiels were baptized and joined the Scotch Baptist Church in Edinburgh.[3] They began to gather with others of similar mind, forming a church in 1804. Some of them remained members at Edinburgh for nineteen years. Their place of worship was a cloth hall until a building was erected in Overhaugh Street which also served as a school. A chapel was erected in Stirling Street in 1842.

In 1798 James Haldane, John Aikman and Rowland Hill preached in Hawick to a large open-air gathering and as a result there were those who withdrew from the parish church. William Thorburn, William Laidlaw, Peter

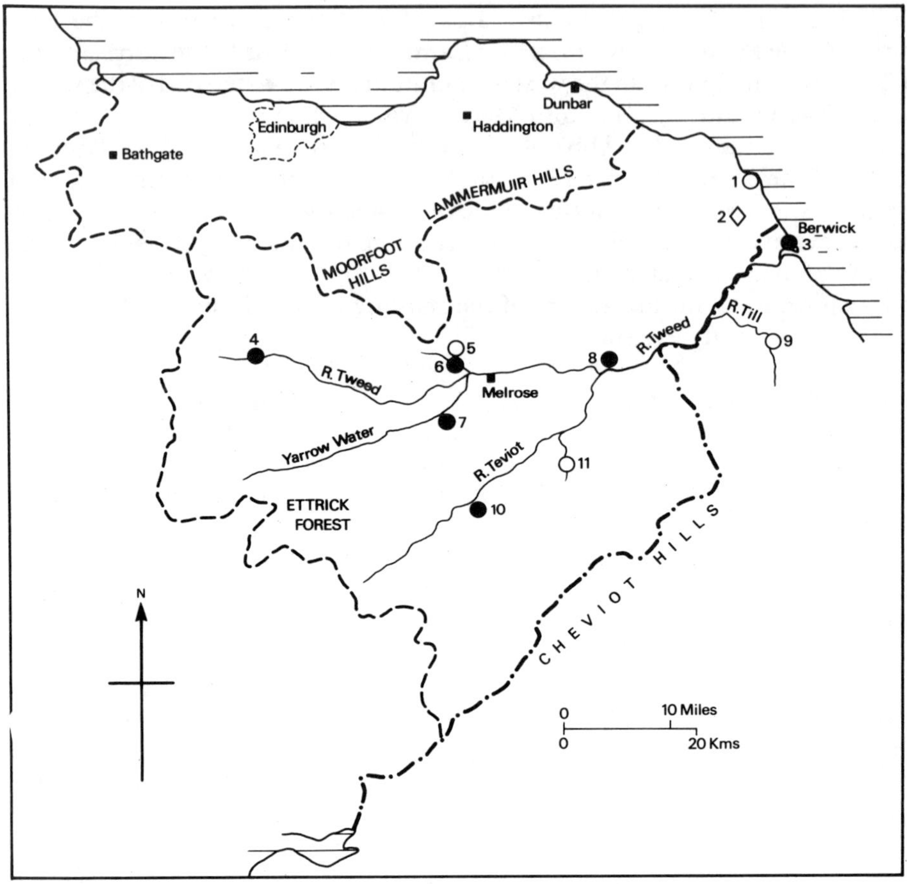

MAP 6 : BORDERS BAPTIST CHURCHES.

Key to Map 6

1. Eyemouth
2. Ayton
3. Berwick
4. Peebles
5. Galashiels : Stirling Street
6. Galashiels: Victoria Street
7. Selkirk
8. Kelso
9. Ford Forge
10. Hawick
11. Jedburgh

Taylor, Robert Leithead and David Dick rented a barn in Backbrae Lane for the purposes of worship. They were served by itinerant preachers until they built the Tabernacle in Kirk Wynd. A church was constituted in 1805, and Charles Gray, a student from Haldane's Academy, was called to the pastorate. When Gray was converted to Baptist views along with the Haldanes themselves, the church (it is said) was as good as swamped in the immersion of its minister.[4] In 1813 Charles Gray left Hawick and the Tabernacle was abandoned and sold. The Baptist group then met in a room in Allars Crescent, becoming a constituted church in 1846 with twenty-three members.[5] There is no doubt that members of these small churches would be noted in Galashiels and Hawick for their consistent lives and that they would be greatly respected as the century progressed.

It is of interest that James Blair of Dunfermline and Francis Johnstone of Cupar conducted an evangelistic tour of the Borders, making a report in 1844. They tell us that Galashiels had forty members and Hawick twelve. At Selkirk they baptized one and had two applications for baptism at Melrose. They preached at Jedburgh in the Odd Fellows' Hall and baptized three. At Kelso they used a building belonging to the Congregationalists for their meeting.[6]

Three other congregations, at Ford Forge, Eyemouth and Aytoun, came within the orbit of the Border churches. Ford Forge, just over the border in Berwickshire, was a coal mining and iron smelting community. The records of Berwick-upon-Tweed Baptist Church tell us that in 1809 Alexander Kirkwood, who had previously held charges in Kilsyth, Ford Forge and Beverley, became their pastor. In a letter to a friend, Kirkwood stated, 'I had preached for 2 years at Ford Forge without stipend, except board and washing and therefore when I married I was without money, without a church, without a bed, without a stool, without a candlestick — having nothing in hand and nothing in hope but one promise — the Lord will provide.'[7] Clearly Ford Forge was a very struggling cause and by 1874 there were only twelve members and forty in the Sunday School.

In the case of Eyemouth, Robert Haldane sent George McLean to do evangelistic work there. He settled in Eyemouth in September 1807 and married a local lady, a Miss Janet Purves, whose father was a small farmer. The congregation met in a house in George Street. The cause was not prosperous, for by 1835 there were only five members. McLean combined the work of schoolmaster with that of being pastor. It is noteworthy that both McLean's sons entered the Baptist ministry. With the death of the pastor, the few members walked to Berwick each Sunday.[8] As for Aytoun, it is known only that it was founded in 1842.[9]

Growth

The coming of the railway was a further stimulus to population increase and trade, and therefore added to the possibilities of growth for the Baptist Churches. From mid-century onwards the railway was to be of considerable importance, replacing horses for the bringing of coal, which was much more reliable than water power for mill development. Galashiels was linked by rail to the Lothian coalfields in 1849, halving the cost of coal. In the same year the railway connected Selkirk and Hawick. The building of a link railway from Hawick to Carlisle in 1862 opened the English markets more easily to Border products. Branch lines linked Jedburgh, Kelso, Peebles and Eyemouth.[10] The railway as an employer would have a number of Baptists on its staff. The Railway Missions at Peebles and Selkirk later provided members for the churches. The railway was the great economic factor which would establish the fortunes of the mill towns and therefore, indirectly, those of the churches.

But it has to be said that prayer and revival did more for the churches than any other factors. At Kelso in the 1859 revival a certain Mrs Binnie, then unmarried, and a Miss Scott Macdougal were converted. Mrs Binnie moved to Edinburgh and for thirty years prayed for revival in Charlotte Chapel. She returned to Kelso in 1875, her husband having died, with her prayer unanswered. She began to pray for a Baptist witness in Kelso so that there would be an evangelistic base in the town. She was to wait another two years for that church in Kelso. Her prayers for Charlotte Chapel had to wait until 1904, when her son-in-law, Joseph Kemp, was pastor there. She was to live to see her three sons-in-law all minister at various times in Kelso.[11] The prayer life of this lady could be echoed again and again in every one of the Border churches. There was certainly much prayer that the revival of 1859 would not leave out this area. It would be true to say that the spiritual fervour of that awakening was to last in some Border churches until 1908. At Galashiels the years from 1869 to 1875 were memorable. An evangelist called Steel visited Galashiels to conduct meetings in 1869. Other evangelists, I.M. Craggie, W.D. Dunn and Richard Hill, carried on a work of revival. In one year fifty-two members were added to the church. A comment at the time was that 'when Pastor Thomson was first connected with Galashiels the congregation took little interest in the winning of souls. The great object was to build up each other. But when Mr Steel came and when their hearts were inflamed with a passion for souls, a change came.'[12]

With Galashiels being so near to Selkirk, spiritual events such as were taking place there inevitably affected the other town. James Brown, a Selkirk blacksmith, and others were influenced and were baptized at Galashiels. He formed a church in 1880 with nineteen members, a figure which was to rise to fifty-four during its second year. A building was bought from the United

Presbyterian Church in 1890.[13]

Hawick in 1873 was visited by the evangelists I.M. Craggie and W.D. Dunn and much blessing came to the church. It was in faith that the church asked for the support of the Home Mission in 1879 and applied to C.H. Spurgeon to send a pastor for full-time work. William Seaman began his ministry in 1880, and by 1883 the church had moved to a new chapel in Bridge Street with sixty-two members.[14]

It was the same spirit which caused Magnus Sandeson of Highlaws to seek to revive the cause in Eyemouth. In 1858 he bought Sorella House and transformed it into a chapel with baptistry and manse at his own expense. John Grant was called and did excellent work as the congregation grew to between seventy and eighty. He resigned in 1866-7.[15]

Patronage was also to help church growth, and particularly was this the case in Kelso. Unlike churches in the other towns of the central Borders whose finances largely came from mill workers, the cause in Kelso was to have a generous patron in Miss Scott Macdougal of the Makerstoun estate. There had been an unsuccessful attempt prior to 1877 to found a Baptist witness in Kelso, and so there was an old disused meeting house. This meeting-house was renovated by Miss Macdougal. She also sent to Wick to see if James Work would try to restart the Baptist cause. She fully supported him, promising £100 per year for ten years for stipend. She found the old meeting-house inadequate and put up a building with stone quarried from her estate on a new site in the same street. This building she gave to the Baptist Union. Near her home she converted a house into a chapel for her estate workers. In her home she had a 'prophet's chamber' which was rarely unoccupied. She was behind many of the cottage meetings held in the neighbourhood and she gave support to the Baptist work in Jedburgh. Believers from the estate were baptized in the Tweed.[16] It is significant that membership rose from thirteen members in 1880 to 106 by 1890. Within two years of Miss Macdougal's death in that year, it had dropped to fifty-seven.

Division is another factor in Border church development, as it produced the Victoria Street Church in Galashiels in 1875. It may be argued that had the congregation at Galashiels stayed together it would have avoided many later problems, but it is also true that friction can sometimes lead to church growth. In 1875 Galashiels was knowing times of revival. The church had up to this point had a plurality of pastors along Scotch Baptist lines.[17] There were many in the church who felt that this no longer met the need and they decided to call a full-time man to the pastorate. The issue was one of principle and as the majority in Stirling Street agreed to this innovation, the dissenting party had no choice but to accept or leave. Those who believed with Alex Thomson, Henry Fleming and George Pennycook that there should still be a plurality of pastors withdrew to form a meeting in Bridge Place Hall and later decided to erect a new building in Victoria Street. This was achieved in 1883 with the aid of a loan from the Union. Alex Thomson, who had served as an elder in Stirling Street for a considerable period, was appointed, along with Andrew Morton, to the joint pastorate. Victoria Street was to rise to a membership of 113 by 1906. Apart from a fall in membership between 1910 and 1920, when it dipped to sixty-one, from 1933 until 1957 Victoria Street retained around a hundred members and was active in evangelizing its area of Galashiels.

At Peebles A.M. Crooks, an insurance agent holding Baptist principles, met with a few of like mind in the Masonic Hall in 1889. Crooks took charge of supplying the pulpit and was for a time honorary pastor. With the membership at twenty, he accepted an estimate for a building to cost £387. The average wage was 25/– (£1.25) per week. The faith of the church was rewarded as there was growth until the membership stood at seventy-five in 1930.[18] The town was also growing at this period, reaching 6,402 in 1931.

It was at this period that Jedburgh also acquired its church. In 1886, twenty-two members formed a church and called George Pennycook from Galashiels as pastor. They were to erect a 'tin tabernacle' as their place of worship.

Many able pastors have occupied Border pulpits. It is impossible to name them all. There was, for example, J.W. Kemp, who held pastorates at Kelso and Hawick (1897-1902), and who was noted as a Bible teacher with a special interest in the doctrine of the Second Coming of Christ. He was a man who placed great emphasis upon prayer and who always wanted to exploit opportunities for God. In 1901, for example, he took a new local theatre for an after-church service before it was used for any other purpose and held a service there which was attended by many who never came to church. He held the audience spellbound. Since it was a new venture he was much criticized by some.[19] He went on from Hawick to Charlotte Chapel, Edinburgh.

William Seaman at Hawick (1880-96) had the blessing of baptizing 170 and, of the 147 members when he left, only nine had been on the roll when he came. He went on to serve as an agent of the Home Mission, but the chapel in Hawick is a monument to his work. Other eminent names include J. Bell Johnstone (1887-96 at Galashiels, Stirling Street), D. McNicol (1903-7 at Hawick), H. Lockyer (1926-30 at Hawick) and G.M. Hardie (1926-30 at Peebles).

Organizations were used in all the Border churches to promote growth.

Sunday School and Bible Class were most common. Christian Endeavour became popular at the beginning of the century, and at Hawick, for example, in 1906 there were a hundred in this organization. Peebles formed a Cycle Club in 1923 to take the gospel to other villages. Total abstinence was strong in all the churches, with members often belonging to Temperance Societies. In 1915 Stirling Street expressed appreciation at the King's pledge of total abstinence and assured the government of its most strenuous support in temperance measures.[20] The churches also added a Women's Auxiliary or Women's Own as well as a Boys' Brigade and Girls' Brigade to their organizations as they found them to be helpful.

Open-air services and missions were also a regular feature, along with extensive tract work. A report on a mission at Jedburgh in 1895 is typical. 'Many fought through snow drifts for 3-4 miles. Several found the Lord. The members were blessed by the visit of G. Whittet and J. Burns. The church wishes to thank the Evangelistic Committee of the Union for sending them.'[21] House groups were also used. Ford Forge had four cottage meetings in 1877, Galashiels two in 1870 and Selkirk two in 1892.

The Borders Baptist Association was founded by J. Bell Johnstone with the aims of fostering fellowship and promoting Baptist work in the area. This took place during his first ministry in Galashiels (1887-96). The association was to intervene in Hawick in 1897 when fifteen withdrew from the church there after criticizing the preaching of James Hodgson. There was eventual reconciliation after the pastor left. The association also tried to maintain the work in Jedburgh when that church appealed for funds in 1915.

Decline

Overall growth continued until the end of the nineteenth century. Stirling Street in 1895 had 297 members. Hawick in 1907 was to reach 277 members, but before the new century dawned Eyemouth had ceased and Ford Forge had already disappeared from Baptist Union records in 1886.[22] The town of Eyemouth was devastated by a storm in 1881 in which half the male population was drowned in the fishing fleet. Yet the decline of the cause there was complete by 1879. It is known that the building later came into the hands of G. Gollan of the United Presbyterian Church, who used it as a Sunday School meeting place.[23]

The reason for the decline of Ford Forge may have been economic, as the coal pits in the area declined until they closed in 1918. This was a struggling cause in a very small community where Methodists and Anglicans were also active. It is known that Louisa, Marchioness of Waterford, who owned Ford village from 1859 to 1891, was a Christian who improved houses, schools and churches. Lady Waterford had much talent in religious art which she used in God's service, painting each person in the village in her many biblical pictures.[24] Maybe religious art was not appreciated by those more noted for plainness of worship. There are those who speak to this day of baptisms in the River Tell, and certainly the old building, now a store, was next to the mill pond.

It is often alleged that emigration out of the Borders caused decline, and it is unquestionably true that young people not desiring to work in the mills had to go elsewhere for employment. With the biggest church, Stirling Street, as an example, it is of interest to know that from 1842 until 1918 116 people came from other Baptist Churches outwith Galashiels to join and 124 left the area. Of those who left, 55 moved elsewhere in Scotland, 18 to other Border towns, 28 went to the United States and 23 to the Empire. From 1917 to 1970 the Stirling Street records show that 75 transferred into the church from outside Galashiels and 13 emigrated. Clearly decline cannot be blamed upon emigration. In fact migration sometimes worked in favour of the Borders.[25]

Yet trade has always had an effect upon the congregation. In 1874 at Hawick the church was asked to receive a Mr Hewison from the Baptist Home Mission and to raise £50 towards his stipend. The members said that 'they were unable because of the state of trade to provide this amount'.[26] Galashiels in 1891 had a population of 17,367. A depression in trade took the population down in that year to 13,613 and left whole streets deserted.[27] The cause was the McKinley Tariff in the United States that restricted the import of textile goods. The ministry of Robert Clark (1896-1900) in Stirling Street saw the congregation rise to 297 and decline to 260 with a downward trend continuing until 1905. The church in receiving the pastor's resignation letter recorded, 'We regret exceedingly that the state of trade has had a depressing effect on the congregation but for this cause we believe your work would have been more encouraging.'[28]

The 1890-1905 trade depression hit all the Border churches, but Galashiels suffered the most. Victoria Street, with 102 members in 1905, was down to 70 by 1911. Selkirk, with 75 members in 1902, had 58 by 1905. Hawick, with 151 members in 1896, had only 110 members in 1897, though it revived to grow to 278 members in 1906. Jedburgh had 35 members in 1892, yet by 1907 had only 15. The trade depression fostered dejection and stopped the progress which had been evident for so long throughout the previous century.[29]

Before the First World War Sunday Schools and Bible Classes had begun to decline. In 1902 Hawick had 143 in the Sunday School; by 1910 there were 129 and by 1918, 45. The Bible Class would reach 100 in 1915 and then drop to 50 by 1918. Stirling Street had 115 in the Sunday School in 1902 and 60 in the

Bible Class, but by 1918 the figures had fallen to 40 and 50 respectively. One of the chief recruitment areas for the churches was diminishing.

The war of 1914-18 inflicted great harm on the churches through numbers of men killed, the disruption of church life and alterations in prevailing attitudes. Hawick, for example, lost eleven men killed and had sixty-six members and adherents serving with the forces. The church hall was used as a recreation room. The church did a lot to help the soldiers. Stirling Street, Galashiels, lost nine men in action. Selkirk lost both secretary and treasurer. The disruption to life meant that by 1918 Stirling Street had 198 members, Hawick 205, Selkirk 23 and Jedburgh 24. It is clear that the war would have an effect directly and indirectly upon Sunday School and Bible Class.

It is said that nineteenth-century revivals were strongly associated with laymen and this was looked on with suspicion by full-time ministers. By 1900 independent lay evangelism had largely ceased. Recruitment became a ministerial function.[30] While Baptist Churches continued to use laymen, it is clear that many of the cottage meetings so characteristic of the churches had ceased. The closure of the Jedburgh Church in 1918 also illustrates the failure of lay initiative. Its last pastor, A.H. Gammage, left in 1917. Between 1913 and 1918 Jedburgh lost twenty-eight members and was down to twenty-four. The church was apparently in very bad shape, with no youth work and services suspended. In 1920 the Hawick Church discussed whether the building in Jedburgh should be re-opened. Its members were quite insistent that the work would not be carried on from Hawick.[31] It is arguable that the Border churches could have maintained Jedburgh, and we can only conclude that either there were insufficient laymen willing to take up the challenge or that the work had simply become much weaker than the last figures of membership suggest. It is clear that the period of growth had given way to a phase in which maintaining numbers was the highest aim.

Theological controversy has not been a prominent factor making for decline. Where controversy has occurred it has usually been over practical matters, as in the split which gave birth to Victoria Street, Galashiels. Hawick had a minor theological controversy over the issue of the open or closed communion table in 1900. Two members believed that the Lord's Supper should be restricted to baptized believers only and strongly made their case. The church however did not agree and the two members resigned. In February 1914 W.A. Ashby, minister at Hawick, was in controversy with a so-called Protestant champion who had come to the town to stir up anti-Roman Catholic feeling. James MacDonald was so inconsistent in life that Ashby felt it necessary to expose him. The church upheld the stand taken, but four members sided with MacDonald and lapsed from membership.

It was most unfortunate that when the First World War had hardly started, in October 1914, Stirling Street, Galashiels, was taken to court. The dispute was over a narrow strip of ground seven or eight inches in breadth down one side of the church. The church intended to lay drains there but the neighbours disputed the ground, which was built over and in which both parties had acquired rights by agreement or acquiescence. The case of William Leithhead against Stirling Street was to reach the Court of Session. Eventually settlement was made in favour of the church with costs.[32]

Did lack of pastoral provision hinder the work? It is not unusual to see a dip in membership shortly after a pastor left, with an upturn on the arrival of his successor. In the earlier part of the nineteenth century it was customary for the pastor to earn his living outwith the church. This was the case in Eyemouth, where Pastor McLean was schoolmaster from 1807 to 1836. It was the same for Hawick when Pastor Hawkins was schoolmaster (1862-71). These churches, it has to be said, did not grow at that time. Yet in Selkirk Pastor Brown, who worked as a blacksmith, saw much growth during his pastorate from 1880 to 1912. His ministry covered the revival years. The great growth in Galashiels accrued to Stirling Street which had chosen to appoint a single pastor. What is clear is that having a full-time pastor gave a certain status to a church in some Border towns. In the course of time all the Border churches decided in favour of having a full-time pastor if at all possible. It is arguable that when a church relied upon students for its supply that church did not see much growth, yet, to be fair, during the last sixty years whether a church has had full-time or part-time ministry the membership graph has continued to dip. The exception to this would be Peebles, which grew strikingly under G.M. Hardie in the 1920s. The experiment of a joint pastorate between Kelso and Selkirk (1974-8) was not what either church ideally wished, and proved to be rather impractical because of distance. The importance of having a pastor, or having several as Victoria Street did for a time, is seen in the allocation of thought, prayer and money to selecting each of them. While the ability of the pastor may have attracted a certain clientele for a time, personality has played less part in church growth than the corporate morale of the congregation.

Decline fostered a certain desire for union. Selkirk discussed a proposed merger with the Congregationalists in 1918 but did not consummate it. In 1921 R.A. Barclay, a Baptist student preparing for the ministry, wrote in his diary of Selkirk, 'Don't see how we will ever have the church packed, place is far too strongly Presbyterian'. Stirling Street invited Victoria Street, which had abandoned Scotch Baptist practices in 1912, to join them in 1919. Victoria Street declined the approach. R.A. Barclay, writing of Peebles in 1920, did not flatter. 'The palace of destitution, like a hen coop. Can cover it in 2 steps . . . Can even count the folk by the drop of the pennies in the plate as they pass it. Treasurer Miss . . . thought I should have finished differently in the morning. I was too abrupt and made them think too much — what are we for?'[33] Peebles at that time had a membership of thirty-five, but during the decade would double in membership and obviously must have greatly improved.

The maintenance of the witness was the prevailing priority up to the onset of the Second World War. Again war brought both disruption and opportunity. Hawick had thirty-two in the forces and eight ladies on National Service. Once again the church hall became a canteen, and ministry was given by the church to the soldiers who came from Stobs Camp. Stirling Street also used its hall as a canteen in 1939. The hall was requisitioned in 1942 for storage purposes. The minutes of churches record visits by soldiers. Kelso, for example, records the baptism of a number of sappers by Pastor A.W. Inglis. All churches played their part in the national crisis. By 1945 Stirling Street had 120 members, Victoria Street 100, Kelso 52, Peebles 42, Selkirk 42 and Hawick 195.

The Post-War Era

It was with optimism that the churches entered the 1950s. In 1955 Scotland was visited by Dr Billy Graham, the American evangelist, and members of the Border churches were to attend the meetings in the Kelvin Hall, Glasgow. Hawick hired a special train for this purpose and there were conversions to encourage the churches. At the end of the decade, however, the pastor at Hawick noted that 35% were over 60 and only 2% under 20 out of a membership of 150.

By this point churchgoing was ceasing to be fashionable. 'Popularity of pleasure motoring on Sunday had been one of the main changes in attitude to Sabbath observance. Cricket matches were held on Sunday afternoons in 1963.'[34] These changes meant that Sunday Schools could no longer be held in the afternoon and there was a further adverse effect on evening attendances.

Population shift away from the centre of Border towns was a further challenge. The process was well advanced before the Second World War, but after the war it accelerated, removing members to the outskirts and making transport a problem. Thousands would move to Tweedbank, Langlee and Darnock in Galashiels, to Burnfoot and Stirches in Hawick and to similar developments in other towns. The two churches of Galashiels recognised the resulting need and in 1960 sought to have a joint evangelistic programme. The minutes of the joint deacons' courts record film services at the central churches, and work with children at Colmslie in 1964. A hall was taken for Sunday School work at Langlee and a site in the Darnock housing estate was considered for a while. Hawick in the 1980s has been experimenting with evangelistic work in the school in Stirches. Peebles has also been using a school for Sunday School work on a local estate rather than the church base.

New church buildings are generally regarded as a great blessing when erected, but they can also become a great problem when they are unsuitable for a congregation. Selkirk had a building which could seat 450 people. In 1974 the church was finding it impossible to maintain and to heat with a membership of twenty. The church therefore sold the building to the town with various restrictions on its use for £811.[35] The church retained part of the building for worship, paying a nominal rent. The town sold the church to an undertaker and joiner. In 1986 the building became dangerous and the church worshipped temporarily in a school. Kelso has also inherited a vast building and faces questions as to how to adapt to present needs with a membership of sixteen in 1986. Peebles, with fifty-one members in 1986, has the problem of a building which is too small for the congregation and which is in need of major repair. Hawick has an adequate building but a very inadequate hall, with no ground on which to build. In December 1985, however, the Hawick Home Mission closed, and the trustees agreed to transfer the property to the Baptist Church. This Mission was the fruit of work by the evangelists Scroggie and Dunn in 1872. The building was erected in 1883 due to public generosity and the help of Lord Polwarth. This gives Hawick an opportunity to develop new halls.[36]

The Galashiels Churches after much heart-searching came together in 1971 as one church. It was agreed they should have a joint pastorate, but the thorny problem of buildings was not settled. It is clear that both churches had declined, Stirling Street having sixty-six members and Victoria Street fifty-five, but Stirling Street had particularly gone down. The years of indecision about joining together, followed by a similar indecision about which building to use, did not help the work or give the church a sense of direction in the community. It was only when Stirling Street had been sold that it became possible to consider erecting a new hall at Victoria Street. The wood and iron hall was demolished and more ground purchased which allowed the church to erect a beautiful new hall in 1983. This further inspired the church to undertake a wholesale renovation of the church building. Galashiels now possesses the best appointed buildings in the Borders.

In 1984 the National Bible Society conducted a census of Scotland. The Border adult population was given as 77,920. There had been a 2% adult population increase over four years and a 6% decrease in the number of children. The combined membership of the five Baptist Churches was given as 310, with a drop of 6% since 1980. There had also been a drop in child attenders by 13% since 1980, giving 140 children. The adult attenders were down by 3% since 1980. The average congregation, taken on the basis of two services each Sunday, was forty-two. All the churches continued to hold midweek meetings at which attendance averaged fourteen. It was of interest that most of the churches used the New International Version of the Bible.[37]

In the early 1970s another group of Baptists entered the Borders. They called themselves Free Baptists, Tabernacle Baptists or Bible Baptists. Those who undertook this work came from America and they tried to establish new causes in Hawick, Jedburgh and Eyemouth. Their basis of doctrine was Conservative Evangelical given in the form of a statement which included such points as the imminent premillennial coming of Christ. They state, 'Independent churches stand as a protest to religious unbelief that has engulfed so many large denominations . . . Independent Baptist churches refuse to co-operate with denominations and councils of churches that condone the presence of such unbelieving leaders.'[38] They would therefore find any affiliation with other denominations difficult, but this does appear to pass unjust comment on existing Baptist work in the area. In Hawick a small house church was developed in Wilton Glebe which afterwards moved to an old post office in Weensland Road and a Sunday School work was begun. In Jedburgh the work has not grown at all. At Eyemouth there was a gathering of about sixty at one point. The pastors who carry on this work are supported from the United States.

In the late 1970s and early 1980s the charismatic movement which had made an impact all over Scotland also made an impression on the Borders. Some Baptists were helped and renewed through it. There were a few, however, who left to join independent charismatic fellowships in Hawick, Galashiels and Selkirk.

It is hard to measure the achievement of the work of the Baptist Churches. From our churches several missionaries have gone out. The names of Adam Dorwood with the China Inland Mission and J.W. Moodie, the soldier-evangelist (from Victoria Street), Miss Joseph with the Zenana Mission to Shantung (from Selkirk) and Dr Jack Gray with BMS in Zaire as well as Lyn and John Collis (from Kelso) are well known. Selkirk at one point supplied many who took part in the Scottish Colportage Society and also sent two men into the ministry. It was from Hawick that T. Kerr Spiers and James Hope Scott, the latter from the Home Mission, went into the ministry. Dr Somerville, a medical doctor from Galashiels, was president of the Baptist Union of Scotland in 1899-1900.

Faithfulness and generosity, often amid great difficulties, have kept alive small causes which might otherwise have been closed. Minute books constantly record collections for all kinds of disasters, be it the devastation caused by the German fleet on the east coast in 1915 or the more recent famines in Africa. Peebles receives Union aid and Kelso did so until 1985 and both have full-time pastors. Selkirk has maintained a student pastor — a quite remarkable achievement for a membership of seventeen.

Growth in our region can certainly be traced to industrial development, but without the spiritual factors of the nineteenth-century revival with an emphasis on prayer and giving, growth would not have blossomed. The negative social factors of the twentieth century have taken their toll, but the door of opportunity is still open. The most recent history of the Hawick Church, published on the centenary of the building, comments that the congregation is of almost the same size as when the church entered its new premises in 1883.[39] What applies to Hawick is true of all the churches. The Baptists are back in the numerical situation that obtained prior to the great revivals of the later nineteenth century. The churches are all concerned about evangelism and the Baptist Union's programme of Scotreach has been taken up in most situations with enthusiasm in the mid-1980s.

Notes

1. J.B.P. Bulloch, *The Third Statistical Account of Scotland: Selkirk and Peebles* (Glasgow 1964), p 308.
2. D. Brewster, *The Edinburgh Encyclopedia*, 10 p 662, cited by Clifford Gulvin, *The Scottish Hosiery and Knitwear Industry, 1680-1980* (Edinburgh 1984), p 16.
3. Stirling Street Baptist Church, Galashiels, Minute Book, 1.
4. Harry Escott, *A History of Scottish Congregationalism* (Glasgow 1960), p 334. 1789, the date for the origin given by George Yuille, ed, *History of the Baptists in Scotland* (Glasgow 1926), p 137, is wrong.
5. *Hawick Baptist Church, its origins and history* (Hawick 1923), p 1 (Public Library, Hawick).
6. *First Yearly Report of the Baptist Union of Scotland* (Cupar 1844).
7. *A Short History of Berwick-on-Tweed Baptist Church* (Berwick-on-Tweed 1971), p 1.
8. Daniel McIver, *Old Fishing Town* (Greenock 1906), pp 308-9.
9. Yuille, ed, *Baptists in Scotland*, p 276.
10. William Peacock, *Border Country Railways* (Hawick 1982).
11. F.G. Little, *Story of a Scottish Baptist Border Church* (Kelso n.d.), pp 6-7.
12. Stirling Street Minute Book, 1872.
13. Selkirk Baptist Church Minute Book, 1.
14. Helen Nisbet, *Hawick Baptist Church: the centenary of the church building* (Hawick 1983).
15. McIver, *Old Fishing Town*, pp 308-9.
16. Little, *Border Church*.
17. Yuille, ed, *Baptists in Scotland*, p 136.
18. Peebles Minute Book.
19. Winnie Kemp, *Joseph Kemp: the record of a Spirit-filled life* (London n.d.), pp 12-17.
20. Stirling Street Minute Book, 1915.
21. *Scottish Baptist Year Book (SBYB)*, 1895, p 69.
22. *SBYB*, 1886.
23. McIver, *Old Fishing Town*, pp 308-9.
24. *The Lady Waterford Hall, Ford, Northumberland* (Berwick-upon-Tweed 1980).
25. Stirling Street Roll Book.
26. Hawick Minute Book, 1874.

27. Bulloch, *Selkirk and Peebles,* p 267.
28. Stirling Street Minute Book, 1900.
29. Gulvin, *Hosiery and Knitwear Industry,* p 81.
30. Robert Currie, *et al., Churches and Churchgoers: patterns of church growth in the British Isles since 1700* (Oxford 1978), p 74.
31. Hawick Minute Book, 1920.
32. Stirling Street Archives.
33. R.A. Barclay, Diary, 1920-22, held by John R. Barclay.
34. Bullock, *Selkirk and Peebles,* p 334.
35. Selkirk Minute Book, 1974.
36. R.E. Scott, *Kirk and Town of Hawick* (Hawick 1982), p 17. W. Landles, 'Hawick Home Mission', *Hawick News,* 29 Nov. 1985, p 20.
37. Peter Brierley and Fergus Macdonald, *Prospects for Scotland: report of the 1984 census of the churches* (Bromley, Kent 1985), pp 62-3.
38. Jack P. Manley, *What is an Independent Baptist Church?'* (n.p. n.d.).
39. Nisbet, *Hawick Baptist Church.*

K.W. McNeish

7. AYRSHIRE, DUMFRIES AND GALLOWAY

The south-western area encompasses sixteen Baptist Churches or fellowships, with five in Dumfries and Galloway and eleven in Ayrshire. The two parts of the region have little in common. Dumfries and Galloway is a sparsely populated region which had only one Baptist Church in Dumfries, 'The Queen of the South', until the 1970s. Four of the five have developed since 1979. Ayrshire, however, is a mixture of rural and industrial areas. Baptists appeared briefly in Ayr in the seventeenth century, but they did not put down roots. They were then absent until the 1840s. The denomination blossomed in the late nineteenth century. The contrast between the two areas is stark and demands explanation. Why was nineteenth-century Ayrshire such a fertile seedbed for Baptist growth, and Dumfries and Galloway so barren?

Historical Background

Baptists were late arrivals in the south-west. The region has Christian roots going back to Ninian, a Briton who evangelized the southern Picts, perhaps at the end of the fourth century. Until the Reformation, Whithorn, where Ninian erected a church, was an important centre for pilgrims. The Church was of continuing importance, as the ruined ecclesiastical monuments of New Abbey, Glenluce and Lincluden mutely witness.

After the Reformation, Presbyterianism put down deep roots in the south-west. Although there were English Baptist soldiers in Ayr during the Cromwellian era,[1] they seem to have had little influence in the town, and Independency of any kind was unwelcome. Presbyterianism may have been torn by dissent, but the area remained doggedly faithful to the Established Church in the face of an alien religion peddled by an occupying power.

The Restoration of Charles II posed a threat to Presbyterians. Those who had entered the ministry since 1649 were ordered to be episcopally ordained. Two hundred and sixty-two Presbyterian ministers refused and were expelled from their parishes.[2] Many of these were from the south-west and they included all the members of the presbyteries of Stranraer, Kirkcudbright and Wigtown. The Solemn League and Covenant was held to be binding. Undaunted, the Covenanters met in open-air conventicles. Government soldiers ruthlessly hunted them down. Their gravestones remain in the hills to this day. A stern form of Presbyterianism was tested and survived. It became deeply ingrained, and the folk memory lives on. In this environment, Baptist ideas made little impact.

By the mid-eighteenth century the Established Church was losing its grip on society as splinter groups seceded. As the nineteenth century approached, Ayrshire had forty-eight congregations of the Church of Scotland and twenty-five other Presbyterian Churches. The Disruption further eroded the position of the Established Church. Sixteen of the fifty-six Ayrshire ministers joined the Free Church. In 1851 the Church of Scotland had fifty-four congregations, other Presbyterians had seventy-six and there were thirty-eight other churches.[3] The hitherto weak Episcopalian witness in Ayr had been strengthened and had spread. Irish Roman Catholics had arrived, as had the Baptists. The Presbyterian monopoly was broken.

Between 1803 and 1809 Baptists were recorded in Auchencairn, Sanquhar, Dumfries, Kilwinning and Saltcoats. All these fellowships except Irvine, the continuation of Kilwinning, died out, so that there is little record to explain why they developed just after the turn of the century. It is known that the Haldane brothers actively visited the area between 1798 and 1803 on evangelistic tours. They advocated lay preaching which was novel and excited much controversy. However, it was not until 1808 that the brothers adopted Baptist views, so that they cannot have been directly responsible for founding Baptist causes. Nevertheless, they were stimulating interest in non-Presbyterian forms of Evangelical Christianity, and were behind the growth of Independent Churches at Ayr, Muirkirk, Sanquhar and Dumfries.[4] Indirectly, this was to help Baptist causes.

In Kirkcudbrightshire an isolated witness grew up at Auchencairn (1808), a small rural community. The main impetus here was the pastor, David Gibson (1778-1853), who established it in the unlikely setting of a parish which had only 1,692 inhabitants in 1841.[5] Very little seems to be known about it, and it appears to have ended with Gibson's death in 1853.[6]

Around the same time a church developed in neighbouring Dumfriesshire, in the small upper Nithsdale mining town of Sanquhar. It was a coal mining community with a population of 3,268 in 1831. In the 1790s the only Dissenters noted in the town were a few Anti-Burgher Seceders and some McMillanites.[7] The cause from which the Baptists sprang was begun in 1807 under Haldaneite influence. Following the adoption of Baptist views by the Haldanes, most of the Sanquhar Church took the same step in 1809.[8] William McLintock was pastor there for thirty years from 1830.[9] Their place of worship is noted in the New Statistical Account of 1841 as a chapel 'in which a few Anabaptists meet for divine worship'. The account also says, 'The number of families in the parish attending the Established Church is 551; attending the Secession chapels and the chapel of the Anabaptists, 164.'[10] It is interesting because the writer may have been precise when he refers to them as Anabaptists. It is likely that many would be 're-baptized', after being initiated into other denominations, since it was a first-generation Baptist

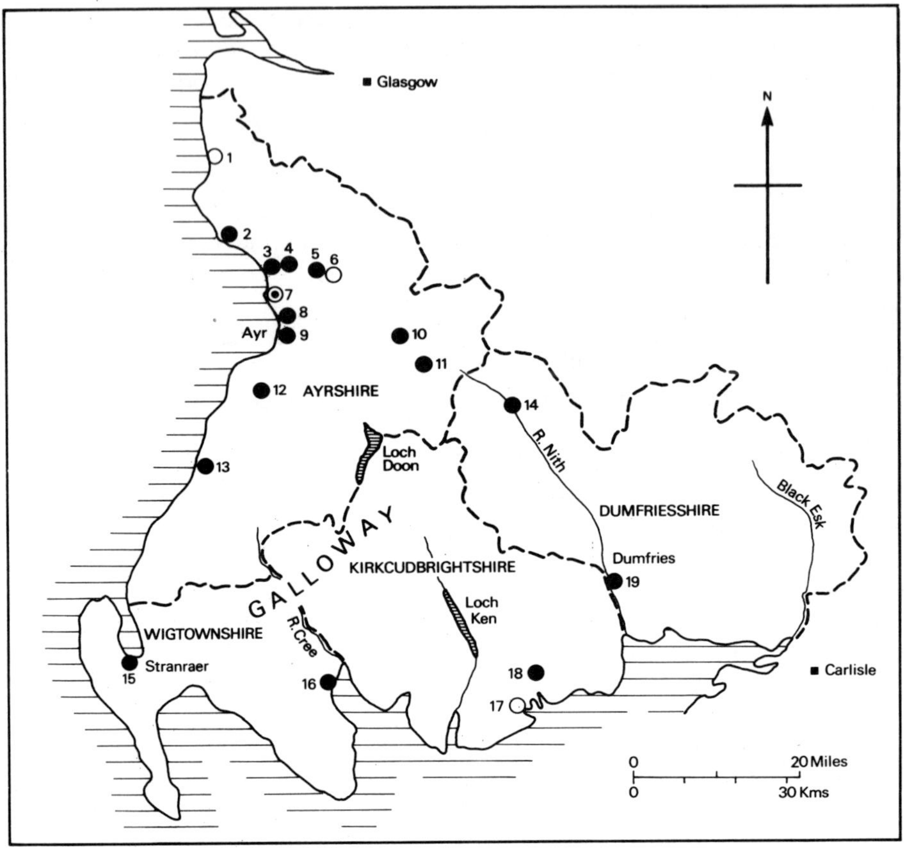

MAP 7 : AYRSHIRE, DUMFRIES AND GALLOWAY BAPTIST CHURCHES.

Key to Map 7

1. Largs
2. Saltcoats
3. Irvine
4. Bourtriehill
5. Kilmarnock
6. Newmilns
7. Troon
8. New Prestwick
9. Ayr
10. Old Cumnock
11. New Cumnock
12. Maybole
13. Girvan
14. Sanquhar
15. Stranraer
16. Wigtown
17. Auchencairn
18. Dalbeattie
19. Dumfries

---

cause.

This church persisted until quite late because it is mentioned in a book published in 1891:

> A small body of Anabaptists met for worship for many years in a chapel which they built, but they received no accession to their numbers and through death and removal they gradually diminished to a mere handful of worshippers. Last year owing to the death of the elder, who conducted the service, their weekly meetings were abandoned, and the chapel sold and converted to a dwelling house.[11]

Ineffective evangelism failed to reverse the attrition and seems to have doomed the church. The present Sanquhar Church has no links with this early group. Its roots, although dating back to the eighteenth century, are from a Presbyterian tradition.[12]

Around 1800 there was also a Baptist group in Dumfries, with a building and baptistry in Three Crowns Court which it was forced to relinquish in 1816. By 1832 they were led by Pastor Thomas Young. The cause seems to have lacked vigour. The New Statistical Account lists ten churches in the town, including the Methodists and Independents, but Baptists are not mentioned. There is, however, a record in 1860 which describes a small community with no pastor or building.[13] No link is known with the present congregation, which was founded twelve years later, but it is possible that the latter contained members from the earlier group.

The enduring monument of the early work in the south-west is not in Dumfries and Galloway, but in Ayrshire. George Barclay of Kilwinning trained as an Independent preacher, and then turned to Baptist views.[14] On 12 December 1803, with twelve others, he founded a church in his home town, and for eighteen years they worshipped, appropriately enough, in an upper room. In 1822 they moved to Irvine, where most of the members lived, and the present church in that town traces its origins to this time.[15] Barclay had a lifelong ministry to the area and, together with Christopher Anderson, evangelized in Galloway, Perthshire and even Ireland. He was minister for thirty-six years, during which 200 members accrued to the cause.

The work in Saltcoats, a town on the coast near Kilwinning, started in 1804. By the 1830s the cause was evidently weak. From 1831 James Blair ministered there as an agent of the Home Mission, but in 1836 he was moved to Ayr. This was because it was more central for future expansion in Ayrshire. The church in Saltcoats disappeared around 1840.[16] At Ayr Blair founded a church with ten members. He conducted meetings in the Black Bull Inn and baptisms in the River Ayr. He remained as pastor until 1841, but the cause was not firmly established. The church died out in about 1850, and it was not until 1886 that Baptist work was re-established there.[17] Likewise a church at Kilmarnock supported by Blair during his Ayr ministry petered out around 1845.[18]

Socio-Economic and Geographical Influences

It is hard to discern any pattern in early Ayrshire developments except that the most solid advances were in the larger communities. Even here Baptist roots were so shallow that reverses meant the collapse of the cause rather than the later pattern of set-back and recovery, or the common English pattern of deserting to another Baptist cause.

An example of the weakness is Newmilns, a small Ayrshire cotton-weaving town east of Kilmarnock. This had a congregation from about 1830 to 1840.[19] Little is known about the church, but we know the character of the place. In 1820 it had been described as seething with revolutionary madness, and in 1838 Norman MacLeod, who came to Loudoun as a young minister, commented:

> But Newmilns! What a place! Never, never was there such desecration of the Lord's Day, dozens and dozens of lads walking about and trespassing on fields and insulting the people and fearing neither God nor man. A large proportion of the population are born before marriage. The mass of the youth are sent to work before they can read, and in a few years are independent of their parents. In short, between drunkenness and swearing and Sabbath breaking, the village is in a dreadful state.[20]

The Baptist Church obviously made little impact and withered away. The residue was not even strong enough to revive when the Irvine–Kilmarnock railway line was extended to Newmilns in 1850 with its promise of better contact with other fellowships.

The reasons why Baptists became established in nineteenth-century Ayrshire but languished in Dumfries and Galloway seem to be rooted in their contrasting economic and geographical structures. Dumfries and Galloway is a long, sprawling region, 110 miles across from the Anglo-Scottish border to near the Irish coast. It is thinly populated, with very poor road and rail services. Rail travel between the two major towns of Dumfries and Stranraer today demands a long detour into Ayrshire. The A75 Stranraer-Gretna road, which carries Irish traffic into Europe, tortuously circumnavigates obstacles like Loch Ken and the deeply indented coast and has had to wait until the late 1980s to by-pass major towns en route. The area is underdeveloped. Even today the major towns are small, with Dumfries having a population of around 30,000, Stranraer around 10,000 and the old county town of Kirkcudbright 2,700. There is no strong regional centre.

In these circumstances it is not surprising that only Dumfries could sustain a viable Baptist Church in the nineteenth century. At that time Stranraer was less important as the Irish packets left from Portpatrick where there was a connection to London by daily stage-coach. Lack of support from Baptists elsewhere must have contributed to the fading away of the church in Sanquhar. Similarly David Gibson's work in Auchencairn must have struggled in the parish of Rerrick with a small population and two competing churches. Despite Gibson's personal energy, the Baptist cause succumbed to the dominant Presbyterianism. Isolated and remote, it was unpromising from the start.

Ayrshire Baptist causes enjoyed much more propitious circumstances. The county is mainly an area of coastal plain cupped between high hills. It is compact and fairly densely populated. In the nineteenth century the total population rose spectacularly. Irish immigration was substantial at the same time as the area was industrializing. Textiles, leatherwork and coal expanded. Mining towns sprang up among the rural estates. Ayr grew from a population of 2,000 in 1750 to about 28,000 in 1901. Kilmarnock and Irvine became large towns and Glasgow was not far away to serve as a regional focus.

Baptist work was more at home in this social flux. The old order based on the parish church crumbled and old loyalties weakened as newcomers came into the area. Even small towns like New Prestwick and Old Cumnock grew and were able to support Baptist congregations, together with a multiplicity of Presbyterian Churches. Internal communications improved with the establishment of turnpikes. In 1839-40 rail links between Irvine, Ayr and Glasgow were established. Three years later there was a link from Dalry to Kilmarnock. At this time passenger steam services linked Glasgow to the Ayrshire coast. All this made Baptist workers in Glasgow and Ayrshire more mobile and made mutual support easier than in Dumfries and Galloway.

Seven Ayrshire churches were founded in the period 1876-1900. Most were fostered by links with other churches. Better communications are not a complete explanation, but they are certainly part of the reason why the region developed before Dumfries and Galloway. The Kilmarnock cause was re-established in 1865. It grew and by 1886 its minister was visiting Ayr to baptize,[21] just as James Blair of Ayr had nurtured the earlier work in Kilmarnock. The move of two Kilmarnock members to the hamlet of Gasswater in the east of the county led to the creation of a new church. They held successful evangelistic meetings, taking the new believers back to be baptized at the mother church twenty miles away. These formed the nucleus of the church at Old Cumnock (1876). That church in turn started missions at New Cumnock and Taiglaw.[22] Kilmarnock also helped New Prestwick (1889) in its early days.

This pattern would not have been possible in Dumfries and Galloway. The towns were too small, and too far apart. It is inconceivable that regular pastoral support from Dumfries could have promoted work in a place like Newton Stewart, even had there been sufficient population. Certainly the long-distance pulpit supply of the Wigtown cause in the 1970s by Girvan, thirty-seven miles away, and Dumfries, about sixty miles away, would not have been possible. Even the support of Dalbeattie (founded 1978) by Dumfries, fourteen miles away, would have been difficult by road, even if there had been a demand.

Irish immigration into the south-west affected the social make-up of the area, but it is difficult to see any direct link with Baptist work in the nineteenth century. Most were Ulstermen, crossing from Antrim to Portpatrick and heading for Ayrshire. However, in the twentieth century, strong links between Ulster and the Wigtown Church have been established, with regular evangelistic support from groups such as the Lurgan Christian Police Mission in 1980 and the Lurgan Busmen's Mission. The Baptist Union observed that Ulster Christians emigrating into Wigtownshire in the 1980s might be sympathetic to Baptists and recommended that local churches be alert to their presence.[23]

Overseas aid has been a major source of support in Wigtown. The Foreign Mission Board of the Southern Baptist Convention in the USA sent Dr Robert Ford, previously minister of First Baptist Church, Woodland Mills, Tennessee, to give pastoral oversight from the foundation of the work. The Wigtown Church has satellite meetings at Newton Stewart and Port William. The Dumfries Church enjoyed the fellowship of a Southern Baptist Church choir from South Main Baptist Church, Houston, and an evangelistic team from Loganville and Walnut Grove near Atlanta, Georgia, in 1986. While the long-term effects of these ministries cannot yet be assessed, these options were totally unavailable to Galloway in the previous century.

Ayrshire, on the other hand, with better communications, could enjoy stronger links internally and with other Christian groups. When the Irvine Church had difficulties during a vacancy in 1884 it obtained pulpit supply from students of the Scottish Baptist College. This occurred again in 1892. In 1899 further problems developed and the Baptist Union gave advice on the situation. Baptist College students again provided pulpit supply. Eventually the church dissolved, but the Union was active in reviving the church in 1901 under the leadership of Hugh Henderson.[24] Similarly in 1894 the Home

Mission helped New Cumnock during a vacancy, and in 1904 the Union assisted Ayr in a difficulty by taking over the building and making an allowance for the retiring minister.[25] Good links with other fellowships assisted the establishment and survival of churches.

Church Life

History, geography and economics are only the constraints within which Baptists have worked. The advantages of situation enjoyed by Ayrshire and the town of Dumfries are incomplete explanations of church establishment and growth. The vitality of their religious life is crucial.

When the second wave of church planting affected Ayrshire in the 1860s, its origins seem to have been in a small group of Christians meeting for Bible study in Kilmarnock. In 1864 they were baptized by James Paterson of Adelaide Place Church, Glasgow. In 1865, seventeen believers founded a church, which took root under the strong leadership of E.J. Stobo (1866-72) and later William Donald (1884-1910). Financial assistance was provided by Thomas Coats of Paisley.[26] This pattern of a promising environment, a committed core of believers, good leadership and external assistance is repeated in many of the other successful causes.

Ayr, beginning to be a seaside resort for the people of Glasgow as well as a county town, was an obvious place for a Baptist presence. The present Ayr Church was founded in 1886 with twenty members. Eighteen of them had been baptized by William Donald of Kilmarnock and they formed a strong core. An energetic first minister was found in John Horne, who had just completed training at Spurgeon's College. C.H. Spurgeon himself provided financial assistance to the new cause. The result was dramatic growth. By the pastor's second anniversary the membership had increased to 145 and during his ministry, which lasted until 1892, 280 people joined the church. A less effective successor to Horne meant that the early prosperity fell away.[27] There was a second Baptist cause in Ayr, at Allison Street, just before the First World War, a sign of the town being fertile ground for the denomination,[28] but it was not until the mid-1920s that the church again reached the membership level it had attained under Horne. His role was clearly decisive.

Early church life often has a vitality that ebbs in later years. Fired with this vigour, in 1890 the Old Cumnock Church, then only fourteen years old, started a mission at nearby New Cumnock, based on twelve core members from the mother church. They held a successful outreach campaign in which forty were converted. Early in 1893 a new church was constituted at New Cumnock and later in the year it called its first minister, James Adair.[29]

Migrant Baptists seem to be a vital ingredient in setting up new churches, both today and in the nineteenth century when the ripple effects of Kilmarnock's foundation were not yet exhausted. The process is well illustrated by the foundation of the New Prestwick Church. Thomas Young, a solicitor in the Ayr Church, moved to New Prestwick, and, finding no suitable place of worship, set up a house group in his own home in 1887. Conversions followed and an open membership church was formed in a wooden hall with Young himself as pastor (1889-1907).[30]

The last of the Ayrshire churches founded in the final quarter of the nineteenth century was Maybole. In 1898 non-denominational evangelistic services were held in the Methodist Church. As a direct result a Baptist Church was founded in 1900 with fourteen members, led by Pastor Thomas Ramsay (1900-1919). It was admitted to the Baptist Union the following year.[31]

In 1919, Ramsay became Pastor Emeritus of Maybole, and was actively involved in collaborating with the Ayrshire Baptist Association to promote a new cause at nearby Girvan. Like Maybole, Girvan seems to have been a 'cold start' without a core of believers and so a mission was held and then, in 1920, a church started with seven members. Here the building was a problem and so meetings were held in various civic halls. Then the Union offered a corrugated iron building previously used by the Jedburgh Church. The Girvan Church had to pay transport and erection charges of £700. This solved the problem.[32]

After 1920 the causes of the Ayrshire Association area consolidated. Most major towns had Baptist Churches, the exceptions being Saltcoats, Troon and Largs. Eight churches were firmly established in the county. Four had been wound up, but Ayr and Kilmarnock had been re-established. The only churches to have failed irredeemably were Saltcoats and Newmilns.

In Dumfries and Galloway the Dumfries Church had failed, but it was re-established in 1872 by five men whose aim was 'our jealous observance of His will — viz., The New Testament — as our more particular rule of faith and practice'.[33] The isolation of this outpost from mainstream Scottish Baptist witness, or from nearby English Baptist witness, is shown by the fact that George Anderson, a Presbyterian, served as an evangelist, having previously worked with the former Dumfries South UF Church. By 1876 the members were able to call their own pastor, Lachlan McPherson. The church prospered, although information is scarce since the records were destroyed in a fire. Under Alex Bremner (1887-97, 1923-32) there was a packed building with men sitting on the window sills.[34] Dumfries and Galloway saw the establishment of no new churches until the late twentieth century.

Twentieth-Century Developments

The First World War involved many. Forty-five members and adherents of the Ayr Church served in the forces and seven died on active service. Its minister, W.C. Charteris, distinguished himself as a military chaplain and was absent for most of the war. Despite this trauma, when he left in 1921 the church had 111 members and all its debts cleared.[35] At New Prestwick James Scott's ministry, which encompassed the war years, saw membership doubled, and at Irvine many of the soldiers in the area were attracted to visit the church.[36] However profound the effects on national religious life in the long term, Baptists in the south-west responded vigorously to the challenge of the war and emerged in a determined frame of mind.

The distinction of being the first president of the Baptist Union from the south-west came to Thomas Ramsay, the retired minister of Maybole, in 1921-2. Only two others from the area have been president since: Alex Bremner of Dumfries (1924-5) and W. Wallace Muir of Kilmarnock (1941-2). Here, once again, is a sign of the relative isolation of the area.

The inter-war period was a difficult time economically and Ayrshire industry suffered. Little happened by way of church planting until the eve of the Second World War, when a church was founded at Troon in 1938. In 1942 it had twenty-two members and although it joined the Ayrshire and Dumfriesshire Association it remained outside the Baptist Union. Alex C. Wilson was the minister from 1945 to 1949, when membership rose to thirty-two. It ended in 1965 after a prolonged vacancy. The Union was involved in the disposal of the feu.[37]

Wartime pressures did not prevent the foundation of new causes. The Largs (Brisbane Road) Church was set up in 1940 with J. Campbell as minister. It was a non-Union church and had about twenty members in 1942. It later joined the Union but after a vacancy ceased in 1948. Its building was subsequently sold. The existence of a strong Brethren community in Largs may have inhibited its growth.[38]

In the year after the creation of Largs there was a fresh initiative in Ayrshire. It was a bleak period in British history with Dunkirk a recent memory, Yugoslavia and Greece invaded by the Nazis, HMS Hood sunk and clothes rationing just introduced. Nevertheless the Irvine fellowship led by Archibald Speed decided to start outreach work in Saltcoats in 1941. The previous cause had died out a hundred years earlier, but a newspaper advertisement stirred interest and a group met for two years in a Masonic Hall.

They were very determined. A Tuesday prayer meeting called 'The Twelve O'Clock Vigil' raised £1,000 for a building. This was in spite of Baptist Union discouragement, with suggestions that the meetings be suspended for the duration of the war unless the members particularly wished to continue. They did. On 3 June 1944, as invasion fleets were poised for D Day in Normandy and Rome prepared to capitulate to the allies, the Saltcoats Church bought premises in Union Street. By the end of the war it had thirty-seven members. In 1948 it joined the Baptist Union, and about a year later the local association. The church acquired a manse in 1952. In 1965 it moved to its present building and by 1966 it had ninety members.[39]

Meanwhile Dumfries and Galloway remained a desert for Baptist work. The sole oasis, the Dumfries Church, had nearly dried up in the 1950s and 1960s when membership fell to six and there was serious discussion about the possibility of closure. In the 1950s a report on the social composition of Dumfries by the Glasgow University Department of Extra-Mural Studies revealed a wide range of religious groups, but the presence of Baptists was not even noted.[40] Presumably the church was not sufficiently significant to appear in the survey.

All churches go through difficult ministries from time to time, but the problem with the Dumfries congregation was where to turn for help. The Union offices in Glasgow are seventy-five miles away and Ayr is only a little nearer. Pulpit supply is difficult. Mutual support for congregations and ministers is more difficult. In fact the geographical remoteness of the church made links with England a more practical alternative, although this seems never to have been adopted. From about 1962 the tide began to turn. The haemorrhage of members was staunched by energetic incomers in mobile occupations such as nursing and teaching. These people brought new vitality, and the church expanded, attracting among others many nurses from the local hospital. During the ministry of Sandy Greig (1973-85) the Dumfries Church prospered, becoming the evangelistic centre of its locality.

The reinvigoration of Dumfries marked the beginning of a new phase of Baptist advance in the region. The enterprising Girvan Church saw the opportunity of starting a work in Wigtown (population about 1,100) when some of its members went to live there in the 1970s. Despite the intervening thirty-seven miles, Girvan was able to nurture the group and to provide a preacher every month, often their minister, Ian Cameron. Some preachers helped Wigtown from Dumfries, about sixty miles to the east, and Noel Kirkman of Dumfries provided active encouragement. A crucial event was a visit by a team from the World Evangelization Crusade. This was followed by diligent visitation, and the core of the fellowship grew. The church in Wigtown was formally constituted in 1983.[41]

In an economically disadvantaged area such as Wigtownshire, the provision of a building can be a headache. This was dealt with at Wigtown by meeting in homes and later by hiring a room. Rural unemployment is also a problem, and there is a shortage of men in full-time employment on the membership roll. As a result building a church will be more of a problem than in nineteenth-century Ayrshire, where industrialization created a larger wage-earning population to draw upon. Nevertheless Wigtown looks outward, with two branch meetings and regular visits to Penninghame Prison.

While driving from Dumfries to Wigtown, Noel Kirkman noted the absence of Evangelical witness in Dalbeattie (population about 5,000). Six members of the Dumfries Church lived there, a valuable nucleus. Outreach work began in Dalbeattie in 1976. Visitation was done, and in 1981 a closed membership church was constituted with twenty-seven members and Kirkman as minister. Sunday morning congregations average forty or fifty people.[42]

Dumfries was also pivotal in establishing a Baptist Church in Sanquhar. A congregation there had withdrawn from the Church of Scotland over merger proposals in 1974. After several years as an independent church served by United Free ministers, numbers declined. The Dumfries Church, however, offered support, and in 1984 the cause in Sanquhar was reconstituted as St Ninian's Baptist Church on a closed membership basis with about twenty members.[43] In 1986 Malcolm Brand, a retired Baptist minister, became pastor.

Ayrshire's evangelistic zeal was not eclipsed by its neighbour. In 1968 land was bought for a church at Bourtreehill near Irvine. In 1974 pioneer work was started there by R.H. Swanson and by 1975 services were being held at Towerland School. Affairs progressed well and by 1978 a new building was opened. In the following year a church was constituted with thirty-five members. Morning services regularly had attendances of a hundred or more.[44] Swanson was minister from 1980 until his death in 1982. In 1985 the cause was still receiving Union assistance.

The Ayrshire and Dumfriesshire Association had long hoped to establish a church in Stranraer. It is strategically situated with road links from Glasgow and Ayr, and from Carlisle and Dumfries. It has ferry links with Northern Ireland and it is the second largest town in Dumfries and Galloway, with a population of 10,000. In 1973 the association tried to find a Baptist nucleus there and failed, but in 1980 a group of Evangelical Christians in the town asked the Girvan pastor, Ian Cameron, to help start a Baptist work. Afternoon services were begun. In 1983 Ian Cameron retired there to nurture the cause.

When morning services were launched, some support fell away due to conflicting loyalties with other churches, a phenomenon also noted at Wigtown. Nevertheless the church was founded in January 1985 with thirteen members.[45] Churches as small as this are vulnerable and it has since suffered loss by members leaving for employment reasons. Such mobile people have started a number of churches in the Ayrshire and Dumfriesshire Association and helped revive others, but the untimely departure of Baptists from smaller causes can be damaging.

Conclusion

The present state of the South-West Baptist Association area is encouraging, with sixteen churches established. Of these, five are in Dumfries and Galloway and the remainder are in Ayrshire. Old Cumnock and New Cumnock are outside the Baptist Union. They withdrew in 1969 over the Union's membership of the Scottish Churches' Council, which at that time might possibly have included Roman Catholics. This rift remains unhealed. Old Cumnock is also outside the association.

On the positive side, the Carlisle Baptist Church has just joined the South-West Association. Also there are still areas which could support a Baptist Church, given a committed nucleus of members and assistance from neighbouring churches. A new work has apparently started in Troon and is understood to be a non-Union project. Possibilities include Annan (6,000), Newton Stewart (2,000), Largs (9,000) and Kirkcudbright (2,700). Communications are less of a problem than in the past and a wider range of external resources for leadership and evangelistic help is available. Neither should Baptists be put off by the possibility of failure. Some of the area's strongest churches have been built up in towns where a previous work had collapsed, such as Dumfries, Kilmarnock, Ayr and Saltcoats. Union counsel helped Irvine survive at a time of crucial difficulty and the Scottish Baptist College provided pulpit supply. The Dumfries Church helped Wigtown, Dalbeattie and Sanquhar. Girvan assisted Wigtown and Stranraer. With this web of mutual support, causes in difficulty can be nursed back to strength. This applies throughout the area, but particularly in Dumfries and Galloway where some churches are likely to remain small, financially weak and vulnerable to ministerial vacancies, membership losses and splits which larger churches could shrug off. If Baptists in the south-west live up to their history, the future could see consolidation of present gains as well as future growth.

Notes

1. George Yuille, ed. *History of the Baptists in Scotland* (Glasgow 1926), p 29.
2. Rosalind Mitchison, *A History of Scotland* (London 1970), p 251.

3. John Strawthorn, *Ayrshire: the story of a county* (Ayr 1973), pp 134, 138.
4. Harry Escott, *A History of Scottish Congregationalism* (Glasgow 1960), pp 326, 330, 331.
5. *The New Statistical Account of Scotland: Kirkcudbright* (Edinburgh 1845), p 366.
6. Yuille, ed, *Baptists in Scotland*, p 276.
7. Sir John Sinclair, ed, *The Statistical Account of Scotland, 1791-1799: Dumfriesshire* (East Ardsley, Wakefield 1978), p 476.
8. Escott, *Scottish Congregationalism*, p 331.
9. Yuille, ed, *Baptists in Scotland*, p 288.
10. *The New Statistical Account of Scotland: Dumfries* (Edinburgh 1845), pp 311-12.
11. James Brown, *The History of Sanquhar*, 2nd edn (Dumfries 1891), p 393.
12. Kenneth Stewart, 'St Ninian's: latest Baptist cause in Scotland.' *Scottish Baptist Magazine (SBM)*, Jan. 1985, p 2.
13. J.A. Andrew, 'Workmen uncover Baptist history', *SBM*, Apr. 1986, p 3.
14. See cap 2, p 33.
15. Neil McLauchlan, *Irvine Baptist Church, 1803-1978: 175 years of Christian service* (Irvine 1978), p 5.
16. Yuille, ed, *Baptists in Scotland*, pp 205, 288.
17. ibid, pp 205-6.
18. ibid, p 209.
19. ibid, p 286.
20. Strawthorn, *Ayrshire*, p 138.
21. Yuille, ed, *Baptists in Scotland*, p 206.
22. ibid, pp 212-13.
23. Unpublished notes of the Rev Ian Cameron.
24. McLauchlan, *Irvine Baptist Church*, p 15.
25. Yuille, ed, *Baptists in Scotland*, pp 211, 206.
26. ibid, p 209.
27. H.S. Muir, '*Hitherto*': *Ayr Baptist Church, 1886-1946* (Ayr 1946), pp 7, 9. G.B. Hossack, *Ayr: our Baptist story* (Ayr 1986), p 7.
28. *Scottish Baptist Year Book*, 1912, pp 105-6.
29. Yuille, ed, *Baptists in Scotland*, pp 210-11.
30. ibid, pp 211-12.
31. ibid, p 210.
32. ibid, p 211.
33. *Dumfries Baptist Church Centenary Brochure* (Dumfries 1972).
34. ibid.
35. Hossack, *Ayr: our Baptist story*, p 9.
36. Yuille, ed, *Baptists in Scotland*, p 212. McLauchlan, *Irvine Baptist Church*.
37. Unpublished notes compiled by the Rev and Mrs A.T. Peck.
38. ibid.
39. Unpublished papers in the possession of the Saltcoats Church Secretary, Miss Jean Harper.
40. John Highet, *Dumfries Speaks Out* (Glasgow 1951), p 29.
41. Information from Mr and Mrs D. King.
42. Personal knowledge.
43. Stewart in *SBM*, Jan. 1985, p 2.
44. Unpublished notes in the possession of Mrs Swanson, widow of the late R.H. Swanson.
45. Information from the Rev Ian Cameron.

J.A. Andrew

8. RENFREWSHIRE

Renfrewshire is a small but important Division of Strathclyde Region. It runs west of Glasgow for thirty miles on the southern bank of the widening Clyde estuary and rises to bleak moorland 1,700 feet high only eight miles inland. Its largely urban population numbers about a third of a million souls. One in fifteen of the population of Scotland lives in Renfrewshire and about one in fourteen of the Baptists in Scotland lives there.

There are twelve Baptist Churches in Renfrewshire itself, but the one at Rothesay on the Isle of Bute is also in the Renfrewshire Baptist Association. Today there is no Baptist Church between Port Glasgow and Johnstone, but there used to be Baptists in Kilmacolm and Kilbarchan. Formed in 1809, the tiny Kilmacolm congregation, which never had a minister, had nine members in 1846 but ended in 1870. 'They were an exceedingly worthy set of people', said a parish minister.[1] Formed in 1810, the Kilbarchan Church had twenty-three members in 1846 and ceased about 1850. Re-formed, however, in 1904, it reached 113 members and 298 Sunday School scholars in 1911 before falling to seventy members in 1916 and turning Congregationalist soon afterwards.

A Baptist Church began at Millport on the small island of Great Cumbrae in 1818 and had a minister for most of the last century, but ended soon after 1940 when there were only six members. In the early years of the last century Baptists worshipped at Port Bannatyne on the Isle of Bute, but had not met for twenty years or so when the nearby Rothesay Church was formally constituted in 1855. From 1973 to 1986 a group of Baptists with a commendable outreach towards children met in Wemyss Bay.

Renfrewshire's largest town, Paisley, has four Baptist Churches — The Thomas Coats Memorial, George Street, Victoria Place and Glenburn. The second largest town, Greenock, has two — Orangefield and George Square. These, with Gourock and Port Glasgow, are the only four mainland churches in West Renfrewshire or Inverclyde District.

Two Baptist Churches are of old foundation and two are new. Coats Memorial was begun by Scotch Baptists as Storie Street Church in 1795, when Renfrewshire's population was less than a quarter of its present total. The original members of the Storie Street Church had come from the Abbey Close Independents in Paisley and never joined forces with the Pen Folk, the members of the church in Pen Lane in Paisley who adopted believer's baptism in 1797 but slowly died away in the 1820s. Orangefield began in 1806, at a time when half of Greenock's population of 20,000 went to church on a

Sunday. Linwood began in 1968 in a new town of about 8,000 and Erskine began in 1975 in a new community of about 7,000.

There were distinct phases in the relationship of church membership to population. Between 1801, the first census year, and 1871, the adult membership of the churches did not rise as steeply in proportion as Renfrewshire's population. Between 1871 and 1931, membership rose considerably more steeply than population. Since 1951, however, membership has plunged while population has gone on increasing. The total Baptist membership in Renfrewshire and Bute today is no more than it was in 1903.

Leadership

A primary factor in church growth has been good leadership. This is the quality, at once spiritual and practical, that delegates and gets things done. Good leadership can spring from the minister, the diaconate or the congregation. A General Secretary of the Baptist Union of Scotland has written, 'In every area of church growth, success or failure depends mainly upon the quality of church leadership.'[2]

Example of life, as well as vision and forward planning, is an aspect of leadership. George Cowie was the Port Glasgow minister from 1952 to 1966 and again, during a hard time, from 1973 to 1976. He and his wife Ena had a fine pastoral influence and a caring concern for the whole church. They also both served on the town's Old People's Welfare Council. One minister ironed the washing for a lady member who was ill, another made a point of buying from his members' shops, another after a Sunday morning service came round to fix the plumbing in a member's kitchen — these are things long remembered. Of another minister it was recalled, 'If you were ill he was on the doorstep. Both he and his wife knew everybody and spoke to everybody.'

Every church has had its leaders — women and men, Sunday School teachers and deacons — and it is perhaps invidious to select just a few. Coats Memorial had three outstanding ministers in Oliver Flett (1860-94), Walter A. Mursell (1898-1920) and W. Vaughan King (1922-42), who gave a marked sense of continuity to the church. Flett was an Orcadian, strong and sincere, who was given a DD by Glasgow University for his services to Baptist education. He was a 'true original, full of personal and mental vigour, with more than a dash of Dr Samuel Johnson in his nature'.[3] In their different personalities, Mursell and King proved eloquent and industrious successors. King 'gave every ounce of his strength . . . he was faithful in everything . . . an indefatigable pastor, especially in sickness and sorrow'.[4] Paisley people in the 1930s crowded on Sunday evenings to hear this orator's sermons on topical

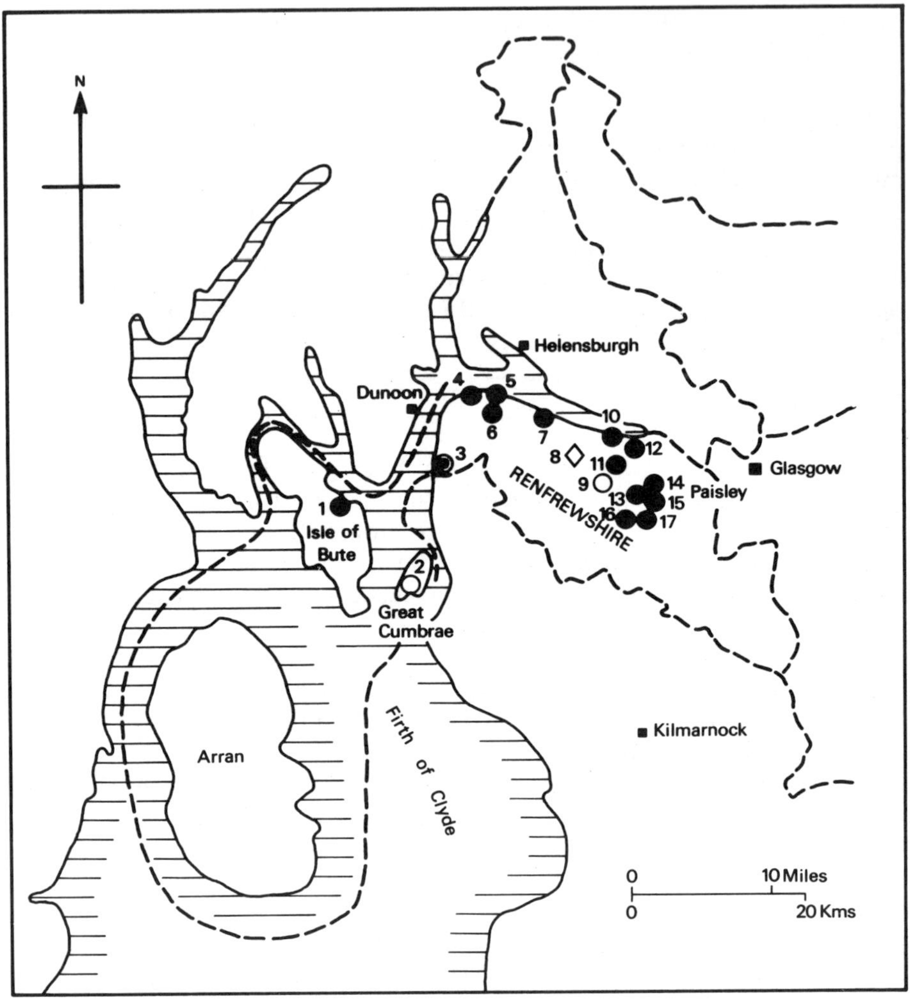

MAP 8 : RENFREWSHIRE BAPTIST CHURCHES.

Key to Map 8

1. Rothesay
2. Millport
3. Wemyss Bay
4. Gourock
5. Greenock: George Square
6. Greenock: Orangefield
7. Port Glasgow
8. Kilmacolm
9. Kilbarchan
10. Erskine
11. Linwood
12. Renfrew
13. Paisley: Victoria Place
14. Paisley: Thomas Coats Memorial
15. Paisley: George Street
16. Johnstone
17. Paisley: Glenburn

subjects and to hear the professional performances of the church choir.

Victoria Place also had three important pioneer ministers who each became president of the Baptist Union of Scotland. John Crouch (1866-96) was an emotional expository preacher and was keen on photography, astronomy and continental travel. He first married when 68. Robert Glendening (1896-1923) came from Cornwall, married Emily Coats and died in office. John Stark (1924-49), a joiner by trade and a university graduate who was badly wounded in the First World War, served on the Renfrewshire Education Committee. He was portrayed as a 'preacher of marked individuality. Less doctrinal than his two predecessors, he makes his constant theme the Christian life.'[5]

Thomas Watson McAlpine was unpaid pastor at George Street from 1846 to 1877. Benjamin Cole (1897-1913) was loved by his Orangefield congregation and Peter B. Watson Cowie (1920-36) was another outstanding Orangefield minister. John Moore (1931-47) came to George Square when its spiritual morale and finances were low, but he was an exciting forthright gospel preacher and leader, and with his great-hearted wife saw the church experience some of her finest days. James B. Coull (1937-50) of Johnstone knew many folk in the town as he went everywhere on foot and gladly stopped at the homes of strangers to tell them about their sick relations whom he had just met when visiting his own members in hospital.

Faithfulness and long service are great virtues in church secretaries. S. Swan (1915-42) of Renfrew, William Cartner (1951-78) of Port Glasgow and William McNeill (1949-60; 63-69) of George Square were three such secretaries who provided a continuing rallying-point for the Baptist cause. Swan and McNeill each enjoyed or endured seven ministers. In Rothesay Thomas Fyfe was treasurer for almost forty years, Charles Muir, JP, was treasurer for forty-one years and George Maitland, Snr, was secretary for over thirty years.

Outreach

The next section also concerns good leadership — in starting and sustaining various successful ventures of outreach. This has always been central to church growth. 'Leaders who do not aim at growth through evangelism do not really lead the church anywhere.'[6]

There have been successful efforts to bring children to Jesus over the decades, whether in the form of special intensive campaigns or week-by-week instruction by Sunday School and Bible Class teachers. Walter J. Main's mission to Renfrew in 1933 produced 'great enthusiasm . . . many conversions'. James Kennedy's mission in Johnstone in 1942 saw sixty children profess conversion to Christ. In 1968 Bill Freel led a mission in Glenburn. Over 400 children came the first day. About forty children trusted the Lord at a World Evangelization Crusade mission in Linwood in 1975. Johnstone's week-long Vacation Bible Schools in the 1970s reached up to one hundred children at times.

Presenting the claims of Christ to adults has been no less important. The Gipsy Smith mission in Greenock Town Hall in 1902 had useful results for the local churches. After the Welsh Revival of 1904, Orangefield held thirteen weeks of meetings called 'Welsh Revival Services' the next year and these brought much blessing. About the same time Port Glasgow held special open-air and church meetings and saw 'many precious souls gathered in' and had to record the happy lament '. . . the sitting accommodation at some of the services was not at all pleasant for some'.[7] In 1930, when seventy-six, John McNeill, a famous Presbyterian evangelist born and bred in Renfrewshire, drew crowds to Coats Memorial and did the same again the next year.

National missions too have been used as a means of outreach by Renfrewshire churches. In 1903 Torrey and Alexander had a month-long mission in Glasgow and in 1914 Chapman and Alexander included Paisley in their evangelistic tour. More recently, Baptist Christians have been mobilized and trained to serve as counsellors and stewards at the Glasgow Crusades led by Billy Graham (1955), Luis Palau (1981) and Dick Saunders (1983). At a more intimate and local level, house groups and church groups, some of which are charismatic, have invited and attracted non-Christians to their weeknight or Sunday meetings in recent years.

Not nearly enough social service has been done in the community in the name of our churches themselves. One present exception is Victoria Place's participation in the Paisley Christian Action Centre. With other denominations, Baptists have been taking their turn in helping the residents of a hostel for the homeless in this form of outreach.

Tremendous social service was done for Scotland by William Quarrier. Born in Greenock, Quarrier rose from nothing to become a multiple shop owner and a great philanthropist. Best of all he was a Christian and a man of faith, vision and prayer. His Orphan Homes outside Bridge of Weir consisted eventually of a hundred buildings spread over 390 acres, and over 25,000 children have passed through the solid, spacious, detached cottages since 1878. Converted in a Glasgow Baptist Church and later a deacon of the Adelaide Place Church, Quarrier helped to start Baptist Churches in Dunoon and Kilmarnock. Into his large church in the Homes he introduced open communion. He was the friend and inspiration of many Renfrewshire

Baptists.[8]

Most churches have seen members leave for overseas work. From Rothesay Mrs Donald Smith went out to serve God for forty years in China with the Baptist Missionary Society, long after her husband died as a result of the Boxer Rebellion of 1900. Interned by the Japanese in the Second World War, she finally returned to Rothesay in 1945. Herbert Dickson of Port Glasgow served God in the Qua Iboe Mission in eastern Nigeria for fifty years from 1922 and did a spell of service as late as 1979. Over £2,500 has been contributed to his memorial fund to provide Bible training for Nigerians. Tom Houston's first pastorate was at Johnstone from 1951 to 1954. Then he became chaplain at Quarrier's Homes. In 1984 he was Chairman of Mission England during Billy Graham's visit. Today he is President of World Vision International and based in California.

By bringing together people of similar interests and possibly of the same sex and age-group, church organizations, whether uniformed or not, have played a major role in producing Christians and in encouraging them to grow — in discipleship, fellowship, involvement, service and witness. Often the Women's Auxiliary group has been the largest or most flourishing organization in a church. At Johnstone in 1930, when there were only seventy-six church members, 120 attended the WA meetings each week.

Sunday Schools have also been a powerful growth factor. Nine of the thirteen churches have on occasion had over one hundred children in their Sunday Schools. Storie Street in the 1880s and Victoria Place in the 1890s each had responsibility for over 450 children. And these numbers exclude the Bible Classes run by ministers or deacons that also sometimes topped the hundred mark.

The Christian Endeavour Society at Renfrew from 1908 to 1985 proved a source of great blessing to the many members who passed through its ranks. Committee work and chain prayers were engaged in by the teenagers for whom membership of the CE was a teaching and training ground. Youth work at Johnstone progressed during the Second World War. Half an hour of Bible project work was followed by half an hour of games and half an hour for tea, when a free cake with jam on it meant much to wartime youngsters. The young people of Port Glasgow in the 1970s ran the church magazine, visited older folk, painted the church hall, ran a missionary evening, did street advertizing, witnessed from a coffee bar, went on sponsored walks and generally helped and encouraged the whole congregation. There seemed to be no generation gap. Several of the young people's friends were converted one by one at the Sunday evening services.

Senior Citizens had their own Monday afternoon tea meetings, complete with a Christian message in word and song, at Johnstone from 1970 to 1983, with up to a hundred attending. In some ways these happy occasions were reminiscent of the Saturday evening deputation tea meetings between the wars or the love feasts of coffee, bread and cheese of the last century held in churches like Storie Street and George Street between Sunday services.

Another organization that can be an avenue of service and an inspiration to its members and a drawing power to others is the church choir. Port Glasgow in the early 1930s had a flourishing choir which, accompanied by the new organ, rendered cantatas. Victoria Place at least once gained first place among church choirs in the annual Renfrewshire Music Festival. George Square in the 1950s had a fine choir with Albert Peterson as the organist. George Street and Coats Memorial have managed to sustain their choral tradition to this day.

In the 1920s it seems that Coats Memorial had as many as twenty-one organizations or sections, namely The Social Club with its Musical, Instrumental, Orchestral, Natural History, Photo and Athletic Sections, the Choir, the Literary Society (over 500 members), the Debating Circle, The Baptist Missionary Society, Wolf Cubs, Scouts, Brownies, Girl Guides, Boys' Brigade, Ladies' Work Party, Sabbath Morning Association (10 a.m.), Sunday School (3 p.m.), Bible Class (150 members) and the Penny Savings Bank. Obviously the church satisfied the intellectual, recreational and social needs of many by these organizations.

Growth through Weakness

There is more to growth than ministerial leadership, preaching and pastoral visitation. Growth can be measured in terms of warm fellowship and congregational co-operation as well as in baptisms, per capita giving and full-time Christian workers going out from a church.

Vacancies can also give opportunities for growth. A vacancy between ministers can be a time of decline, of course, but if the last minister has left in satisfactory circumstances and the congregation rallies round the church secretary and deacons, there can be advance — and not just in financial terms. One instance of such a vacancy was Glenburn's in 1972-3. It lasted for nineteen months after Alan Stoddart's departure for pioneering work in Erskine, but a remarkable unity and love prevailed as Sandy Mackeith of Govan acted as a wise moderator.

Nor are spiritual disagreements always totally bad. Schisms from the original Storie Street Church led to the formation of the George Street and

Victoria Place Churches in 1842 and 1866 respectively. However, the original 'mother' church did not suffer unduly, but pressed on to exceed 200 members by 1881, 300 by 1890 and (as Coats Memorial) 470 by 1935. Ostensibly the cause for the 1842 secession was doctrinal differences between the Calvinism of the old Scotch Baptists and the newer theology that was gaining ground in Scotland. Personality clashes and the generation gap may also have played their part. The flashpoint was the assertion of non-Calvinist views by Adam Tennant. From the 'Notice' written immediately after the schism by the two seceding elders and five seceding deacons we learn that up to 1839 in the Storie Street Church 'there had been agitation . . . upon what is called Arminianism, Rowism and Morrisonian Doctrines, free will — Mans ability — calling in question Election, the necessity of divine influence or power accompanying the word to make it effectual for the conversion of sinners — and the Doctrine of Universal Atonement, or of Christ dying for All — for every Man — All these in opposition to what they call Calvinism.'[9]

Finally on 12 June 1842, when less than half the membership was present, a vote was taken and it was agreed by 57 to 39 votes to tolerate the controversial views of Tennant. The defeated, disgusted and possibly out-manoeuvred Calvinist minority soon withdrew and so reduced Storie Street's membership to eighty-four. Tennant went on to become the Storie Street secretary, while John Taylor, styled an elder and pastor since 1819, became one of the George Street elders. Only four years after the schism Storie Street recorded a membership of 119 and George Street one of 126.

In 1866, when Paisley had 50,000 people and over sixty places of worship, seventy-two members of Storie Street resigned to form Victoria Place Baptist Church. They had already engaged for the past three Sundays as preacher a student from the London college of C.H. Spurgeon, who had visited Glasgow a month before. The gifted John Crouch preached first in the Swedenborgians' church at 12 George Street — when all three Paisley Baptist Churches were hardly a stone's throw from each other — and remained as minister of Victoria Place till 1896. Though today in Lady Lane, almost literally in the shadow of the soaring Coats Memorial Church, Victoria Place raced with Storie Street in growth to reach 150 members by 1871, 250 by 1886 and 400 by 1905.

Meanwhile Pastor Flett of Storie Street seized the occasion of the 1866 schism to get three changes voted in — that business matters be transacted on week nights only, that the Lord's Supper be observed at the end instead of the start of the afternoon service and that a public confession before the church be no longer compulsory on the part of baptismal candidates. The one person who did not vote for these changes was Elder Gibb, the secretary, who soon left the church, leaving Pastor Flett as the church secretary for the next twenty-seven years.

Open communion Baptists in Greenock started what became George Square in 1884, leaving the established Particular or Calvinistic Baptist Orangefield Church at the other end of Nelson Street. But Greenock was big and ready enough for two Baptist Churches. Orangefield went from 187 members in 1884 to 258 in 1893 and to 301 in 1910, while George Square with 43 members in 1886 reached 159 in 1915 and 200 in 1935. Pastor Flett and members of the Coats family in Paisley helped greatly in establishing the young congregation of George Square and in financing the building of its church.

Sometimes schism comes from the independent spirit of Baptists that can make for contention and bitterness. G.W. Landels resigned in 1885 as pastor of George Street in Paisley after only two years there. On his resignation the membership was drastically reduced from 160 to 44. Probably many went on to attend, if not join, the two nearby Baptist Churches. The George Street minute book is strangely quiet about the cause of Landels's resignation, though a year before a deacon had accused him of reading 'sermons which were not his own, an action which I firmly hold to be a grievous sin in the sight of God', to which Landels replied that he would continue to quote extracts from his father's sermons.

New Churches, Finance and Co-operation

Growth has also come from new churches being founded in recent years to serve expanding centres of population. After the Second World War Paisley took over Glenburn district to build a new housing scheme on it. Bailie Semple of George Street helped to ensure that one of the three new churches in the scheme would be a Baptist cause. Successful children's work under James Todd and John Grant led to Sunday morning services for adults and in 1956, having been helped by the Paisley Baptist Churches, Glenburn Church was formally constituted with twenty-four members. Unhappily, few members lived on the new scheme itself. The pleasant church building and halls were opened in 1959. By that time Derek Murray was the first minister.

Linwood Church started from a local paper advertisement put in by James Todd of Glenburn and James Young of Renfrew. As a result a small group met in Mrs Olive Davison's home on 14 October 1966. Soon a Scout hut was hired, but when it burnt down the members of the fellowship bought the main shell of a large wooden hut and worked hard to make it into their own hall, with extra rooms for teaching children, a kitchen and toilets. A fire engine obligingly filled up the concrete tank for the baptisms on Guy Fawkes night

1969! In that year Linwood Baptists, still few in number, did a big house visitation campaign when Bill Galloway was lay pastor. Tom Lannigan became Linwood's first minister in 1972 and a year later the new church building was opened.

In the starting of Erskine Church the Renfrewshire Baptist Association came into its own. It organized financial support and ministers to take services in the new community of about 3,000 that was rising up close to the Clyde. The Baptist Union also played a valiant part in establishing and financing an initial pastorate in 1972. The ever-helpful Alan Stoddart came from a pastorate at Glenburn and stayed ten pioneering years. The Baptist cause was the first church in the new community. Services moved from a community hut to a community centre to the present fine church building, which was opened in 1978. In 1975 the church had been constituted with twenty-seven members and seventeen associate members (professing Christians from other denominations who have a voice and a vote at church meetings on all matters except constitutional issues). Weekly offerings increased from £20 in 1978 to £315 in 1986 and membership rose to 104. Jim McGillivray (later minister of Rothesay), Bill MacDonald, Fergus Stokes and Stephen Younger all served in turn as student assistants to the pastor, with Fergus Stokes eventually staying on as pastor. Helped by a spirit of renewal and activities that included a youth coffee bar at the nearby Park Mains School, Renfrewshire's youngest church put down strong roots.

Financial support has sometimes been crucial in church life and growth. Thomas Coats, the thread manufacturer, died in 1883. He had been a generous member of Storie Street Church for forty-four years. His family opened his memorial church in 1894. This is a giant red sandstone 'cathedral', which is approached by thirty steps forty-five feet wide and has a crown tower 220 feet above Paisley's High Street that can be seen ten miles away. Inside, the intricate work in stone, wood and mosaic is quite astonishing.

The church buildings stayed in the hands of the Coats family who undertook their upkeep and the expenses of the caretakers, the organist and the choir. The halls underneath the church were not to be used for Sunday School work but for Bible Classes only and social meetings. The Coats family reserved the right to use the church on weekdays for organ recitals and other musical services of a religious character. The new church had a splendid organ, a fifty-strong choir and its own hymnal and psalter, which were compiled by the organist, Montague Smith, Snr, whose son followed as another accomplished and long-serving organist. The choir performed cantatas, to which 1,200 people paid entry on occasions, and in 1939 an operetta.

In its heyday Coats Memorial was closely identified with public life. In 1906 two MPs were church members and in 1938 the provost of Paisley was the church secretary. Over the years famous preachers spoke from the marble and alabaster pulpit — Graham Scroggie, Leslie Weatherhead, Lord Soper, Martin Niemöller, Richard Wurmbrand.

Members of the large Coats family that worshipped first at Storie Street and then at Coats Memorial extended their munificence to other churches also. George Square benefited greatly in its early years, and in 1912 Sir Thomas Glen-Coats gave the fine old Storie Street organ to George Street.

The Coats family contributed more than money and organs to the Baptist cause. Jervis Coats of Storie Street was its first organist. Then in 1872 he became minister of the Govan Church and in 1914 the principal of the Baptist Theological College. He gave invaluable service to the churches and the Baptist Union. In the 1930s another Coats, W. Holms Coats, was principal of the college.

The Rothesay Church also benefited from family generosity. It was bought in 1847 from Congregationalists by the widowed Mrs Sheriff, whose daughter transferred her interest in the property to church trustees in 1886. At her death she bequeathed her house as a manse.

Gourock Church, started in 1895 by seven ladies, some of whom came from Orangefield Church, found a novel source of income for itself. In 1922 Alex Paterson, a Baptist Union ex-president, became Gourock's minister and within three years seventy-eight people were added to the membership roll. So Paterson suggested that the church's sloping front garden should be the site for a new church, under which three small shops facing Shore Street would be built. The rent from these shops, which still exist today, would then help towards the cost of the new church.

Co-operation between the churches, which has contributed to growth, has been expressed largely through the Renfrewshire Baptist Association (RBA). Some critics have wondered if people from both ends of the county can be expected to meet occasionally. Others have believed that the churches have problems enough of their own and cannot spare their few willing horses to represent them on the RBA committee. But since its start in 1922 the RBA has proved a financial encouragement and help in several ways to the churches. Johnstone was helped as the congregation sought a new church and finally bought and decorated the Liberal Club halls in Church Street in 1930. Port Glasgow was aided with its new church in 1949. Especially did the RBA help the new pastorate at Erskine in the 1970s. Perhaps the RBA functioned best when stable, settled ministers encouraged fellowship and support among the churches.

Like the RBA, the Baptist Union of Scotland has been a financial help or life-saver, with all the psychological boost that means to the churches, as well as being a focus of unity and strength. In return the churches have supplied eight past presidents, though not one since 1944, and three WA national presidents. Loans have been made to several of the churches down the years since 1869, including one of £300 to George Street in 1912. Loans were given to Renfrew early this century for its church, then its manse, then an interest-free loan for new halls in 1937 and a loan for the new manse in 1947. Help was given to Johnstone in the difficult 1920s. More recently Glenburn and Erskine Churches were greatly aided by the Baptist Union. Advice on legal, building and insurance matters has been made available for many years.

Church Decline

Leadership has been as powerful an influence for decline as it has been for growth. Over the years some ministers have, for different reasons, been asked to resign by their churches. Others have resigned before they were asked. Some no doubt have departed because they judged their congregation was too hidebound, too poor (or mean) or too lacking in vision. Several ministers have gone on to other denominations, several have left the ministry itself, at least six in each instance. Some perhaps have lacked perseverance or the fillip that comes from seeing good results. Poor leadership or misguided leadership has not, of course, been a monopoly of ministers. Church deacons, members and adherents have also failed by providing inadequate leadership or by tolerating it.

Another factor in church decline was war. During the two World Wars most churches suffered difficulties arising from the disturbed and changing conditions — irreparable loss of life, an extra shortage of manpower, men on Sunday work, longer working hours in industry, blackouts, food shortages, bomb damage and buildings taken over for the war effort. In the terrible First World War Victoria Place lost twenty-five men killed and Coats twenty-four, each figure representing about 6% of the membership. George Street and Orangefield temporarily surrendered their ministers when they served overseas as army chaplains.

Johnstone wondered whether to close during the First World War owing to the depleted number of men, and in the Second World War had its church hall commandeered by the War Department. Because windows could not easily be blacked out, an afternoon service replaced the evening service on Sundays. Coats replaced its evening service in 1940 with one at 3 p.m. and then with one at 2 p.m., but results were discouraging. Coats even lost its great minister, W. Vaughan King, when he died from an injury received in the blackout on leaving Orangefield on an exchange pulpit Sunday in 1942.

However, adverse effects of the war years must not be exaggerated. It is good to read in Port Glasgow's records of 1919 that 'no formal meetings were held but a general oversight was faithfully maintained and no part of the Church was overlooked or in any wise suffered through the long break in stated meetings of Office bearers. We desire to put on record our deep thankfulness to God, for His great mercy towards us during the weary war years.' It is also good that George Square in the Second World War saw an influx of visitors, Baptist fishermen turned sailors from the Moray coast included, from ships calling at Greenock. Five out of ten churches had a larger membership in 1920 than in 1915 and four had a larger membership in 1945 than in 1940.

The last century has seen a sad and serious decline in traditional crafts and industries. In 1921 more tonnage of shipping was built on the Clyde than in the rest of the world put together. Today the once bustling shipyards of Greenock, Port Glasgow and Renfrew are hardly a shadow of their former glory. The once powerful sugar industry in Greenock has also fallen on hard times, though since 1951 electronics firms have provided thousands of new jobs in Inverclyde District with its population of 100,000. In Paisley the rich Coats family, largely Liberal in politics and Baptist in denomination, endowed the town with a library, museum and observatory, as well as the huge Baptist Church. In 1896 the two firms of Coats and Clark amalgamated to become the world's largest thread-making operation. Today their vast Victorian factories lie empty and vandalized. The big car plant at Linwood began as Pressed Steel Ltd in the 1940s and employed 7,000 in the 1970s but closed in 1979, leaving little of a manufacturing nature to take its place.

Inevitably these industrial changes have had socio-economic repercussions, for good as well as for ill, on the Renfrewshire churches as regards the employment, movement and finances of their attenders. Churches lost people who decided to emigrate or to seek work elsewhere in Britain because they had been made redundant at home. Yet it was not inevitable that churches should lose members or that finances or morale should fall in hard economic times. Some churches doubled or trebled membership in the times of depression. Yet, though it is impossible to prove, on balance industrial depression in Renfrewshire was probably a factor making for church decline rather than for church growth.

Accommodation and Other Problems

Accommodation difficulties and dilemmas frequently afflicted the churches.

Buildings sometimes became too big, too old or too costly to maintain, while others were destroyed or proved too small. Port Glasgow's problem in 1938 was the destruction of its building in Chapelton Street by fire. This necessitated splitting up the church's activities and more than one move, and the new building, to the erection of which twenty-two Baptist Churches contributed, was not opened till 1949. Port Glasgow's problem after 1950 was that its membership went downhill as the town's population went uphill! All the post-war housing schemes are up at 300 feet. Finally the church amalgamated in 1983 with Ferguson Memorial Mission (begun 1902) and occupied its building, which is up the town hill a little but at the top of a steep incline and with parking space for only five cars.

Port Glasgow has not been alone in having an ageing congregation. Orangefield and some of the Paisley Churches have been in a similar position. This has raised big questions like 'Should Orangefield and George Square in Greenock unite?' and 'Should Victoria Place and Coats unite?' and 'Should George Street and Glenburn unite?' Orangefield and George Square have held joint services in July in the past and once ran the Sunday School at Ravenscraig between them. Their union was mooted as an option as far back as 1960. The three Paisley Churches of Coats, Victoria Place and George Street have seen the inner town centre gradually depopulated as the new estates on the edges of the town were built. Yet today the three churches share the same main road bus stop. The church at George Street is old, having been opened in 1861. In 1978 Coats and Victoria Place voted on the proposal that they should unite, with the new church having an assistant minister who would be in charge of a social action centre in the old Victoria Place buildings, but while Coats voted overwhelmingly in favour of such a union, Victoria Place was split down the middle with 62 in favour and 62 against.

Johnstone's problem was that it moved in 1965 into a vacated Church of Scotland building which started life as a Relief Church in 1828. Being tossed from the horn of maintaining an ancient building to the horn of necessary modernization is a painful experience.

Pastorally Renfrewshire has had its share of long vacancies, some extending up to three years. Over six years in the early 1980s only Johnstone had the same minister for the whole period, the evangelistically-minded George Cruickshank having worked there since 1970. Much depends on why a vacancy occurs as to how it affects the church. If it occurs in unhappy circumstances or is the second or third vacancy in a short space of years, fringe attenders and newcomers to the area may well worship elsewhere under a settled ministry. Much too depends on the spiritual and moral fibre of the church secretary and his or her deacons as to whether or how quickly a vacancy becomes an advantage to a church's growth in all the directions that matter. Continuity of preaching and pastoral visitation so often suffer during vacancies.

In the last century taverns, theatres and sport as well as churches drew the crowds. In this century increased leisure time has not necessarily led to more church work being done. First cinemas and then television and home videos proved serious rivals to church services and meetings, even for Christians. On top of that cars made many more mobile and offered a wider choice of churches. Families became much smaller than a century ago, which partly explains the sad fact that Coats in 1875 and Victoria Place in 1893, for instance, each had more Sunday School scholars in their charge than all the thirteen churches put together in 1985.

Gone (for the time being) are the days when a coachload of forty from Irvine would come up to take a Saturday evening deputation at Renfrew and give a string of stirring testimonies. Gone are the days when churches were trusted more than banks (the City of Glasgow Bank failed in 1878) with poor people's savings — the Penny Savings Bank at Victoria Place functioned from 1877 to 1946. Gone are the evenings when 150 lively youngsters attended Band of Hope meetings for instruction in temperance principles and 125 came to the mid-week prayer and Bible study meetings in Rothesay. Are the days also gone when the preached word is discussed on the way home or over lunch? Do Baptists keep only the Lord's half-day now? The judgment has been made by a Scottish Baptist that 'it is the indifference of Christians that stifles the growth of the Church, not the indifference of the unbeliever'.[10]

False growth occurs when spurious commitments are made by people who are baptized, become church members and boost church rolls only to drift and drop away, often within three years, not only from their own church but from any church at all and sometimes from any profession of following Christ. Spurts of growth in the 1970s were seen in Linwood and later in neighbouring Johnstone. Linwood had earlier held two successful Witness Involvement Now schools for training in personal evangelism. Over fifty people of all ages and mostly from a non-Christian background were added by baptism to the church, yet within five years perhaps only 60% were still members. The missing members had not all moved house, but seem to have grown lukewarm or worse in serving Christ. Perhaps this was because there was little attempt at systematic teaching and fellowship follow-up for the new converts. Was it because they had not fully understood the nature of Baptist church membership or even the Christian life?

Possibly the main reasons for the general decline of Renfrewshire churches since 1950 have been a dearth of spiritual leaders and the prevailing social climate. Men and women with the cutting edge of conviction and urgency seem to be largely missing. Prayer that prevails, sermons that save and relationships that are costly in love are relatively rare. The churches themselves have partly lost their vision of a risen and returning Son of God. In an increasingly permissive society people pursue pleasure and money rather than principles and morals. There appears to be greater scope for temptations and fewer people believe in any life after death. Yet older congregations can be revived by God's Spirit, new churches can be started and enthusiastic outreach can be effective in bringing people to the Lord Jesus.

Notes

1. James Murray, *Kilmacolm* (Paisley 1907), p 164.
2. A.D. MacRae, *Your Church must choose* (London 1982), p 40.
3. *The Thomas Coats Memorial Baptist Church, Paisley, Jubilee Book, 1944* (Paisley 1945), p 78.
4. *The Memorial Church Monthly* (Feb. 1942).
5. *The Torch: Victoria Place, 1866-1966* (Paisley 1966).
6. MacRae, *Your Church*, p 19.
7. Port Glasgow Church Minute Book.
8. See, e.g., Alexander Gammie, *William Quarrier* (London n.d.).
9. George Street Church Records.
10. MacRae, *Your Church*, p 17.

D.R. Reeves

9. GLASGOW AND DUNBARTONSHIRE

Since the eighteenth century, Glasgow has been the heartland of Scotland's industry and population. As such it has formed the centre of the work of Baptists in Scotland. Not only has its association possessed the largest number of members, but also it has come to house the Baptist Union of Scotland offices and the Scottish Baptist College. This chapter shows the development of the Baptists from a tiny meeting that was formed in 1770 to a situation where in 1985 Baptists had churches in almost every large community in the area.

By the mid-eighteenth century, Glasgow was a small, elegant city of about 20,000 people. Its life revolved around the ancient university, the cathedral and, increasingly, the trade flowing through its growing docks and the production of its cotton mills and coal mines. A new economic order was bringing about the rise of a body of businessmen who no longer took the old ways of Presbyterianism for granted. Many of them, together with their employees and associates, were prepared to consider new interpretations of the Christian faith and new forms of church order. Thus George Whitefield, who visited Glasgow in 1754, made sufficient impact to inspire a mob to burn down the theatre.[1] A succession of non-Presbyterian churches emerged. The Glasites set up a congregation in 1761, the Old Scots Independents in 1769 and the Bereans in 1780. A Scotch Baptist Church came into being in 1770 as a congregation gathered around one of the founders of the Edinburgh Scotch Baptist Church, Archibald McLean, a printer and bookseller in Glasgow. The church was set in order as a branch of the Edinburgh Church in March 1770, meeting in the heart of Glasgow in a building in High Street with Archibald McLean and George Begg as co-pastors. The focus of the church's beginnings was a series of baptisms in the River Clyde, and, once formed, and despite opposition, it grew rapidly. In 1776, its numbers were reinforced by the addition of a large contingent of the Old Scots Independent Church who had adopted Baptist views. In 1802, the congregation was sufficiently large (it reportedly had around 250 members) and wealthy to erect a church building in George Street that attracted the congratulations of the local magistrates on its elegance.[2]

Urban Boom and Baptist Division, 1800–1860

In 1801, the census recorded 77,058 persons living in Glasgow within an area now regarded as the City Centre and Calton. In an unprecedented spurt of growth, by 1861 there were no fewer than 395,503 persons living within the city boundaries — a five-fold increase in sixty years. The engine of this growth was the process of industrialization whereby Glasgow was developing rapidly the classic Victorian industries of coal mining, iron and steel making, engineering, paper making, shipbuilding, railway engines, clothing and textiles around the core of the old city. This jobs boom, combined with substantial improvements in communications through the advent of steamships, railways and turnpike roads, drew population from all over Scotland (particularly the Highlands) and Ireland.

Urban growth was compact, however. Housing the immigrants was achieved in tightly packed tenements which were driven east and west on the north bank of the Clyde. To the east, housing for the poor stretched into Bridgeton and Calton. To the north, Cowcaddens and Garnethill were built. To the west, the wealthy moved into the newly built elegant suburbs of Park Circus, Blythswood Square and Woodlands. Straggling industrial quarters developed to the south in Laurieston, Tradeston and Hutchesontown. Some of the villages and small towns around Glasgow also began to grow, particularly those with favourable sites for shipbuilding such as Dumbarton, Clydebank and Govan, those on the coalfield such as Kirkintilloch and those places especially suited for paper making and textiles on fast flowing rivers such as in the Leven Valley. The extension of ferry services and the railway created new resort suburbs at Dunoon and Helensburgh.

Whilst this explosion of industry and population was going on, for most of the period non-Presbyterian churches made slow progress. Early in the century, Robert Haldane made a powerful impact through his evangelism in Glasgow and he built a Tabernacle in Ann Street, off Jamaica Street. This became an Independent Church under Greville Ewing in 1800. Within three years, it had divided to found a second congregation which met in North Albion Street. This congregation, in turn, split over the issue of believer's baptism and a large group joined the George Street Scotch Baptist congregation. Haldane closed down the Tabernacle in 1809 when he adopted Baptist views and the congregation built a separate chapel in West Nile Street. This latter moved to West Campbell Street and finally became Hillhead Congregational Church. It may be said that the Haldane revival mainly benefited Independency in Glasgow rather than the Baptist cause.[3]

The Scotch Baptist Church which had built up during the late eighteenth century manifested a tendency to divide and correspondingly weakened itself. Its rigid form of Calvinism also made it unlikely to respond vigorously to the massive urban growth going on around. In 1810, 160 members of George Street seceded to form a separate church, meeting first at the Trades Hall, then Morrison's Court (off Argyle Street) and finally North Portland Street. This group followed the lead of Dr James Watt, previously an ordained minister of the Secession Church, who had more liberal views about the circumstances of observing the Lord's Supper than the traditional Scotch

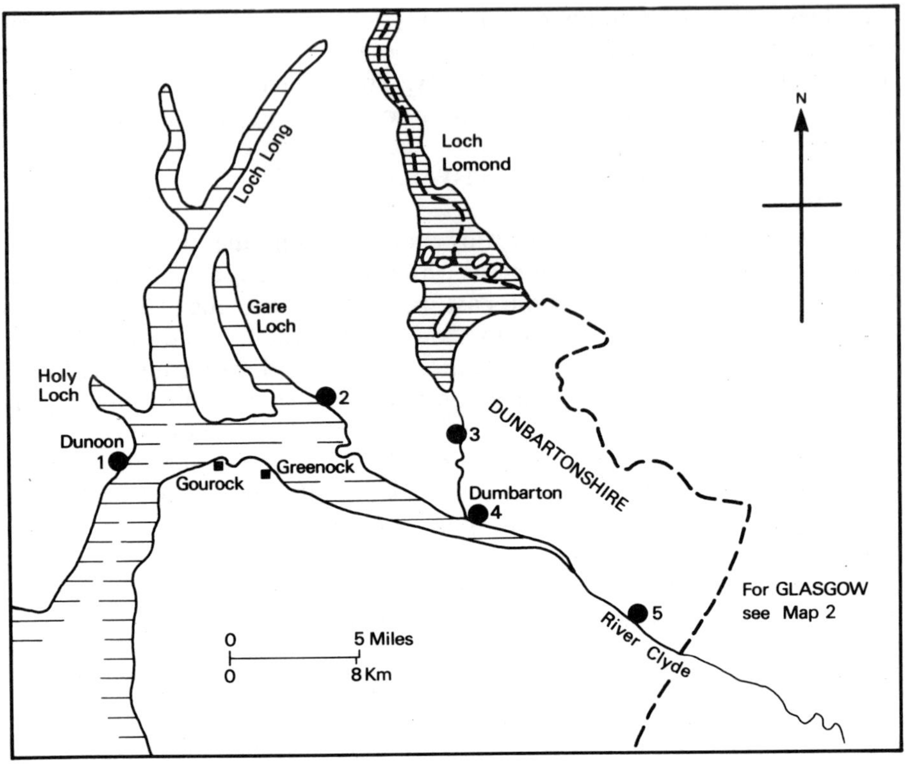

MAP 9.1: DUNBARTONSHIRE BAPTIST CHURCHES.

Key to Map 9.1

1. Dunoon
2. Helensburgh
3. Alexandria
4. Dumbarton
5. Clydebank

Baptist position. Most of those joining this fellowship were in the group that had seceded from the North Albion Street Independent congregation. A further secession from George Street took place in 1834 when disputes over church order again broke out and those taking the strict view separated to form a new congregation which first met in the Andersonian Hall of the university and then built a chapel in Brown Street, Anderston. A further Scotch Baptist congregation emerged independently in 1823, led by a Church of Scotland minister who had adopted Baptist views. This was William Shirreff, formerly of St Ninians, near Stirling, and the church met at Albion Street. In 1841, it merged with North Portland Street, which in turn merged with George Street. This perhaps reflects the weakening of Scotch Baptist principles and perhaps the diminution of numbers in these congregations. It did, however, enable the united congregations to build a new chapel which was completed in 1845 at John Street, near George Square.[4] This merger may nevertheless have caused another division, since another congregation, probably of Scotch Baptist order, was formed in Hill Street, Garnethill, in 1844.

The pulse of Baptist growth in Glasgow was quickened by 'English'-order churches possessing a single pastor and reflecting the new eagerness for mission of the epoch. The first 'English' Church was formed in 1801 with James Lister as sole pastor. It established links with the English Particular Baptists, but closed in 1806. A second attempt was made in 1820 by a missionary, Alexander McLeod, who had worked for Christopher Anderson's Baptist Itinerant Society. This church met at first in George's Place and then in South Portland Street. It ministered essentially to the Highlanders living in Glasgow and held its services in Gaelic. In 1829, a missionary of the Glasgow City Mission, James Paterson, became unhappy with the Calvinist Albion Street meeting he attended and set up a new church in a hired hall. This was probably a professedly General Baptist cause possessing an Arminian theology heavily influenced by Methodism. By 1835, this congregation had grown rapidly as a result of Paterson's evangelism and had sufficient resources to build its own chapel at Hope Street (now part of the Central Station site). By this time, congregations were up to 1,000 people and baptized members numbered 260. Hope Street Church's vision for the growth of the city in the East End led it, in 1845, to encourage a group of members to establish a new congregation in Blackfriars Street.[5] A secession from this church in 1851 established a further congregation which met initially at Trades House, Glassford Street, and which later, in 1859, erected a church at North Frederick Street. The 62 members constituting this new church at its formation had become 243 by 1860.[6]

Outside the city, two small churches existed for a time. In Helensburgh a church was set up and pastored by a retired Glasgow businessman, Robert

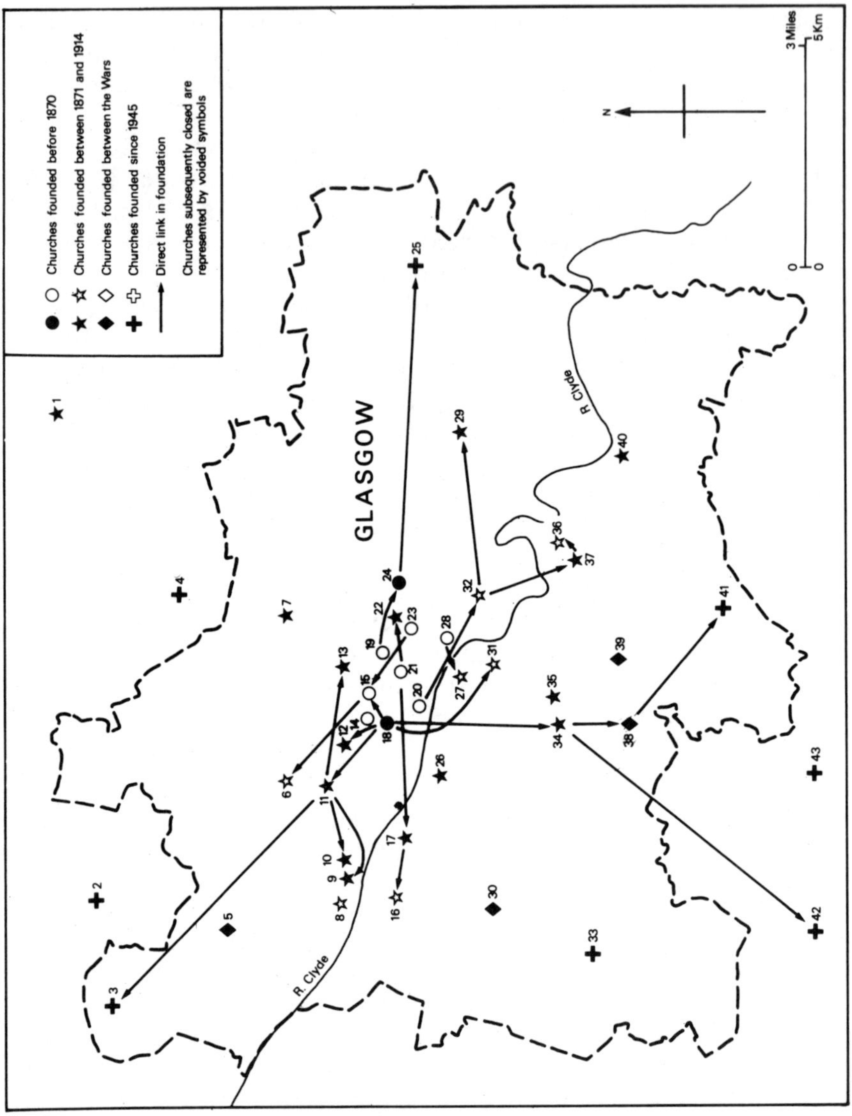

MAP 9.2 : GLASGOW BAPTIST CHURCHES.

Key to Map 9.2

1. Kirkintilloch
2. Bearsden
3. Drumchapel
4. Bishopbriggs
5. Knightswood
6. Kelvinside
7. Springburn
8. Whiteinch
9. Partick Mission
10. Partick
11. Hillhead
12. St. Clair Street Mission
13. Port Dundas Mission
14. Hill Street
15. Cambridge Street
16. Govan West
17. Govan
18. Adelaide Place
19. Frederick Street
20. Brown Street
21. John Street
22. St James Road Mission
23. John Knox Street
24. Dennistoun
25. Easterhouse
26. Harper Memorial
27. Victoria Place
28. South Portland Street
29. Shettleston
30. Mosspark
31. Huchesontown
32. Bridgeton
33. Pollock
34. Queen's Park
35. Hermon
36. Rutherglen West
37. Rutherglen
38. Cathcart
39. King's Park
40. Cambuslang
41. Castlemilk
42. Newton Mearns
43. Clarkston

Dickie, between 1833 and 1870.[7] Dumbarton too had a fellowship established in 1823, but it died out in 1866.[8]

By the sixties, Baptist witness in Glasgow had become well founded, with seven churches in existence, three Scotch Baptist and four 'English' Baptist in basis. Overall numbers were, however, tiny when compared to the size of the population and the size of the Presbyterian and Roman Catholic Churches. Nevertheless, the pace of growth had quickened as the century wore on. Revival and the stimulus of the Moody and Sankey missions were to result in far greater advance in the latter part of the century.

Urban Growth and Baptist Multiplication, 1860–1914

Between 1861 and the beginning of the First World War, the city of Glasgow and its satellite industrial towns grew apace, though more slowly than in the first half of the century. Glasgow's population tripled from 395,503 in 1861 to 1,034,174 in 1921. Similar rates of growth took place in Clydebank, the Leven Valley and in the small towns on the fringe of Glasgow such as Bishopbriggs, Kirkintilloch, Cambuslang, Rutherglen and Milngavie, whilst Helensburgh and Dunoon established themselves as fashionable middle/upper-class commuter suburbs and resorts.

The industrial boom of the Victorian period continued to be the driving force. All the major heavy industries grew. New iron and steel works were built, notably the giant Dixon's Blazes Works in Polmadie, Parkhead Forge and the Clyde Iron, Clydebridge and Hallside Works around Rutherglen. The period was the heyday of the shipbuilding industry with the development of the Denny Yard at Dumbarton, the John Brown Yard at Clydebank and the string of famous yards north and south of the Clyde in Glasgow. Large engineering works were built, while chemical works, textile mills, railway workshops and the port itself, together with related industries such as grain storage and food processing, also grew.

The population attracted by this massive development of factories was housed in rapidly built tenements laid out in grid form across the flat farmlands north and south of the Clyde as well as around the centres of the previously established towns. During this period, the large, mainly industrial working-class communities of Scotstoun, Clydebank, Whiteinch, Partick, Govan, Kinning Park, Maryhill, Govanhill, Springburn, Shettleston, Parkhead and Tollcross emerged, each around its industry. Hillhead, Dennistoun, Pollokshields, Shawlands, Mount Florida, Kelvinside and Cathcart meanwhile developed around squares and parklands as higher-class housing for Glasgow's managerial, professional and clerical workers. The physical extent of the city grew apace, swallowing up countryside. As urban growth developed, Glasgow absorbed the surrounding burghs. On a smaller scale, this kind of sprawl also took place along the valley of the Leven between Dumbarton and Balloch.

Although the pace of growth quickened, so too did popular interest in Christianity. Evangelical Nonconformity was at its height in England and Wales, and its influence spread north of the border. There was vigorous mass evangelism by the Americans Moody and Sankey. Calvinism continued to fade as a major force and Baptist thinking, praying and effort centred on witnessing, evangelism and church planting. Congregationalism and the related Evangelical Union built twelve new churches in Glasgow between 1870 and 1914.[9] Similarly a combination of a surge of population with a quickening of faith made this a major era of Baptist advance.

Twenty-five churches or missions were formed in the period and five relocated. Baptist membership, estimated as around 1,000 in 1861, had risen to 6,241 in 1921, a rate of growth well beyond that of the population. The pattern of church development behind these statistics reveals a picture of great dynamism and deserves careful examination. The new causes may be divided into four categories: relocated churches; new independent foundations; missions established by the other churches; and independent missions.

Five of the seven existing churches in central Glasgow relocated, with John Street staying on the site where the reunited congregation had built its own church in 1845 and Hill Street closing about 1870. The remaining churches that emerged in the early nineteenth century moved out from the centre.

Movement was to some extent forced by commercial pressures, but also reflected the desire by congregations to go to where their members and the general population lived. The centre of the city at the time (i.e. the area bounded by Hope Street, the River Clyde, High Street and George Street/ Cathedral Street) was being steadily taken over by administrative buildings (such as City Chambers and the various law courts), commercial premises, the great railway stations and yards, factories and warehouses. In some parts, there was planned redevelopment of the worst housing by the City Improvement Trust. The central churches were therefore becoming isolated from the people they served and their sites were becoming more valuable. The growth of their congregations required larger premises. It may also be surmised that the Baptists desired to be known as a respectable denomination equal in stature to the Church of Scotland and its offshoots. No longer was a compact, square meeting-house adequate. A spacious, lofty building with fashionable Gothic architecture more closely matched their ambitions.

The Blackfriars Street Church moved from its site in 1877 (as a result of negotations with the North British Railway over the building of their goods yard and warehouse complex) to John Knox Street near Glasgow Cathedral. By the 1870s the Hope Street congregation was very conscious of its cramped premises and the problems arising from its very rapid growth. From 1870 to 1877 it grew from 239 members to 668, nearly trebling its size! It sold its site to the Caledonian Railway Company in 1874, and with the proceeds bought a site and erected an elegant church at Adelaide Place in the residential Blythswood Square area to the west of the city centre. Ironically, this move marked the peak of the size of the congregation. Thereafter it declined through losses of members to the new churches in the suburbs.[10] The Frederick Street congregation took a similar decision to move at a later date. In 1900, the church resolved that 'considering the depopulation of the locality and the conversion of the district into a business centre, it is expedient and desirable that the Church should remove to another district'.[11] The congregation selected a new site well to the east in the high-quality residential area of Dennistoun. It built an attractive and stylish church in 1909 to suit the congregation's size and vigour. Significantly, this move resulted in a sharp increase in membership. Prior to this, Frederick Street had been losing numbers.

The two smaller churches also moved, by a series of changes of place of worship. The Brown Street congregation established a branch meeting initially (in 1860) in Stockwell Street which subsequently (in 1861) moved to Rutherglen, and then (in 1870) to Bridgeton. This new meeting flourished, and by 1878 had secured larger premises (at London Road) in which a baptistry was installed. At this point, Brown Street congregation (or what was left of it) transferred to the new church in Bridgeton, leaving the use of its premises to Adelaide Place Baptist Church for its mission and Sunday School work in Anderston. The new Bridgeton congregation did not look back. In 1883, helped by Adelaide Place, it purchased a small building from the Church of Scotland at Canning Street and two years later added a hall.[12]

The South Portland Street congregation (later called the Baronial Hall meeting) evidently started to dwindle in the late 1860s for similar reasons that impelled the other congregations to move out. In 1873, it transferred across the River Clyde to meet in Clarence Hall in Kingston. By 1875, however, its pastor had resigned and it gave up meeting, with many of its members transferring to other churches such as Hope Street. The following year, however, the newly formed Glasgow Baptist Association, recognizing the needs of this large and rapidly growing area and the existence of a Baptist nucleus, stepped in and organized services once again. This rapidly resulted in the formation of the 'South Side' Baptist Church which, after a period of using public halls, built its own temporary premises in 1877 and finally erected a building in 1898 at Victoria Place, Govanhill. By this time, the church had around 250 members.[13]

A strength of a Baptist Church is its ability to develop gradually from an informal and independent association of believers living in a particular district. This ability created the impetus for the formation of nine churches. These new churches were generally encouraged by the existing fellowships, and, in part, were fed by members leaving them to help pioneer new work. They were not, however, deliberate offshoots.

The first new independent congregation arose through the concern of members of the existing 'English' Baptist Churches of Hope Street, Blackfriars Street and North Frederick Street to reach the growing Cowcaddens area immediately to the north of the present city centre. A group met in 1861 and formed a church the following year. It led a precarious existence through lack of permanent premises and settled ministry until 1876, when the congregation managed to build a church at Cambridge Street and acquire an effective pastor. Its numbers remained relatively small until the aggressively evangelistic ministry of Edward Last from 1891 to 1900 resulted in a trebling of its membership to 376 by 1901.[14] His departure, however, and the declining population of the immediate area meant that soon this congregation began to lose members.

The rapidly growing south-side suburbs of Glasgow in Crosshill, Queen's Park and Pollokshields were attracting a large number of members of the central churches, particularly as the housing being developed was essentially for the middle classes. It was not therefore surprising that a group gathered to hold services. Despite some difficulties over church order (some were Scotch Baptist in origin), a church was constituted in 1878, a pastor called and Sunday Schools organized. Membership rose quickly from thirty-one founder members to around 200 in 1887, when their new church at Queen's Drive was opened. This was soon called Queen's Park Baptist Church.[15]

A similar development took place in the burgeoning high-class suburbs being built along Great Western Road to the west of Charing Cross. The residential district naturally attracted the well-to-do from more central parts, Baptists among them. In 1882, a group of members from Adelaide Place Church started services in Hillhead Burgh Hall, constituted a church in the following year, built a hall at Cresswell Street in the next year and the church finally in 1885. This rapid pace (the church had 300 members in 1888) is a comment on the fertility of the area for a Baptist Church as well as the evident quality of leadership of the original members and its first minister, F.H. Roberts. Neither did the pace slacken, as, by the end of the century, Hillhead Church had 639 members and was by far the largest Baptist Church in Glasgow.[16]

In the growing towns around Glasgow, six congregations were formed through independent efforts. Groups of Baptist members attached to the city churches assembled to hold services and to evangelize their growing areas. This usually led quickly to the formation of a church and the building of a hall for the congregation. This pattern of church planting took place in Cambuslang (formed 1881), Kirkintilloch (1887) and Shettleston (1899).

In Dumbarton, a group of Baptist believers arose, not from an existing nucleus, but from a group of people converted during the visit of Moody and Sankey in 1874. They were helped to set up a Baptist Church by a missionary, John Downie, drafted in by the Baptist Union. This church was constituted in 1876.[17]

The growing resort and commuter suburb of Helensburgh (whose development quickened after the completion of the railway in 1858) had had a small Scotch Baptist Church. A new start was made in 1880, when this remnant decided to hire the Masonic Hall in Helensburgh and hold services. This led to the formation of a church in the following year. The first pastor was appointed in 1883. He established the church on a firm footing so that by 1886 they had sufficient resources to erect a building.[18]

Dunoon had many similarities to Helensburgh, becoming a fashionable seaside, commuter and retirement resort for Glasgow people in the middle of the century. It developed particularly quickly once the railway link was established to Gourock and steam paddle-driven ferries were providing an efficient form of access to the town. A Baptist Church which had existed there in the early years of the century had long since disappeared. In 1862, it was decided by a group of eminent Glasgow Baptists (among them William Quarrier) to open a Baptist Church for the convenience of summer visitors and a few local Baptist people. It was run by a board of trustees and served by lay preachers from Paisley, Edinburgh and Glasgow until 1883, when the resident Baptists felt sufficiently strong to form a properly constituted church.[19] Its second pastor, Duncan MacGregor (1886-1909), established the church and built up its membership from an initial 35 members to a peak of 170 in 1903, when a new building was opened.

Part of the reason for the considerable growth of the Baptist Churches during this period was their urge to evangelize new areas. It could indeed be said that the period from about 1880 to the end of the century was a period of missions, when the existing churches made formidable efforts to plant new churches or at least run subsidiary worship meetings/gospel services, women's meetings and Sunday Schools in a separate place. The common characteristic of these missions is that they were established through a deliberate effort by another church to organize services, provide premises and pay full-time workers, generally in one of the new industrial areas growing up in or around the city of Glasgow. These were areas of rapidly growing housing for those working in the booming heavy industries of the time, but not to be regarded as natural Baptist territory. If no deliberate efforts had been made, there would not have been a spontaneous formation of an independent congregation such as has been described already.

The first of these missions was in Govan, where people from the Frederick Street and John Street Churches operated a mission station with the full support of both parent churches. This resulted in the formation of a church in 1872 with seventy members. Originally it used a local hall, and then took over a redundant United Presbyterian Church. Finally, in 1876, its own building was erected. Growth came steadily as a result of the lifetime work of its first pastor, Jervis Coats (later Dr), who built the church up through his forty-two-year ministry in Govan.[20] In turn, this church established a mission church that ran for seven years from 1902 in West Govan. Similarly, in 1878, Adelaide Place Baptist Church started a South Side mission in the Norfolk Hall in Tradeston. This was in addition to its mission which had recently been formed in the old Brown Street premises. The missions had Sunday School meetings, women's meetings and gospel services and were organized by a team of people led by lay missioners.

In 1882, the South Side mission was in crisis. Formation of other churches south of the Clyde, notably at Queen's Park and Victoria Place, clearly were persuading the Adelaide Place deacons of the redundancy of this effort; however, the missioner at the time, Charles Donald, had other ideas. In the face of opposition from the parent church, he resigned and set up the mission as a church in the following year in Hutchesontown. The congregation had 117 members in 1891 and had managed to erect its own 'iron hall'. Meanwhile, Adelaide Place Church had turned its attention north of the Clyde to the Maryhill area, where tenements for the working classes were being built apace. In 1883, a mission had been formed and a hall built in St Clair Street, near the Maryhill Road. Lay missionaries and leaders from the parent church developed a growing number of activities, subsequently including Sunday worship, a women's meeting, a Band of Hope, Sunday School and Bible Classes.[21]

Also in the north and west, the newly formed Hillhead Church turned its remarkable energies and resources to mission work. In 1885, one of the leading members set up a Sunday School, young people's activities, a Band of Hope and a range of other organizations ministering to the needs of working-class people in the newly developed Partick area. A hall to accommodate this work was built by Hillhead Church in 1895 at Douglas Street (subsequently renamed Purdon Street), Partick, and a full-time missioner, David Miller, was appointed in 1898. Services were started in 1899, and from these a separate church was formed in 1904 with Miller as pastor. Partick Baptist Church managed to complete its own building in 1907. The formation of this church received considerable support and financial assistance from the Glasgow Baptist Association, which raised part of the money for its new halls in 1909. Hillhead Baptist Church also directed its energies towards the area north of the city centre known as Port Dundas. This had become a populous working-class area and the church established mission activities and a Sunday School there in 1886. Various rented premises were used until 1911, when a hall was built in Canal Street.[22]

The central Cambridge Street Church made its contribution by establishing mission work in the extreme north-west part of the city. During the dynamic ministry of Edward Last (1891-1900), it detailed thirty of its members to work with the Pioneer Mission (a national evangelistic church planting mission) to establish a cause in the rapidly growing tenement areas straggling up the Maryhill Road. The new church was constituted in 1897 with fifty members. Initially it occupied various halls including Maryhill Burgh Hall, but in 1903 it erected a hall at Queen Margaret Drive, North Kelvinside. A church seating 550 people was added in 1908, when membership had reached one hundred.[23]

In the eastern part of the city even the conservative John Street Church became alive to the need to evangelize. As early as 1855, it had had outreach Sunday Schools and preaching stations, but in 1886 it built its own mission hall for Sunday Schools and gospel services at St James Road, Cowcaddens. Frederick Street also established a mission at Balmano Street in 1889. The dynamic Bridgeton congregation, once it had become established, by 1889 was holding mission services in Rutherglen, where a group of its members lived. In 1893, members of this congregation detached themselves from Bridgeton and formed a church meeting in the lesser Town Hall. It grew rapidly despite a split in 1901, when a second 'West Baptist Church' was formed. By 1911, Rutherglen Baptist Church had 161 members. Growth continued, not least through the ministry of the controversial Charles Donald (the promoter of the Hutchesontown congregation), who was pastor from 1907 to 1914. The West Church, however, reunited with it in 1915.[24]

Finally, the Dumbarton Church contributed to church planting in similar vein during this period. It was not large, nor had it been long established, when its third pastor, John McLean, who ministered between 1884 and 1889, developed an evangelistic ministry in the surrounding area. In 1887, he and some of his members who lived in the district organized mission meetings in the Vale of Leven. The church, a rich donor and the Home Mission together raised sufficient money to a fund a missionary for three years. Their efforts led to the formation of a string of three Baptist Churches, one in the Leven Valley at Ferry Loan which met in an iron hall and was known as 'the Wee Tin Kirk', and the others at Bonhill and Susannah Street, Alexandria. In 1907, the Ferry Loan and Susannah Street meetings amalgamated and in 1908 the other church joined them in a single cause. In 1911, the church found its present home when it took over the premises of an old United Presbyterian Church at Bridge Street, Alexandria.[25]

In 1889, shortly before he moved to Victoria Place, Glasgow, John McLean also organized a new mission church in Clydebank. This quickly developed and was constituted a church in 1890 with about fifty members. It called a pastor in 1892 and built the current premises in Alexander Street in 1894. Membership grew steadily to 142 members in 1911.[26]

Several churches began during the period as independent missions, again serving the industrial communities developing within Glasgow. The Evangelism Committee of the Baptist Union identified the need to plant a Baptist Church in Springburn in 1891 and started regular services in a hall in Station Road. This progressed into the formation of a church of twenty-seven members in 1892.[27] Progress was good, membership being 162 by 1901, and the church needed larger premises. An iron hall was acquired initially, but then, in 1904, the church erected its own building, funded in part by gifts from the proprietor of the nearby Caledonian Railway Works. An independent evangelistic mission was started in Govanhill in 1896 that only at a later stage became Baptist. This became Hermon Baptist Church, located in Cathcart Road, in 1923.[28]

The Pioneer Mission also was significant in planting two churches. It supported a young preacher and evangelist John Harper in his efforts to commence a Baptist evangelistic mission in 1895. This centred on the Gordon Halls in Paisley Road and soon a church of twenty-five members was formed, known as Paisley Road Baptist Church, with Harper as pastor. The need quickly arose to build a church and a site was acquired in the Plantation dockside district of Kinning Park, on which, in 1901, an iron hall seating 600 was built, funded in part by the Pioneer Mission. Growth was such (by 1905, the Church had 445 members!) that this hall needed extensions, which were completed in 1905, accommodating a further 400 people. A permanent church building was then planned but the lack of resources of this working people's mission and the intervention of the First World War delayed its construction until 1921.[29]

In Whiteinch, another working-class riverside community on the north side of the Clyde, the Pioneer Mission also developed a Baptist cause in 1906. It started with but fourteen members using the Whiteinch Burgh Hall for services. In 1908, an iron hall was built and growth of the congregation ensued to a membership of one hundred by 1910.[30]

By the outbreak of the First World War, the Baptists in Glasgow and Dunbartonshire had established a church in all communities of any size following a considerable and sustained effort of mission, particularly since 1880. Baptists had proved themselves to be responsive to the rapid growth of the communities of the industrial conurbation, not least in establishing missions in the most deprived working-class areas of Glasgow. Twenty-seven churches and five missions were in existence, which should have formed a strong base for further advance once the World War was over. This, however, was not to be.

Consolidation, 1914-1945

Glasgow and its surrounding towns entered a new era once hostilities commenced in the autumn of 1914. All resources focused on the war effort and building stopped in the city. The economy boomed as the steel, engineering and shipbuilding industries tried to keep up with the requirements of the armed services. When the war ended there was a brief reconstruction boom, but then economic slump in those same industries ensued until re-armament in preparation for the Second World War renewed demand. The general economic depression halted population growth and remarkably, compared with the Victorian era, the population of Glasgow remained at about the same level for thirty years. Such growth as took place from excess of births over deaths was counteracted by emigration to places of greater economic opportunity such as southern and midland England, the United States and Canada.

Within Glasgow, however, shifts of population were taking place. The housing within the 'inner city' was becoming notorious for its insanitary and overcrowded condition. Glasgow Corporation had new powers through a succession of housing acts to deal with it and the task was tackled with energy. Slum clearance schemes took place in the Calton, Mile End, Anderston, Cowcaddens and Gorbals districts, whilst new tenements were built in Possilpark, Springburn, Maryhill, Yorkhill, Parkhead and Polmadie. More imaginatively, new garden suburbs were built to provide attractive and spacious housing on the edge of the city at Yoker, Whiteinch and Knightswood in the west, Mosspark and Craigton in the south-west and Riddrie and Sandyhills in the east. Glasgow's inner-city population dropped by one fifth whilst the city continued to spread. Private housing developers made some contribution to the city's growth in new fringe garden suburbs in Cathcart, King's Park, Giffnock, Netherlee and Bearsden.

Within this context, Baptist progress faltered. The mood of the nation after the shocks of the First World War and rising materialism resulted in people becoming noticeably less receptive to the message of the gospel, and churches had diminished zeal for worship and evangelism. The heavy casualties amongst Scottish regiments in the First World War deprived many churches of the rising generation of male leaders. Constant economic hardship also limited the resources churches had to pay their pastors and keep their buildings. Funds were less available for mission. The halting of population growth reduced the need to plant churches. The result was that membership of Baptist Churches, which had peaked in 1921, remained at about the same level throughout this period.

An overall static situation conceals the fact that many changes were taking place within church life. Inner-city population decline was reflected in most of the central churches, and it soon began to appear that there were too many. All the central city churches lost numbers. Bridgeton and John Street had less than half the members in 1941 that they had possessed in 1921. Cambridge Street, Victoria Place and John Knox Street also lost significant numbers. Kelvinside declined, probably because its ministry was not consistent and because it was overshadowed by the extremely vigorous Hillhead Church not far away, which was experiencing a halcyon era. One inner-city church closed: the small mission cause at Hutchesontown, which had been losing numbers steadily since 1900. It did not appear to survive the dislocations of the First World War. The picture of deprivation so well known in Govan and highlighted there by the work amongst the unemployed of Dr George MacLeod was reproduced widely in other Clydeside industrial communities. Clydebank, Govan and Cambuslang Churches all experienced sharp decline, probably because of the extreme economic depression of their local communities at the time.

Several of the inner-city churches remained static. Harper Memorial and Adelaide Place retained their numbers through their vigorous evangelism and strong ministry, despite the population decline in their immediate areas. Queen's Park, Rutherglen and Partick Churches all had hinterlands that were growing in population and so they retained their membership.

Expanding churches tended to be in areas of population growth such as Springburn, Whiteinch, Kirkintilloch, Dunoon, Dumbarton and Dennistoun. Hillhead was the exception. Though in a static or slowly declining part of Glasgow, its membership grew by over 250 during this time as it became one of the major centres for evangelism and fine preaching in the city during the ministry of Dr John MacBeath (1929-42).

The new housing areas being developed on the fringe of Glasgow attracted concern and mission by the existing Baptist community. Soon after the war, attention was given to the needs of the growing southern suburbs around Cathcart and Muirend. Effort by members of Queen's Park Baptist Church, supported by the Glasgow Baptist Association, enabled a new church to be formed at Cathcart in 1923, meeting in the Couper Institute. Funds from the Baptist Union Twentieth Century Fund and churches in the Glasgow Baptist Association permitted the purchase of a site at Merrylee Road and the building of a hall in 1925. Thomas Stewart, the secretary of the Baptist Union at the time, was also interim minister for the church's first three years.[31]

This momentum of joint effort between the association and the Union was continued when several Baptist families who had recently moved into the new Glasgow Corporation garden suburb of Mosspark in the south-west of the city sought assistance to develop a new church. While still meeting in a house, a church was formed in 1924. Local halls and a school were used until, in 1925, a building was opened in Corkerhill Road. Loans for the building and grant aid towards a stipend for a pastor were provided by the Baptist Union whilst the Glasgow Baptist Association raised funds to pay off the debt on the building.[32]

Glasgow Corporation had commenced another major garden suburb on the north side of the River Clyde in the green fields west of Anniesland Cross in 1925. This major scheme, soon to be known as Knightswood, constituted a new challenge to Baptist witness. Soon Baptist families were moving into the new housing, and, supervised by J.A. Campbell of the John Street Church, services were begun in a hall opposite Knightswood Hospital in 1927. The Baptist Union took over responsibility for the work in 1929, seconding T.A. McQuiston, the Baptist Union evangelist, to superintend the work. A site for a church was soon secured at Knightswood Cross and a building was opened in November 1929. Seventy-four members formed the church, a group which grew rapidly to 200 by 1941.[33] The progress made in developing these churches by joint effort was not sustained in other corporation estates such as those at Riddrie, Possilpark/Milton or Craigton. This may be a reflection of a lack of resources or the fact that in each case a Baptist Church was not too far away.

In the 1930s, the main progress was in the formation of three small and struggling churches in the growing privately developed suburbs on the south side of Glasgow. Within the Glasgow boundary, a church commenced in King's Park and was constituted in 1934. Further out, a small Baptist cause was started at Stamperland, Clarkston, in 1937. It met in homes and then occupied a succession of premises in the district including a private school, a tea room, a Scout Hall and then Stamperland Institute. It was to acquire its own hall only in 1955.[34] Another Baptist Church was briefly established in Giffnock from 1938, but this fellowship did not survive the adversities of the Second World War.

Thus in overall terms it can be said that the Baptists held their own in the inter-war years, albeit in adverse circumstances. Advance continued to be made in establishing fresh churches in new housing areas, though activity lost momentum as the period wore on, not least due to the very trying economic circumstances prevailing in Glasgow. The period of the Second World War provided many problems for church life with the absence of younger members in the forces, many ministers becoming chaplains, the blackout and military and civil use of buildings restricting activities. Three churches were actually badly damaged by bombing — John Street, Harper Memorial and Clydebank. The stress of the war formed inauspicious circumstances in which to face the future.

Decline and Recovery, 1945 to the Present

To the Victorian city fathers whose energies were centred on coping with the population explosion of Glasgow, it would have seemed incredible to see the city population dwindle year by year, as happened throughout the post-war period. In 1951, Glasgow was a 'million city' with 1,090,000 inhabitants; thirty years later, it scarcely topped the ¾ million mark at 760,000.

Two forces lie behind the stark statistics. The city's economic base soon started to crumble once the post-war reconstruction boom had run its course, and throughout the fifties and sixties its shipbuilding, engineering, locomotive and textiles industries steadily declined, as did its docks, warehouses and shopping centres. These trends became even worse in the seventies and eighties, only being counteracted by the rise in public services and office and other commercial employment. The inflow of light industries from England and the USA experienced in other parts of Scotland mostly bypassed the city. Its economic base shrank, leaving dereliction and a steady rise in unemployment. Population loss has followed as people have left to find job opportunities in England, the oil centres of the north-east and overseas.

Economic decline was accompanied by a deliberate effort at 'thinning out' the city during the late fifties and sixties. The appalling housing conditions of the inner city had not been solved and the corporation started a massive redevelopment programme in 1955 with the first scheme (Gorbals) being completed in 1958. Twenty-nine areas were to be dealt with. The task involved wholesale demolition and rebuilding of all the districts around the city centre (Anderston, Woodside, Townhead, Cowcaddens, Royston, Calton and Gorbals) as well as parts of Partick, Maryhill, Springburn, Whiteinch, Pollokshaws, Kinning Park, Govan and Bridgeton. Neighbouring authorities also drew up schemes in the centres of Clydebank, Dumbarton, Rutherglen and Cambuslang. Between 1958 and about 1975, this massive programme of demolition was substantially completed, allied with the removal of housing to insert new dual carriageway roads and motorways to ease the increasing pressure of traffic in the city and its surrounding towns.

Demolition was accompanied by an equally massive programme of new housing. Initially this took place in new estates on the fringe, but later it took the form of the organized transfer of people to New Towns around Glasgow (East Kilbride, Cumbernauld, Erskine, Irvine) and further afield (Livingston in West Lothian and Glenrothes in Fife). As the inner areas were cleared, so new housing was later built at a lower density to replace it. Glasgow thus declined in population but extended its area as the four large housing estates of Drumchapel, Pollok, Easterhouse and Castlemilk were built between 1952 and 1973 as well as lesser estates on the fringe around Springburn, Summerston, Knightswood, Hillington and Darnley. Rutherglen, Cambuslang, Dumbarton, Clydebank and the Vale of Leven towns also had their smaller equivalents.

As the century wore on and the better-off working people and middle classes gained higher living standards and different social aspirations, demand for private housing grew. The lack of available land in Glasgow itself and the opposition of the corporation initially drove the private developers to the fringe of the city and they proceeded to build on the green fields in Bearsden, around Milngavie, in Bishopbriggs and Kirkintilloch to the north of the city and in Whitecraigs, Newton Mearns and Cambuslang to the south. Latterly, new inner-city private housing developments have been taking place in some of the cleared sites within Glasgow.

This situation of dramatic urban upheaval and extension constituted an extremely unsettling context for church life and also offered a major challenge to the ability of Baptists to change, relocate and plant churches in new areas. Not only was the city in transition but also churches faced problems of increasing apathy towards spiritual matters, theological uncertainty, rising inflation and ageing buildings (mostly built in the last two decades of the nineteenth century). Strong faith and great vision were needed to cope with the demands.

At first, it appears that Baptists failed to meet this complex of challenges. There were serious losses to their numbers during the period. Membership stood at a peak for the century of 6,413 in 1941. By 1985, there had been a loss of 45% to 3,499. However, when one considers that the main centre of Baptist membership was in Glasgow, which lost 30% of its population in the same period, these losses do not seem quite as bad, particularly since the number of churches in existence in 1985 was about the same as in 1945.

The loss of population in Glasgow's centre and inner city took its toll on churches as members moved out to the fringes, to the New Towns or emigrated altogether. This was particularly marked in the later 1950s and 1960s. Most churches experienced a serious decline in that period. Typically, those that survived had half the members they possessed prior to the Second World War. Some fared even worse. Adelaide Place, for example, had lost 63% of its 1941 members by 1971. Even the churches in the more stable suburban areas where redevelopment was not proceeding such as Knightswood, Cathcart and Shettleston felt the draught. Of the existing churches in Glasgow only Mosspark, Hermon and King's Park remained stable, and, in the Leven Valley, the Dumbarton and Alexandria churches remained about the same. Some causes had to survive the trauma of the redevelopment of their buildings, notably the Govan and Springburn Churches, or the need to rebuild bomb-damaged buildings (Harper Memorial, John Street and Clydebank).

It was inevitable that there should be closures within the city centre and redevelopment areas. The historical development of churches in the early nineteenth century had left too many central churches, and their decline which had set in during the inter-war period was completed in the 1950s. John

Knox Street finally closed in 1959 as its building reached a state of disrepair and was bought up by Glasgow Corporation. Cambridge Street closed in 1963 and John Street in 1969 under similar circumstances. The proceeds of building acquisition were, however, used by the Baptist Union for other church building. For example, the John Knox Street money helped fund the Drumchapel Church and John Street's money paid for the Castlemilk building. In the redevelopment areas, Victoria Place (close to Hutchesontown and Gorbals) closed in 1959, Bridgeton in 1967, Whiteinch in 1962 and Kelvinside finally in 1982. Most of the congregations had long since moved away, though the Victoria Place remnant joined Queen's Park Baptist Church. Other losses were the inner-city missions of Hillhead Baptist Church — Partick, which closed in 1962, and Port Dundas, in 1958. Adelaide Place closed the St Clair Street Mission in 1952.

Only three churches existing before the war grew after it. The inner-city Queen's Park Baptist Church declined like the rest until the early 1970s, when, arising from a vigorous programme of evangelism, modernization of its organization and the strong ministries of Brunton Scott and Edwin Gunn, it embarked on a new era of steady growth. It gained 150 members between 1971 and 1985, few of them by transfer. Kirkintilloch Church has also grown steadily, reflecting strong leadership as well as the rise in the population of the town through the building of private housing estates. Helensburgh Church reflects similar trends, though the new private housing has accommodated not only Glasgow commuters but also the personnel of the growing naval establishments at Faslane and Holy Loch.

Seven new churches have been established in these years. The Baptist Churches of the city and the Union quickly became aware of the needs of the growing peripheral housing schemes Glasgow Corporation was building. The Pollok Church was the first to be established in 1952.[35] This started with twenty-four founder members and showed the wisdom of church planting in that it had grown to a peak of 202 members in 1958. James Findlay of the Dennistoun Church, alongside some members of Cathcart Baptist Church, developed a Sunday School and services in the Easterhouse estate in 1960 and soon formed a church, which also grew rapidly to one hundred members by 1969. Cathcart Baptist Church took responsibility for starting work in Castlemilk in 1961. Services and a Sunday School were first held in a school and then in the YMCA Hall. Despite faithful effort and the labours of the first pastor, A.L. Price, progress was slow and the church became firmly established only when it acquired its building in 1977.[36] Hillhead Church detached a group of its members and commenced a Sunday School, youth work and services in the northern part of Drumchapel in 1961, using Lochgoyne School. This emerged from the consideration of the future of the Partick Mission, where declining attendance at its organizations and worship were suggesting its days were numbered. The proposal was made to transfer the work to a new housing area and indeed the equipment as well as the proceeds of the sale of the Purdon Street Mission Hall helped provide for the new Drumchapel Baptist Church. This was formally constituted in 1962 and its building was opened in 1966.[37]

As private housing has been built in the suburbs around Glasgow, particularly in the late 1960s and 1970s, so Baptist members have moved out. Many have commuted back on Sundays to support their original churches in the city, but others have responded to the need for a local witness and three churches have emerged. In Bearsden, in 1973, a group of people from Adelaide Place and Hillhead Churches began to meet in a house and then in a converted community centre at Bearsden Cross. In 1975 they called their first pastor, G.H. Ritchie, and soon established a branch Sunday School and services at Castlehill in the western part of the town, where several estates have recently been developed. The church has grown rapidly through evangelism and attracting Evangelical Christians to a total of 148 members in 1985. At Bishopbriggs, a group who were originally members of various churches began meeting in homes and rented premises. In 1980, the fellowship built its own Church Centre complex, and by 1985 membership had risen to ninety-seven. Strongly committed to charismatic renewal, the church has developed a series of remarkable ventures including a small housing estate, a Christian Conference Centre and a complex of sheltered housing for the elderly. On the south side in the sprawling suburbs of Newton Mearns, Queen's Park (reflecting its own vigour) detached a group of its members to form a church in 1983. This grew rapidly to eighty-three members in 1985, appointing Deans Buchanan as first minister and identifying and acquiring a site for its own building.

The post-war period has been a time of trauma, change and challenge to the Baptist Churches, particularly in Glasgow. Apart from the pressures of increasing secularization, the period between 1955 and 1975, when vast swathes of the inner city were being demolished, caused a major crisis for the Victorian-built churches in their areas. Meanwhile, the massive developments of new housing, within the city by the corporation and outside by private developers, constituted another major challenge to be met by evangelism and church planting. One feels that those in leadership at this time in the Baptist Union, the Glasgow Baptist Association and the churches took good decisions. An orderly rationalization of the central churches took place , and the Adelaide Place decision to stay and minister to the central city needs was justified by subsequent success. Each new housing area has had a church planted, though the fellowships in the peripheral housing schemes have had a hard time after initial success. The surviving inner-city churches have begun to recover from the decline in membership of the sixties and, in any case, may soon be able to recoup the losses of the past as the renovation and rebuilding of the inner city bear fruit. The city population has begun to stabilize and may soon even begin to grow. It is not insignificant that overall membership of churches in the Glasgow Baptist Association has begun to increase again since 1980.

Retrospect and Prospect

The industrial cities of Great Britain have never been easy situations for the Christian Church. This has proved to be the case for the Baptists in Glasgow as much as anywhere else. The denomination had a late start in Scotland and its growth did not become substantial until the mid-nineteenth century. The achievements of the latter part of that century, however, could only be described as very remarkable and an important lesson in church planting and evangelism through the effort of individual churches and, in some cases, relocation. The 1920s demonstrated the value of inter-church and Baptist Union co-operation in setting about meeting the challenge of the new council estates. The 1960s and 1970s showed the need to accept the closure of a church in one area to focus resources and effort in areas of population growth and opportunity. Perhaps, however, more would have been achieved if churches had been less tenacious about their historic sites and even more ready to move. The lesson is extremely clear from the Glasgow experience that church planting brings real growth. Sensitive and visionary adjustment to the constantly changing urban scene brings real fruit for the kingdom.[38]

Notes

1. David Daiches, *Glasgow* (St Albans 1982), p 98.
2. George Yuille, ed, *History of the Baptists in Scotland* (Glasgow 1926), p 179.
3. Harry Escott, *A History of Scottish Congregationalism* (Glasgow 1960), pp 297-310.
4. Yuille, ed, *Baptists in Scotland*, p 180.
5. ibid, p 181.
6. ibid, p 173.
7. ibid, p 192.
8. *Dumbarton Baptist Church Centenary Souvenir Programme, 1976* (Dumbarton 1976).
9. Escott, *Scottish Congregationalism*, pp 297-310.
10. Adelaide Place Baptist Church Minute Books, 1871-1877.
11. Yuille, ed, *Baptists in Scotland*, p 174.
12. G.H. Ritchie, *Bridgeton Baptist Church: these hundred years, 1860-1960* (Glasgow 1960), pp 7-9.
13. Yuille, ed, *Baptists in Scotland*, p 186.
14. Alexander Clark, *Cambridge Street Baptist Church, 1862-1924: a historical sketch* (Glasgow 1924), pp 2-6.
15. W.W. Murray, *Queen's Park Baptist Church: a history of the church's first hundred years* (Glasgow 1978), pp 9-25.
16. Anne M. Semple, *At Work in the World: the centenary booklet of Hillhead Baptist Church* (Glasgow 1983), pp 3-5.
17. *Dumbarton Centenary.*
18. Yuille, ed, *Baptists in Scotland*, p 192.
19. *Dunoon Baptist Church Centenary Brochure* (Dunoon 1963).
20. Yuille, ed, *Baptists in Scotland*, p 175.

21. Adelaide Place Baptist Church Minute Books, 1878-1883.
22. Semple, *Work in the World*, pp 18-21.
23. Yuille, ed, *Baptists in Scotland*, p 182.
24. ibid, p 184.
25. John McDiarmid, *Vale of Leven Baptist Church History, 1887-1952* (Alexandria 1980).
26. Yuille, ed, *Baptists in Scotland*, p 191.
27. Dudley Reeves, *Consider the Years: Springburn Baptist Church, 1892-1967* (Glasgow 1967), pp 7-12.
28. Yuille, ed, *Baptists in Scotland*, p 176.
29. *Harper Memorial Baptist Church Souvenir Brochure, 1897-1947* (Glasgow 1947).
30. Yuille, ed, *Baptists in Scotland*, p 187.
31. G.M. Hardie, *Cathcart Baptist Church Semi-Jubilee Booklet, 1923-1948* (Glasgow 1948).
32. Stewart Crabb, *A History of Mosspark Baptist Church* (Glasgow 1974), pp 3-5.
33. *Knightswood Baptist Church: these twenty-five years* (Stirling 1954), pp 10-12.
34. William Kater, *Clarkston Baptist Church: Operation Hazard: prospecting for God* (Glasgow 1955), pp 1-5.
35. W.G. Pert, *Pollok Baptist Church Silver Jubilee Year, 1952-1977: 25 years of Christian witness* (Glasgow 1977).
36. Correspondence with the church secretary, Dr K.J. Baxendale, and information from Ronald Armstrong.
37. Semple, *Work in the World*, pp 25-6.
38. I am grateful for oral evidence from G.H. Ritchie, Dr C.D. Anderson and Dr D.B. Murray and for invaluable typing help from Ms Nan Cordiner.

D.R. Watts

10. LANARKSHIRE

Lanarkshire cannot be described as natural home territory to Baptists. It is entirely different from the historic centres of the Home Counties, West Country, East Anglia and the East Midlands. It is mainly industrial, developed in the last hundred or so years and predominantly working-class. Yet there are now sixteen churches possessing over 2,000 members. The churches have shown and still show vigour and vision, a group in a county that had but three churches and 300 members a century ago.

The Background, 1800–1870

Lanarkshire was a 'boom' county in the early and middle part of the nineteenth century. When the century began, it was almost entirely a farming area, the biggest settlement (apart from Glasgow) being the county town, Lanark, with 4,700 people. Industrial development was just beginning in the north-west corner along the new Monkland canal which linked the coalfield with Glasgow. Collieries and ironstone quarries were being developed on a small scale, a harbinger of the future economic base of the county.

The transformation of the county was begun through the development of iron quarrying and coal mining. By 1851 there were 139 collieries employing 16,000 people. Then came in succession an iron industry and a steel industry of increasing scale. These spawned railway wagon building and various engineering industries throughout the coalfield area. Industrial growth drew workers from all over Scotland, from Ireland and from England. The county's population multiplied from 60,000 in 1801 to 204,000 in 1871, that is by three and a half times. By 1871, the towns of Airdrie, Coatbridge and Wishaw had about 20,000 people each and the villages around Bothwell, such as Uddingston, Bellshill, Holytown and Carfin together had 20,000 people resident. This represented a rapid sprawl of housing spreading across the North Lanarkshire countryside amongst pits, quarries, iron works and factories, the whole area becoming interlaced by the new road and railway network. The rest of the county also grew in population, benefiting from the demands of the neighbouring conurbation for dairy produce and fruit.

The churches developed during this time quite quickly. Most progress was achieved by Presbyterians and Roman Catholics. In Coatbridge, for example, the pattern of provision was that the United Presbyterian Church, Church of Scotland and Free Church of Scotland built churches in 1839, 1836 and 1844 respectively and the Roman Catholics erected a chapel in 1848. The Episcopalians built a church in 1841 and the Congregationalists started in 1860.[1] In various permutations, this was a characteristic pattern throughout

MAP 10 : LANARKSHIRE BAPTIST CHURCHES.

Key to Map 10

1. Coatbridge: Lugar Street
2. Coatbridge: West Canal Street
3. Airdrie
4. Harthill
5. Uddingston
6. Bellshill
7. Shotts
8. Cleland
9. East Kilbride: East Mains
10. East Kilbride: Calderwood
11. High Blantyre
12. Hamilton
13. Motherwell
14. Wishaw
15. Cambusnethan
16. East Kilbride: Westwood
17. Larkhall
18. Carluke
19. Stonehouse
20. Lanark

the coalfield.

The Baptists were more or less unknown in the area at this time. As a denomination, if that is the right word, they composed a group of struggling, highly independent churches in Glasgow with little thought of evangelism to areas beyond. Their only contribution to the spiritual needs of the booming Lanarkshire area was indirect.

Robert Haldane founded a church jointly with John Calder in Airdrie that existed from 1817 for some years. This was revived in 1842 through the work of Francis Johnstone of Cupar, who was also secretary of the short-lived equivalent of the Baptist Union at the time. He led a mission which resulted in the adoption of Baptist views by the Congregational minister, James Taylor, and a part of his flock. This group built a church in 1843, but Taylor left for the pastorate of the newly formed Blackfriars Street Church in Glasgow. Thereafter, the Airdrie Church had a struggling existence until 1869 when it appointed a full-time pastor, William Fulton.[2] At this time, the fellowship remained small, with only sixty-one members, the only Baptist witness outside Glasgow in a county of 200,000 people. It would have seemed at that time unlikely that, within fifty years, these members would have risen to over 2,000 in fourteen churches.

Establishment, 1869–1921

The momentum of industrial growth continued through the development of coal, steel, engineering and related industries. In some parts of the North Lanarkshire coalfield, the pace of industry quickened, notably in the establishment of the major steelworks of such firms as Stewarts and Lloyds at Airdrie and Coatbridge, the Clydesdale Company at Bothwell, the Coltness Iron Company and Glasgow Iron Works at Wishaw and Colvilles in Motherwell.

The continued expansion of coal mines throughout the area from Bothwell to Shotts also added to the booming industrial conditions. The number of collieries grew from 151 in 1881 to 257 in 1895 and employment in coal mining quadrupled from 1851 to 1921. Population growth continued apace. The number of people in the villages round Bothwell tripled from 19,000 to 60,284 between 1871 and 1921. Shotts, Wishaw, Coatbridge, Blantyre and Larkhall doubled in size. Motherwell grew from a village of 9,175 in 1871 to a large town of 49,600 in 1921. Outside the coalfield, however, population grew only slowly. The county area (excluding what is now Glasgow) rose in population from 204,000 in 1871 to 457,000 in 1921, an increase of two and a half times.

Church development to match this urban growth was vigorous enough, with new churches being added steadily in new areas both by the Presbyterians and by new groups such as the Brethren, the Salvation Army and the Pentecostal Church of Scotland. Whilst the Presbyterians were uniting in stages, the non-Presbyterians fragmented. The atmosphere for non-Presbyterians was nevertheless improving as the west of Scotland benefited from the great increase in evangelism surrounding the Moody campaigns and their imitators.

This was a period of great vigour for the Baptists. They had broken out of a period of isolationist, introspective theology and had become an active evangelizing force. The Baptist Union's formation in 1869 was an expression of the new attitudes of the churches, which became more interested in church planting, mutual support, co-operative effort, training men for the ministry and the preaching of the gospel. This new fellowship and drive for evangelism brought results in Lanarkshire. Church formation came through three different sources: through the efforts of key individuals, through the outreach work of the Baptist Union and, most significantly, through offshoots of existing churches.

The first independently formed church was that at Coatbridge where, in the wake of the 1859 revival, a group of Evangelical believers gathered to study the Bible and worship together. Separate from the Presbyterian Churches, they were all convinced of the importance of believer's baptism. By 1869, the group was using a local Temperance Hall and had drawn in the assistance of William Fulton, the Baptist minister of Airdrie, and Baptist College students to take services.[3] By 1874 it had come under the direction of the Home Mission with an appointed evangelist, J.M. Hewson.[4] The church at High Blantyre emerged similarly from a small group of Evangelical believers in the village. Walter Wilson, a recently converted layman, had initially joined the Free Church but became exercised about the importance of believer's baptism and, with the help of A.A. Milne, the Cambuslang Baptist minister, formed in 1896 a church of fourteen members, meeting in the local Christian Institute.[5] In 1899, a group of sixteen members of other Baptist Churches in Uddingston village decided to form a church there. They were given pastoral oversight by W.J. Millar, the agent at the time for the Baptist Industrial Mission. By 1900, this group had fifty-four members and had managed to build its own iron hall.[6] In 1911, a group similarly came together in Lanark, gathered by the work of J.R. Chrystal, who had recently retired to live in the town from his long and successful ministry at Hamilton Baptist Church. By 1916, the church had become established enough to open its own building.[7]

The direct efforts of the Baptist Union were responsible for four churches in the county. In 1871, three Baptist families who had just moved to Wishaw from Glasgow appealed to the Baptist Union to help them start a church. The Union responded by providing them with the services of J.M. Campbell, whose work quickly led to the constitution of a church of twenty-seven members in 1872. The church used public halls until 1875, when a building was constructed with the aid of the Union's funds.[8] In 1886, in Hamilton, the Baptist Union and Home Mission jointly invited J.R. Chrystal to commence work to form a Baptist Church. Chrystal was a local Church of Scotland minister who had recently become convinced of the importance of believer's baptism and so had left his charge. His work soon bore fruit and a church was formed in the same year with twenty-seven members.[9] The churches in Shotts and Larkhall also emerged as the direct work of the Evangelistic Committee of the Baptist Union. Shotts began in 1908, when the Union appointed a pastor-evangelist, J.S. Russell, to conduct outreach in the village.[10] Services were launched at Larkhall in 1918, and in the following year, with support from Hamilton, a church was formed with twenty-two members.[11]

Four churches and one mission emerged in Lanarkshire as the result of the work of existing churches. Of particular significance was the work of George Whittet, the energetic minister of Wishaw Baptist Church from 1876 to 1917. His evangelism soon stretched beyond the village into surrounding districts. In 1882, this work led to the formation of a group in Motherwell which became a constituted church of thirty-seven members in 1887.[12] Monthly Sunday afternoon services conducted by Whittet led in 1889 to the start of a church in Carluke, which had its own building and pastor by the next year.[13] A further outreach emerged in about 1900 when the Wishaw Church started a Sunday School, women's meetings and services in halls in Cambusnethan.[14] The evangelistic vision that had resulted in the Motherwell Church was not lost once that church became established, for within six years of its formation, a group of its members living in Bellshill decided to start a cause in their village. Initially, the Motherwell minister, John Connor, gave assistance, but the new church soon appointed its own pastor. By 1900, it had erected its own building.[15] The Shotts Church, hardly established itself, spawned in 1917 an offshoot of five members in Harthill, to the east of the town. The pastor and various members from Shotts established this church, which met initially in a school and then purchased its own hall.[16]

Once established, these churches enjoyed a period of steady growth. They set to the development of their organizations, the elimination of the debt on their buildings and the support of their pastors. A typical example is Hamilton. From a founder membership of twenty-seven in 1886, it had grown to eighty by 1891 and then trebled within twenty years. Initially, the congregation rented a hall, then purchased a disused church before finally erecting a new building for 600 with a suite of halls in 1909.[17] All increased membership quickly, with the churches in the largest towns rising to well over

200 by the time the First World War broke out. Motherwell and Wishaw had 368 and 312 members in 1921, Coatbridge had 215, Bellshill 230, Airdrie 215 and Hamilton 243. One can attribute this development to the vigour of the congregations, but it must not be forgotten that they were situated in areas where the population was growing rapidly. Most churches, however, grew more rapidly in percentage terms than the local population. The only development to mar this scene of co-operation, growth and activity was that in 1900 the church at Coatbridge split, with forty or so members breaking away to form the Coats Church meeting in Lugar Street.[18]

By 1921, there were fourteen churches in Lanarkshire with no fewer than 2,091 members. All major settlements in the county now had a Baptist Church, and it may have been thought that the advance would continue after the war. This was not to be the case, for a number of reasons.

The Twenties and Thirties

The industrial scene changed quite abruptly after the First World War. A reconstruction period until 1922 brought a false dawn, but during the remainder of the period the local economy plunged into a period of closures, sackings and industrial strife. The steel and heavy engineering industries cut production and rationalized plant so that by 1939 Bairds, Colvilles and the Shipbuilders' Consortium owned most of the main works in the area. One major steel company, Stewarts and Lloyds, moved a major part of its works from Coatbridge to Corby in Northamptonshire in 1935. The local coalfields were becoming exhausted and some, like those around Larkhall and Hamilton, had entirely closed. The 210 collieries open in 1920 had declined to seventy-eight by 1954. Few new industries sprang up to replace the old. Unemployment spread. This industrial scene reversed the pre-war population growth. A rising number of people left the area (130,000, 1921-51). Broadly, the population hovered at about 500,000 between 1921 and 1951. The churches were all affected by this time of decline and unemployment, which was compounded by a growing materialism and a different attitude to spiritual matters that affected the life of the nation as a whole after the First World War.

Baptist witness likewise faltered. The general disruption caused by the First World War had done damage and many of the churches forfeited some of their most promising young men in the carnage of the Western Front. Motherwell Church, for example, lost twelve young men in the war and Wishaw thirteen. The impact of rising unemployment and general trade depression had very tangible results too. Most churches experienced a steady drain of members through emigration, generally to Canada or Australia. In some cases, it was nearly catastrophic, as for example in 1923, when Wishaw lost over a hundred members in the one year due to the closure of two iron and steel works in the town.[19] Most churches found finance tight, and they generally struggled to find even sufficient to pay their pastors. The smaller churches, in particular, experienced hardship, and help had to be sought from the Baptist Union. The consequences of these trends were that church membership in general in Lanarkshire remained static and only one new church was formed.

Within this overall picture, there are some interesting variations. Most churches in the main coalfield area — Airdrie, Coatbridge, High Blantyre, Bellshill, Wishaw and Carluke — remained about the same size. This can be regarded as quite an achievement considering the emigration that was taking place. Vigorous ministries and consistent evangelistic effort were resulting in a steady stream of baptisms and new members which was counteracting the losses from people leaving. The Motherwell and Hamilton Churches, however, experienced sharp decline. Motherwell bore the brunt of the industrial decay in the area, and it was also suffering from a movement of population to the outskirts of the town. The Hamilton Baptist Church had a different story. Under the successful ministry of George Douglas the church grew steadily from 1921 to 1930. In 1931, however, the congregation removed him from the pastorate, a decision that resulted in mass resignations. Of the membership of 304 in 1930, only 120 were left in the following year. T.W. Lister, a retired minister, stepped in to help the church through the crisis, and the subsequent pastor, R.F. Conway, called in 1934, helped rebuild the congregation.[20] By the time he left in 1940, membership had recovered to 240.

The difficulties of the time did result in some withdrawal of work. Wishaw carried on its Cambusnethan Mission for much of the period, but eventually closed it. The small church at Harthill did not fulfil its initial promise and was finally closed in 1938. The Coats Church in Coatbridge also closed in 1924, re-uniting with its parent.

On the other hand, Lanarkshire Baptists did continue to grow in some areas. A new church was established in Cleland in 1935, when members of the Wishaw Baptist Church took over a vacated Congregational Mission, revived its work and purchased the property.[21] Growth also took place in the small churches that had been established just before the First World War — notably Shotts, Larkhall and Lanark. Shotts had no stability of ministries, but nevertheless grew from a membership of sixty in 1921 to just over 200 by the outbreak of the Second World War. Its iron hall became inadequate and in 1935 it converted an old cinema into a permanent building. Larkhall grew steadily from 1923 when it first obtained a full-time minister. Support was given until 1937 by the Baptist Union in a contribution to the minister's stipend and loans for its building. Lanark had a chequered history. Its strong start in the early 1920s faltered to a point where it ran only a Sunday School in 1931. Thereafter its work was rebuilt so that by 1938 it had advanced to a position of having seventy-two members. Uddingston maintained a vital witness during the whole period through successive ministries, but particularly through the outstanding work of A.D. Law between 1928 and 1945. The strength of the fellowship was such that, despite the financial strains of the time, when its temporary building had become so dilapidated that it threatened to be unusable in 1933, the congregation managed to raise sufficient funds to rebuild it the following year.[22]

Overall, the Baptist Churches just about held their own during this time despite the economic problems of the period and the steady emigration. Wartime and the period thereafter were to bring an improved position in employment, but also an acceleration of secularization and more movements in population.

The Second World War to the Present

Industrial prosperity returned as the Lanarkshire coal, iron, steel and engineering industries contributed to the manufacture of armaments, which grew rapidly from 1936. After the war the slump in production in these industries hit Lanarkshire, but not too badly, as the area received an infusion of new industry from England and the USA, resulting in particular from the regional assistance policies of the Attlee Government. A key focus of industry became the New Town of East Kilbride, designed to cater for Glasgow's overspill population and to function as a growth point for the area. New places of work were created by the government's Industrial Estates Corporation at Coatbridge, Newhouse, Bellshill, Blantyre, Bothwell, Carfin, Chapelhall and Larkhall. Major factory developments took place at Shotts and there was investment in the steel industry at Ravenscraig, Clydesdale, Gartcosh and the Coatbridge works. A wide range of new light industries was also attracted. These included aerospace, electronics, commercial vehicles, clothing, confectionery, precision engineering and pharmaceuticals. The resulting employment opportunities were counteracted by the continued loss of jobs in the coalfields, where the seventy-eight pits existing in 1954, providing 10% of the jobs in the county, had all closed by 1983. The general momentum of growth gradually petered out as the industries moving into the county steadily declined. Unemployment began to rise in the 1970s as some of the post-war industries joined the traditional engineering, steel and coal industries in their story of closure and redundancies.

Housing developments took place on a considerable scale, to some extent reflecting this industrial transformation. There were three significant changes. First, Glasgow's need for housing overspill to relieve its overcrowding led to the building of East Kilbride New Town. This started in 1948 and by 1981 had 81,000 people. Secondly, the burghs, the National Coal Board and Lanarkshire County Council put great effort into replacing the poor mining cottages hastily built in such large numbers during the development of the coalfield. This led to the emergence of many small housing estates on the periphery of Coatbridge, Motherwell and Hamilton and between Bellshill and Shotts. Thirdly, new social trends favouring home ownership have encouraged housing developers to build private estates in various areas of existing towns and villages such as Motherwell, Hamilton and Uddingston to cater for people unable to find private housing in Glasgow. Together these developments helped stabilize the population as a whole and caused some limited growth, notably in East Kilbride.

The churches have been active in responding to shifts in population. In 1960, it was noted that since the war, nine new Church of Scotland congregations had been formed in the county, four by relocation. At this time an estimate of church membership and congregations was as follows:

Church of Scotland:	173 congregations and 105,400 members
Roman Catholics:	48 congregations and 130,000 members
Others (excluding Baptists):	25 congregations and 10,400 members
Baptists:	15 congregations and 2,200 members

East Kilbride was a special focus of activity. By 1960, this New Town had four Church of Scotland parishes and Episcopalian, Roman Catholic, Church of Christ and Congregational Churches.[23] The New Town also became a focus for work and development by the Baptists.

Initially, no church was intended by the Baptist Union because it did not wish to compete with the Churches of Christ which had already started work and were similar in theology and practice. The Lanarkshire Association, however, took a different view and pledged finance and support from its ministers to start a Baptist Church in the new town.[24] Eventually, a new Baptist witness in East Kilbride emerged in 1952 through the work of a joint extension committee representing the Union, the Lanarkshire Baptist Association and the Cambuslang and Rutherglen Baptist Churches. Meetings were held in the town to gauge interest and visitation was carried out by members of surrounding churches (notably Cathcart and High Blantyre). Services began in the YMCA hall. Initially it was hard going, but then a student pastor, James Graham (now of Gold Hill Baptist Church, Buckinghamshire), was found to help develop the congregation. In 1954, twenty-four members constituted the church. In 1955, the first full-time pastor, Peter Barber, was called. Rapid growth in membership ensued as he and the congregation seized the opportunity offered by the growing town. After using several community halls, in 1960 the church finally acquired its own building, a surplus Church of Scotland parish church in the old village of East Mains. By this time it had 170 members. In 1964, services were begun in the district of Westwood at Canberra School, by the original Baptist Church, which sent a section of its congregation to start the new work. A second church was soon constituted in 1965 with a full-time minister, Alex Rodger, and it achieved sufficient momentum to be able to erect its own building in 1968, supported by aid from the Baptist Union. The impetus was maintained with the two other churches co-operating in 1966 to form a third congregation in Calderwood through holding services in Allens School. Soon Calderwood acquired a pastor, James Hamilton, who was inducted in 1971. The church was constituted in 1974, and a new building was opened in 1976 with eighty-three members.[25] In 1976, a further church was considered for the East Kilbride satellite town of Stonehouse, and meetings were held for a time. These were abandoned when the proposals to extend the New Town were dropped soon after. It is a measure of the achievement of these congregations, the vision of the first minister and the backing given by the Baptist Union that by 1981 the churches in East Kilbride had 470 members, apart from large numbers of young people and children. This strength now amounts to one quarter of the total membership of the Lanarkshire Baptist Churches.

The other congregations in Lanarkshire had varying fortunes. Most churches lost members after the war as the disruption caused by the great shift of people had its impact. Many who had gone to the forces for the war never returned, finding jobs in more prosperous parts of Britain or overseas. Some returned from the war but did not go back to their churches. Nevertheless some causes experienced steady growth. Hamilton Baptist Church is the most notable case. The effect of its pre-war difficulties seemed to linger as membership dipped sharply to a new low of 137 in 1952 (from, it will be recalled, 304 in 1930). Thereafter membership remained about the same until the late 1960s when, through a combination of effective leadership, capable preaching and wide-ranging evangelism under the pastorates of Gordon Heath (1969-76) and Alastair Begg (1977-83), the church grew rapidly to its 1985 size of 374 members.[26] A similar pattern can be seen in Carluke and Cleland, where there were static numbers in the 1950s and 1960s, but where marked growth has taken place since about 1971.

Coatbridge, Larkhall, Bellshill, Airdrie and High Blantyre Churches have held their own with fluctuating but broadly static memberships during the whole period. These towns have been at the heart of the considerable changeover of employment and housing in the Lanarkshire coalfield, yet have managed to attract new members and converts to compensate for those who inevitably move elsewhere from areas such as these.[27]

The remaining fellowships have gone into decline. Both the large churches of the Motherwell area, in central Motherwell and Wishaw, have lost members quite considerably, not least as a result of the growing crisis of jobs in the area as steel plants have shed capacity. Shotts Baptist Church, which had grown to 215 members by 1951 following its firm establishment in the 1930s, has gradually declined. Despite vigorous ministries and gains made through evangelism, there has been a steady loss of numbers as the coal mines have been run down and closed with consequent transfers, notably to Fife.[28] Uddingston's history is somewhat similar. Its membership, which tended to hover around one hundred during the 1950s and 1960s, has gradually fallen in the 1970s to its 1985 figure of fifty-four. Likewise Lanark after its great vigour in the 1930s has steadily decreased in strength.

A key problem in most areas was that because the churches had mostly been built at the peak of nineteenth-century development in new town or village centres, they were now, as a result of changing housing patterns, becoming isolated from the main concentrations of population. In some towns such as Motherwell and Coatbridge, local authority housing redevelopment has taken place and removed the local residential areas from which congregations drew many members, adherents and children. Private developers and local authorities have recently built large new estates well away from the churches' location. The only solution has been for churches to reach out to these new housing estates, and many congregations organized Sunday Schools in an effort to reach the people who lived there. The longest running effort has been the work at Townhead, on the north-west side of Coatbridge, which has been going for thirty years or so. Airdrie Baptist Church similarly has had various Sunday Schools in parts of the town during the period. Currently there are two. Motherwell has had Sunday Schools at Ladywell (on the north-west side of the town) and in 1980 it established its outreach in a house in North Motherwell, providing a playgroup, youth club and Sunday School. Hamilton established a Sunday School at Udston Primary School in the Hillhouse area in the 1960s, transferring it to Townmill more recently. High Blantyre has established a similar outreach Sunday School in another part of its area. At various times in the 1950s and 1960s, Carluke, Shotts and Bellshill also ran Sunday Schools in outlying parts. None of these efforts has, however, issued in a 'daughter church' as has been the case (and deliberate intent), for example, in East Kilbride. In retrospect, it can be seen that the establishment of nothing but Sunday Schools, intended to feed the main churches with new converts, did not really work, not least because most of the housing estates in which these efforts were made soon contained relatively few children. The lesson from history is that growth comes from deliberate church planting and a specific effort to develop work amongst all ages.

Conclusion

Despite a late start, the Baptists took root in Lanarkshire and now have a strong network of churches through the northern industrial part of the county. The creation of a Baptist witness in East Kilbride is an inspiration to any interested in evangelism and demonstrates that Baptists are capable of building strong churches in rapidly growing urban areas in a secular society.

Issues remain. Lanarkshire churches have yet to grasp the needs of *declining* industrial areas where the dominant mood is economic gloom and out-migration. Many are beginning to become isolated from these spreading communities. They may need to develop a more radical and flexible approach in order to reach the new private housing estates and the increasingly deprived peripheral local authority housing schemes.[29]

Notes

1. Andrew Miller, *The Rise and Progress of Coatbridge and Surrounding Neighbourhood* (Coatbridge 1896).
2. George Yuille, ed, *History of the Baptists in Scotland* (Glasgow 1926), pp 214-15.
3. S. McCarroll, 'A Brief Summary of Some Events extracted from the History of Coatbridge Baptist Church' (Typescript 1969), pp 1-2.
4. Edward Campbell, 'Coatbridge Baptist Church' (Typescript n.d.).
5. *Cameos of Our Church: the jubilee of High Blantyre Baptist Church, 1896-1946* (Blantyre n.d.), pp 3-5.
6. *Uddingston Baptist Church Jubilee Souvenir, 1899-1949* (Uddingston n.d.), pp 4-5.
7. Yuille, ed, *Baptists in Scotland*, p 220.
8. *Wishaw Baptist Church* (Wishaw 1971), pp 7-8.
9. *'Surely the Lord is in This Place': Hamilton Baptist Church: Golden Jubilee of church building, 1909-1959* (Hamilton 1959), p 3.
10. *Shotts Baptist Church, 1908-1958, Jubilee Celebrations Souvenir Programme*. Yuille, ed, *Baptists in Scotland*, p 222.
11. *Fifty Years of Witness: Larkhall Baptist Church Jubilee, 1919-1969* (Larkhall 1969). Yuille, ed, *Baptists in Scotland*, p 220.
12. *One Hundred Years of Baptist Witness in Motherwell, 1882-1982* (Motherwell 1982), p 5.
13. Yuille, ed, *Baptists in Scotland*, p 216.
14. *Wishaw Baptist Church*, p 9.
15. Yuille, ed, *Baptists in Scotland*, pp 215-16.
16. ibid, pp 218-19.
17. *'Surely the Lord'*, pp 3-4.
18. Yuille, ed, *Baptists in Scotland*, pp 217, 277.
19. *Wishaw Baptist Church*, pp 12-13.
20. D.B. Murray, *The First Hundred Years: the Baptist Union of Scotland* (Glasgow 1969), p 101. *Scottish Baptist Year Book*, 1931-5.
21. Information from Mr D.S. Marshall, church secretary.
22. *Uddingston Baptist Church*, p 14.
23. George Thomson, ed, *The Third Statistical Account of Scotland: The County of Lanark* (Glasgow 1960), pp 124-7, 441-3.
24. Personal communication from the Rev. J.M. Dines.
25. J.I.D. Hamilton *et al.*, 'East Kilbride Baptist Church Silver Jubilee, 1954-1979' (Typescript 1979).
26. Personal communication from Messrs D.R. Quinn and J.H. Thomson, Hamilton Baptist Church.
27. Personal communication from the Rev Hugh Robinson.

28. Personal communication from Mr Henry Inglis, church secretary.
29. I am grateful to Mrs S. Lindsay for typing support.

D.R. Watts

11. CENTRAL

The area covered by the Central Baptist Association, coinciding roughly with Central Region, lies between Strathclyde and Lothian Regions and owes something to both. Barring Cumbernauld, all of the churches affiliated in 1986 fall within what was once either Stirlingshire or Clackmannanshire. The major dividing line is not one of local government, however, but the natural barrier of the River Forth. Cumbernauld towards the western boundary was once a Dunbartonshire village, but is now a Glasgow overspill New Town. Bo'ness to the east, looking more to the mining communities of the Lothians, has been a coal-exporting town since medieval times.

The major population centres within the region are Stirling, Falkirk, Grangemouth and Alloa. While Stirling has long been important for military and administrative reasons, Falkirk, Alloa and Grangemouth are all products of nineteenth-century industrial development. Falkirk particularly has been described as a nineteenth-century 'boom town', and between 1871 and 1901 tripled in size, largely due to the success of the Carron Iron Works, once the largest iron foundry in the world. Modern Scottish history has been dated from the founding of the Carron Company in 1759.[1] Grangemouth, once the port for Falkirk's industry, has become a major petrochemical centre, and has nearly doubled in population within the past sixty years.[2] Alloa, the principal burgh north of the Forth, prospered with the fortunes of textiles, mining, brewing and related service industries. Its once busy harbour, plagued with problems of mud banks, eventually closed in 1962.[3]

The smaller towns have reflected the varying fortunes of their larger neighbours. North of the Forth, Tillicoultry and Alva grew with the yarn and woollen trades, and, like Alloa, also had local brewing.[4] Denny and Larbert south of the river shared in Falkirk's ironfounding. The Denny area has had coal mining, brewing and paper mills, benefiting from the proximity of the Forth and Clyde Canal. Larbert also owes much to the 'Falkirk Tryst', a massive livestock and trading fair once held in the Larbert parish. Both Denny and Larbert are now primarily commuter towns for employment outwith the locality.

Baptist work in Central Region has experienced two periods of church planting and growth. The first period, in the nineteenth century, was the time of beginnings and rapid growth. Twenty-four churches and mission stations were established, nine of which remain. The second period commenced in the early 1960s. Since then four further churches have been founded, and church planting continues.

Baptist Beginnings

Although details are inevitably lost, there are certain clear points of comparison in the formation of the first two local Baptist Churches. In 1801 Stirling and Falkirk, with populations of 5,256 and 8,838 respectively,[5] had most potential for pioneering Baptist work. Despite this the causes were initially small and owed a great deal to Baptists from outwith the area. The first Stirling Church had contact with Archibald McLean from Edinburgh[6] and the Falkirk work was brought into being under the direct influence of the Haldanes.[7] Although plagued in early days by division, which at times led to multiple Baptist Churches in each town, both fellowships did eventually consolidate under strong leadership to form what became the present churches.

In 1805 a Scotch Baptist Church was formed in Stirling. Although this church was destined to remain small, other groups splitting off were responsible for forming another three Baptist Churches in the town. The parent church, after a number of moves, appears to have survived to about 1850, a few members transferring to the second cause.

In the period 1809-10 a group led by Peter Grant, a lawyer, left over a dispute regarding communion to form a church of 'English' Baptist practice. Without a building of their own, several moves were made before they settled in Murray Place in 1854.[8] This second group also had two splits. In 1839 a number of members including the pastor left to form another church. A further split, probably in 1844, again under Peter Grant, led to the brief existence of a fourth church in the town, meeting in the Guild Hall. In that year this fourth church, with sixteen members, was in fact larger than the second with thirteen.[9] The second church, however, strengthened by the return of the members of the fourth, was to be the enduring Baptist cause in Stirling. A major factor in this success was the commencement in 1850 of the first of two long and successful ministries. James Culross served for twenty years, being followed in 1870 by George Yuille, pastor for forty-three years.

The offshoot group of 1839 eventually moved to the outlying district of St Ninians, at one time reporting 51 members. In 1880, however, on the death of the pastor who had served since 1843, the church withdrew from the Baptist Union of Scotland and soon disappeared.[10]

A visit to Falkirk by the Haldane brothers in the late 1790s led in 1803 to the establishment of an Independent Church. In 1808 many of the members followed the Haldanes into Baptist views and formed the first Falkirk Baptist Church, which seems to have followed an 'English' Baptist pattern. Without

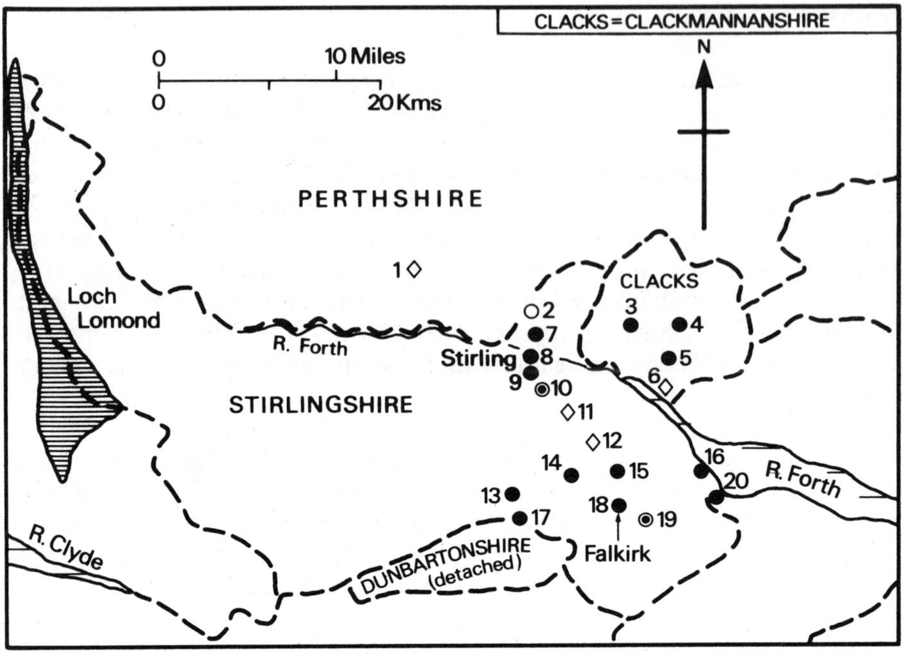

MAP 11 : CENTRAL BAPTIST CHURCHES.

Key to Map 11

1. Callander
2. Dunblane
3. Alva
4. Tillicoultry
5. Alloa
6. Kincardine
7. Cornton
8. Stirling
9. Stirling: Bible Baptist
10. St Ninians
11. Bannockburn
12. Plean
13. Banton
14. Denny
15. Larbert
16. Grangemouth
17. Cumbernauld
18. Falkirk
19. Polmont
20. Bo'ness

its own property, the church met first at Brown's Rooms and subsequently in Kirk Wynd. The first pastor was Daniel Dunbar, a local schoolteacher, who ministered for twenty-six years.[11]

By 1820, however, two additional Baptist Churches had come into being in Falkirk, both of the Scotch Baptist order. In 1826 these united into a single fellowship. Meanwhile the Kirk Wynd Church had split into two, and the proprietor of the Ship Inn where the church was meeting, anxious not to lose custom, added an extra storey for the breakaway group, complete with its own separate entrance! This new company became known, not surprisingly, as the 'Split Baptists'. In 1839 the Baptist Churches of Falkirk united under a Scotch Baptist pattern with forty-three members, and three years later a place of worship was opened in Callender Riggs. By 1850 membership had risen to sixty-three, including ten transfers from yet another Baptist Church, of unknown origins, which had become extinct. In 1864 the church decided to build again, this time in the Howgate. Part of the feu contract stated that the church would hold 'those views of Divine truth commonly called Arminian, in common with the "General Baptists" of England',[12] clearly departing from the Scotch Baptist tradition.

Despite this new building, part of the congregation remained in the Callender Riggs and attempts at union remained unsuccessful until 1868. The renewed union was short-lived due to a dispute over property, and the Callender Riggs congregation soon withdrew, leaving thirty members in the Howgate. The Howgate minister resigned soon after, feeling that the church could not support a paid pastor. In 1883 a union of the various Baptist groups in Falkirk did eventually take place, producing a single congregation with a membership of 107. Like the Stirling Church, it was greatly helped by a long and stable pastorate, that of Alexander Paterson, who served for thirty-three years (1889-1922). Early in this pastorate, in 1897, the church moved to its present site in Orchard Street. It was a measure of the success of the united Falkirk Baptist Church that by 1904 new halls and transepts were required, funded to a large extent by the proceeds of a three-day public bazaar in 1906.[13]

Church Planting

Following the establishment of the Stirling and Falkirk Churches, the next largest town in the area was ready to receive an indigenous Baptist witness. In 1838 members of the Stirling Church formed the Alloa Baptist Church. This set the pattern for church planting north of the Forth along the line of the Ochil Hills, known locally as the Hillfoots. In 1882 Alloa members living in Alva established a church there, and in 1893 a group of Alva members did the same in Tillicoultry. In 1891, Alva also had a hand in the formation of the church in Denny. Although the populations of Alva, Tillicoultry and Denny were small, this was clearly a time of great spiritual awakening.

In 1838 six members of the Stirling Church living in the Alloa area met in Mar Street, Alloa, for the purpose of forming a Baptist Church. James Scott was designated to serve as lay pastor, becoming full-time in 1854, and even then partly supported by the Baptist Union and by Bristo Baptist Church in Edinburgh. The church initially continued to meet in a home in Mar Street, but this soon became too small and after several further moves it acquired the Episcopalian Chapel in East Vennel. After a number of years this was enlarged to double the seating capacity to two hundred. By 1881 the congregation had grown sufficiently to allow a new building in Ludgate, which remains the home of the present congregation.[14]

Besides the spiritual awakening of the time, the formation of the Hillfoot churches was clearly aided by the economic boom being experienced by the textile trades in which these communities specialized. This was not to last, however, and textile depressions in the late nineteenth and early twentieth centuries led to mass emigration to Australia and America causing setbacks in church work, though this affected Alva and Tillicoultry more than Alloa.[15]

In the early part of the nineteenth century Alva was a small agricultural village, but all this was to change with the coming of the textile trade. A ready supply of water power from the Ochils encouraged the development of woollen milling and the associated trades. As a result of this the 1841 population of 1,500 had become 5,300 by 1891.[16]

In 1882, eight members of Alloa Baptist Church and six other local people, concerned over the lack of Christian teaching in the town, decided to found a new Baptist Church in Alva. One of the Alloa members, D.W. Laing, who had been trained by C.H. Spurgeon, was appointed pastor, continuing as such until 1904. Membership soon increased with transfers from Alloa until from meeting in the Christian Institute, members went on to purchase the local parish school in 1886 and refit it to seat 120, the membership at this time being sixty-seven.[17]

Within ten years, however, as Alloa members had previously been travelling from Alva, so now Alva members were travelling from the similarly growing textile town of Tillicoultry. Hence, in 1892, the Alva Church purchased the Hamilton Street Halls in Tillicoultry to found an extension Baptist cause. The following year Tillicoultry Baptist Church was formally constituted, and in 1894 the twenty-eight members issued a call to J. Mathan Holden.[18]

Alva's endeavours to establish new Baptist work soon spread beyond its immediate area. One of Laing's many Christian friends was a Denny businessman by the name of William Wright. Formerly a member of the Free Church, by 1888 he had adopted Baptist views, and his friend Laing baptized him and received him into membership of Alva Baptist Church. In 1891, at Wright's invitation, Laing conducted a mission in Denny at which many professed faith in Christ. From this group the Denny Baptist Church was formed. The church met first in the Lesser Town Hall, but growth was such that permanent premises were required and the present building was erected in 1905. At one of the number of missions held during this year, at least seventy people experienced conversion, and over the next three years the church more than doubled in membership. Wright was clearly the natural leader, and in 1910 he devoted himself to the work on a full-time basis until his death in 1922.[19]

Not all such efforts of this period, however, were equally successful. Missions established in 1890 by the Alva Church in Callander and Dunblane struggled for a few years before succumbing.[20] Neither town shared extensively in the industrial developments of the time.

The last major church planting initiative of the nineteenth century took place in Grangemouth, another emerging industrial centre. In 1894 the rapidly rising population attracted a Baptist presence with help from Falkirk Baptist Church. In the initial stages this effort went well, and in 1895 the church was formally constituted. Despite a rising population in the area, by 1909 the membership had declined to such a level that the work was wound up. This may in some measure have been due to the fact that the church never enjoyed its own premises.

In 1926 on the initiative of the Baptist Union an investigation was made into the possibilities of recommencing work, but no firm action was taken. In 1938 a further attempt was made, this time the initiative coming from Baptists in Bo'ness, but in the following year the church again closed. In 1948 work in the town was again under discussion, but the matter was left in abeyance. Today there is once again a small Baptist fellowship in Grangemouth, formed in 1974 by local Christians meeting in homes and hired premises. Growth, however, has never paralleled the expansion of the town. Hence despite rapid population growth and good local employment, Grangemouth remains something of an enigma when viewed against the pattern of Baptist growth in the region.[21]

By the start of the twentieth century there were seven well established churches and over 800 members. The churches that proved successful were all in the industrial and commercial centres. Besides marking nearly one hundred years of Baptist work in the area, this was also the point at which church planting practically came to an end for many years. Only another three churches — Banton, Larbert and Bo'ness — were to be established over the next sixty years, all three between 1903 and 1906, at about the time that the effects of the Welsh Revival were being felt. Outreach work also flourished for a while in Bannockburn, Plean and Kincardine, but never led to constituted churches.

Alone amongst the Baptist Churches of Central Region, Banton Baptist Church, established in 1903, has survived in a rural community and has never joined either the local association or the Baptist Union of Scotland. Numerically the fellowship has remained small, but perhaps not out of proportion to the scattered population of the area.[22]

The next place to find itself with a Baptist presence was Larbert, also a rapidly growing community. The 1790 population of 400 increased tenfold inside forty years. By the time the church came to be founded in 1904 the local population stood at almost 12,000, largely resulting from the prosperity of the nearby Carron Iron Works.[23]

In 1904 a meeting was held in Stenhousemuir (separate from Larbert only in name) 'to consider the planting of a Baptist Church in the district'. Twelve men attended this meeting, some from Falkirk Baptist Church and others from local non-Baptist churches. At a second meeting it 'was agreed to begin as a mission church'. An opening meeting was soon held with over sixty present. Seven months later deacons were elected and the church began life proper.[24] The first years seem to have seen good progress, and in 1906 William Wyse was called to be the first pastor, continuing until his death thirty-six years later. By 1912 the need for a building had also become clear and the forty-one members acquired the Larbert Foundry Company reading rooms, which is where — many changes on — the church still meets today.

Baptist work was also soon afoot amongst the 12,000 people of the port town of Bo'ness. By the early twentieth century, the once large whaling fleet and substantial coal mining industry were already on the way to decline. The Bo'ness Baptist Church owes its origins to the endeavours of three local couples who in 1906 became the founder members. The opening meeting took place in the Lesser Masonic Hall, with twenty present. Early indications in the work seemed quite promising, despite a lack of premises, and by 1914 a membership of sixty had been achieved.[25]

The Second Phase

The 1960s saw the commencement of a second round of church planting.

Cumbernauld, up until the mid-1950s a small village but then developed as a New Town, saw the first new Baptist Church in the region for many decades. In 1955 the Cumbernauld Development Corporation started business, aiming for a population of 70,000. By 1986, the town was only 20,000 short of this.[26] Among those moving in were some with Baptist convictions, and the first service was held in Kildrum Primary School in 1961. The work made steady progress and within a year a church was formally constituted. By 1962, it had installed its first pastor, Peter Bryan. As the cause progressed the need for permanent accommodation became clear and by 1965 a new building was in use. Archie McColl, inducted in 1967, is still the pastor. For the first ten years the church grew steadily, in the early days receiving a number of transfers. In 1975 a peak membership of 106 was achieved.

One of the interesting features of the Cumbernauld Church is the help and support received from various Baptist organizations. The churches of the region gave considerable help in the early days through the association, and help and encouragement were also received from the Baptist Union. The Women's Auxiliary movement had already been busy in raising funds to celebrate its jubilee, and £18,000 was donated towards the Cumbernauld building.

The other new Baptist work of this period was in the rapidly expanding Cornton housing estate in Stirling. In 1959, the Murray Place Church began a Sunday School in Cornton, attracting over a hundred to the first meeting. This was followed two years later by a meeting under the auspices of the Murray Place Women's Auxiliary. In 1965 a crisis occurred when the Community Centre where they met was due for demolition. No other premises were available in the area, but a member of the Murray Place Church stepped in with the gift of £9,000 — which was added to on two other occasions — for the building of a hall in Cornton. This was eventually opened in September 1966. At this point, Cornton welcomed J.M. Weiland, a Baptist minister engaged in further studies. He was the first of a series of student pastors and served the church for two years.[27] In 1978 the work in Cornton was constituted as a church. David Bowker was called as the first full-time minister in the following year.

Growth and Consolidation

Although church planting ceased between 1906 and 1961, the churches were not inactive, one of the most notable joint efforts being the formation in 1909 of the Stirling and Clackmannanshire Baptist Association. The aims of the association were to encourage fellowship between churches and to further the principles and work of the denomination, mainly by joint evangelistic efforts. Under the leadership of George Yuille of Stirling, the first president, the churches set themselves the task of discussing how best these aims could be achieved. By the end of the association's first year, only Banton remained unaffiliated.

The first joint effort of significance was an attempt to establish a Baptist presence in Plean, a mining community midway between Stirling and Larbert. This work did seem to prosper for a while, but appears to have eventually joined with a local Brethren assembly. An interest was also shown in mission work in Bannockburn, with the Stirling Church taking special responsibilty. The association seems to have displayed a lively and at times practical interest in the many evangelistic missions being held in member churches, at one time considering employing its own evangelist. Concern for the local area did not lead to neglect of the wider Baptist scene, and in 1911 two delegates were appointed to attend the Baptist World Congress in Philadelphia, USA. Now known as the Central Baptist Association, this body continues today, but since the close of the Second World War the local churches have generally shown a declining interest in its activities.

Individual church growth did continue in the pre-war period, notably in Stirling and Alloa, due in some measure to rapid population expansion. In the period 1891 to 1911 the population of the Stirling area increased by 51%, and the Alloa area population by 25%. Both churches also benefited from a high number of transfers, Stirling receiving 117 and Alloa 108 members from Baptist Churches elsewhere. During this period the Alloa Church was particularly active in evangelism, holding quite a number of cottage meetings in the town and surrounding area. By 1911 Alloa was the largest Baptist Church in the region with 232 members.

Falkirk, Alva and Tillicoultry peaked in membership around the turn of the century. In Falkirk population still continued to grow and local industry to expand. This was in contrast to Alva and Tillicoultry. In Alva, the local population first began to drop just after the beginning of the twentieth century and in Tillicoultry population fell steadily from the 1890s. This was closely related to industrial factors and particularly to the failing fortunes of the textile trade, which was to have even more serious repercussions subsequent to the First World War.[28]

Larbert and Denny continued to grow during the pre-war years, both as towns and as churches. Within a seven-year period, the Denny Church practically doubled in membership from twenty-five to forty-nine.[29] In Larbert growth was slower but steady, closely reflecting population trends until the late 1950s. Although the town of Denny was only half the size of Larbert, the membership figures of the two churches were broadly similar in this period.

The effects of revival, particularly in Stirling and Denny, must not be overlooked. In 1905, a two-month mission held by the Stirling Church yielded 600 professed conversions. By the following year over 500 of these had been followed up, but only a small proportion became church members. In the same year Denny was also reporting 'revival in embryo', with over seventy conversions as a result of a short mission. One of the features of these times of awakening was co-operation with churches of other denominations, often taking the form of joint prayer meetings.[30]

The war years (1914-1918) saw varied fortunes amongst the churches. Stirling, Alloa and Alva continued to grow, Stirling and Alloa still receiving a high number of transfers. Falkirk, Larbert and Tillicoultry remained static in membership, but two of the smaller churches reported a drop which gauged on a percentage basis showed quite significant membership losses. In 1917 the association reported 291 members and adherents in the forces. Regardless of losses during the war, such an exodus could hardly fail to have its effects in terms of continuity of membership and attendance. One possible spiritual gain of the time was the military presence in a number of towns, which besides commandeering the use of church property meant that certain churches now found themselves with army church parades and boosted congregations.

Despite problems of finance and emigration, the years immediately following the First World War were good years for the churches, a number of the churches and towns continuing to grow. Stirling in particular experienced a housing explosion between 1919 and 1939, when over 2,000 new houses were built. The 1920s period also saw an increase in motor transport, allowing travel to churches beyond walking distance.[31] Between 1925 and 1935 a number of the churches recorded their highest membership figures to date.[32]

Some explanation for this may be in the number of evangelistic missions being held. Some churches held two or three each year. 1932 was a particularly active year, with missions in Alva, Larbert, Alloa, Stirling and Falkirk. The association gave financial help to the smaller churches to enable them to employ an evangelist as needed. This was also a time of meetings for the deepening of the spiritual life, both locally and on an association basis.

Despite some rising memberships, however, the churches were not immune to the industrial recession round about. The most obvious effect of this was the financial problems experienced by some churches, ranging from the industrially inclined Falkirk Church to the smaller semi-rural Alva fellowship. In some cases these continued even into the 1940s and a period of fuller employment.

In 1939 Britain was once again at war and before long the effects were felt even in Central Scotland. Although the total number of men called up seems to have been less than in the First World War, weaponry had developed considerably and the fear of aerial attack meant that now thought had to be given to blackout regulations, devouring many hours of discussion at deacons' meetings.

Despite the effects of the conflict on church life, membership levels did not suffer unduly during the war, and by 1945 some churches had actually grown. Of the eight churches, Alloa, Falkirk, Larbert and Bo'ness remained static in membership, while Alva, Tillicoultry and Denny showed gains. Only Stirling lost members, though this was more due to an internal problem than to the effects of war. By 1945 the Denny Church had increased by nearly 60% and could now be self-supporting. Though not rising particularly in numbers until later, Larbert was also able to become self-supporting.

Social Issues

Considering that most of the churches were well on their way to stability and permanence, two World Wars and the intervening years gave opportunity to think about issues wider than mere survival. The advent of the First World War saw interests developing in new areas. A number of churches became involved with army units stationed in their locality. Stirling, Falkirk, Tillicoultry and Larbert reported to a 1915 association meeting that they were sharing in the responsibility of caring for the welfare of soldiers stationed in their towns.[33] In 1918, a number of ministers were given leave to work amongst troops in Europe.

During the Second World War this interest in the welfare of those on active service was revived and in many cases specific financial provision was made. Falkirk, Stirling and Denny all set aside funds for 'comforts for the church boys in the army'. At the same time a great emphasis on prayer continued along with gospel campaigns and meetings for the deepening of the spiritual life.

Another developing interest during the First World War was in the total abstinence movement. In 1915 the association sent a letter to the Prime Minister expressing gratitude at George V's example in forbidding alcohol in the royal household. It also urged the government to prohibit the sale of alcohol during the war. Significantly the evangelist chosen to conduct local missions on behalf of the churches was from the Total Abstinence Society. This was also a peak period for the Band of Hope societies, originally a junior temperance movement, though latterly often functioning purely as a children's meeting.

Of all the churches in the region, Alloa, situated in a brewing and distilling town, took the strongest line. Letters were sent to the government protesting against the liquor trade and in 1911 the church came close to introducing teetotalism into its constitution.[34] Another effect of this controversy was that many churches changed to non-alcoholic communion wine.

During the Second World War the problem of alcohol still continued to be a matter of protest from some churches and correspondence again flowed between the region and Whitehall. Whether this was entirely to do with Christian concern for health and welfare or more a matter of attention to the war effort must be open to some debate. After all the sober man is a more effective soldier!

In 1913 the Alloa Church had protested to the government over the sale of opium to China.[35] The spirit of protest also extended to such issues as gambling and Sunday opening of cinemas. Not all social action was protest, however, and many of the churches had by this time instituted a relief fund for the poor.

Another feature of the inter-war years was the proliferation of church organizations catering for all ages and needs, due to both spiritual and social concern. In 1929 Falkirk Baptist Church boasted Sunday School, Christian Endeavour, choir, Boy Scouts, Bible Class, Baptist Missionary Society Collections, Women's Auxiliary, Girls' Guildry, Band of Hope, Baptist Medical Mission, Young Worshippers' League, Women's Sewing Meeting and Zenana Mission Collection.

Up to Date

Immediately following the war years, the populations of the towns by and large show an upward trend, at least until the early 1950s. In some cases, as in Stirling, this was fuelled by industrial development. In response to this a building boom took place. Significant areas of housing included suburban developments in Sauchie serving the Alloa area, and Cornton and St Ninians serving Stirling.[36] The relationship between area population and church membership, up to the present day, however, is not particularly clear. Membership in some churches, such as Tillicoultry, fell as the area declined. Other causes, such as Larbert, rose with the local population. Others again, such as Falkirk, did the opposite of the expected — in this case growing as the area population fell.

Following on from the earlier trends of consolidation, a campaign called 'Baptist Advance' was set in motion in late 1951. With hindsight both the attendance and concrete results would appear to be somewhat disappointing. A few years later the 1955 interdenominational Tell Scotland campaign also saw local Baptist involvement.

Growth was by no means uniform throughout the region in the 1950s and 1960s. In particular the three churches north of the Forth, at Alloa, Alva and Tillicoultry, all experienced falling membership. In Alva and Tillicoultry this followed the trend of declining area population, itself the product of industrial changes, while in Alloa the area population remained fairly constant during these twenty years. Bo'ness similarly was tending to fall in population and church membership. The fact that there was little work to be had in these areas particularly hit the number of transfers of membership. An important spiritual factor to bear in mind was that this was also a period during which the affluent and permissive societies were developing and the gospel did not seem to be making as much impact as in previous years.

In Falkirk, membership figures were still rising over against a slight decline in the population of the town, but this must be set against the fact that in 1971 approximately eighty names had to be removed from the church membership book in a roll revision. In Denny, the town population rose very sharply in this period, largely due to Glasgow overspill resettlement. This did not initially affect the church and very few transfers or converts were gained, despite an overall population increase of almost 50% in twenty years. In 1967 Stirling became a university town and was also rising in its non-student population. The church experienced a very steady growth during both the 1950s and 1960s, benefiting both from transfers and conversions. From this point up until the present day, the Stirling Church has attracted a number of students from the university, although few come into membership. The village of Larbert was also increasing in size at this time and the church was also growing both by transfers and conversions, particularly during the 1950s.

For many of the churches the fifteen-year period 1970-85 has been a time of falling membership, but also, for some, one of exciting new initiatives. Membership has continued to decrease amongst the three churches at Alloa, Alva and Tillicoultry, as has also been the case in Larbert, Cumbernauld and Stirling. Some of Stirling's losses during the 1970s can be accounted for by transfer of membership to Cornton, however, and during the 1980s membership has begun to rise again. Some additions were drawn from a mentally handicapped Bible Class attached to the church. The town of Stirling also supported from the early 1970s a Bible Baptist Church of American origin which migrated several times before settling in a building in

St Ninians.

Where growth in membership has occurred, namely in Bo'ness, Denny and Falkirk, this has been for a variety of reasons. Particularly in Bo'ness, the background to this is far from straightforward. For many years the church had been suffering from declining local population, and a move in the main residential area of the town both reduced the number of nearby potential members and led to the church premises becoming isolated from where most people lived. This situation had by 1978 become so serious that membership stood at only eight. At this time a decision was made to give the use of the church building to the local Salvation Army corps whose own building was being demolished.

Meanwhile, however, a new group of Baptists was meeting in the town, unaware of the existence of the original church. This led eventually to the church being approached by the Baptist Union with the aim of integrating the two groups. A joint meeting held in 1979 led to an amalgamation under the title of the Bo'ness Baptist Fellowship. Later that year Bryan Jago was inducted as initial pastor. In 1981, with membership standing at twenty-three, a new constitution was agreed. The following year the previous church premises were finally sold and a new building was eventually acquired in Boundary Street. Membership in 1985 was thirty-six.

Throughout the 1970s, membership of the Denny Church remained practically static, but by the commencement of the 1980s the church was again benefiting from transfers and a number of converts, many of them having moved into the town as a result of the Glasgow overspill. By 1984 the membership stood at eighty-five, its highest point in fifty years.

After a slow fall in numbers during the 1970s, Falkirk also moved into a new era in the early 1980s. Despite the continued decline in population of Falkirk and the frankly devastating effects of the failure of much local industry — particularly including the famous Carron Iron Works — the membership of the church has grown quite dramatically. From 1981 to 1986, the increase was 56%. Developments in Falkirk which have contributed to this include the church's outreach to a whole new sector of the community through its 'Open Door' cafe for the unemployed. Recently the church has also been using Falkirk Technical College for worship meetings every six weeks.

One encouraging theme common amongst a number of the churches in recent years has been a need for increased accommodation. Alloa was first with new halls in the 1960s, both Larbert and Denny following suit in the 1980s. In Larbert this was desirable because falling membership was balanced by rising church attendances. The most significant development along these lines has yet to take place, as the Murray Place Church in Stirling is due to transfer in 1988 to a renovated Church of Scotland building on the opposite side of the street to its former premises.

While much of the emphasis so far has been on the work of the churches, this is not to ignore the significant contribution made by individuals. Included in these must be men like Laing with his burden for church planting, William Wright who gave much financially and spiritually, and laymen like J.D. Taylor of Larbert and Jack Carr of Stirling, who served as presidents of the Baptist Union. Special mention must also be made of George Yuille, the pastor of the Stirling Church for over forty years, the first president of the association, second secretary of the Union and editor of the *History of the Baptists in Scotland*. His present-day successor, James Taylor, was the youngest president of the Union up to that point when he held office at the start of his Stirling ministry in 1971-2.

The 1980s has also seen all the churches entering into the three-year Scotreach programme of planned evangelism and consolidation. One aspect of this common involvement was a united association outreach weekend through the Hillfoot churches in 1985.

The churches of the Central Baptist Association now find themselves on the brink of a more promising period than for many years. Memberships in the two largest churches are increasing, generally congregations seem to be growing and extension fellowships are underway in St Ninians in Stirling (not to be confused with the smaller Bible Baptist cause) and in Polmont near Falkirk. At the same time, however, problems of finance do persist in the smaller churches and nominal membership is far from unknown. In this respect while some churches are facing the future with new vision and expectation, the next few decades will be crucial for others. As throughout Baptist history, the issues will be decided by factors primarily neither economic nor demographic but spiritual.

Notes

1. Nigel Tranter, *The Heartland: Clackmannanshire, Perthshire and Stirlingshire* (London 1971), p 215.
2. *Census 1981: Report for Central Region*, 4 (Edinburgh 1983), p 1.
3. D.W.G. Timms, ed, *The Stirling Region* (Stirling 1974), p 182.
4. *The New Statistical Account of Scotland: Stirling* (Edinburgh 1845), pp 187-8; *Clackmannan* (Edinburgh 1845), pp 51, 73.
5. *New Statistical Account: Stirling*, pp 427, 13.
6. George Yuille, ed, *History of the Baptists in Scotland* (Glasgow 1926), p 229.
7. ibid, p 227.
8. Stirling Baptist Church Minute Book, 1, pp 58-9.
9. *The First Yearly Report of the Baptist Union of Scotland* (Cupar 1844), p 20.
10. Yuille, ed, *Baptists in Scotland*, p 288.
11. *Falkirk Baptist Church Book of the Bazaar* (Falkirk 1906).

12. ibid.
13. ibid.
14. Yuille, ed, *Baptists in Scotland*, p 224.
15. R.C. Rennie and T.C. Gordon, ed, *The Third Statistical Account of Scotland: The Counties of Stirling and Clackmannan* (Glasgow 1961), pp 553, 566.
16. ibid.
17. Yuille, ed, *Baptists in Scotland*, p 225.
18. ibid, p 231.
19. A.D. Gillies, ed, *Pastor William Wright: some memories and memorials* (Denny 1927).
20. Yuille, ed, *Baptists in Scotland*, pp 276, 278. For the Crieff Church, which joined the Central Baptist Association in 1987, see cap 13, p 240.
21. Stirlingshire and Clackmannanshire Baptist Association Minute Books. Information from the Rev. Douglas Crisp.
22. *Scottish Baptist Magazine (SBM)*, Nov. 1905, p 6.
23. Rennie and Gordon, ed, *Third Statistical Account*, p 392.
24. Larbert Baptist Church Minute Book, 1, 3 May, 10 May and 29 Sept. 1904.
25. Bo'ness Baptist Church Minute Book, 1.
26. The Cumbernauld Historical Society, *Historical Cumbernauld* (Cumbernauld [1968]), p 6.
27. P.C. Coles, 'To God be the Glory: retelling the story of The Cornton: a church within a community' (Typescript 1974).
28. Rennie and Gordon, ed, *Third Statistical Account*, pp 555, 565.
29. *Scottish Baptist Year Book (SBYB)*, 1905-11.
30. *SBM*, Apr. 1905, p 7; Sept. 1905, p 4; Nov. 1905, p 7.
31. Gavin Booth, *Alexander Coachbuilders* (Glossop 1980), p 7.
32. *SBYB*, 1925-35.
33. Stirlingshire and Clackmannanshire Baptist Association Minute Book, 1.
34. Alloa Baptist Church Minute Book.
35. ibid.
36. Timms, ed, *Stirling Region*, pp 197, 205.

L.N. Cowan
F.C. Wright

12. FIFE

'"Fife" is a name which usually stands alone as sufficiently distinctive. In the mind's eye of any Scot it conjures up a vision of the peninsula on the east coast of Scotland, lying betwixt the Firths of Forth and Tay, and separated from the rest of Scotland across the neck of the peninsula by the rampart of the Ochils.'[1] So wrote Alexander Smith in the opening paragraph to his volume *The County of Fife*, published in 1952 as part of the Third Statistical Account of Scotland. What Smith said thirty-four years ago is still true today, save for the opening up of the old county by the road bridges over the Forth and Tay in the 1960s. He was referring to its distinct 'dog's head' shape on the map and its strategic importance as a power base because of its relative isolation. One recent historian of early Scotland has suggested that Fife was to Scotland what Kent was, in strategic and economic terms, to England.[2]

The natural barriers of the firths and the hills have only relatively recently lost their formidable nature. When one considers the fact that for long the interior of the peninsula was covered by woods, lakes and swamps and that, as a result, movement was difficult, it comes as no surprise to find that Fife has a very distinct identity to its history. That distinctiveness persists even today in the title of 'The Kingdom of Fife' and the fact that it survives as one of the nine regions of Scotland despite the recommendations of the Wheatley Commission that it should be divided between Tayside and Lothian.

Having reached a position of some prominence by the tenth century, Fife became an area which flourished during the Middle Ages. With both the chief seat of the court and a significant bishopric, it gained a position of some importance in temporal and ecclesiastical affairs. Economic activity was also considerable, demonstrated in the number of Royal Burghs found within its bounds, mostly along the northern shores of the Forth.

Decline, however, came in the seventeenth century, with the removal of the court to London, the ravages of Cromwell's armies and the crippling of trade by the combined effects of the Dutch wars and the Navigation Acts. Following the Act of Union in 1707 the imposition of a salt duty hampered trade in fish and salt.

Recovery was slow during the eighteenth century, though new farming methods saw improvement in the efficiency and prosperity of agriculture. Industry was slower in growing than in the rest of central Scotland and the effects of industrialization were not felt until well into the nineteenth century. Two industries in particular are worthy of note. One is linen production, a traditional industry which was becoming increasingly mechanized only by the 1850s. Factories were built in Kirkcaldy, Dunfermline, Cupar, Newburgh and Auchtermuchty. Their numbers grew throughout the remainder of the century.

Coal, another traditional industry, also expanded steadily, though at a slow pace compared to other areas. This was caused by the difficulty of working the large deposits of coal, the West Fife coalfield particularly being much broken up by faulting. The expansion of the coalfield therefore came late in the nineteenth century, though when it did, it was with great suddenness. Between 1851 and 1881 numbers in the industry rose from 3,200 to 5,900. In the next thirty years they had risen to 27,000. This rapid growth shifted the hub of economic activity to the west of the county and saw the growth of numerous communities such as Lochgelly, Bowhill, Cardenden and Cowdenbeath.

The present century has seen the construction and growth of the naval dockyard at Rosyth, which today employs more workers than any other industry in the region, and within the past twenty years, the New Town of Glenrothes has grown with the development of electronic and micro-electronic factories. It is within this context of increasing industrialization that Baptist Churches have become established in Fife over the last two centuries.

Church Planting

In his 1952 account of the county of Fife, Alexander Smith was drawn to say that within the history of Fife was contained 'the concentrated essence of Scottish history and character'.[3] This is no less true of Scottish Baptist history, for the essence of Baptist progress in Scotland from the Commonwealth to the Scotch Baptists and the Haldanes, to the founding and growth of the Scottish Baptist Union are all to be found here. We must briefly review the different phases of church foundation in order to clarify what will later be said concerning growth and decline.

Following a brief interlude during the Commonwealth when Baptists are recorded as having existed in Cupar, the first period of church foundation was in the late eighteenth and early nineteenth centuries. By 1830, churches existed in Largo, Dunfermline, Kirkcaldy, Cupar and Anstruther. Churches in these places have remained. In three other small towns, Tayport, Kinghorn and Auchtermuchty, churches were also in existence by 1830 but have since ceased to exist. Additionally, the New Statistical Account of 1845 which mentions the 'few Anabaptists, who meet together for worship' at Kinghorn, also refers to a Baptist meeting being held in the parish of Kilconquhar in the north-east of the county, though exactly where in the parish is not recorded.

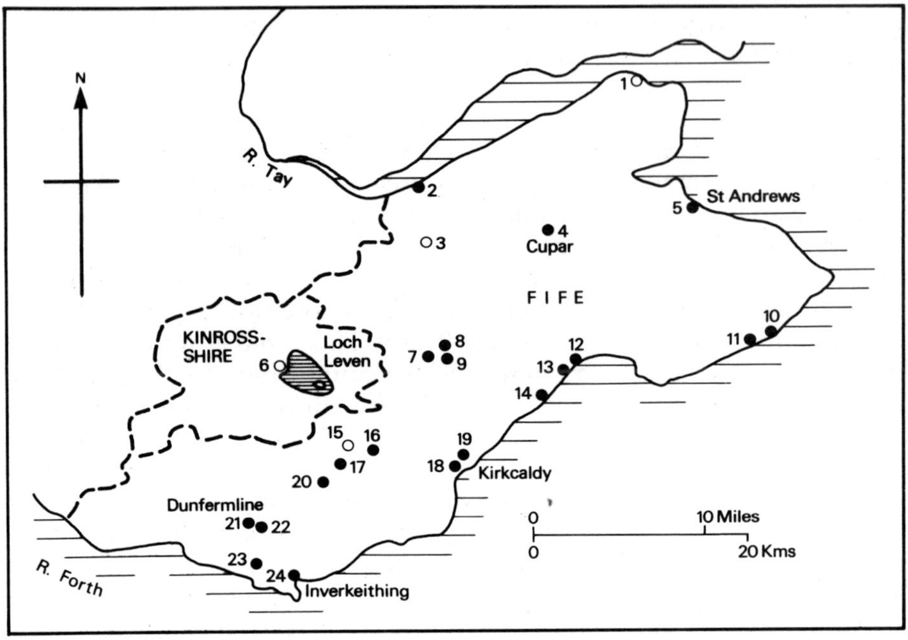

MAP 12 : FIFE BAPTIST CHURCHES.

Key to Map 12

1. Tayport
2. Newburgh
3. Auchtermuchty
4. Cupar
5. St Andrews
6. Kinross
7. Leslie
8. Collydean
9. Glenrothes
10. Anstruther
11. Pittenweem
12. Largo
13. Leven
14. Buckhaven
15. Lochore
16. Bowhill
17. Lochgelly
18. Kirkcaldy: Whyte's Causeway
19. Kirkcaldy: Pathhead
20. Cowdenbeath
21. Dunfermline: West
22. Dunfermline: Viewfield
23. Rosyth
24. Inverkeithing

The mid-nineteenth century saw what might be described as a realignment of already existing churches leading to the formation of the present churches at Viewfield in Dunfermline and Whyte's Causeway in Kirkcaldy. It is to this period that the present churches date their origin, rather than to the earlier 'Scotch' Churches. To these we may add the church at St Andrews. The third phase, marked by the increasing economic growth in the locality, saw churches founded at Cowdenbeath, Leslie, Leven and in Dunfermline, where a second church was founded after a dispute in Viewfield. These churches were formed between 1873 and 1897.

In the early twentieth century, under the twin impulses of continued economic growth, particularly in the central Fife coalfield, and church planting activity on the part of the Fife Baptist Association, churches were constituted at Pathhead in Kirkcaldy, Pittenweem, Inverkeithing, Bowhill, Buckhaven, Lochgelly, Rosyth and, briefly, Lochore within the first two decades. This dramatic burst of activity was followed by a period of stagnation in church foundation which was to last some thirty-five years until a church was established in 1956 in the New Town of Glenrothes. A further twenty-five years passed until a second church at Collydean in the expanding north of the town was commenced in the early 1980s.

Having sketched the steps in the founding of the churches, we must turn our attention to consider the reasons why, over the past two centuries, the Baptist Churches in Fife have grown, and, where there has been decline, investigate the causes. That there has been general growth is undoubted. Numbers have increased from the founding of the first church in the 1780s to around 650 in 1850, if we use Francis Johnstone's estimate of the number of Baptists in Scotland, to some 1,400 by 1900. Thereafter membership rose to 2,125 in 1925, declining to just under 2,000 in 1930 and reaching its peak of 2,135 in 1935. Since the mid-thirties the trend has been downward in spite of small increases between 1955 and 1965 and since 1980.[4]

In looking into the reasons for such growth and decline, one factor must ever be at the forefront of our minds. This is that, in terms of membership, there is no such thing as a 'standard' Baptist Church in Fife — or elsewhere. No church accords with the membership graph of Baptists in Fife and, indeed, no two membership graphs of the various churches appear similar. Many reasons for growth are therefore to be found in the local situation and personalities of the individual churches, rather than in regional or national factors.

With this in mind, we turn first to consider the early growth of Baptist Churches within Fife, which came about for fairly distinct reasons. The eighteenth century saw a widespread disaffection with the Established

Church in Scotland, and, whether as a reaction to the system of patronage or as a result of doctrinal disagreement, numerous secessions from the Church of Scotland took place. In time, further secessions from these breakaway churches also occurred. It is within this atmosphere that Baptist Churches began to grow in Fife. These first churches, at Dunfermline (1780), Kirkcaldy (1798) and Largo (1791), were of Scotch Baptist pattern. All had links with the Edinburgh Church and with earlier Independent Churches in these areas.

In addition, there is evidence of the strong impact individuals could have on the setting up of a cause. In Kirkcaldy, William Peddie, who had trained for the ministry of the Secession Church, was one of two elders who took the lead in organizing the church, while in Largo it was the local practitioner, Dr William Goodsir, who took the initiative in both founding the church and ministering to it until his death in 1816. Clearly it was his standing in the town which helped the fellowship here, by no means one of the larger communities in the area, to flourish. Similarly, in Cupar it was largely because of the activities of one man, Jonathan Watson, a druggist from Montrose, that the church was organized. Watson was a man with considerable gifts as a preacher and while in his first year in the town spoke regularly on 'Baptist principles', the result being the meeting of a few folk on a regular basis, with Watson himself as minister, in 1816.

Newburgh, though tracing its history to a visit by Archibald McLean in 1808, had Baptists within the parish over ten years before this date. Writing his parish description for Sir John Sinclair's Statistical Account of Scotland, the Established Church minister Andrew Ireland recorded that, 'The Unitarians do not exceed four; and the Anabaptists are not double that number. The Anabaptists are connected with a church of the same description, at Dundee.'[5] Little else, however, is known of the small group of Baptists in Newburgh during this early period.

It was in the main centres, on the whole, that these early churches grew, and were sustained, though short-lived churches existed also at Auchtermuchty and the two villages at either end of the Fife Turnpike, Kinghorn and Tayport. By 1840, churches existed in Dunfermline, Kirkcaldy, Cupar, Newburgh and Anstruther, besides those mentioned previously. In the cases of Dunfermline, Kirkcaldy and Newburgh, it can hardly be coincidence that they were centres for the manufacture of linen, and there is some evidence that a number of the early members were involved in the weaving trade.[6]

In our day it would be regarded as a major disaster in church life for a congregation to be so divided in its opinions that one group felt obliged to 'withdraw' and form another church. Earlier generations were not so perturbed at such a prospect. Indeed, Scotch Baptist organization, with an emphasis on unanimity of mind in church meetings, made the likelihood of such withdrawals more common. By the mid-nineteenth century, there was something of a reorganization in the Fife churches. Secession and schism continued to have an effect on their life.

At St Andrews, Baptists had worshipped as part of the Independent congregation until, in 1841, one young man, William Noble, was baptized by the pastor of the Cupar Baptist Church. He was apparently treated with some intolerance, and the church produced a statement on the position of those of Baptist persuasion within the congregation. This was unacceptable, and so the Baptists withdrew to form their own congregation with a membership of eight.[7]

In the same year there was disagreement in the Scotch Church in Dunfermline. A later *Historical Sketch* records that 'a feeling of dissatisfaction arose among several of the members regarding the method of conducting public worship and they deemed it their duty to begin a distinct effort and form a church on different principles'. It appears, from a letter written by the pastor, James Blair, that he and they were unhappy about the practice of public exhortation which, he stated, 'at times gave rise to unedifying scenes'.[8] The result was that some nine men and twenty-three women left to form an 'English' Baptist Church which was to become, after later removal, Viewfield Place Baptist Church. Nor was this apparently the only secession from the church in 1841. Peter Chalmers, minister of Dunfermline Abbey, who produced a model account of the parish for the New Statistical Account, notes two separations in 1841. He records that one was under Blair and the principles of this body were 'those of the English Baptists'. The other, he continued, 'was of persons who take the designation "Christians" from Acts XI:26, who have no creed, oral or written, but the Bible. They are usually styled *Campbellites*, after a Mr Campbell in America, to whose opinions regarding the influence of the Spirit, and instrumentality of the Word, in conversion, they are understood to be favourable.'[9]

Kirkcaldy also saw its Scotch Baptist Church subjected to division when, in 1852, an elder, three deacons and thirty members of the Scotch Church withdrew to 'meet the next Lord's Day in the room formerly occupied by Philp's School, to observe the Ordinances appointed by the Head of the Church'.[10] The small body formed a strong nucleus and within two years had built and opened the church at Whyte's Causeway. At first, however, church government remained much as it had in the older Scotch Church, with the elders responsible for preaching and administering the sacraments and with mutual exhortation being practised. Several secessions occurred from the young church at Whyte's Causeway, one such in 1855 leading to the withdrawal of one elder and twelve members, joined shortly by another five and subsequently forming a Church of Christ in Pathhead.[11]

Anstruther represented another strand in Scottish Baptist history. Work began in the town in 1812 after a visit by James Haldane. Following that, meetings were held in the Tabernacle until a dispute in 1839 saw a split between Baptists and paedobaptists. Though for some time they continued to worship together, an Independent chapel was built in 1853. The twenty remaining Baptists continued to meet and, by 1859, feeling it advisable to have a pastor solely devoting his time to teaching and pastoral work, it was decided to form a church — though only after James Cumming Brown from Regent's Park College had arrived.[12]

In some places, Dunfermline being a good example, secession could almost be regarded as the norm of church experience whatever the denomination. Dispute arose among the Baptists of Dunfermline in the 1890s. On this occasion it was the question of whether the Lord's Table should be open to all believers from which the problem arose. Within the Viewfield Church the question dragged on for nearly a decade. In 1888 and 1890 the matter was discussed but not resolved. Finally, in 1896, in a ballot some 126 voted for open communion and 124 for closed. Reconciliation proving impossible, 110 members resigned to form the New Baptist Church, later known as the West Baptist Church. Clearly the dispute was serious and Viewfield's most recent historical booklet records the inevitable result that 'the church was weak and lacked vitality, and it was some time before the effect of such a split was overcome'.[13] Nevertheless, in the longer term, the result was two strong churches in Dunfermline. By 1903, Viewfield had 246 members, and the West 241. Twelve years later, in 1915, Viewfield numbered 291 with West membership having risen to 275.

Leadership

Good leadership within the congregation is clearly a factor in church growth. Churches throughout Fife, as elsewhere, can record expansion during the period of particular ministries. In the ten years of T.W. Lister's ministry in Leslie between 1880 and 1890, for example, some 216 members were placed on the roll. Of these, only twenty had transferred from elsewhere, the remainder being what we might term 'conversion growth'. Ten years further on, only a further fifty names had been added.[14] It is a remarkable testimony to Lister's work, and amply justifies the praise lavished on him from all parts of the community when he left for Rattray Street in Dundee.

Other churches at different times could give similar testimony to the importance of the pastor. Cupar in its early days was blessed with a number of notable and effective ministries in those of Jonathan Watson, Francis Johnstone and William Landels. At Viewfield, from 1875 and including the period of recovery from the dissension of 1896, considerable increase in size necessitating the building of a new church was due in large measure to the gifted leadership of J.T. Hagen. In Leslie in the 1930s the ministry of John McBeath saw sustained growth, the minute books recording applicants for baptism and church membership coming hard on the heels of one another, a situation not in evidence before or after McBeath's pastorate. At about the same time in Lochgelly John McKendrick's ministry was producing similar results. A few years earlier St Andrews had seen much the same occur during the incumbency of R.F. Conway.

One of the most noteworthy instances of sustained growth is in the Leven church where T.G. Esplin became pastor in 1926. The membership then stood at 114. Between 1926 and 1940 the membership grew every year, reaching 214 by the latter year. It then fell back slightly in the 1940s, but still stood at 194 when Esplin retired in 1948. A graph of the Leven membership shows clearly this steady increase, and, just as clearly, the steady decrease since that time. (See Figure 12.1.)[15] More recent examples of such situations can be found in Viewfield under the ministries of James Graham and William Freel, Rosyth under J.W. Tyrrell and Ronald Marr and in the 1970s and 1980s the ministries of William Cowie, Ian Paterson and William Wright in Leslie, Inverkeithing and St Andrews respectively.

Such ministers did not lack assistance. In almost every case we could enumerate those in the churches who gave them support, whether as church office-bearers or as leaders in Sunday School, Band of Hope, Christian Endeavour, Women's Auxiliary and choir or in organizing social outreach activities and open-air evangelistic events. In its early days Viewfield was fortunate in having at its disposal the services of James Robertson and William Mathewson, both of whom were representatives of the manufacturing class and whose wealth and considerable local esteem were of use in the growth of the church. Others, such as James Westwater at Lochgelly, H.F. Seager at Rosyth, Thomas G. Henderson, long-serving secretary at Buckhaven and Fife Association treasurer, and Peter Thomson at Anstruther, used their considerable gifts within their particular localities. Indeed, Thomson, who was provost of the small burgh of Kilrenny in 1900 and church secretary at Anstruther for over fifty years, was also superintendent of the Sunday School which was so popular that it was known as 'Peter Thomson's Sabbath School'. It met on a Sunday afternoon and was the only one in the town to do so. The result was a large attendance, many parents being glad of the opportunity to deposit their children out of the way.

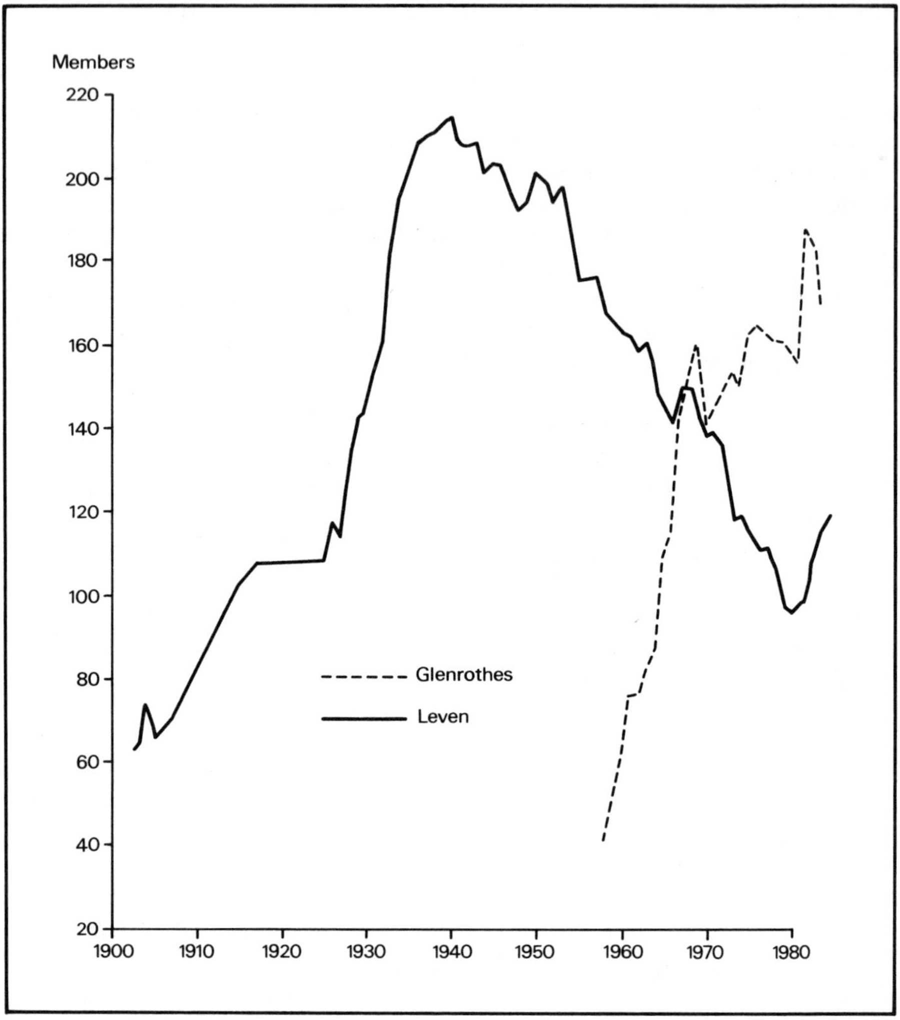

FIGURE 12.1: MEMBERSHIP GRAPHS FOR TWO FIFE BAPTIST CHURCHES SINCE 1900.

Economic Factors

There is little doubt, when we look at the growth of the Fife churches, and particularly their foundation, that economic factors played a considerable part. It is hardly a surprise to find that most of the early churches were to be found in the manufacturing towns of Dunfermline, Kirkcaldy and Newburgh, together with the county town of Cupar and the university town of St Andrews. Apart from these, and the peculiar exceptions of Largo and Anstruther, growth came with the expansion of the Fife coalfield in the late 1860s and 1870s. Cowdenbeath, at the heart of the mining area, saw a considerable influx of population from Fife and other parts of Scotland, and a church was formed in 1873. As the coalfield expanded north and east, so new towns and villages were constructed at Lumphinnans, Lochgelly, Ballingry and Cardenden. This growing population was fertile ground for church growth and in the early years of the present century churches were established at Lochgelly and Bowhill to serve these communities.

Further east, with more coalfield growth centred on the activities of the Wemyss Coal Company and later the Fife Coal Company, churches were founded in Leven and Buckhaven. These churches, 'in the midst of a teeming and growing population',[16] provided fertile ground for church planting — growth which was effectively exploited by the young Fife Baptist Association.

Ample testimony to the scale of this growth of population is given by successive reports of the Fife Association and of the Fifeshire Joint Committee to the Baptist Union of Scotland. Growth in the Fife population between 1901 and 1911 was of the order of 25%, and this considerable increase gave hope of opportunity. In 1908 the committee reported that the Lochgelly district was 'growing rapidly, a result of the development of the coal fields, and it is believed that there is an opening for a church here'.[17] The following year there was further comment. 'The population in the county continues to increase at an abnormal rate, owing to the rapid development of the coal mines, and the problem of how to meet the religious needs of the unshepherded multitudes is daily becoming more perplexing and oppressive. We are called upon as an Association to attempt great things for God.'[18]

In 1903, the Government, requiring a new dockyard to repair Dreadnought battleships, and concerned at the growing threat from Germany, announced a plan to construct a yard at Rosyth on the north shore of the Firth of Forth. Slow progress was made, and by the outbreak of war in 1914 the dockyard was still in no state to receive ships. It was opened in 1916 in time to carry out vital repairs following the Battle of Jutland. From 1917 the whole of the Grand Fleet was based on Rosyth. By 1913 there were some 3,000 men employed in 'Tin Town'. Among the workforce were a number of Baptists from Chatham who took a lead in organizing services locally. The work begun in 1918 was expected to flourish — a correspondent to the *Scottish Baptist Magazine* noting the enthusiasm of the people at Rosyth and its unique and promising situation.[19]

Since the Second World War, the most prominent point of population growth has been around the New Town of Glenrothes. Looking at a graph of the Glenrothes church membership since its foundation in 1956, we see a fairly steady growth which is not found in any other church in the region over the same period of time. (See Figure 12.1.)[20] Clearly, the situation of a New Town with not only an incoming Baptist population but also an area where people have few 'roots' or settled church connections is a fruitful area for growth. This is seen not only in the Glenrothes Church and its sister church at Collydean in the more recent and still expanding north of the town, but also in the growth of the Leslie Church, which is situated on the north-west edge of Glenrothes and which draws roughly half its membership from the New Town.

Working Together

The exploitation of areas of population growth has been ably assisted by the Fife Baptist Association and, to a lesser degree, by the Baptist Union of Scotland, though 'church planting' had been actively undertaken in Fife many years before the association came into being. The church at St Andrews had considerable help in its early years from the vigorous church at Cupar.

The association was formed as a 'District Union' of churches in 1895, though a year earlier the Leslie Church had hosted a 'Conference of the Baptist Churches in the County of Fife'. In a programme advertizing this, David Kerr the pastor and James Robertson the secretary stated, 'From the correspondence we have already had in connection with this conference, it appears that there is a decided desire on the part of the Churches to have an Association or District Union, such as has been recommended by the Union.' Churches were asked to authorize someone to be present to represent them on a committee to be formed after the conference to consider the matter further.[21]

From early in its existence the Fifeshire and Clackmannanshire Association was involved in starting causes, often in co-operation with the Union. In 1908 it reported to the assembly that, together with the Baptist Union of Scotland, an agent had been placed in Lochgelly. Co-operation of the Union was recognized in the setting up of the Fifeshire Joint Committee comprising the office-bearers of both Union and association, together with the treasurer of the Union's Extension Fund, Dr Jervis Coats, and six members (three ministers and three laymen) of the association. The committee initiated work in some areas such as Lochgelly (1908) and Bowhill (1904). It seized the initiative when local revival necessitated organization to follow up evangelistic effort, which happened at Inverkeithing in 1905, and it aided efforts which had been started by other churches, such as that at Pathhead, where the Whyte's Causeway Church had set up a mission in the latter years of the nineteenth century.

Both these churches, along with the association, gave great assistance in the founding of the Buckhaven Church in 1910. Indeed the association's involvement is recorded in clause 9 of Buckhaven's original constitution, which states, 'The Fife Baptist Association has guaranteed the Pastor's salary for a period of five years from this date.'[22]

Similar co-operation can be observed in the two most recently founded churches in the region, at Glenrothes. The Leslie deacons' minutes for January 1956 record that an approach was to be made to Fife Education Committee regarding Preston School 'for the purpose of holding a Sunday School'. The school was, however, already being used by the Salvation Army, which caused further thought. On 21 February 1956, the Leslie deacons met again, when the following was minuted: 'The Pastor suggested, and it was agreed that a meeting be called of all Baptist families residing in Glenrothes with a view to discussing the forming of a Baptist Cause.'[23] Within a few months the Fife Association had circularized the churches in fellowship with it to raise contributions for the new work.

In March 1980 the association was involved in discussions with the Glenrothes and Leslie Churches about work in the expanding northern area of the New Town. At the initial meeting on 17 March, the Glenrothes and Leslie Baptist Fellowship committee, later to become the Collydean Steering Committee, had even considered suggestions of union between the churches to further the extension cause. The background was outlined by James Thomson, the secretary of the committee, in a letter to Andrew MacRae, the soon-to-depart General Secretary of the Baptist Union of Scotland: 'When Glenrothes and Leslie churches decided on extension work in untouched but needy areas of the New Town, it was immediately realized that some kind of joint action was envisaged, between two churches with reasonable relations but with no great history of collaboration.'[24] He went on to outline how the churches' representatives, together with those of the association, one of whom was Thomson himself, as current president, had agreed to consider unified action, the possibility of acquiring buildings and a pioneer/team ministry for the area. Following much discussion and the gathering of sound advice, at a meeting on 13 October 1980 the ideas of a team ministry and a unified church were dropped, a discussion document not having commended itself to the diaconates of either Glenrothes or Leslie. It was agreed, however, 'That a meeting be called of all those resident in the Northern Precincts, with a view to the formation of a Collydean Baptist Fellowship', and 'That action be taken immediately, without waiting for the acquisition of a building.'[25] Some years and much hard physical effort in converting a disused granary given by the local Development Corporation were to follow before the Collydean Church, constituted in April 1983, met in its present setting.

Some years earlier, Leslie Church, with association support, had been involved in an abortive attempt to form a church in nearby Kinross. In 1977, the Leslie fellowship, which had several members resident in Kinross, formed a house group there, as one of several midweek house groups within the church. It was realized, however, that there were other Baptists in the community and attempts were made to form a fellowship and hold services, the Leslie deacons' minutes recording in February 1979 that 'services at Kinross were continuing to grow in strength'. This was, however, the only reference to Kinross, and the cause was soon abandoned, factors being the removal of personnel, isolation from effective support from other churches and the fact that there existed in the town an active and Evangelical Church of Scotland.

Mission Activity and Buildings

Apart from the early Scotch Churches, the churches in Fife, as elsewhere in Scotland, have sought to cater not only for deepening the fellowship between their members but also for providing evangelistic opportunities into the surrounding communities. As a result a wide variety of organizations has been constituted for particular groups. The Viewfield Church gives an example of the breadth and variety of such organizations, its 1984 short history listing over thirty, ranging from choirs through the Women's Auxiliary, a Business and Professional Women's Group, pre-school play-group, Girl Guides, Girls' Brigade, Boy Scouts, youth club, Christian Endeavour and Band of Hope to a Senior Citizens' Group and a Men's Fellowship. Various techniques have also been used to spread the gospel including village missions, a Young Life week, a Sunday Club and a drama group. Other churches could list similar activities and add a few more.

Local evangelistic outreach has been a sustained dimension of local church life. The largest increase in the membership of a Fife Church in a single year was eighty-nine, reported by Lochgelly for the 1925 *Year Book*. Sixty-nine people had been baptized in the same year. Reference to the Lochgelly minutes for this period, however, provides little enlightenment as to the reasons. Certainly the increase appears to have been received with remarkable calm. There seems to have been little activity by way of special efforts. There were missions, but these were a regular feature of the life of the church in the twenties and thirties, with one being held every three or four months. Most other churches at different periods can point to successful increases in membership following local outreach initiatives, though none as large as that mentioned above.

Fife churches have also participated in nationally organized evangelistic events, perhaps the most notable in this respect being the Tell Scotland Crusade led by Dr Billy Graham in the early summer of 1955. Fife churches were active before the event took place. In Lochgelly the January 1955 meeting of the deacons saw concern about increasing attendances sandwiched between the need to purchase teaspoons and the pastor sharing with the deacons the inconvenience of not having a telephone. The secretary minuted the following report: 'How to increase numbers at services was raised after some discussion it was agreed to hold a four night mission from April 12th to 15th.'[26] The April meeting reported that those efforts had been very successful and the deacons also approved a retiral offering for the All Scotland Crusade. By the autumn, results were being seen in the number of folk coming forward for baptism. The church, at this time, minuted in some detail its interviews with baptismal candidates. Of one candidate, it was reported that 'Miss Wilson made her decision for Christ at the Glasgow Crusade held in the Kelvin Hall conducted by Dr Billy Graham. She felt that for some time back, she would have made the decision, it only needed someone to take the lead.'[27]

Similar reports were heard throughout that autumn and winter. Other churches in Fife also reported fairly large increases in membership following the crusade. Other churches reporting higher membership included Anstruther, Bowhill, Buckhaven, Cowdenbeath, Pittenweem and Rosyth. We must also record the fact, however, that this growth was not sustained and, indeed, in succeeding years, some of these churches found their membership decrease as quickly as it had risen in 1955-6.

Church buildings among Baptists in Fife have on occasion spurred on the progress of the church. Certainly, in Leslie, the opening of the building in 1886 was followed by considerably increased membership in the succeeding year. In other areas, buildings have been more of a sign of prospering churches. From 1841, the Viewfield Church met first of all in a furniture warehouse and a number of other locations until Provost Robertson, one of its members, purchased the Maygate Chapel, first renting it, then gifting it outright, to the church. After 1875, under the influence of the vigorous and talented leadership of J.T. Hagen, membership increased to over 250, necessitating a further move. A site was purchased at Viewfield Place and a building opened with seating for 600.

In the same period, Anstruther was also seeing much growth. Partly this was due to personal evangelism in the town by the members, partly due to the inspired preaching of Harri Edwards, but also because the town was the main centre of the herring fishing. This resulted in large numbers from fishing communities in the north-east and from England converging on Anstruther for periods in both summer and winter. The original chapel seating 220 had to be enlarged by an extension for 120 additional seats in 1882. In 1902 an extra schoolroom was also added. In between, in 1889, the church had bought a hall in nearby Pittenweem to begin Sunday School and mission work.

In recent years, an imaginative project was undertaken in Glenrothes. In 1979, because of increasing numbers, the Glenrothes Church came to an agreement to exchange buildings with the Episcopal Church in the town, which found its building too large. Within a short time the two churches had agreed terms and the exchange had been carried out, aiding the continuing growth of the Baptist cause.

Decline in the Twentieth Century

However tempting it might be to dwell on the growth of the Fife churches, we must also look at the decline in membership. Even a glance at a graph of Fife Baptist membership will show that the overall trend since the second decade of the twentieth century has been downward, and we must attempt to discern the reasons for this. (See Figure 12.2.)[28]

One of the main factors is clearly the economic one. Whereas at the beginning of the twentieth century the growth of the central Fife churches had much to do with the health and expansion of the mining industry, the converse also holds true as we approach the present day. In the early 1950s, Smith, in his Fife volume of the Third Statistical Account, describing the prospects for coal mining, could still look ahead with confidence. 'An expansion of mine working there will be', he could say.[29] This was a statement of expectation based on the prosperity of the time. Since then, however, there has been a considerable contraction, notably in central Fife, where, following the tragic mining dispute of 1984-5 only one pit, at Seafield, Kirkcaldy, remains, and that with an increasingly uncertain future. From the early 1960s, accelerating towards the end of the decade and through the 1970s, the churches associated with the central Fife coalfield and particularly those in Bowhill, Cowdenbeath and Lochgelly have experienced great decline.

The fishing villages of the East Neuk also suffered from economic adversity, though at an earlier period. Smith describes the 'very depressed period of the 1920s',[30] and this can be traced in the membership of both Anstruther and Pittenweem Churches, where there was a sharp decline in

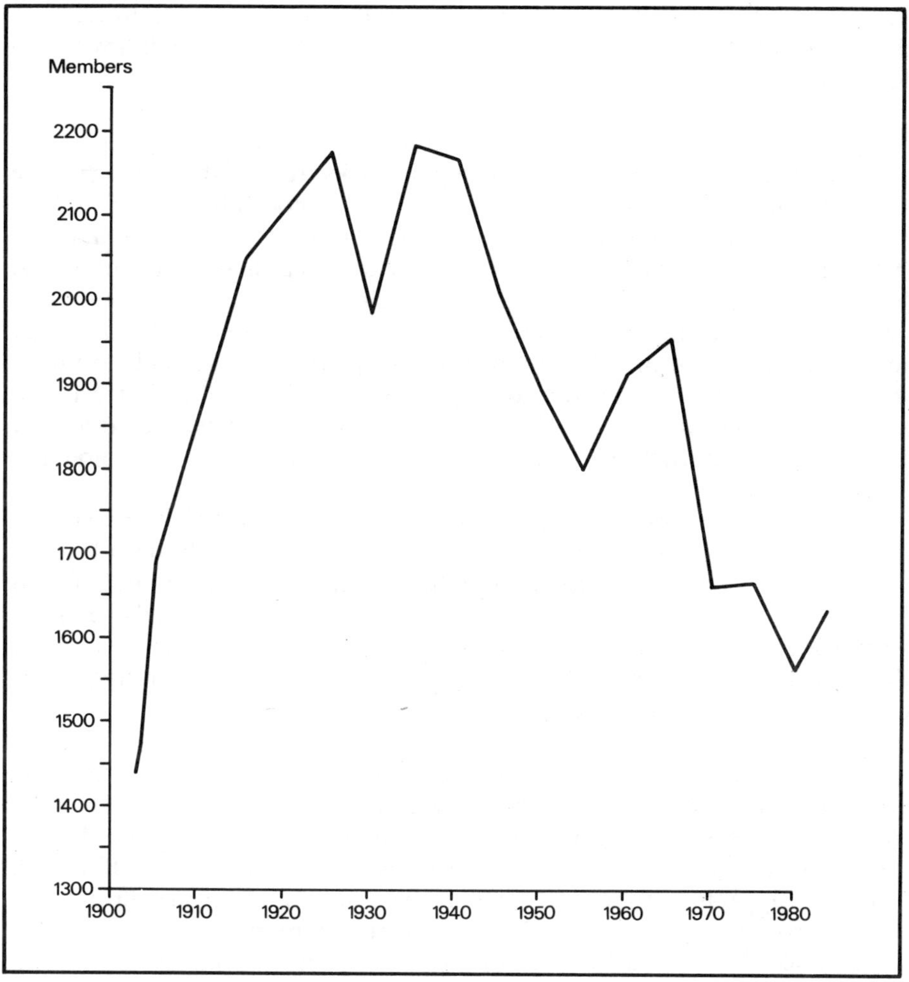

FIGURE 12.2: GRAPH OF TOTAL MEMBERSHIP OF FIFE BAPTIST CHURCHES SINCE 1900.

1924-5. In Anstruther there was a recovery in the thirties to be followed by a further decline in the forties and fifties, a pattern which largely followed the fortunes of the fishing industry.

The twenties also saw difficult times for the very young Rosyth Church. Despite being the most modern royal dockyard in the country, the Government, in 1925, decided to use it as a 'Care and Maintenance' facility. Many of the workforce were moved south, houses stood empty and the Admiralty was forced to reduce their rents. The effect, catastrophic for social life in the young community, was felt in the church where, in the course of a year, membership fell from seventy to thirty-eight. Worse was the fact that many who left were in positions of leadership, and it is difficult to find a month in the minutes when a deacon or Sunday School teacher was not returning to the south of England. Gradually the church recovered as folk from the surrounding area took over tenancy of the now low-rent houses.

In an earlier period it is significant that Leslie recorded its maximum population in 1881, the year after the church was founded, in the decade when T.W. Lister added so many to the church. Similarly the largest population in both Cupar and Newburgh was in 1851, when the churches in these towns were vigorous. Economic decline and changing population patterns within the region had a clear effect on the health and even the viability of the churches within the affected area.

Effective leadership, or perhaps, in the context of church decline, its absence, is another factor in falling membership rolls. This can be difficult to trace, for whereas during a particular ministry there may be evidence for the growth of a church, a decline is sometimes not so discernible. It would, however, appear to be the case that where there was a vacancy in the pastorate, particularly when this was prolonged, membership rarely increased at a steady rate. This is clearly demonstrated in the fairly recent history of the Inverkeithing Church, where the arrival of the present pastor in 1977 has seen a dramatically increased membership, which had been static at a low level for a number of years when the church was without a minister. Undoubtedly this has also been because of the impact of charismatic renewal within the Inverkeithing Church and the close proximity of a rapidly expanding community in Dalgety Bay, where there was some talk of establishing a new fellowship.

It is also hard to resist the suggestion that when a church declines to the extent of having around only twenty or so members, recovery is very difficult. In part this must be because the pool of labour from which the leadership of the church is drawn is too narrow. The recent fortunes of the churches at Largo, Pittenweem and Newburgh fit into this argument, though we have to say also that these communities are not the most thriving within the region and are also fairly settled, with static, or even declining population.

One means of dealing with apparent decline is to unite two churches in neighbouring towns together in one cause. Though never carried through in Fife, the idea has been proposed in various forms. The possibility of closer relationship between Pittenweem and Anstruther has been suggested. Such a policy, however, overlooks the fact that traditionally the two communities are quite different and retain the differing outlook to this day. The result has been to maintain the existing position. A suggestion has also been made in recent years to link Bowhill with Leslie and Glenrothes in some way. Again, however, Bowhill has little in common in either character or proximity to the other two.

Possibly the best example of such a scheme and the reasons for not carrying it through are provided in a letter dated 24 December 1945 from George Smith, the secretary of the Rosyth Church, to Dr Scott, then secretary of the Baptist Union. The letter was in response to proposals put by the Union representative at a conference of the Dunfermline and district churches in October of 1945. These proposals were for closer co-operation between the churches by means of a joint advisory council, which the Rosyth Church supported, and for uniting the Rosyth and Inverkeithing Churches as part of a circuit. This was rejected and for detailed reasons, which not only cast light on the general argument against such links, but also provide an insight into the position of a dockyard town church at the end of the war. Mr Smith wrote:

> We feel sure that such a scheme would work out to the detriment of both churches. (a) Rosyth and Inverkeithing communities have almost nothing in common. Inverkeithing is an old Scottish burgh with rather staid ways, while Rosyth is a modern suburb, cosmopolitan in composition and progressive in outlook. There are little comings and goings between the two towns. The whole tone and outlook in the two churches reflects the divergence in their respective communities. During the war as the population of Rosyth has become decreasingly Scottish this divergence has been accentuated still further.

With perhaps one or two minor amendments such a statement would have been made in other areas where such links had been mooted.

Secondly, it was suggested that such a scheme had been attempted before and failed. In the 1930s it had been proposed when Donald Dron became minister at Rosyth that he should also have pastoral oversight at Inverkeithing, which at the time had a student pastor. Practical co-operation had not been forthcoming and it was felt that it was most unlikely for such a scheme to succeed in 1945.

Smith's third point concerned the feeling that to ask one man to tackle the work in both towns would be unjustifiable and unfair to both the minister and the churches. He proceeded to outline the work of the Rosyth pastor:

> The work of the Minister of Rosyth Church involves not only the pastoral work of the congregation but also the officiating chaplaincy of the Navy. This means visiting the neighbouring naval establishments of H.M. Dockyard, R.N. Air Station, Donibristle, Port Edgar Hospital, and H.M.S. Waxwing, Dunfermline. As well as that there are numerous calls made on our minister's time by the floating population which inevitably exists in a dockyard town, whose names do not swell the official statistics but whose demands occupy pastoral time.

Finally, he was critical of the shortsightedness of the Baptist Union in failing to see the future potential of both churches. The Union, and in particular the Sustentation Committee, had failed to gain up-to-date knowledge of the situation in Rosyth and the whole matter 'had the effect of giving the impression to new members and office-bearers that the Sustentation Committee are interested mainly in financial economy'.[31]

Such a sustained plea did not fall on deaf ears. A meeting was held with representatives of the Sustentation Committee. Some months later, in March 1946, it is recorded in the church minutes that 'the suggestion from the Committee that the two churches, i.e. Inverkeithing and Rosyth, be under one Pastor was turned down'.[32] Arrangements were at once set in train for a married minister to be called to Rosyth. The idea of combination has not been revived since, and the two churches at different times have fulfilled the potential suggested in George Smith's 1945 letter.

A further influence on declining figures has been the changing social conditions of the twentieth century. Before the First World War the membership trend in the Fife churches was on the increase. Since then the trend has been downwards. The Great War certainly produced difficulties for the churches, though, as we have seen, in the case of Rosyth it saw the birth of a new fellowship. Most of the churches saw men join the forces, though this hardly dented membership rolls. In many churches the war is scarcely noted in the minutes and the Viewfield historians record that, 'There is no indication of the life of the church "just ticking over" during the war years. Hardly a month passed without baptisms and there was a good spirit in the fellowship . . . .'[33]

Perhaps the worst affected in Fife were the churches in the fishing towns of the East Neuk. The secretary of the Anstruther Church reported in an article in the *Scottish Baptist Magazine* for September 1915 the disaster that had come upon the town: 'One of the busiest of the smaller fishing towns on the east coast a year ago, it is now a dead city (industrially) and a fish is one of the last things you see.'[34] In December 1914, the minutes of the Pittenweem Church record 'the great crushing depression so very much felt in our district caused by the war'.[35] These comments apart, the war appeared to have little effect on the life of the churches.

Nor is there any evidence of decline in the post-war period. The life of the churches continued as normal. A look at a graph of Baptist Church membership shows decline between 1925 and 1930, but recovery between 1930 and 1935. When we examine individual churches, we may conclude that fall in the late twenties was as much a result of the economic situation as of anything else. Membership decreased in Anstruther and Pittenweem, where fishing declined, in Rosyth, where the dockyard was run down, and in Cowdenbeath, in the heart of the central Fife coalfield, in a period when the coal industry was suffering from severe dislocation.

The real slide in membership came between 1940 and 1955 and between 1965 and 1970 for Fife as a whole. Attempting to discern reasons for this is peculiarly difficult, since churches, in their minutes, hardly comment on the subject, and individual churches experienced different circumstances, with some even increasing their membership during this period.

It would appear that the Second World War had a greater effect than the First. It led to a greater dislocation to established living. More people were mobilized and movement became more common. That situation, along with what might be called the 'Spirit of the Age', lasted long into the post-war period. Certainly there was a feeling, latent perhaps, that it was harder to communicate the gospel.

Other social factors have also had an effect on church life since the war. The availability of transport, increasingly by car, has perhaps had an effect on the smaller churches, especially in an area such as Fife where distances between the churches are relatively short. It is sometimes attractive for a family to by-pass a small church with only twenty or so members for the opportunities of a larger one only ten to fifteen minutes away. The advent of television and the increasing lack of community spirit are also factors which the churches have wrestled with over the past forty years — with what success it is difficult to say, for the churches have adapted their life and work to changing circumstances.

Membership in Fife over recent years has been on the increase and it is too soon to assess the effectiveness of the three-year Scotreach evangelism programme, though this has stirred a number of the Fife churches to increased activity and awareness of their communities. There is no doubt, however, that they have much to learn in discerning areas of economic and demographic expansion within the region, in developing effective leadership in the churches, in pursuing evangelistic opportunities and in supporting each other within the bonds of the local association. These have been some of the chief pathways to growth over the past two centuries.

Notes

1. Alexander Smith, *The Third Statistical Account of Scotland: The County of Fife* (Edinburgh 1952), p 2.
2. A.P. Smyth, *Warlords and Holy Men* (London 1984), pp 39-40.
3. Smith, *Third Statistical Account*, p 34.
4. *The First Yearly Report of the Baptist Union of Scotland* (Cupar 1844), p 20. Subsequent figures are based on returns from churches to the Baptist Union of Scotland and reported in the *Scottish Baptist Year Book (SBYB).*
5. Sir John Sinclair, *Statistical Account of Scotland, 1791-1799: Fife* (East Ardsley, Wakefield 1978), p 680.
6. George Yuille, ed, *History of the Baptists in Scotland* (Glasgow 1926), p 149, records details of weavers in title deeds of Whyte's Causeway Church.
7. ibid, p 157.
8. *Viewfield Place Baptist Church, Dunfermline, Historical Sketch, 1841-1909* (Dunfermline 1909), sheet 6.
9. *The New Statistical Account of Scotland: Fife* (Edinburgh 1845), p 899.
10. Matthew McLachlan, *Whyte's Causeway Baptist Church: the first hundred years, 1852-1952* (Kirkcaldy 1952), pp 4-5.
11. ibid.
12. Archibald McColl, *A Brief Review of the History of Anstruther Baptist Church* (Anstruther 1960).
13. William Bathgate and Graham Fotheringham, *Viewfield Baptist Church, 1884-1984* (Dunfermline 1984), p 4.
14. Roll of Membership in Leslie Baptist Church, 1880-1920.
15. The source for the graph is *SBYB.*
16. Yuille, ed, *Baptists in Scotland*, p 155.
17. *SBYB*, 1909, p 69.
18. *SBYB*, 1910, p 76.
19. *Scottish Baptist Magazine (SBM)*, Aug. 1918.
20. Glenrothes (Church Street) has enjoyed the services of the same minister, Alexander Wright, ever since its inception in 1956.
21. Programme for Conference of Baptist Churches in Fife, Saturday 10 Nov. 1894, attached to Minute Book of Leslie Baptist Church, May 1890 to June 1904.
22. T.G. Henderson, *Buckhaven Baptist Church Jubilee Newsletter*, Feb. 1960.
23. Leslie Baptist Church, Deacons' Minutes, 1956.
24. Letter to A.D. MacRae in possession of Leslie, Glenrothes and Collydean Baptist Churches.
25. Minutes of Glenrothes and Leslie Baptist Fellowship committee, 13 Oct. 1980.
26. Lochgelly Baptist Church, Minute Book, 6 Jan. 1955.
27. ibid, 27 Nov. 1955.
28. The source for the graph is *SBYB.*
29. Smith, *Third Statistical Account*, p 249.
30. ibid, p 225.
31. Letter from deacons of Rosyth Church to Baptist Union of Scotland, 24 Dec. 1945.
32. Rosyth Baptist Church Minutes, Mar. 1946.
33. Bathgate and Fotheringham, *Viewfield*, p 8.

34. *SBM*, Sept. 1915, p 142.
35. Pittenweem Baptist Church Minutes, Dec. 1914.

S.D. Henry

13. TAYSIDE

Bordered by the Grampian Mountains to the north and west and the Ochil Hills and Firth of Tay to the south, Tayside is a relatively small area of land running in a south-west to north-easterly direction on the eastern side of Scotland. The Sidlaw Hills provide the backbone of the region and the major rivers are the Tay, Earn and Almond, flowing from the mountains in the west to feed the major estuary of the Firth of Tay. Sheltered from the west by the mountains and favoured by rich soil, the area is productive in arable farming, particularly in the Strathmore Valley, which lies between the Grampian Mountains and the Sidlaw Hills.

The major cities are Dundee, on the northern shore of the Tay estuary, with 275,000 people, and Perth, an ancient capital of Scotland strategically positioned between the Ochil and Sidlaw Hills, with 45,000 people. Industrial development was primarily linked to the flax, linen and eventually jute trades. The smaller towns such as Forfar and Arbroath, as well as Perth and Dundee, were involved in what was mainly a domestic flax industry. In the late eighteenth century this industry became centralized in Dundee, which was strategically placed to receive flax from Europe and the Baltic, and, in the 1830s, jute from the Indian sub-continent.

Flax was used to make sail canvas, coarse linen shirts for the army and clothing for negro slaves in America. Dundee was the focal point for the resulting prosperity. Between 1815 and the early 1830s not less than £250,000 had been spent on the harbour. There was a ferry across the Tay, a paddle vessel running to Perth and a daily coach to Glasgow.[1] The Dundee to Newtyle railway, opened in 1831, preceded the more successful Dundee and Arbroath Railway, which began in 1839.[2] It is not surprising that Dundee's population rose from 30,000 to 50,000 between 1816 and 1833.[3]

The industrial base for textiles was already well established when the jute industry mushroomed in Dundee. In 1833 there were 300 tons of jute imported into the town. Ten years later there were 4,858 tons. By 1863, 46,983 tons of jute were imported and Dundee was already a major centre of commerce. In 1851 trade in Dundee exceeded that of any other Scottish town except Glasgow. The city's industry fared particularly well in times of war, the demand for tents, sails and clothing being then high. Thus the Crimean War and the American Civil War benefited the city. As well as attracting people from the countryside to live and work in the city, industry drew in Irish immigrants whose trials in their homeland had been very great. In 1830 there were 2,000 Irish in Dundee. In 1840 there were 7,100 in Angus as a whole. By 1861 there were 14,366 Irish in Dundee, not including second-generation immigrants. Most of these worked in the linen trade. In 1901 31% of the total female population (73% of all employed females) worked in textiles. Similarly, 17% of the total male workers (26% of all employed males) worked in the industry.[4]

In times of boom and growth in the industry this was of great advantage, but there were also times of recession, especially when manufacturing moved to India, leaving many in great hardship. Opportunities for mission and ministry amongst the millworkers were there, and taken by the churches through their mission halls, but they also had the disadvantage of relating to a large Irish Catholic population which maintained a ghetto-like resistance towards those outwith their community. The Dundee churches faced many of the problems of urban mission.

Early Baptists

The presence of Baptists in Tayside is first recorded during the Commonwealth period of Cromwell's government, when a garrison was established in Perth. The effect of English Baptist soldiers upon a resistant Presbyterian community appears to have been minimal and passed when the Commonwealth era ended.[5] Tayside can with some justification, however, argue its case for being the seedbed of the Baptist movement in Scotland. The rise of the Glasite Churches within the region provided a forum for further Dissent and the subsequent emergence of the leadership of the Scotch Baptist movement.

In 1792 one in twenty of the population of Dundee attended a Glasite Church.[6] Robert Carmichael, originally the minister of the Anti-Burgher Secession Church at Coupar Angus, eventually came over to Baptist views, initially influenced by Glas's teaching and his friendship with Archibald McLean. Carmichael settled in Dundee in 1769 to set the small group of Baptists in order as a church.[7] Until then those who were persuaded of Baptist views, like others from Glasgow and Montrose, had to travel to Edinburgh for baptism.

Carmichael's influence led in 1770 to a small church being formed in Montrose, originally from a Glasite congregation, when seven men and two women were baptized by McLean in the River Esk. John Greig was appointed an elder by Carmichael, followed later by David Mill and Thomas Wren. This church continued for twenty years and then declined. The decline was no doubt encouraged by the doctrinal dispute that arose between Archibald McLean in Edinburgh and Neil Stuart, an elder of the Glasgow congregation, over the position of Jesus Christ within the Godhead. Stuart visited Dundee and Montrose to canvass support for his views. The church at Dundee was

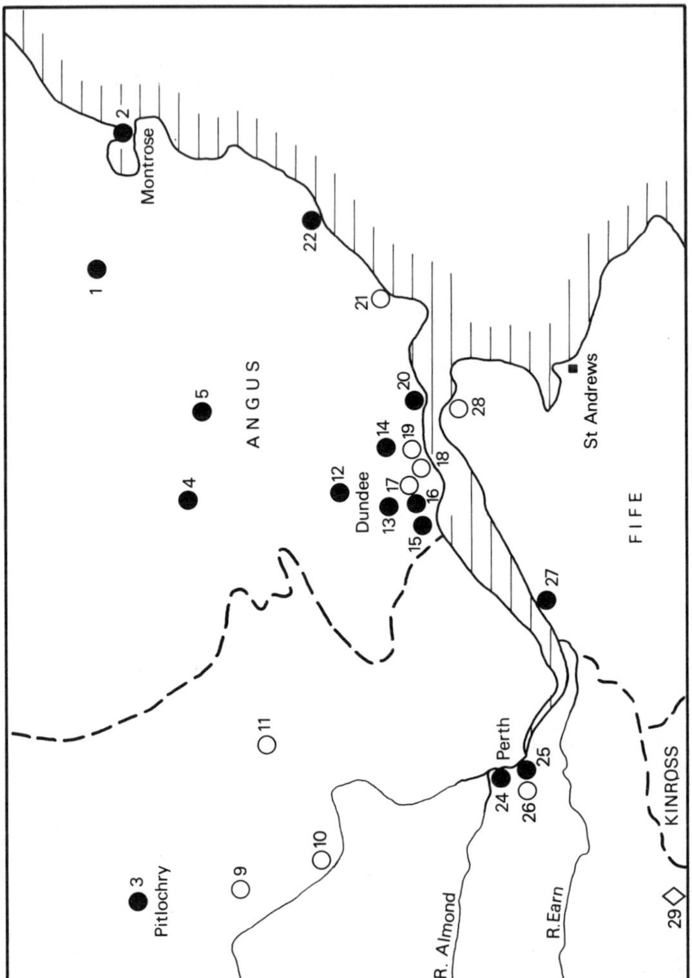

MAP 13 : TAYSIDE BAPTIST CHURCHES.

Key to Map 13

1. Brechin	11. Blairgowrie	21. Carnoustie
2. Montrose	12. Dundee: St Kilda Road	22. Arbroath
3. Pitlochry	13. Dundee: Lochee	23. Crieff
4. Kirriemuir	14. Dundee: Maxwelltown	24. Perth: Evangelical Church
5. Forfar	15. Dundee: Hawkhill	25. Perth: Canal Street
6. Killin	16. Dundee: Ward Road	26. Perth: West
7. Lawers	17. Dundee: Rattray Street	27. Newburgh
8. Aberfeldy	18. Dundee: North Seagate	28. Tayport
9. Tullymet	19. Dundee: South Seagate	29. Auchterarder
10. Dunkeld	20. Broughty Ferry	

more perplexed than convinced about the issue, but the small congregation at Montrose was largely ready to side with Stuart. After some time most of the congregation in Montrose recanted, but not without doing much damage to their credibility.[8]

Carmichael's sojourn in Dundee was short-lived. Returning to Edinburgh because of ill health, he died in 1774. This left the Dundee Church without leadership, and again it had to look to Edinburgh or Glasgow. Andrew Swanston, who had formerly been a Burgher Seceder, was baptized in Glasgow, although he came originally from Newburgh in Fife. For four years he preached in Dundee and Newburgh, and the results of this itinerant ministry were evident when several people from Dundee and Perth were baptized in 1784. Nevertheless, the numbers of the Dundee congregation were still low, and the church possessed no elders. Thirteen years after Carmichael's death, W.M. Dickie, who had been a deacon in the Edinburgh Church, was called to Dundee to the office of elder and in 1787 the church was set in order. James Duncan, one of the members, was chosen as a colleague for him, and in 1794 David Miller was also appointed.[9]

The growth of these Baptist causes was encouraged by such leadership, but as long as Edinburgh, as the 'Mother Church', insisted on exercising authority over them, that growth was stunted. Long before the Haldane influence touched these churches, the issue of what properly constitutes a church exercised the minds of their leaders. Andrew Swanston was swayed by the thinking of William Hynd of Newburgh, who argued that it was the duty of disciples to observe the Lord's Supper whether numbers were great or not, even in the absence of elders. Edinburgh held firmly to the Glasite view that elders were essential for the service, and in 1784 Hynd was expelled. Swanston, perhaps disillusioned by the dispute, went on an itinerant preaching ministry, independent of the Scotch Baptist movement.[10]

Controversy surfaced again when the Haldane churches adopted Baptist principles. Although the fresh wave of evangelism gave rise to new congregations, such as that in Arbroath (1810), the division of the Haldane churches into two parties — Independent and Baptist — left both factions weak. Perth, however, is a notable exception. The group that had arisen in 1784 from Andrew Swanston's itinerant ministry remained small, for even when constituted as a church in 1808 there were only twelve members. By 1810, as a result of additions from the old Independent and Tabernacle Connexions, it consisted of eighty members with four elders, four deacons and two preachers.[11]

As Baptist work expanded in Perth, so it grew in Dundee when William Innes of the Tabernacle Church and brother-in-law to the Haldanes adopted Baptist views. Most of the congregation maintained their paedobaptist stance, but they were evicted, as in Perth, to allow the minority who had followed their pastor to keep the premises. The Christian witness in Dunkeld suffered a great deal through the disruption of the Tabernacle congregation by J. McLeod who, even before he became a Baptist by conviction, proved a very forceful pastor. His successor, Robert Kinniburgh, found that most of the leading members had adopted Baptist views and that McLeod, by frequent return visits to Dunkeld, was encouraging others to take the same attitude. It seems that the Independent Church survived this onslaught, as it resumed meeting in 1813 under the leadership of John Black until his death in 1857. The Baptist witness, however, seems to have dissolved as quickly as it had started.[12]

As well as the Scotch Baptist movement and the Haldane phenomenon, another major factor in the early fostering of the Baptist cause in the region was the influence of the Baptist Itinerant Society and the Baptist Highland Mission.[13] These organizations and their successors sustained small congregations in rural Perthshire as well as elsewhere in the Highlands and Islands. In addition to the congregations at Killin (1808), Lawers (1808) and Aberfeldy (1846) which received support from the Home Mission, there was the commencement of work in Crieff by Alex McLeod, who was placed by the Baptist Itinerant Society in Perth in 1808. He moved to Crieff in 1810. Though this small town was to play host to such itinerant preachers, the nature of their ministry left the church pastorless for long periods at a time. James Scott of Alloa visited Crieff and Auchterarder periodically, but it was through the plea of the small Crieff congregation to the Home Mission that Alex Kirkwood was appointed in 1845 to sustain the congregations at Crieff and Auchterarder, with memberships of fifteen and sixteen respectively.[14] Most of these Perthshire congregations remained small in membership, but their influence in the community, often enhanced by the failure of the Established Church to sustain weekly services in remoter areas, was wider than such membership statistics would suggest.

Up until the beginning of the nineteenth century, the Baptist presence in Tayside was mainly in the larger towns. The congregations were small, often lacking in leadership of any calibre or theological training. The emphasis on itinerant evangelism which they shared with the Haldanes, however, led the movement into the smaller communities of Tayside. Attendances at these preaching stations could often be large. Duncan Cameron of Lawers recorded that at Aberfeldy in 1845 the Independent minister allowed the use of his chapel because the Baptist meeting house was too small for those wanting to hear.[15] Despite the popularity of such gatherings, the resultant membership of the churches was not large. In the first yearly report of the Baptist Union in 1844, out of a total of 662 members for Dundee and Perthshire, Tullymet was the largest cause with 131. This is exceptional, as it outstripped what was afterwards for many years to be probably the strongest Baptist Church, Meadowside in Dundee, which had 109. In comparison, Lawers had 38, Killin 22, Montrose 17, Glenlyon 12, Rannoch 17 and Aberfeldy 20.[16]

Although it could be said that the Baptists have had little foothold in predominantly agricultural areas, the reasons for this are more than the traditional outlook of rural communities. The fact that when the parish minister was absent from his church the congregation would attend services led by the Baptist preacher indicates a desire for the continuity which a settled ministry would provide. This lack, coupled with depopulation through emigration and the shift from the rural to the growing urban areas, set the seal on the Baptist Churches never being an integral part of rural life. It is in the largest towns that we find the chief growth of Baptist witness, especially in the latter half of the nineteenth century. From that growth we can discern factors at work that were absent in the smaller villages of Tayside.

In the early period of Baptist witness in Dundee, the appearance of new churches was due to dispute and division rather than planned evangelism. The issue of the observance of the Lord's Supper in the absence of elders, which affected many of the Scotch Baptist Churches in 1810, divided the Baptist community in Dundee into two. The Rattray Street congregation could trace its descent from those who felt such observance was legitimate and subsequently met in loft premises in Baltic Street from 1810 to 1835. By 1842 there were recorded three Baptist congregations, one attended by about 300 (the precursor of Rattray Street), the other two averaging thirty to fifty each (the North and South Seagate Churches).[17] The North Seagate congregation, begun in 1834 as a split from South Seagate over the re-opened communion dispute, came to an end in 1857, but not before having conformed to 'English' Baptist practice in 1849 by calling a salaried minister, the first being Thomas Henderson. After a succession of short-term pastorates, the church dissolved and the assets were given over to the Baptist Association of Scotland. The South Seagate Church closed in 1855 and discharged the debt on its chapel in 1856. Thus the initial dissenting group from the original Scotch Baptist congregation, moving from its Baltic Street premises to Meadowside in 1835, outlived the others.

Leadership

Although the Meadowside congregation had formerly taken issue with the Scotch Baptist principle of no communion without the presence of elders, it still held firmly to the plurality of non-stipendiary elders. This policy was pursued when two men from the Independent Church at Temple Lane, David Mills and David Lindsay, were invited to join James Law as co-pastors not long after their baptisms in 1831. Only when Lindsay emigrated to America in 1843 did Mills agree to join Law as co-pastor. He was already a successful businessman and was to typify the kind of leadership that the church was to inherit until it changed its policy regarding paid pastors. Though Mills later left the Meadowside congregation in 1856 over an unspecified divergence of opinion on doctrine, he went on to establish another church on 14 June 1863 in Constitution Road. He had exerted a useful ministry that braced the Meadowside congregation for the doctrinal difficulties.[18] Although two groups left the Meadowside congregation to meet in the King's Road Hall and in Salem Chapel, the church remained vigorous.

Though the plurality of elders may have posed its own temptation of jockeying for position, it also safeguarded the congregation from being totally leaderless if there happened to be a dispute. The Meadowside congregation survived Mills's departure and continued to grow numerically and in stature within the wider community. It was one of its most gifted and honoured elders, Sir Charles Barrie, knighted by King George V in the spring of 1919 in recognition of his services to the city, who first introduced the possibility of a trained pastor. He wisely smoothed the way by remaining co-pastor with the first salaried minister, T.W. Lister, who was called in 1890.[19] Active businessmen found it difficult to keep pace with the growing congregation and the subsequent strains of the pastorate. The reluctance to accept salaried pastors amongst Scotch Baptists, at least in Dundee, was more than a suspicion of the theologically trained. It also had its roots in the financial burden such men would be on the congregation. This is borne out by the example of John Gilbert, who led the South Seagate congregation for about fifty years until his death in 1848. He had formerly been an Independent minister in Queensferry. On coming to Dundee he was baptized and took up the post of unpaid preaching pastor while earning his livelihood as a teacher.[20]

Although the trend was to favour a salaried pastor, this did not always lead to runaway church growth. This can be seen in the demise of the North Seagate congregation mentioned above. Thomas Henderson, who in less than a year accepted a call to Elgin, where he also remained less than a year before moving to Glasgow, showed that a church which looked outwith the community for its pastor could also suffer, as the pastor's roots were not always put down in any particular place. Sadly for that congregation, its next pastor, James Blair, who had been the Baptist Association evangelist based in Dundee, had to resign through ill health after serving just over two years. The inability of the congregation to repay debts outstanding on its building finally led to its closure. The former members did regroup to form the Bell Street congregation, but again the first two pastors remained for only a year in total. Subsequently, J.O. Wills was called as pastor and, within three years of his ministry commencing, a congregation of thirty, giving £50 per annum, had increased to 150, giving £150 per annum. This was not to assure the Bell Street congregation of a future, for when the Police Commissioners served the 1870 Town Improvement Act upon the congregation, it was to lead to the church's demise.[21] The Meadowside congregation was to survive this same upheaval by moving to the present building in Rattray Street.

Why did one congregation ride the storm and the other founder? Perhaps the Bell Street congregation had no length of time to establish itself firmly. It had to depend on the Lochee Church to hold its baptismal services until a legacy of £50, together with two communion cups and books from 'the English Baptist Church which had at one time met in Seagate', was received.[22] Financial difficulties were never far away and perhaps the strain of supporting a pastor as well as maintaining property was too much.

J.O. Wills's successful ministry in Lochee previous to Bell Street shows that factors have to be considered other than leadership alone; however, the relationship between the progress of the Baptist cause and the movement of pastors cannot but be directly linked. A remnant from Bell Street continued to meet and in 1874 called J.Cumming Brown to be pastor. Brown had already exercised a strong and fruitful ministry in the Perth Church. After six years of his ministry, the congregation was considerably strengthened and meeting in its own premises in the Long Wynd. William Tulloch, whose leadership ability was widely recognized within the denomination, was to follow a short ministry by Charles McAlpine. After Tulloch's ministry of nearly six years (1883-9), David Clark came to the Long Wynd. Under his stimulating influence the church expanded, was resited in a new building in Ward Road, and established another congregation in the Maxwelltown district. Clark, whose sole ministry was that in Ward Road, gave ten years to establishing it as the leading church within Tayside (1889-1900). This was further consolidated by his successors, A.T. Walker, who remained seventeen years (1901-17), and D.D. Smith, thirty-one years (1918-49).[23]

Although there are other factors in the development of these churches, the leadership they received, both ministerial and lay, was an essential ingredient. Itinerant preachers or short-term pastorates did nothing towards establishing a lasting witness that could withstand the variety of fortunes each congregation had to face.

Liberality

There is evidence that liberality amongst the Baptist groups was crucial in the consolidation of strong congregations. Although the Bell Street congregation, under the gifted leadership of J.O. Wills, had increased in membership five-fold, its giving had only trebled. Initially there was a heavy financial input into the property by William and Alexander Gourlay, shipbuilders, and Robert Anderson, millspinner, but this came to an end with the Town Improvement Act of 1870.[24] In both the key churches in Dundee there were men of means who underwrote the liabilities. Sir Charles Barrie was eventually to gift the Rattray Street building to the church in 1916, having previously paid the cost of the manse. His concern was that despite the low rental of the buildings, the 'membership was largely composed of the working class'. He felt that it was therefore the more necessary to own the property.[25] This kind of liberality was matched elsewhere. James Lawson, who was a deacon and eventually became treasurer of the Ward Road Church, largely underwrote the stipend of the Maxwelltown cause in its early years. Of an annual salary of £100, John Dick received £80 from Lawson.[26] This generosity was duplicated by the Lawson family in later years in offering to pay the salary of a church sister to aid the minister in pastoral work. Both Barrie and Lawson were named in the *Dundee Courier* report on the Baptist Union Sustentation Day, 22 April 1914. Dundee gave £3,380 and took third place in Scotland. Of this amount Barrie gave £600, his wife £150 and Lawson £500.

Outwith Dundee there were similar situations. The Perth Church was favoured with the interest of Sir Robert Pullar of the famous cleaning and dyeing empire based in the town. He purchased the former Baptist Church in South Street and donated it to the City Mission. He also contributed generously to the purchase of the church's extensive property in Tay Street, the former Perth Theatre and Opera House.[27] Similarly, the congregation received the manse as a gift from Peter Campbell, a sweet manufacturer, in 1906.

In Broughty Ferry, the fashionable suburb east of Dundee, a new work was begun through members of the Tayport Church on the opposite bank of the River Tay. Once more the church depended on a person of means, the building being constructed in 1881 on land donated by Miss Cumming, who also left her house for use as the church manse.[28] The gift of manses was to be a considerable asset, particularly to the smaller churches, as they had difficulty in securing pastors if no accommodation was available.

In his presidential address to the District Association meeting at Rattray Street in March 1924, Councillor William McFarlane appealed for greater sympathy between the large and small churches. Smaller causes both deserved and needed assistance. They acted as feeders to the town churches as the young people grew up and an exodus took place to the cities. Meanwhile emigration to the colonies, coupled with congregations being predominantly female, left the churches weak in leadership.[29] Whilst it has been shown that those with financial means were liberal beyond the confines of their own church fellowship, it was certainly to the larger congregations' advantage to secure more eminent preachers for their pulpits and so retain their membership. Money helped to maintain the size of the bigger congregations. Conversely the lack of a firm financial foundation contributed to the decline — or at least non-growth — of the smaller, rural churches in the later nineteenth and early twentieth centuries.

Evangelism

Expansion was very much on the minds of Baptists in the second half of the nineteenth century. They benefited from the impetus of the 1859 revival. The period following the revival saw the establishment of a number of churches — Lochee (1865), Blairgowrie (1867), Carnoustie (1868), Forfar (1872), Broughty Ferry (1876) and Pitlochry (1881). Forfar and Lochee were the result of preaching tours. Richard Steel came south from Grantown-on-Spey and saw twenty-three converted and later baptized in the mill dam at Carsebank Farm, Forfar, amidst rowdy scenes.[30] Lochee, similar to Forfar in that the principal industry was jute weaving and spinning, also received a preaching visit, this time from the far south, in the person of T.W. Medhurst, the first student trained by C.H. Spurgeon at the Metropolitan Tabernacle in London. Although the outcome of this preaching and lecturing tour was only a small group gathering in the Weavers' Hall, it soon consolidated the work and called its first pastor.[31]

The Forfar congregation was subject to sharp criticism from the community due to its proselytism within what was a smaller population than Lochee. Despite this, baptisms in the Reid Hall, which could hold 1,400, were often crowded affairs. In August 1876 the members opened their own premises, seating 300, but not before the firm of building contractors had gone into liquidation, leaving them to complete the work themselves.[32]

The Lochee congregation seemed to establish a firmer footing. At its annual social in December 1869 there were about 200 present, and the members were in good heart despite the departure of J.O. Wills, to Bell Street, Dundee. Their offerings in the previous year had reached £200, and their activities in the arduous work of tract distribution amongst 'the most wretched of the village' were being 'blessed'. Again the leadership of the church was in the hands of local merchants, there even being an address given that afternoon by a Mr Scrymgeour of Tayport entitled 'Business and Religion'.[33]

There is little known of the church at Carnoustie. It disappeared from the local association records by 1899, when the church declined association help to find pulpit supply due to its 'accommodation problems'.[34]

The Pitlochry situation appears to run contrary to the tide of population drift. Its population was growing through its attraction as a health and holiday resort, not unlike Crieff, and the churches at Blair Atholl and Tullymet sustained services in a joiner's shop which had been converted into a little chapel. In 1881 the church was constituted and three years later in July 1884 it opened its own building on a site that was to prove more important in recent years.[35]

Another enterprise which proved short-lived was the beginning of a congregation at Blairgowrie. It grew from the transfer of eight members of the Tullymet Church in 1867. It had two pastors — from 1867 to 1872, David Young, and from 1873 to 1880, Finlay Forbes. Thereafter the Baptist presence in Blairgowrie becomes hazy. Ten years later it was noted by Grant Robinson of the Perth Church that there were 'a number of Baptists' there, including one of his own deacons recently removed from Perth. Auguries for progress, however, did not seem favourable, either from the newly resident deacon or from the Baptist Home Mission, which declined to contest the ownership of property once belonging to the Baptist cause.[36]

Meanwhile town-dwellers were seeking ways and means of developing Baptist witness within the city limits. The churches in Perth and Dundee worked in the impoverished areas of their towns, from which they gained many children for their Sabbath Schools. The Rattray Street Church maintained a mission, originally in the Miller's Pend, Brook Street, though it was moved to the West Port and known as the 'Caley Mission' in Caledonian Road. Similarly the Long Wynd Church had a missionary vision, evidenced in its taking over the service previously run by the YMCA in Kinnaird Hall for a month's trial.[37] Whether this work continued or not is uncertain. Obscurity also surrounds the Henderson's Wynd Mission which appears in the minutes of a church meeting on 27 February 1879. It was decided to dispose of it at the next church meeting. Both these activities disappear from the church records.

New activities do appear — such as the mission started in Session Street in connection with the Tract Society, and the Open Air Mission held at the top of Long Wynd before the evening service. The decision, taken on 13 February 1890, to commence a mission in Wellgate Hall during David Clark's ministry, was to prove a significant step not only for Long Wynd/Ward Road, but also for Dundee as a whole. From the successful evangelistic work in the Wellgate in the early years came the beginnings of the church at Jamaica Street in the Maxwelltown Halls district. This mission was aided greatly by the church's Tract Society, which visited homes in eight districts in the Wellgate neighbourhood. Two years later, a further enterprise was begun with the hiring of a room in Todburn Close for 'Gospel work'. This, like others, disappears from the church records, but it indicates the zeal for evangelism that prevailed at the time. To distribute 40,000 tracts and circulate 116 printed sermons in a year is a considerable feat.[38]

The Wellgate Mission flourished, thus making it possible for the church to make the sacrifice of purchasing the Maxwelltown Halls from Ex-Provost Hunter for £1,275 in 1898. A significant aspect of this extension work was that Ward Road, even in the loss of thirty-four members who founded the church at Maxwelltown, did not suffer unduly and was set for future growth itself. The Maxwelltown Church also grew by leaps and bounds under the ministry of John Dick. In the course of his ten-year ministry he baptized 321 persons and received into membership 495. There were 350 members in the church on his departure.[39] This kind of success was never to be realized again.

Another mission was begun by Ward Road in the Cowgate. The work continued throughout the Great War, but in August 1919 the 'Evangelistic Section' of the mission resigned en masse. The church recognized that continuing the work was a fruitless effort in an area which was greatly depopulated due to the expansion of commercial premises. It was decided to maintain the youth section but to look for alternative premises. By 1922 it was back in the Wellgate opposite Morrison's Court. This property fell into disrepair and the mission was again on the move, eventually settling in 1925 at 45 Arbroath Road. It continued there until the Second World War, when it was finally closed. Though served and aided by the sponsoring church, it never reached the point of being an independent fellowship, though it had many of the characteristics of a church — Sunday School, Bible Class, Sunday evening service, Thursday Prayer Meeting and 'Saturday Gospel Tea

Meeting'.[40] It was sustained by a loyal group of Ward Road members and acted as a 'feeder' for the main church. Through a lack of initiative from the main congregation and a different social climate from that of the late nineteenth century, it survived and no more.

Baptist Co-operation

The greatest attempt to unite energies and resources came through the establishment of the District Committee of the Baptist Union in December 1892. In its early years this was an extension arm of the Union and it sought to meet the opportunities and tackle the difficulties of an increasing population. It soon turned into a District Association for Angus and Perthshire. Its high hopes were rarely fulfilled. In November 1896, for instance, it planned to hold a series of evangelistic services. Five churches applied. Only two campaigns, at Pitlochry and Broughty Ferry, actually took place, though there was a 'gratifying amount of blessing'. A resolution of 1906 to establish one new church every ten years was more than optimistic.[41] An over-ambitious view of the likely number of conversions in the community, coupled with the restrictions that the Great War introduced, curtailed many of the aspirations of the zealous.

There were occasions when the churches maximized their advantage independently, such as when Ward Road pioneered the new cause at Maxwelltown. An attempt to imitate the Maxwelltown success in the Hawkhill district of Dundee, however, was a protracted failure. Alex Piggot, minister of Leven in Fife, began a Sunday service by advertizing in the newspapers. Grossly inadequate premises were found in Hawkhill. Though a church was formed in 1903, its membership never rose above forty-eight and steadily declined until it was next to closing in the autumn of 1926. Through appeal to the association and eventually the Union, there were concerted efforts to revive the work. As Piggot's health was failing, it was decided by an association sub-committee to ask him to resign 'almost immediately'. This was to open up the way for a future settlement and an appeal was made by the Baptist Union to the larger Dundee Churches to transfer members to the Hawkhill Church.[42]

The whole situation indicates some of the strengths and weaknesses of Baptist life at the time, and perhaps inherently. It would appear that Piggot, the initiator of the work at Hawkhill, was now an obstacle to its progress. The association appeared to be the saviour of the small church. Its direct involvement in the affairs of the smaller congregation, even at its own request, pointed out the need for stronger links with other Baptists. Because of the Baptist practice of independency, however, the association could not make 'executive' decisions. This was the conclusion of the Ward Road Church when it received the request from the Baptist Union in December 1927 to transfer members to Hawkhill. The deacons voted by ten votes to four to take exception to the procedure. They declined to bring the request to the church meeting (though in the course of that year thirteen members were transferred to Hawkhill!). The reason given was the lack of consultation with the two other churches in the area, coupled with the general decline of interest in the city that meant other churches were struggling for existence. Co-operation was not always a Baptist strength.[43]

The association sub-committee considered all sorts of approaches to maintain the Hawkhill witness. One suggestion was a diaconate consisting of two deacons from each Dundee Church including two from Hawkhill if any were available. The Baptist Union was prepared to grant a sum of £500 over four years if it were matched by Hawkhill and the association.[44] The church did survive these difficulties, calling J.S. Andrews of Whiteinch, Glasgow, to be pastor, but it was never to gain the strength of the Maxwelltown congregation to which it had been compared.

In the years between the wars the association again attempted to challenge the community with the gospel in a Dundee District Campaign. It commenced in 1924, using the Baptist Union evangelist, T.A. McQuiston. After three months of ten-day missions in many of the churches in Dundee, the conclusion of the mission committee in May 1925 was regret that it failed to reach the 'outsider'. The committee also felt it would be a mistake to assume that each church would support another during its use of the evangelist. Nevertheless, there was a great deal of co-operation. There were two united services held in Rattray Street and Ward Road on Sunday evenings and a united young people's meeting which filled Ward Road with upwards of 700 youth from various Sunday Schools and Bible Classes of the Baptist Churches in Dundee and Lochee.[45] Despite the obvious uplift the mission brought to the Baptist community, the conversions and baptisms which did result from the campaign were mainly from within the church congregations.

According to the 1925 report of the association, the overall membership of the churches had increased, but only marginally, yet in contrast the Sunday Schools had decreased in membership by about 150.[46] This was part of the overall trend in Scotland at this time. One explanation, it may be argued, was that evangelism was not accompanied by attempts to relieve many within the populace of financial hardship. One other factor lay in the timing of the Baptist Union Mission. It followed on from an evangelistic campaign led by Gipsy Smith, the celebrated evangelist, in October 1924, this being a united church effort. It is possible that Gipsy Smith's campaign could have prepared the ground for future worthwhile mission, but the evidence does not bear this out. The Baptist Churches were heavily involved in the united mission and perhaps this was reflected in the lack of commitment to the other churches during McQuiston's mission.

War and Unemployment

Although the textile industry was boosted during the years of the war effort, such prosperity was short-lived. The first fifty years of the twentieth century were unparalleled for their social upheaval, which had an impact on the Baptists in much the same way as it affected the other denominations. Two World Wars and a major industrial recession took their toll on the evangelistic optimism of the late nineteenth century.

Even the First World War had blackout restrictions, which often meant using church halls for evening services in the winter. By 1918 the Baptist Union was requesting names of men willing to give pulpit supply, as ministers were not to be excluded from 'call-up duty'.[47]

The immediate post-war years brought their difficulties too. The industrial slump and growing unemployment brought a despondency to all areas of society. Yet for the strong churches such as Ward Road the situation was not too bad. At an Annual General Meeting in February 1921, the pastor, D.D. Smith, reported 'notwithstanding the social unrest in the country, he could say without affectation or flattery that the church had been alive to its spiritual purpose and had justified its existence'. The treasurer echoed this in his statement that 'not another church in Dundee had a like satisfactory report, the year's accounts being square with a slight surplus'.[48]

Instead of the economic gleam becoming brighter, it of course dimmed. The pressing need of the populace, in the eyes of most in the city, was not salvation, but work. In 1929 Ward Road agreed to have a collection for the Distressed Miners' Fund. By 1934 a motion was brought before the Ward Road Church that more time be given in the Baptist Union Assembly to discussing social service. The outcome was a public meeting arranged for September 1934 under the auspices of the association's Unemployment Economic Committee. R.C. Duffin, a member of Ward Road, championed this cause, travelling to the Glasgow and Fifeshire Associations to speak on 'The Church and Unemployment'. The attempts to rouse the church into action, both politically and socially, were preceded by the activity of Maxwelltown Baptist Church. With the innovative ministry of David Kyles commencing in September 1931, there began a craft class to counteract the demoralizing effects of unemployment. This was an opportunity for both men and women to make saleable articles, though it was not designed to be commercially viable. It was a precursor of the community service of today, but it was funded by non-government aid. Despite the fact that this was the first class of its kind in Dundee, the work was not on the Prince of Wales's schedule when he made a visit to the city in March 1933. The reason for this was the church's withdrawal from the scheme co-ordinating such classes, as money was received from a well known betting shop for the benefit of these efforts for the unemployed. When the Prince of Wales inquired as to which of the many craft and occupational classes was the first to be started in the city, the officials were embarrassed to find that the Maxwelltown Church's name was not listed for a visit. The Prince of Wales, however, insisted on seeing the pioneering class even though it was outwith the original itinerary.[49]

It is a relfection of the overall concern of the Baptist community — albeit taking the lead from other denominations such as the Congregationalists and the Church of England — that they tried in some way to alleviate the suffering which the Depression had brought. Maxwelltown Baptist Church could guarantee an attendance of 200 men at the special weekly meeting for the unemployed, over and above the twice-weekly craft class. There was no deflection from the spiritual concerns of the church in its recognition of the needs of the physical man.

The sorrows of the Depression were soon to be eclipsed by the darkness of the Second World War. As in the Great War, many of the churches found their best young people joining the forces, and this time the civilian population was even more involved in the war effort. One elderly gentleman of 88 years, a member of Ward Road Church, was commended for having knitted 140 pairs of socks over a two-year period![50] It was a time of great uncertainty. Churches refrained from repairing their property because of government restrictions and the threat of air raids.

The blackout conditions meant a decrease in evening attendance at church and a subsequent fall in overall giving. The immediate post-war years were no less difficult. A growing concern for the integration of demobilized soldiers was voiced in the church at Ward Road:

> What is causing concern is what is to be the response of the returned soldiers to the call and claims of the church. Individual members have a responsibility to make the soldiers feel they owe something to the Church and the Christian faith in which they were reared.[51]

By the following year the hope of quickened progress was not realized. Ministry amongst returned soldiers was disappointing: there was 'no small hostility to divine institutions and religion itself'.[52] If this report is a fair indication, then there was a growing gulf between those who served in the forces and those who had remained at home. Within this climate of disillusionment the church sought to minister in the years after the war.

Post-War Progress

In Perth, the long ministry of Grant Robinson came to an end in 1947. For fifty-seven years he had been pastor of the Tay Street congregation. In 1908 its membership was the largest in the association, and it was to peak at 450 in 1918. Although the membership was beginning to grow before his arrival in 1890, there is no doubt that Robinson was an outstanding preacher of the time. His long absences and somewhat eccentric behaviour, however, caused a major division in the church. A large number moved in 1920 to the Guild Hall in the High Street and subsequently to the St John's West Mission Church in the South Street of the town.[53] Whilst it could be argued that the population of Perth could sustain two Baptist congregations, the circumstances were less propitious than at the creation of the Ward Road/ Maxwelltown extension in Dundee.

The Tay Street congregation continued to decline whilst the West Church, as it became known, was consolidated under the ministry of Matthew Cook. When in 1947 both churches fell vacant at the same time, the Tay Street congregation being only a handful of members, Robert Sloan came as pastor on condition that both congregations joined together in the Tay Street building. Its extensive halls, as well as a large auditorium, had the prospect of being developed in Sloan's ministry as a residential centre in what would have been a strategic position in Scotland. Perhaps if the church had not withdrawn under Sloan's influence from active participation in the Baptist Union, it might well, with denominational help, have achieved that end. On Sloan's departure from Perth to join the Church of Scotland ministry in May 1969, a small breakaway group, led by John Davidson, formed the Perth Evangelical Church, which regarded itself as Reformed Baptist. This move allowed the main congregation greater freedom to participate in the life of the Baptist Union once more.[54]

Ministerial changes were also taking place in Dundee. D.D. Smith, who had been an established figure in the city for thirty-one years, retired as pastor from Ward Road in 1949. There then followed a hard time for the church in settling the vacancy. At Broughty Ferry a minister was being sought at the same time, the stipend offered there being £220 per annum, the minimum recommended by the Baptist Union. Ward Road, on the other hand, was debating offering the stipend of £600, plus £50 expenses. One nominee had indicated he would not come from the south of England, where he was at the time, for less than £750 plus expenses. This whole period in Ward Road was difficult financially, for repairs to manse and church had been deferred due to the war. Different attitudes towards the nature of the church also appeared. The constitution had been changed in 1949 to make it a closed membership church after seventy years of open membership. This had been brought about through the efforts of Richard Goddard, who expressed considerable disquiet later that year when it was discovered that since the change there were a number of persons baptized privately, which defeated the purpose of a public profession of faith.[55] With the settlement of Douglas Robb from Dewsbury in 1951, however, the church took up again its city-centre ministry, but was never to reach the strength and influence which it had under D.D. Smith.

The aim of church extension was always at the heart of the association, but never fully realized. This can be illustrated as early as November 1929 when Montrose was especially mentioned in a committee meeting as a town of nearly 11,000 inhabitants, yet without Baptist representation. Nothing was done to further this concern until 1936, when the Montrose Forward Movement received £10 towards its expenses on the casting vote of the chairman. By 1937 Baptists were once again represented in Montrose but to what degree they received real encouragement from the association is difficult to determine.[56] This hesitancy was to be repeated several more times.

In 1955 the Baptist Union accepted a recommendation from the Angus and Perthshire Association that £2,000 from the sale of the Hawkhill Church properties should be allocated to Ward Road for extension activities in the Douglas and Angus area of the city. This work, along with efforts by the association in Menzieshill in 1960 and in Whitfield twenty years later, came to nothing. Part of the problem was that though there were groups of Baptists living in and near these housing estates, the pull of the city centre churches was greater than the desire to have a church in the areas where a large majority of people lived. Though there were some valiant attempts at establishing a new cause, especially in the large estate of Whitfield, the number of Baptists from the churches in Dundee prepared to do the initial pioneering work was small. Attempts to utilize the Baptist Union scheme of pioneer ministry, strongly backed by the Broughty Ferry Church, also came to naught, principally because the Union could not find a man who would be able to tackle the task.[57]

Therefore despite the roles of the association in providing encouragement and a bond of fellowship, it was never able to commence or initiate a church throughout its history. The best initiatives came from individual churches themselves, though even then not all were successful.

One such successful venture was undertaken in the St Mary's housing estate in Dundee, under the leadership of A.W. Inglis of Rattray Street. Beginning with open-air meetings and house-to-house visitations, eventually a large Sunday School and uniformed youth organizations were established using the local school. From the beginning of the work in 1954 it took only two years to open, free of debt, a simple church/hall type building on St Kilda Road. Like Maxwelltown before it, the new cause depended greatly on the leadership of the sponsoring church, Inglis being pastor of both churches until Alex F. Duncan was appointed sole pastor of St Kilda Road in 1960.[58]

Such initiatives were duplicated in housing estates in other towns. The tendency of city councils to build peripheral estates has exercised the Church as to whether it should go to where the people now live or expect them to travel to the centre. The Montrose Church has sought for many years to establish itself in the Borrowfield district of the town, and, despite a lively youth work and Sunday School, has found local authorities non-co-operative in granting permission for the purchase of land to erect a building.[59]

The Perth Church, despite a sympathetic District Council which gave free use of the North Muirton Primary School for Sunday School purposes, was not to see that work consolidated into a church. At the commencement of a vacancy, almost coinciding with the dramatic loss of its church property by fire in July 1984, the Perth Church virtually ceased work in that district.[60]

The latest established cause in the Tayside area was begun at Brechin in November 1974, when a small group of Southern Baptist servicemen based at Edzell began to meet as a fellowship at 22 Church Street in the town. By 1976 they procured the West Street Columba's Parish Church through the Baptist Union. Eventually the church has become less 'Southern Baptist' in character, but it has made no dramatic impact on the town.

Various Ministries

Of all the towns in the association in Tayside, Pitlochry has perhaps made the greatest impact on the Baptist Union as a whole. This was through the development of the Atholl Centre under the inexhaustible leadership of Watson Moyes, the minister there from 1965 to 1983. Gilbert Ritchie, who was Baptist Union Youth Director at the time Watson Moyes was in college, encouraged him to consider the charge at Pitlochry with a view to establishing a denominational training centre. Within four to five weeks of his settlement in the church, Moyes presented the need to his deacons. The small church at Pitlochry did more than what would be considered reasonable over many years of planning, funding and giving hospitality to the many extra visitors. The centre opened in 1971, two years after Atholl Baptist Centre Ltd was formed, and within two years of making a direct appeal to the churches. Moyes, joined by his wife, who was a teacher of hearing-impaired children, planned to equip the centre for a threefold purpose — as a youth centre, a training centre for the wider church and a resource centre for the disabled.[61]

The Atholl Centre was readily 'adopted' by the association as part of its overall ministry, the local churches contributing not only directly but also by specific events to raise funds. Overall, the Centre has kept to the original vision of its founder, but its central position geographically, whilst being attractive for summer pursuits, is a disadvantage in the winter when church life is at its busiest and weather at its worst. Its future is very much dependent on the overall denomination, and, whilst it receives the continued support of members of the local Baptist community, it could not be sustained by them alone. Because it acts as a service arm of the churches in caring work, the Centre reports annually to the Union on its varied programme. In 1987 a new phase of developments was launched.

Much 'quieter' ministries have been undertaken by other association churches. The Arbroath Church maintained a 'Centre' too. This was the Arbroath YWCA, which, on the retiral of its resident missionary, Miss Ann Todd, was sold to the Baptist Church.[62] Miss Todd, who was a member of the Arbroath Church, together with the pastor, Ernest Barnes, were the prime movers in this step of faith. The Centre has been used by many youth groups, and the Baptist Union Youth Camps come regularly to use the facilities. These were very basic until the Centre was recently refurbished, and whilst its uses are limited, there being no resident staff, it has always been in demand both within the denomination and beyond.

Concern for those nearing the end of life has been seen through the ministry of the Robertson Rest Home, Newport, begun in 1947. This work has been supervised by members of the Rattray Street congregation who are trustees of the retirement home in memory of one of their longstanding leaders within the church.

Epilogue

At this present time in the Angus and Perthshire Association, co-operative fellowship is at a low ebb. Meetings of the council and the combined rallies have been suspended in order to analyze the future of the association. To some degree, the association has turned full circle, reverting to the way it began. The positions of leadership which once had a certain esteem no longer appeal to 'modern' Baptists. This is not a local phenomenon, of course, and is part of a nationwide trend. Over the whole period the association has been functioning, there have been repeated calls to the churches for greater input into the affairs of the association. As in most cases, it was those most heavily committed in their own churches who responded to that call.

Outwith the Baptist community linked by the association, other churches with the same broad sympathies exist, and are usually intensely independent. Mention has been made of the Perth Evangelical Church. There is also a Free Evangelical Church in Kirriemuir. Though it is linked to the Federation of Independent Evangelical Churches, its pastor, Albert Norris, meets with the Baptist ministers' fraternal of the association for fellowship and prayer. Forfar, too, has another Baptist witness, Forfar Bible Baptist Church, which has relied on leadership and help from non-Southern Baptists in the United States. Again, this church refrains from association with the other Baptist Churches.

In reviewing the progress of the Baptists in the Tayside Region, it would have to be admitted that expansion is neither apparent nor likely in the present climate. If the past has anything to teach us, the necessary ingredients are strong and dynamic leadership, coupled with financial liberality on a large scale, often by wealthy individuals, supported by a large nucleus of people who make that extension work a personal goal.

The future of the Baptist witness in Dundee at any rate will be coloured by the union of Rattray Street and Ward Road in January 1987 to form the Central Baptist Church. These two fellowships have discussed and rejected merger many times, but since the Ward Road Church was greatly reduced in membership and its pastorate had recently become vacant, it seemed that the time had come for that step of 'rationalization'. The proximity of these two churches of the same denomination has been an enigma to many Baptists as well as others in the City of Dundee. Perhaps under the ministry of James Clarke and the recently appointed associate, Victor Bundock, formerly of Peterhead, the Baptist witness at the centre of Dundee can take a new tack. Thus two churches pursuing different channels for well over a century are pooling their resources and preparing for ministry in the nineties. In the past they have given leadership to the Baptist community of Tayside. It may be that, united, they will fulfil that role again.

Notes

1. W. Howe, *The Dundee Textiles Industry, 1960-1977* (Aberdeen 1982), p 8.
2. S.J. Jones, *Dundee and District* (Dundee 1968), p 165.
3. Howe, *Dundee Textiles Industry*, p 9.
4. W.M. Walker, *Juteopolis: Dundee and its textile workers* (Edinburgh 1979), pp 114, 86.
5. George Yuille, ed, *History of the Baptists in Scotland* (Glasgow 1926), p 29.
6. See cap 1, p 19.
7. Patrick Wilson, *Origin and Progress of the Scots Baptist Churches from their Rise in 1765 to 1834* (Edinburgh 1844), pp 7-8.
8. ibid, pp 9-12, cf cap 1, p 22.
9. ibid, pp 10, 19, 25.
10. ibid, pp 20-3.
11. ibid, p 54.

12. Harry Escott, *A History of Scottish Congregationalism* (Glasgow 1960), pp 268-81. The reference in Yuille, ed, *Baptists in Scotland*, p 279, to a continuing Baptist cause in Dunkeld appears mistaken.
13. See cap. 15, pp 284, 286.
14. *Report of the Baptist Home Missionary Society for Scotland*, 1846, p 19.
15. ibid, p 16. The date of 1846 for the origin of the church at Aberfeldy (Yuille, ed, *Baptists in Scotland*, p 275) is apparently mistaken since one is noted there in the *BHMS Report*, 1843, p 21.
16. *First Yearly Report of the Baptist Union of Scotland* (Cupar 1844), pp 40-1. On Tullymet, see cap 15, pp 287-8.
17. *Ward Road Baptist Church Jubilee, 1873-1924* (Dundee 1924).
18. 'Baptists in Dundee', Dundee District Library Local History Section, 189(4).
19. Yuille, ed, *Baptists in Scotland*, p 162.
20. *Ward Road Jubilee.*
21. 'Baptists in Dundee', Dundee District Library Local History Section, 189(3).
22. *Ward Road Jubilee.*
23. Yuille, ed, *Baptists in Scotland*, p 163.
24. 'Baptists in Dundee', Dundee District Library Local History Section, 189(3).
25. Rattray Street Baptist Church Minute Book, 13 June 1916.
26. *Ward Road Jubilee.*
27. Yuille, ed, *Baptists in Scotland*, p 166. *Perthshire Courier*, 26 Mar. 1891, 1 Jun. 1891.
28. ibid, p 159.
29. Angus and Perthshire Baptist Association Minute Book, 3 Mar. 1924.
30. Yuille, ed, *Baptists in Scotland*, p 164.
31. ibid, p 160.
32. ibid, p 164.
33. 'Baptists in Dundee', Dundee District Library Local History Section, 179(3).
34. Association Minute Book, 1, p 84.
35. Yuille, ed, *Baptists in Scotland*, p 168.
36. Association Minute Book, 1, pp 8, 11, 15.
37. Ward Road Baptist Church Minute Book, 1874-1893.
38. Ward Road Baptist Church Deacons' Minute Book, 1.
39. *Maxwelltown Baptist Church Jubilee, 1898-1948* (Dundee 1948), p 4.
40. Margaret Bibb and Helen Smith, *Those Hundred Years* (Ward Road Baptist Church Centenary) (Dundee 1974), pp 9-10.
41. Association Minute Book, 1, pp 128-9.
42. ibid, 3, 16 Dec. 1927.
43. ibid, 3, 3 Dec. 1926.
44. ibid, 3, 2 Feb. 1927.
45. ibid, 3, 8 May 1925.
46. ibid, 3, 14 Nov. 1925.
47. Ward Road Baptist Church Deacons' Minute Book, 1906-1920, 28 June 1918.
48. Ward Road Baptist Church Minute Book, 1918-1939, 2 Feb. 1921.
49. *Maxwelltown Jubilee*, p 9. Information from Mr J. Dick, deacon of Maxwelltown Baptist Church.
50. Ward Road Baptist Church Minute Book, 1940-1956, 17 Feb. 1943.
51. ibid, 13 Feb. 1946.
52. ibid, 12 Feb. 1947.
53. Yuille, ed, *Baptists in Scotland*, p 167.
54. Personal knowledge.
55. Ward Road Baptist Church Minute Book, 1940-1956, 11 Feb. 1948 and 23 Mar. 1949.
56. Association Minute Book, 4 Sept. 1936, Nov. 1937, 1940, 26 Nov. 1948.
57. Personal knowledge.
58. St Kilda Road Baptist Church Magazine 'Rendezvous', May 1981.
59. Personal knowledge.
60. Information from Mr R. Small.
61. Information from the Rev. T.W. Moyes.
62. Information from Mr R. Halliday.

J. Quinn

14. THE NORTH-EAST

One autumn day in 1651 young Gilbert Burnet, together with the other citizens of Aberdeen, stood watching a sight which was a cause of alarm and puzzlement. Three regiments of English infantry were marching into the city after overwhelming victories over the Scots at Dunbar and Inverkeithing. News of the latest disaster at Worcester had just arrived. Aberdonians decided against resistance after the storming of Dundee by these same soldiers a few days previously. Still, there was cause for alarm, for the city had already experienced invading armies. A royalist army in 1644 had looted the place and left nearly 200 citizens dead in the streets.

This time it was different. As Gilbert Burnet said, 'There was an order and discipline, and a face of gravity and piety among them, that amazed all people.' There was puzzlement as well as alarm. The Scottish army was the army of a covenanted nation. The Covenant made it plain that the nation was to be exclusively Presbyterian; but, if that was the only form of religion acceptable to God, how could the armies of the covenanted nation be overthrown? Theologically it seemed impossible; yet here was an English army in the streets of Aberdeen. Moreover, Gilbert Burnet noted, 'Most of them were independents and anabaptists: they were all gifted men, and preached as they were moved.'[1]

These Baptists and Independents could not be ignored. Andrew Cant, minister in the new town of Aberdeen, attempted to preach against them in his parish church. Soldiers in the congregation soon pointed out the error of his ways. Swords were drawn, although not used, and the army took disciplinary action to prevent further interruptions of civilian services. These men could not be ignored and curiosity led Scots to seek the reason for the behaviour of these unusual invaders. They listened to their preachers, prominent among whom was Samuel Oates, the Baptist chaplain of Pride's Regiment. Soon there were Scots adopting Baptist views.

These early Scottish Baptists were taking a dangerous course. Nine years previously, in 1642, Othro Ferrendaill, an Independent, had arrived in Aberdeen. Apparently he was a refugee from the Irish rebellion who set up in business as a skinner and became a burgess. Soon it was noticed that he was not attending the Presbyterian services and enquiries revealed him conducting secret worship in several houses. Ferrendaill was excommunicated by the Kirk and his life became so intolerable that he was obliged to conform.[2] However, one man, a Baptist, stood firm — Gilbert Garden of Tillyfruskie, near Banchory. He had held services in his farmhouse, morning and evening, for his family and employees. Boldly he declared his principles when brought before the Provincial Assembly, which ordered his excommunication. He was arrested in Edinburgh in 1643 and imprisoned in the Tolbooth. His father was sheriff depute but no influence could save him.[3]

People listened to Samuel Oates and other Baptist soldiers as they sought to know more of their beliefs. Some became Independents; others went further, becoming Baptists. Prominent among these were two ministers — John Forbes of Kincardine O'Neil and William Youngson of Durris. They enjoyed freedom of worship under Cromwell's government and the beginnings of a Baptist Church were appearing.

In December 1653 Cromwell assumed the title of Lord Protector, arousing fierce opposition from Fifth Monarchy Men. The Fifth Monarchy movement was republican and largely Baptist. Its members wanted no kind of king to follow Charles I and they identified Cromwell with the beast who would make war against the saints (Daniel 7/18-22). Samuel Oates was busy, sending letters to the influential Glasshouse Church in London and writing to Baptist officers serving in Scotland, inviting them to meet and decide their response to the situation. The correspondence was intercepted and all officers implicated were arrested. Soon no Baptist, from General Overton down, was left in a position of authority. Samuel Oates was cashiered and imprisoned, and a number of court martial cases were dealt with early in 1655.[4]

Meanwhile the Kirk had not been idle. Already John Forbes had been visited by the presbytery to enquire into his conduct. Probably as one of the influential Forbes family it was difficult to find elders to testify against him. His uncle was a bishop and his father, the builder of Craigievar Castle, one of the wealthiest merchants in Scotland. No further action appears to have been taken. He died in 1657 or 1658.[5] The other minister among the Baptists, William Youngson at Durris, was less fortunate. Having no influential connections, he was ejected from the parish in the autumn of 1656. Losing both home and income, he was in a difficult position and died in poverty some time later.[6] Gilbert Garden died and his farm was sold in 1668.

The infant Baptist cause in Aberdeenshire was thus crushed out of existence through the action of church and state. After the Restoration the new bishop of Aberdeen ensured that there was little trace left.[7]

Students in Aberdeen

For a generation or so Baptists had vanished from the north-east. In England the Clarendon Code sought to achieve the same result. Even when freedom of worship was granted following the Revolution in 1688, Nonconformists were still prevented from graduating in the universities of Oxford

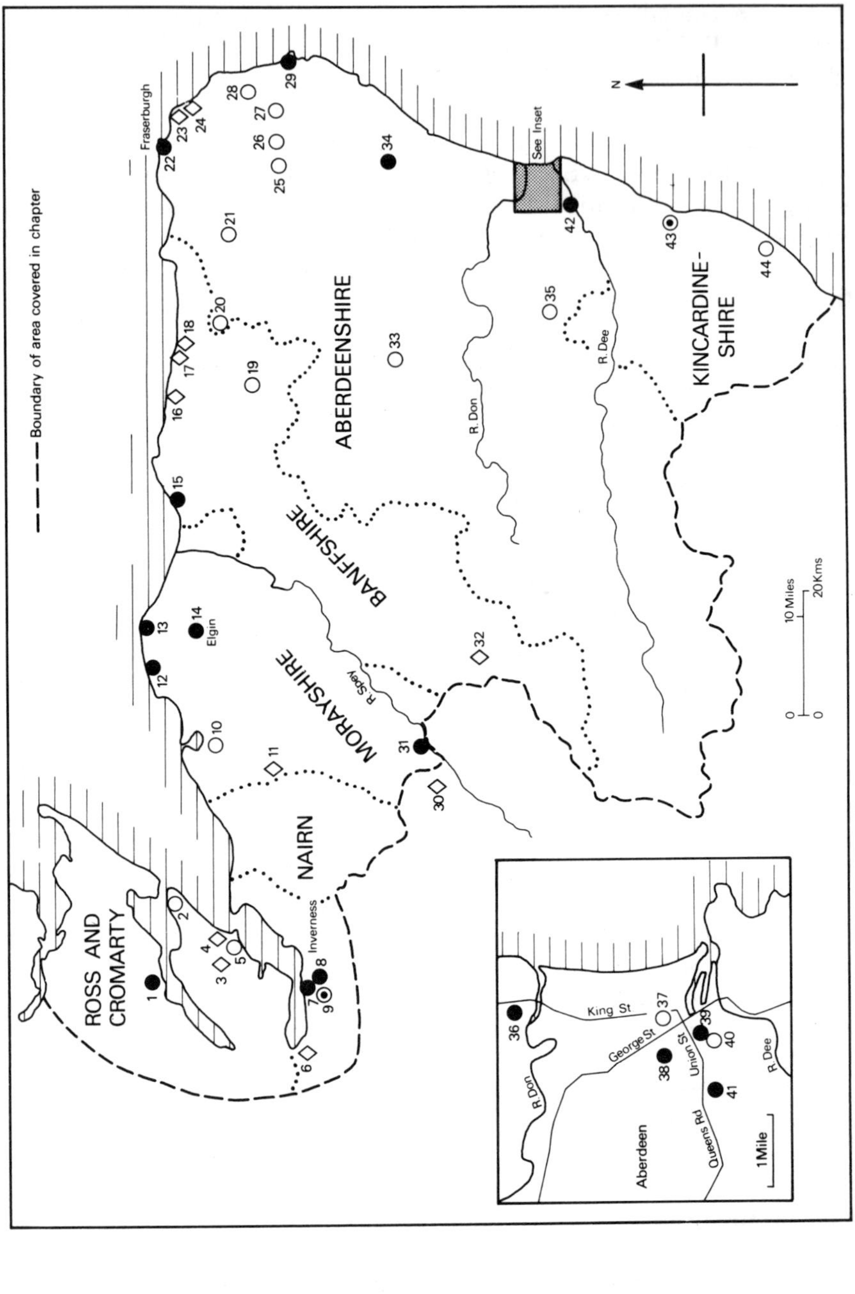

MAP 14 : NORTH-EASTERN BAPTIST CHURCHES.

Key to Map 14

1. Alness
2. Cromarty
3. Killen
4. Rosemarkie
5. Fortrose
6. Beauly
7. Inverness: Reformed
8. Inverness
9. Kinmylies
10. Forres
11. Logie
12. Hopeman
13. Lossiemouth
14. Elgin
15. Buckie
16. Portsoy
17. Whitehills
18. Banff
19. Aberchirder
20. Balmaud
21. New Pitsligo
22. Fraserburgh
23. Inverallochy
24. St Combs
25. Old Deer
26. Mintlaw
27. Longside
28. St Fergus
29. Peterhead
30. Duthil
31. Grantown-on-Spey
32. Tomintoul
33. Insch
34. Ellon
35. Echt
36. Aberdeen: Bridge of Don
37. Aberdeen: Longacre Mission
38. Aberdeen: Gilcomston Park
39. Aberdeen: Crown Terrace
40. Aberdeen: Academy Street
41. Aberdeen: Union Grove
42. International (Cults)
43. Stonehaven
44. Bervie

and Cambridge. From 1728 English and Welsh Dissenters appeared among the graduates of the two colleges at Aberdeen. After 1754 the number of Baptists among them is more noticeable.

In that year John Ward left an endowment for the education of two young men, sons of Dissenters (preferably Baptists) at a Scottish University (preferably Edinburgh). With the perverseness of youth, for the next fifty years most went to Aberdeen. If the Baptist witness in Scotland had been smothered, Scotland was still able to contribute to an educated Baptist witness in England.[8]

Probably the best known Baptist student was Robert Hall, who came from Leicester in 1781 to take an arts course at King's College. Later, when recognized as one of the greatest preachers of the day, Marischal College gave him an honorary DD. He never used the title of 'Doctor', however, and his memorial in Broadmead Chapel, Bristol, simply described him as Robert Hall, AM. Other eighteenth-century Baptist graduates at Aberdeen included Thomas Llewellyn, pioneer of Baptist missions in North Wales; Samuel Stennett, Joseph Hughes and Thomas Chevalier, the surgeon, all from London; and Caleb Evans from Bristol.[9]

A New Beginning

The north-east stretches from Kincardineshire to Easter Ross and from the Highland hills to the sea. It includes the city of Aberdeen, the Highland town of Grantown, the commercial and administrative centres of Elgin and Inverness, and the fishing ports of Morayshire and Buchan. The closing decades of the eighteenth century brought great changes to the area which were to continue well into the next century.

At the outset there were food shortages and riots, particularly in Easter Ross and the Black Isle. Highland crofts were being emptied of their people during the Clearances and large new farms were being created in Buchan and Banffshire. Sheep were being introduced in the Highlands, whilst on the coast larger and better boats were able to fish much farther from the shore and the herring fishery was growing in importance. Numerous little towns and villages were being built or reconstructed. Great civil engineering projects like the building of the Caledonian Canal and Telford's new roads were followed by the early railways. These required a substantial mobile labour force, largely recruited from the counties of Moray, Banff and Aberdeen. Improved communications encouraged movement of the hungry and the dispossessed to the hosiery mills of Aberdeen and the heavy industries of the Clyde. Easier movement of manufactured goods encouraged higher living standards in the north-east. Less tangible, but no less important, was the arrival of new ideas and a new outlook. Into this scene of change, among a people on the move, came an upsurge of evangelism.

1797 was a landmark in the north-east. In that year several individuals felt led to evangelize the area and, when they did so, they found responsive audiences. Opposing the prevailing Moderatism of the Established Church, they proclaimed a gospel which demanded faith and repentance from their hearers. Initially the purpose was not to form new churches or denominations but simply to deliver a message of salvation.

James Watt, an Irishman who later became a minister in Glasgow, came to Balmaud and travelled all over Aberdeenshire and Banffshire, preaching as he went.[10] Some of the hearers were stirred and later, as they thought out the implications, small Scotch Baptist Churches emerged. These included Balmaud (1797), Old Deer (1800), New Pitsligo (1803), Aberchirder (1807), Silver Street, Aberdeen (1807), St Fergus (1809) and Fraserburgh (1810). Some had a brief period as Independent Churches before becoming Baptist.

At this point the Haldanes appeared on the scene. In July 1797, taking a vast stock of tracts and accompanied by two kindred spirits, John Aikman and Joseph Rate, James Haldane set out for the north. Sometimes alone, sometimes as a group, they preached in each town or large village on their route. At Aberdeen they upset the authorities by getting the town drummer to announce their meetings and holding a meeting on university property, in each case without prior permission. Haldane had to apologize, but great crowds came to hear. Proceeding through Ellon, Peterhead, Elgin, Forres and Nairn, they reached Inverness. On their way they preached in the open air, either in market places or from convenient flights of steps. Sometimes ministers of Secession and Relief churches gave the use of their premises. Sometimes they simply preached 'in the street'.

The party now divided. Haldane and Aikman took ship from Burghead for Orkney and Caithness. Returning south by road through Ross-shire, they preached at Tain, Invergordon, Drummond (Evanton) and Dingwall, reaching Inverness on 18 October. Here they rejoined Joseph Rate, who had been engaged in a vigorous mission for the previous seven weeks. Among the hundreds who gathered, a high proportion were young people. Rate had worked throughout the Black Isle and Inverness area, one of his first trips out of town being to Aldourie, home of the Grants who befriended William Carey in India.

At their first meeting in Inverness the congregation filled the Methodist chapel and manse and overflowed into the street. There followed a preaching journey through Nairn, Elgin, Huntly, Aberdeen and back to Haldane's home near Stirling. James Haldane published an account of the tour. His closing remarks concerned the spiritual needs of the people and the necessity for taking action in response. There must be 'the means to send forth labourers into the harvest'. He felt the need was for evangelical preachers and 'Sabbath-evening schools'.[11] Other journeys followed.

Having shown that laymen could preach the gospel effectively, James Haldane now dedicated himself to the development of this work. With his support and encouragement, itinerant preachers made their way into the north-east early in the nineteenth century. They included such men as David McRae, Walter Munro and Lachlan Mackintosh.

David McRae was a Master of Arts from King's College, Aberdeen. He associated with the Independents at Huntly and made his first preaching tour along the coast to Dingwall in 1801. Ordained the following year, he settled at Avoch in the Black Isle. Accepting Baptist principles, he was baptized in 1805 and published *A View of the Old and New Way of Doctrine*. Being obliged to leave the Independents, he now moved to nearby Fortrose, where a Baptist Church was soon formed. It was to continue for almost a century, with preaching stations at Rosemarkie and Killen. In 1812 he moved to Edinburgh and taught students for entrance to the university.[12]

Walter Munro was a great traveller in the Gaelic-speaking areas; but in 1813 he succeeded David McRae at Fortrose. He still went on long tours and visited Grantown in 1818. Inverness became his base about 1820, but his success here was limited, the Evangelical scene being dominated by James Kennedy, the outstanding minister of the Independent Church in Fraser Street. After Munro's death in 1836, the few Inverness Baptists worshipped with the Independents.[13]

Lachlan Mackintosh was perhaps the most promising of the men trained by James Haldane. As an Independent he was responsible for founding a church in Rothiemurchus. When he discovered believer's baptism in 1807, some of the people accepted it too. He went to Edinburgh to discuss the situation with Haldane, who was already interested. In February 1808, Mackintosh was baptized and in March James Haldane followed his example. Returning north, Mackintosh formed Grantown Baptist Church and visited Elgin, where he conducted the first baptismal service. Although supported financially by the Tabernacle in Edinburgh, he encountered many difficulties. He was denied accommodation anywhere in Grantown, and the infant church had to meet in a quarry. It was here that young Peter Grant found them singing in the open air and this most successful of Highland preachers found his Saviour. Whilst based at Grantown, Lachlan Mackintosh still went on preaching tours. Thus in 1818 he visited Elgin, Boyndie, Portsoy, Whitehills, Aberchirder, Banff, Balmaud, Fraserburgh, St Combs and Inverallochy. Dedicated and determined, one day he walked twenty-four miles in continuous rain against a head-wind which prevented him using an umbrella. Returning to Grantown, he baptized three in the Spey. In 1826 he left for Dundee.[14]

Dugald Sinclair, though supported by Christopher Anderson rather than by Haldane, did similar itinerant work. He entered the area in 1810, walking down the new road from Ullapool, preaching wherever he stopped. His route lay through Strathpeffer (where he preached to invalids at the spa), Dingwall, Foulis, Invergordon and Cromarty. At Beauly he met Christopher Anderson from Edinburgh. The scene in the market square must have resembled the meeting of Stanley and Livingstone. Travelling to Inverness they preached simultaneously on opposite sides of the river, each with about 1,500 hearers. Then they travelled south by coach.[15]

Early Churches

So much for a few itinerant preachers and missionaries — what of the churches? In the fluid situation then existing some sprang up for a short time and then quietly disappeared. Often there was no specially constructed building and little visible trace remains.

Thus at Cromarty there were half-a-dozen Baptists who spent much of their time attacking the Church of Scotland rather than seeking sinners. They soon faded away.[16] At Echt, James Wight who farmed at Wester Echt gathered a dozen or so in 1827. They were constituted as a church in 1840 and continued until the farmer left for Aberdeen in 1867.[17] At Fraserburgh a church was formed in 1810 with a pastor named Smith, but it seems to have ceased before 1840. Another farmer, Alexander Morrison, accommodated the oldest church in the north-east at Balmaud, near Macduff, from 1797, when its members encouraged James Watt's tour. There were still Baptists in Balmaud fifty years later.[18] Independents formed a church at New Pitsligo in 1803 which became Baptist in 1805 and continued for some eighty years.[19]

Elgin Baptist Church emerged from the Independent ranks in 1808 and led a struggling existence for many years. In Aberdeen a church continued to meet in an upper room in South Silver Street. In 1821 John Gilmore gathered a church which met in Union Terrace. The members were beset with financial difficulties and had to sell their premises in 1828, moving to John Street. Following unsuccessful negotiations to merge their open membership church with the closed communion Silver Street Church, they ceased to meet in 1837. Just then Alexander Stalker came to Aberdeen for the sake of his health. Within six months the John Street Church was re-formed with Stalker as pastor.[20]

Whilst Fortrose continued in isolation in the Black Isle, a group of small churches in Buchan and Banffshire formed an association. When constituted in June 1832, it was purely an auxiliary designed to raise funds from St Fergus, Balmaud, Aberchirder and New Pitsligo for Haldane's Home Mission. The auxiliary became strong enough to bargain with James Haldane. In return for their continued financial support a missionary should operate in the area for six months each year. Haldane agreed but had difficulty in keeping the bargain. The missionary, James Campbell, was so successful that a new church of thirty-two members was formed at Insch and the other churches complained that he had too little time to work among them.[21]

When Lachlan Mackintosh left Grantown, the members called one of their number, Peter Grant, to the pastorate ,and he was ordained on 30 June 1829. With help from Aberdeen he fitted up a house in Grantown as a place of worship. On fire for the gospel, he preached almost every day and two or three times on Sunday. By 1833 the premises had to be enlarged. In 1848-9 there were so many enquirers that every member of the church was engaged in counselling new converts, and the church became one of the largest in Scotland, with responsibility for seven Sunday Schools.[22]

Near the area of the Buchan churches, but apparently not connected with them, another Baptist cause emerged at Longside, near Peterhead. George Thorne, a Baptist exciseman, was stationed there in 1840. He gathered others for worship in a pair of cottages adapted as a meeting-house. Baptisms took place in his garden where he had an open-air baptistry. When Thorne was promoted and transferred to Edinburgh in 1859, this group moved to Peterhead and formed the present church there.[23]

The Disruption of 1843 had consequences for the Baptists. On a wide front the Free Church became a very influential body, large enough to swamp the efforts of small Baptist groups. However, there was a good measure of co-operation. At Elgin the large Free Church congregation had to build new premises and during construction its members met in relays in the old Baptist chapel. At Grantown the Established Church and the Free Church could hold services only in alternate weeks. As neither congregation would attend worship conducted by a minister of the other denomination, they went to the Baptist chapel when their own minister was absent. For some time Peter Grant had a different congregation every week; but he took no unfair advantage, and when he was ill in 1857 the two Presbyterian ministers took turn in supplying the Baptist pulpit.[24]

In Aberdeen things were different. Dr Alexander Anderson, parish minister of Boyndie, joined the Free Church at the Disruption and came to the Old Aberdeen congregation in 1845. His theological development continued, however. Having discovered the truth of believer's baptism, he was censured by the Free Church Assembly, and adhering to Baptist views, was obliged to resign his charge. He commenced a new Baptist Church at Ross's Hall, George Street, and refusing any payment for his services there, he started a school — the Gymnasium — which gained a high reputation as well as supplying him with an income. He maintained an effective witness at George Street for many years.[25]

1859 and After

A great religious revival began in 1859 in Ireland and soon aroused interest in Scotland. 1860 was a poor year for the Moray Firth fishermen. With time on his hands, James Turner, a fish curer and Methodist lay preacher, embarked on a preaching tour of the Moray Firth ports.[26] The consequences were dramatic. Free Church congregations were much affected and their ministers had difficulty in restraining women from preaching and congregations from singing hymns instead of psalms. The Baptists recognized no such restrictions. Thus a meeting in the Free High Church, Elgin, began at 7 pm and closed at 11. The people then adjourned to the freedom of the Baptist chapel and continued until 4 am next day. The following evening the chapel was packed out, with hundreds standing outside, listening through the open windows. A prayer meeting was to be held in a house but it became so dangerously overcrowded that the police had to clear the building.[27]

At Inverness thousands attended great open-air meetings in Farraline Park. It might have been a wholly Presbyterian gathering, but among the ministers was a Baptist, Ferdinand Dunn from Fortrose, meeting the largest congregation of his life.[28] At Grantown Peter Grant was thrilled to report sixty-one baptisms in the year and the membership fast approaching 300.[29]

The Elgin Baptists had been a mere handful when William Tulloch began his pastorate in 1843, and the work was handicapped further by a controversy about total abstinence. Yet foundations had been laid for further growth, a new chapel had been built and the next pastor, Thomas Vasey (1858-61), joined people who were prepared for action when revival came. Soon twenty-three Lossiemouth people were in membership at Elgin and they formed the new Branderburgh Baptist Church in May 1861.[30] Just over a year previously, led by Robert Stewart, a bookseller in membership at Elgin, a group of Baptists from Elgin and Grantown formed a church in North Street, Forres.

In 1866 Stewart was baptizing in the River Findhorn at Roff's Pool. Early in 1868 he engaged in a series of debates on baptism in crowded meetings at the Independent chapel. By mid-March the Independent minister was fighting a rearguard action.[31] The first Baptist minister, James Scott, arrived in Forres a couple of months later.

The 1859 revival seems to have made little impact at Silver Street, Aberdeen; but, during the pastorate of G.S. Mee (1857-62), the John Street Church emerged with large congregations of well-educated people. Among them were two well known journalists, William McCombie and James Macdonell.[32]

Elsewhere fairly short-lived Baptist meetings arose at Bervie (1862) and Mintlaw (1864). At Inverness, led by a local doctor and property owner, Duncan MacKay, a small Baptist group appeared as a distinct body from the old Fraser Street Independent Church, which ceased in 1875.

Now began a period of construction and development. The Disciples of Christ (Campbellites) had started a new cause in Fraserburgh in 1840, placing their usual emphasis on the absolute need for believer's baptism. By 1859 this had become a Baptist Church which grew considerably during the revival and moved into the Town Hall for services, building its own chapel in 1877.[33] Peterhead Church used Maiden Street Hall and the Pavilion Hall, but constructed its own premises in 1878.[34] Both churches had called their first full-time ministers a few years previously.

The fishermen of Lossiemouth were able to build a little earlier and opened their new chapel in 1868.[35] Forres came later, opening new premises in Caroline Street in 1884.[36] Meanwhile Grantown continued to prosper in the chapel built in 1851 and improved in 1882, whilst operating numerous prayer meetings and schools in the surrounding countryside.[37] During construction of the Highland Railway, Peter Grant's son, William, and Robert Stewart of Forres held many meetings for the navvies.

The fishing ports of the Moray Firth continued to experience revival movements. These were much more local affairs than the great movement of 1859. Thus the Lossiemouth church roll shows great additions to the membership in 1893, 1901 and 1922, with smaller but still marked increases in 1933, 1945, 1955, 1959 and 1961. Similar developments occurred elsewhere in the area. Some were spontaneous movements, others the result of campaigns by evangelists following the visit of Moody and Sankey in 1874. There followed some thirty years of consolidation. Progress was maintained in the towns, but the old Scotch Baptist Churches met increasing problems regarding local leadership and some isolated churches began to decline.

In Aberdeen the neighbouring churches at John Street and George Street came into closer fellowship, holding united communion services. John Street chapel was no longer large enough for the numbers attending. In 1870, at the suggestion of a deacon, William McCombie, editor of the *Aberdeen Free Press*, a building was erected in Crown Terrace, and in 1877 the two churches united on the new site.[38] The Longacre Mission was started in 1871. A Silver Street pastor, John Hagen, was much involved in the campaign conducted by Moody and Sankey in 1874. Many were added to the church, being baptized in the River Dee near Duthie Park. Their premises could no longer hold the growing congregation and so the church moved to the Athenaeum until 1876, when Bellevue Academy in Academy Street was purchased and adapted as a place of worship.[39]

The temperance movement was of increasing interest. Many Baptist Churches had a Band of Hope and Women's Temperance Association, and ministers were expected to speak on the subject. Organizations like the Good Templars and the Free Templars operated across denominational boundaries, becoming a means of closer fellowship between churches. The rally held at Forres on 1 August 1875 was typical of many. A special train brought people from Elgin, Rothes and Fochabers. Headed by their brass band and joined by the Forres contingent, some 500 Templars marched through the town to the Cluny Hills. There they heard five addresses, including one by John Downie, minister of Forres Baptist Church. The addresses were short, humorous and not limited to the drink question, but urged work 'for the social and private life of their fellow men'. The band played, two choirs sang, many danced to the music of pipes and fiddles, whilst others competed in athletic events. Then came the return march to the station. In time-honoured phrase, a good time was had by all.[40]

End of the Century

The closing years of the century were still full of changes. Several small country churches faded from the scene. At Fortrose, Ferdinand Dunn retired on health grounds and the church disappeared about 1890.[41] In Aberdeenshire the last of the country churches ceased to exist. Geographically the Baptists seemed to be shrinking.

Academy Street, Aberdeen, had problems. It was largely a working-class church which had come to depend on the generosity of one family — the Stewarts of Banchory Devenick — for the financial support of the pastorate. It was a closed communion church, but about 1882 John Stewart began to doubt the wisdom of barring any true believer from the communion service. Accordingly he withdrew from the church and his financial support went with him. Never again could Academy Street afford a full-time minister.[42]

However, John Stewart and his financial support were still available for Christian service. Free to consider the whole situation in Aberdeen, he saw the need for another Baptist Church. He approached six other gentlemen and at a meeting at Banchory House it was decided to proceed. Initially services were held in the Northern Friendly Society's hall and later in Ross's Hall in George Street, formerly occupied by Dr Anderson's church. With Stewart's financial support, Alexander Bisset became the first minister and conducted the first service on 17 October 1886, a church of thirty-four members being formed on 26 January 1887. The death of John Stewart occurred soon after, with the consequent loss of his financial support, but the Baptist Union made grants to enable the work to continue. By aggressive evangelism the membership grew to 215 in three years. In 1893 the members obtained a site for their own premises in Gilcomston Park. Generously assisted by John Stewart's daughter, the building was opened for worship a year later.[43]

Crown Terrace had been much involved in launching Gilcomston Park Church and was the source of many founder-members. Within Crown Terrace remained some who felt that yet another Baptist Church was needed. Mrs MacAllan had left a legacy for the purpose. Led by James Crichton of Sandilands Chemical Works, five gentlemen agreed on 25 July 1891 to start a new church for the growing city and contributed the first £325. A site was obtained in Union Grove, and a hall was opened on 14 August 1892. The following January, with a membership of twenty-five, the first minister, S.G. Woodrow, was inducted. There followed a period of steady growth.[44]

During the pastorate of Clarence Chambers, Crown Terrace took a leading part in the formation of the Northern Association of Baptist Churches in 1876. However, this body seems to have lost much of its influence after his departure from Aberdeen. A new association was formed and began to operate in the autumn of 1894, one of its keenest advocates being S.G. Woodrow, pastor at Union Grove. The member churches were almost all in Aberdeenshire and the city churches seem to have dominated the scene. Until 1982 the constitution showed that it consisted of 'the Baptist Churches in Aberdeenshire and neighbouring Counties'.

This reveals a problem which has always troubled the association. It covers a vast area, part being distinctly Highland, part a close-knit group in Moray, but with the city of Aberdeen at the extreme end. The association's activities have tended to be grouped into eastern and western districts, based on Aberdeen and Elgin. The recent introduction of an annual Family Day at Elgin is, however, an influence for unity. Early in its existence church extension was considered, and probably the association was responsible for an advertisement in the *Inverness Courier* in January 1898, inviting Baptists interested in forming a church in Inverness to meet A.S. Sievewright, the minister of Forres, at Macgilvray's Temperance Hotel. Members of Dr Mackay's former Baptist group joined with recent incomers to form Inverness Baptist Church. The first services were held and the church constituted before the month was out.[45] Things moved quickly in those days. The same advertizing approach was used later when exploring possibilities at Nairn and Alness.

Entering the Twentieth Century

The period from 1895 to the First World War was one of mixed success and failure in the midst of public controversy. At Inverness the dynamic ministry of Alexander Bremner ensured a growing church and crowded premises. Originally a temperance agent, he was in constant conflict with the drink trade. There was even one occasion when he expected two angry bailies who were distillers would throw him out of the Town Hall.[46] An active Liberal, he was involved in all the political controversies of the time. Whether marching in workers' demonstrations, addressing meetings or conducting overcrowded services, it was difficult to be unaware of the Baptist Church and its minister.

On the other hand, Forres was facing difficulties and was obliged to close down in 1902. Aberchirder, in a district with a shrinking population, survived the war but had to close in 1921. Academy Street, Aberdeen, had problems of finance and leadership, with the war creating further difficulties. The church ceased to exist about 1921.

Along the coast lay the fishing village of Hopeman. First John Garden and then John Sutherland and his wife, undeterred by threats of stoning, had been baptized and joined the church at Lossiemouth in the 1860s. A few others joined them in their six miles' walk to worship as years passed. From 1893 new members from Hopeman were added every year. In consequence a branch cause was organized at Hopeman in 1896. Following an evangelistic campaign by James McKendrick of the Baptist Pioneer Mission, a number of people were baptized at Hopeman by Alexander Bremner of Lossiemouth. The Hopeman cause was constituted as a separate church on 9 September 1900 with twenty-four members.[47]

Meanwhile the fishing port of Buckie was growing, and in December 1903 the Baptist Home Missionary Society sent Alexander Bremner and W.J. Lippiatt to spend three weeks there. Before they left, a group of Buckie people agreed to form a Baptist Church. They met in the Volunteer Hall and moved to the Good Templar Hall before building their own premises in 1910.

At Crown Terrace the long pastorate of W.S. Chedburn ended with his death in 1909. Not only had the church taken the lead in the formation of Gilcomston Park and Union Grove Churches, but it had the first Christian Endeavour Society in Scotland.[48] Chedburn's son, Jackson, became minister at Union Grove in 1924. Crown Terrace next called to the pastorate Forbes Jackson, principal of Harley College, the training centre for the Regions Beyond Missionary Union. He was active in the religious life of the city and beyond. Meanwhile Union Grove had Birch Hoyle as pastor, a man prominent in the YMCA movement and still remembered as the translator of the hymn, 'Thine be the glory'.[49]

At Gilcomston Park, Grant Gibb began a vigorous evangelistic ministry which included large open-air meetings held regularly in Correction Wynd. The Welsh Revival of 1904-5 aroused great interest and Gibb went to Wales to see what was happening. On return he launched an outreach programme at Gilcomston Park with fruitful results. The Inverness Baptists mounted their own campaign, but the main benefit came to the Presbyterian Churches of the town. Alexander Bremner commented, 'We cannot benefit from a movement like this to the same extent as churches with an unconverted membership, but we had a share of the blessing'.[50]

To temperance must now be added the suffragette movement as an external influence with which the churches became involved. Thus D.L. Richardson, minister of Inverness, took part in a meeting at the Town Hall arranged by the Scottish Churches' League for Woman Suffrage in 1913. This came soon after Forbes Jackson of Crown Terrace had been mistaken for Lloyd George and attacked by an angry young woman with a whip.[51]

War broke out in 1914 with little warning. Its immediate effect on the churches was a sudden loss of manpower as the Territorial Army and Royal Naval reserves were mobilized. Fishing vessels were requistioned for patrol and minesweeping activities. Inverness became a military centre, and sometimes the preacher was a soldier in uniform. There was a limited blackout of lighting, initially applicable only to premises visible from the sea. The drain on manpower continued throughout the war. Thus, in July 1915, the Buckie Church reported that three more men had recently joined the Royal Navy and two women left to work at a Dundee ammunition factory. The pastor was writing to another man in hospital in France and 'almost every home connected with our church has someone away on war service'.[52] W.J. Batters was still reporting in 1917 that more had just gone to the forces and that the town 'is nearly depleted of eligible men'.[53]

Not all who left returned. The memorial in Lossiemouth chapel shows twenty-six names. Fraserburgh Church lost ten.[54] William Corner of Inverness lost two sons killed and another severely wounded early in 1915. Some who returned had lost their faith; many were unemployed. Faith and finance were in short supply.

Between the Wars

1919 marked the silver jubilee of the Northern Baptist Association and Mr and Mrs F.J. Scott tried to revive the pre-war interest. In November they gave a lunch for the association council at the Grand Hotel, Aberdeen, and a public meeting followed.[55] Sadly, two of the thirteen churches ceased to exist in less than two years.

An unexpected figure appeared on the scene at this point. A tough young cooper from Wick, Jock Troup, was in Yarmouth in a poor season for herring. He began preaching in the open air to Scottish fisherfolk visiting the port in October 1921 and the result was almost like another 1859 revival. The Yarmouth churches became involved, with a Baptist minister, Douglas Brown, taking a lead in the proceedings. Many hundreds accepted Christ as Saviour.

Then Jock Troup had a vision of a man praying for him to visit Fraserburgh. He had never been there before, but he caught the first available train and went. Reaching Fraserburgh on a cold night, he began to preach in the square in Broad Street. A crowd gathered and someone suggested that they adjourn to the Baptist chapel. They arrived as the deacons were finishing a meeting where they had decided to invite Jock Troup to Fraserburgh. To their amazement the man was there already and, to his amazement, one of the deacons was the man Jock Troup had seen in his vision.

Soon the premises could not contain the crowds. Fishing vessels came home at the end of the season, often with whole crews, converted at Yarmouth or on the voyage, singing hymns as they entered harbour. The revival movement swept along the Moray Firth coast and others joined in preaching the message of salvation.[56] Various denominations reported increases in membership. At Hopeman the Baptists doubled their numbers, forty-nine being added. Lossiemouth gained eighteen in 1922 and fifty-eight more in 1923. Inland at Elgin the Baptists saw congregations of 300. At Buckie, Baptists and Methodists combined for the first time in an evangelistic campaign. Jock Troup was a frequent visitor to Inverness, leaving a lasting mark on the day his powerful fist emphasized a point and split the wooden pulpit.

Recovery after the war took time; rising unemployment affected church finances and most efforts at evangelism were small-scale and local. There was a growing tendency to co-operate with other denominations. A striking example occurred at Inverness where the corrugated iron chapel was becoming very dilapidated. Not only the Union and the assocation, but virtually all the Protestant churches in the town, combined to raise the funds for a new building. Civic and religious bodies united to complete the move from Friars Lane to Castle Street in 1933. The following year all the Inverness churches gained from a mission conducted by Lionel Fletcher. The Baptists had probably the only Christian Endeavour Society in the town and, as new converts were urged to join, the society grew considerably in numbers and activity.[57]

The fishing ports were in difficulty. The herring were forsaking the old fishing grounds and by 1926 many boats were working at a loss. There was a tendency to stay longer away from home in the hope of a better catch and there was a steady flow of young people to the south or emigrating. All the coastal churches were hard hit and strenuous efforts were made in open-air meetings to win others and make good the losses. At Lossiemouth there was an innovation in 1918 when a lady — Miss Jane Henderson — was called to the pastorate. Elgin, apparently prosperous in the 1920s, suffered a serious decline so that by 1939 the church could no longer support a full-time pastor.

The Second World War and After

Once again, on the outbreak of war the fishing ports lost many of their men and boats for service with the Royal Navy. However, this war brought considerable aerial activity and numerous RAF and Royal Naval air stations were constructed. Those at Kinloss and Lossiemouth are still in use today. Forces personnel were brought into the north-east and some began to attend nearby churches. Often their stay was brief, but a new element was being introduced into church life, particularly at Hopeman, Lossiemouth and Elgin.

Union Grove saw many changes. The basement of the building became an air raid shelter and one room was a permanent air raid warden's post. The evening service was transferred to the afternoon to avoid the blackout regulations. At Inverness the minister (William Fisher) died suddenly, just after the outbreak of war. His successor, John McBeath, however, carried on a vigorous evangelistic ministry and the church continued to grow.

The end of the war found a number of churches revising their membership rolls and emerging with numbers much reduced or steadily shrinking. Buckie and Union Grove were in a poor state and membership at Gilcomston Park fell to just over one hundred by 1963. At Lossiemouth the shortage of men contributed to the appointment of ladies as deacons. Amongst other changes, the herring had moved to the west coast and the boats stayed there for the season, but the crews came home at the weekends. As a result Hopeman found increased attendances. Buckie may have benefited also. It also had the same pastor, Alex Barr, for thirty-three years, with a reputation for always being on the spot when Buckie folk were facing trouble or adversity. Fraserburgh had been a church of fishermen, but since the war many have been employed on shore. In the post-war period the BBC was much concerned about pirate radio stations. The fishermen of Moray and Buchan had their own, broadcasting hymns and testimonies over the ship's radio. However desirable, this was illegal and had to stop.

The slow growth and recovery had new impetus from evangelistic campaigns, particularly those led by Luis Palau and Billy Graham, who visited the north as well as having meetings relayed from Glasgow and elsewhere. The decline in membership at Gilcomston Park was halted in 1963, when George Balmer became pastor. When Raymond Inkster succeeded him in 1970 there was a considerable increase in the number of students attending services. This growth added to the pastoral work and it became necessary to ordain three elders to assist the minister. Youth organizations were revived or increased and a number of Home Bible Fellowships were commenced. More recently, an assistant pastor has been appointed.[58]

Growth at Peterhead, Buckie and Union Grove was striking. Peterhead benefited from the work of faithful and dedicated ministers in the post-war period. The impact of the Billy Graham broadcast relays, coupled with a growth in population connected with the oil and fishing industries, contributed to this becoming the largest church in the area. New halls were opened in 1959, a gallery constructed in 1966 and the halls extended in 1982. At Fraserburgh growth was such that a new hall was constructed and opened in 1962. Union Grove opened a new hall in 1978. There was a continuing movement of population from town centres to housing estates on the outskirts. Baptists at Inverness, Elgin and Peterhead opened Sunday Schools in these suburbs to maintain contact with the children. At Inverness a small group left the church in 1969 and founded the Reformed Baptist Church in Telford Road.

At the centenary of the Baptist Union in 1969 the associations were asked to consider the possibilities for new churches. This coincided with plans for the industrial expansion of Invergordon and, by 1972, attention was focused on Alness, soon to be expanded to accommodate the workforce. At the end of 1975 a house was allocated for a minister, and William Clark was inducted at a service in Church of Scotland premises. A Bible study group in his house grew rapidly; he began teaching in the local school and working with a youth club. The Inverness Church helped with visitation. Soon services commenced and in 1977 baptisms took place in the open-air. The church was constituted in 1978 and the premises were opened in March 1980 with the enthusiastic support of the churches at Ayr and Inverness (then outside the Union) and the Northern Baptist Association.[59] Since then an industrial recession and high unemployment have not helped, but expansion has continued.

North Sea oil attracted people to Aberdeen. Some came from other parts of Britain and some from the United States. Among the Americans were Southern Baptists who found it difficult to settle in the existing churches when they arrived in 1975. At first they travelled to an American-style church in Brechin, but this was not a satisfactory arrangement and they began meetings in their homes for prayer and Bible study. Americans working in the oil industry were then invited to Cults, where they obtained the use of the West Church on Sunday afternoons. Following discussions with the Baptist Union and the Southern Baptist Convention, it was decided to attract British residents as well as Americans. James Spaulding arrived from USA in July 1977 as the first minister, and the International Baptist Church was constituted in January 1979. The church moved to Woodside and whilst there a site at Bridge of Don was purchased with funds from the Southern Baptists. A second minister from America, Loren Turnage, arrived that September to begin work at Bridge of Don. Following a review of the situation it was decided that the International Church should move back to Cults, leaving the Bridge of Don site available for another new church. By January 1982 the membership was one-third British, and a new minister, W.G. Slack, was inducted. In 1985, the International Church moved into newly constructed premises at Cults.[60]

Meanwhile the Bridge of Don site was not to remain vacant. Led by Loren Turnage and his wife, a few Baptists began meeting fortnightly in each other's homes in January 1979. Numbers grew and, in conjunction with the Luis Palau Crusade at Pittodrie, regular Sunday morning services began at Old Machar community centre. Children's work commenced and evening services started. Bridge of Don Church was constituted in March 1980, just a week after the opening of the premises at Alness. After a move to larger accommodation at Glashieburn School, a manse was purchased in 1981 and Douglas Hutcheon inducted as minister. The growing numbers necessitated a move to Old Machar Academy and, as a further development, the Turnages started a new work at Ellon. Following a financial appeal by the Baptist Union, Bridge of Don Church expects to have its own buildings in 1988.[61] The year previous saw the formal constitution of the church at Ellon, where twenty-eight founder members signed the church covenant, and the inauguration of a Baptist group in Stonehaven. Inverness Baptist Church has recently decided to sponsor new outreach work in the suburb of Kinmylies.

Conclusion

A brief glance at the map shows that the north-east has been spattered with Baptist activities in the past, but that most have long ceased to exist. There appear to be two principal causes.

The old Scotch Baptist Churches in Aberdeenshire were fairly easily launched, usually with two pastors in each, men who earned their living in secular occupations. These pastors co-operated with one another and there was no stipend to pay from church funds, enabling financial resources to be concentrated on the early erection of chapels. Over the years the initial enthusiasm could not always be maintained and an increasingly educated and prosperous part of the community preferred a more highly trained ministry. In these circumstances, one by one, ageing memberships faded away.

The other factor in the situation is the response of local people to revival movements and evangelistic campaigns. Itinerant preaching, in particular, made a considerable impact, especially in the early years of the nineteenth century when Elgin, Fortrose and the Scotch Baptists of Banffshire and Aberdeenshire had their origin. About the middle of the century revivals led to the formation of churches at Fraserburgh, Lossiemouth and Forres. The evangelistic campaigns of Moody and Sankey brought growth in Aberdeen, but the less publicized Baptist Pioneer Mission and men like Alexander Bremner were successful in bringing churches into being at Hopeman, Inverness and Buckie. In time revivals and campaigns lose something of their impetus. Coupled with the steady drain of population to the south and overseas, this led to diminishing congregations between periods of great prosperity. The slogan 'Evangelize or Perish' is one particularly appropriate to the area.

The churches of the 1980s (see Appendix) appear to have achieved a greater stability than existed a century ago and the Third Statistical Account acknowledges that Baptist influence is greater than numbers suggest.[62] Statistics show that this is an area of church growth with the Baptists making a steady advance.[63] The recent Scotreach movement has proved them responsive to a challenge and a lead.[64]

Appendix

Membership of North-Eastern Baptist Churches in 1985

Aberdeen:	
Bridge of Don	148
Crown Terrace	151
Gilcomston Park	188
International	125
Union Grove	34
Alness	43
Buckie	123
Elgin	92
Fraserburgh	84
Grantown	14
Hopeman	52
Inverness:	
Castle Street	170
Reformed	36
Lossiemouth	67
Peterhead	290

Notes

1. Gilbert Burnet, *History of His Own Time*, 6 vols (Oxford 1833), 1 p 107.
2. John Spalding, *Memorials of the Trubles in Scotland and in England, AD 1624–AD 1645*, 2 vols (Aberdeen 1851), 2 pp 187, 202-3, 217, 226, 241.
3. Spalding, *Memorials*, 2 pp 203, 271. Alistair and Henrietta Taylor, *Valuation of the County of Aberdeen for the Year 1667* (Aberdeen 1933), pp 61-2. George Yuille, ed, *History of the Baptists in Scotland* (Glasgow 1926), pp 25, 33.
4. C.H. Firth, *Scotland and The Protectorate* (Edinburgh 1899), pp 238-42, 251-3.
5. Alistair and Henrietta Taylor, *The House of Forbes* (Aberdeen 1937), p. 321. *Fasti Ecclesiae Scoticanae*, ed Hew Scott, 7 vols, (Edinburgh 1915-28), 6 p 101. *Selections from the Records of the Kirk Session, Presbytery and Synod of Aberdeen*, ed John Stuart (Aberdeen 1846), p 225.
6. *Fasti*, ed Scott, 6 p 53. Yuille, ed, *Baptists in Scotland*, p 33.
7. *Aberdeen Records*, ed Stuart, pp 270-1.
8. Norman Moon, *Education for Ministry* (Bristol 1979), p 118.

9. Graham Hughes, *Robert Hall* (London 1943), pp 33-4.
10. A.B. Thomson, 'Some Baptist Pioneers in Scotland during the Eighteenth Century and the Early Years of the Nineteenth', *Scottish Baptist Year Book (SBYB)*, 1900, p 14; 1904, p 127.
11. J.A. Haldane, *Journal of a Tour through the Northern Counties of Scotland and the Orkney Isles in Autumn 1797* (Edinburgh 1798), pp 49-97.
12. Thomson, 'Baptist Pioneers in Scotland', *SBYB*, 1904, pp 126-30.
13. *Inverness Courier*, 18 Jan. 1837, p 1. *The New Statistical Account of Scotland: Inverness* (Edinburgh 1845), p 29.
14. Yuille, ed, *Baptists in Scotland*, pp 58, 72-4, 94-5. Annie Grant Robinson and J.A. Grant Robinson, 'Life of Peter Grant', in Peter Grant, *Dain Spioradail* (Glasgow 1926), pp 17-19. Lachlan Mackintosh to James Haldane, 4 June 1818, Waugh Papers, Baptist Union of Scotland Records.
15. Dugald Sinclair, *Journal of Itinerating Exertions in some of the more Destitute Parts of Scotland* (Edinburgh 1814), pp 18-21. For Sinclair, see D.E. Meek, 'Dugald Sinclair: the life and work of a Highland itinerant missionary', *Scottish Studies*, (forthcoming) and cf cap 15, pp 284, 289, 292.
16. Hugh Miller, *My Schools and Schoolmasters* (Edinburgh 1869), pp 474-6.
17. *The First Yearly Report of the Baptist Union of Scotland* (Cupar 1844), p 21. Alexander Gammie, *The Churches of Aberdeen* (Aberdeen 1909), p 269. *Baptist Manual*, 1846, p 35.
18. *New Statistical Account: Aberdeen*, p 283. *First Yearly Report*, p 21.
19. ibid. Harry Escott, *A History of Scottish Congregationalism* (Glasgow 1960), p 258.
20. *The Free Communion Baptist Church* (Crown Terrace, Aberdeen) (Aberdeen 1939), p 12. Gammie, *Churches of Aberdeen*, p 272.
21. Minutes of the Buchan Auxiliary of the Baptist Home Missionary Society of Scotland, 3 June 1833, Waugh Papers.
22. *Baptist Magazine*, 1848, p 690; 1849, p 167.
23. Yuille, ed, *Baptists in Scotland*, p 99.
24. Robinson and Robinson, 'Life of Peter Grant', p 19.
25. G.N.M. Collins, *The Heritage of our Fathers* (Edinburgh 1976), p 87. *Free Communion Baptist Church*, pp 17-21. Gammie, *Churches of Aberdeen*, p 273. Yuille, ed, *Baptists in Scotland*, p 89.
26. *Third Statistical Account of Scotland: The County of Banff* (Glasgow 1961), pp 163-4.
27. *Inverness Advertiser*, 30 Mar. 1860 and 18 Apr. 1863.
28. ibid, 13 July 1861.
29. *Report of the Baptist Home Missionary Society of Scotland*, 1861, pp 10-12.
30. J.A. Dunlop, *History of the Baptist Church in Elgin* (Elgin 1908), pp 15-16. *Centenary Booklet: Lossiemouth Baptist Church, 1861-1961*, pp 7, 11.
31. *Inverness Advertiser*, 4 Sept. 1866, 24 and 31 Jan., 11, 14, 21 and 28 Feb., 6 and 13 Mar., 1868.
32. *Free Communion Baptist Church*, pp 27-30.
33. John Cranna, *Fraserburgh Past and Present* (Aberdeen 1914), p 170. Yuille, ed, *Baptists in Scotland*, p 96.
34. ibid, p 100.
35. ibid, p 98. *Lossiemouth Baptist Church*, p 8.
36. Robert Douglas, *Annals of the Royal Burgh of Forres* (Elgin 1934), pp 260, 486.
37. Yuille, ed, *Baptists in Scotland*, p 96.
38. ibid, pp 89-90. *Free Communion Baptist Church*, pp 20-1.
39. Gammie, *Churches of Aberdeen*, p 269.
40. *The Highlander*, 7 Aug. 1875.
41. *Inverness Courier*, 28 Aug. 1906.
42. Gammie, *Churches of Aberdeen*, p 270.
43. ibid, pp 276-7, *The Jubilee History of Gilcomston Park Baptist Church*, p 3.
44. Yuille, ed, *Baptists in Scotland*, p 91. Gammie, *Churches of Aberdeen*, pp 279-80.
45. *Inverness Courier*, 11 Jan. 1898 and 3 Feb. 1899.
46. ibid, 20 Mar. 1908.
47. Yuille, ed, *Baptists in Scotland*, pp 96-7.
48. *Free Communion Baptist Church*, p 24.
49. *The Baptist Hymn Book Companion* (London 1962), p 168.
50. *SBYB*, 1905, p A15.
51. *Inverness Courier*, 14 Feb. 1913. *Free Communion Baptist Church*, p 24.
52. *SBYB*, 1915, Home Mission Reports, p 14.
53. *SBYB*, 1917, Home Mission Reports, p 15.
54. S.D. Henry, 'Scottish Baptists and the First World War', *Baptist Quarterly*, 31 (1985), p 63.

55. *SBYB*, 1920, p 80.
56. J.A. Stewart, *Our Beloved Jock* (Philadelphia 1964), pp 8-15. Jackie Ritchie, *Floods upon the Dry Ground* (Peterhead 1983), pp 14-53, 57-63, 72-3. *Christian Herald*, 5 Jan. 1922, p 2.
57. J.S. Fisher, *From Friars Lane to Castle Street* (Inverness 1983), pp 12-30.
58. Muriel Cantlay, *Together with God, 1886-1986* (Aberdeen 1986), pp 21-30.
59. Minutes of the Northern Baptist Association.
60. *Scottish Baptist Magazine (SBM)*, Oct. 1985, p 10. *Press and Journal*, 27 Oct. 1977, 6 Jan. 1984.
61. Bridge of Don Baptist Church, *News Bulletin No. 1*, 1985. *SBM*, Feb. 1986, p 3.
62. Henry Hamilton, ed, *Third Statistical Account of Scotland: Moray and Nairn* (Glasgow 1965), p 61.
63. Peter Brierley and Fergus Macdonald, *Prospects for Scotland: report of the 1984 census of the churches* (Bromley, Kent 1985), pp 70-5.
64. Further written information was kindly supplied by the following: Rev. Alexander Barr, Mr Stanley Barnard, Mr James Innes, Mr Ian Jardine, Mr J. McPherson, Mr Lewis Ritchie, Rev. Loren Turnage and Mr Charles Welch, MBE.

J.S. Fisher

15. THE HIGHLANDS

In the present-day Highlands (consisting of Western Isles Region and Highland Region, and also including Argyll and Bute), Baptists constitute a very small proportion of the total membership of all the denominations — about 0.8%, or some 630 members out of 80,500, according to a survey conducted in 1984.[1] This statistic may give the impression that Baptists in the Highlands are an insignificant minority whose history should merit no more than a paragraph in a wider analysis of the development of the denomination in Scotland, and no more than a footnote in a survey of Scottish church history as a whole. Yet a century ago Baptists were a major force in the religious life of the Highlands, and as recently as 1921 the evening congregation at a Baptist Church in Tiree could be expected to reach about 200 (compared with the present Sunday average of fifty-seven for Highland Baptists).[2] The Baptist congregations which are found today in the Gaelic-speaking West Highlands — in the Inner Hebridean islands of Mull (at Bunessan), Islay (at Bowmore and Port Ellen), Colonsay and Tiree — were once part of a very much larger family of churches sharing an Evangelical faith which was expressed primarily through the medium of Gaelic. At its fullest extent, this family stretched from Fortrose in the north to Port Bannatyne (Bute) in the south, and from Tiree in the west to Tullymet in the east. Because of their Gaelic cultural identity, the Highland Baptist Churches formed a distinct group within the Scottish denomination, and their maintenance was a special concern of the Baptist Home Missionary Society for Scotland. As the area of Gaelic speech receded progressively westwards in the course of the nineteenth and twentieth centuries, the mainland churches gradually turned to English as the language of worship.[3] Even in the islands, no Baptist Church now uses Gaelic in regular worship, although the Tiree congregation held its morning service in Gaelic until about 1965.

The replacement of Gaelic by English in the life of the Highland Baptist Churches is indicative of, and consequent upon, social change within the region. The most obvious manifestation of this change is rural depopulation, which has continued relentlessly since the early nineteenth century. In the Highlands the Evangelical faith which is central to Baptist witness was embraced most firmly by the ordinary working people — crofters, cottars, fishermen, landless labourers — who were to emigrate in large numbers as social pressures increased during the nineteenth century and persisted into the twentieth. The appeal of the Baptist message to what may loosely be termed 'the crofting class' is made abundantly clear in the surviving evidence; its acceptability is reflected in major spiritual movements which affected most localities where Baptist preachers were active before 1900, and which continued after that date in the Inner Hebrides, especially in islands such as

Tiree where a substantial crofting population had managed to maintain itself in spite of large-scale emigration.[4] Emigration from the Highlands thus helps to explain the sparsity of Baptist Churches in the area in the present day and the smallness of existing memberships. The removal of the earlier population has led to the encroachment of English on the domains of Gaelic and to the introduction of new social and ethical values. As a sense of community has declined, it has become more difficult to light the spark of revival, and, as the twentieth century has worn on, Baptist pastors have often found themselves struggling to maintain their small flocks in the face of increasing apathy, a problem which they share with other denominations and other parts of Britain.

Baptists were not, of course, uniformly strong throughout the Highlands. Historically, Baptist believers have been most plentiful in the Gaelic areas of Perthshire and Argyll, and in the Inner Hebrides including Skye. In the Outer Hebrides and the north-west mainland, where there are today strong bodies of Evangelical Presbyterians, Baptists have been unable to establish a lasting presence. The reasons for the acceptance of Baptist principles in some districts and their rejection in others, as well as the factors which have influenced Baptist development in the Highlands, will be among the topics considered in this chapter.

Early Evangelists

Baptist missionary activity in the Gaelic-speaking districts can be traced back to about 1801 on present evidence, and is attested initially in the islands of the Clyde estuary and on mainland Argyll. In 1801 Donald McArthur, originally a cobbler who was later employed as a curer and carrier of herrings around the Kyles of Bute, abandoned his occupation and became an evangelist. At the same time he discovered believer's baptism.[5] A vignette of McArthur is provided by a 'Lay Member of the Established Church' who was writing in 1827:

> During the time he was in Bute, Mr Donald McArthur, the baptist, a powerful Gaelic orator, was preaching in the island, and in the neighbouring districts of Cowal, Arran etc. Many were so affected under his preaching, as to fall down and cry out. He made many converts throughout these places. He planted a baptist church in Port Bannatyne, which is still in existence. He went to America many years ago. It is said that a short time before he left the country he adopted erroneous notions of some Scripture truths.[6]

Following his ordination in Frederic MacFarlane's church in Edinburgh on 29 August 1804 'as a Baptist preaching elder, pastor, or minister, by persons of

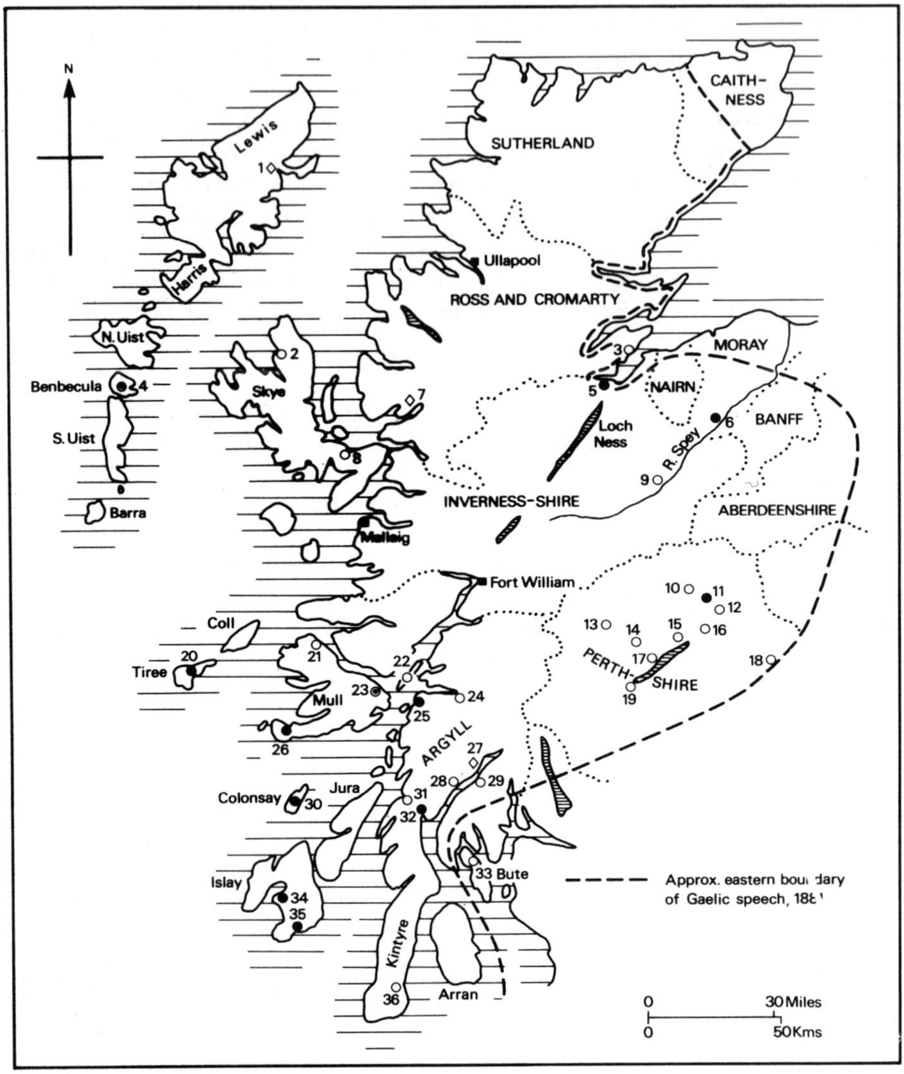

MAP 15 : HIGHLAND BAPTIST CHURCHES.

Key to Map 15

1. Stornoway	13. Rannoch	25. Oban
2. Uig	14. Glenlyon	26. Bunessan
3. Fortrose	15. Fortingall	27. Inveraray
4. Benbecula	16. Aberfeldy	28. Furnace
5. Inverness	17. Lawers	29. Strachur
6. Grantown-on-Spey	18. Dunkeld	30. Colonsay
7. Lochcarron	19. Killin	31. Bellanoch
8. Broadford	20. Tiree	32. Lochgilphead
9. Kingussie	21. Tobermory	33. Port Bannatyne
10. Blair Atholl	22. Lismore	34. Bowmore
11. Pitlochry	23. Craignure	35. Port Ellen
12. Tullymet	24. Taynuilt	36. Campbeltown

that persuasion', McArthur formally became the pastor of the 'dissenting congregation' at Port Bannatyne,[7] but as the quotation indicates, he preached extensively elsewhere. He may have established a Baptist congregation at Strachur (north Cowal) as early as 1801, and his influence contributed to the establishment of churches at Dunoon and Greenock (Orangefield).[8] The evidence suggests that McArthur had links with 'English' Baptist Churches in the Lowlands, the earliest of which was founded in Glasgow in November 1801 with James Lister as its pastor.[9] The Glasgow Church was visited by Andrew Fuller in the summer of 1805. Fuller noted in his diary that 'this little church also supports a mission, in the highlands of Scotland, where a new society has lately been formed'.[10]

Although little is known so far about the 'new society' to which Fuller refers, the Glasgow Church was concentrating its Highland missionary efforts on Bellanoch, a village at the western end of the recently opened Crinan Canal, and Fuller was in touch with the missionary stationed there, Donald McVicar. McVicar, a former itinerant with the Haldanes' Society for Propagating the Gospel at Home, was evidently at Bellanoch by 1801, and by 1804 the nucleus of a Baptist Church had been formed.[11] It was formally constituted, and McVicar ordained as its pastor, on 27 April 1805.[12] There is a strong possibility that the 'new society' mentioned by Fuller was based at Bellanoch, and that it contemplated an extension of its missionary work by 1806, when a Bellanoch member, Dugald Sinclair, was sent to Bradford Baptist Academy to train as an itinerant missionary. Sinclair had been baptized in Glasgow by James Lister in March 1801, a few months before the formation of the Glasgow Church, and he had begun to preach immediately after his baptism, probably in his native district, Mid-Argyll.[13]

McVicar's ordination at Bellanoch was attended by two men closely associated with the 'English' Baptist Church in Glasgow — James Deakin, a deacon of the church, and Christopher Anderson, who was a member of the church for a brief period.[14] Having trained for a year in England, Anderson returned to Scotland in the autumn of 1806, gathered a fellowship in Edinburgh of which he became pastor in 1808,[15] and with the help of George Barclay of the 'English' Baptist Church at Kilwinning, initiated a 'cause' for the promotion of 'the knowledge of Christ Jesus . . . in the dark and most destitute parts of their Native Country'. Barclay and Anderson began this work late in 1807, and by 1808 they were sustaining a full-time Gaelic-speaking missionary, Alexander McLeod, based first at Perth and then at Crieff. By 1810 they had enlisted a second missionary — Dugald Sinclair of Bellanoch, who had newly completed his training. Sinclair operated from the Bellanoch area, and by means of the financial support which was provided by Anderson's church in Edinburgh and by interested friends in Scotland and England, he exercised an itinerant ministry which was of great importance for the establishing of Baptist witness in the Inner Hebrides. In this way the plan of a Baptist mission to the Highlands, which had evidently lain behind the founding of the Bellanoch Church, was further developed.[16]

In Argyll and Bute, Baptist Churches were emerging at the same time as Independent Churches under the leadership of Haldane-trained itinerants such as Archibald McCallum of Kintyre. The development of the one group must have influenced the other, but there is no clear evidence of a Baptist fellowship growing from an earlier Independent foundation at this stage (up to 1808). [17] In Perthshire, however, Baptist Churches were pre-eminently the result of dissension within existing Independent Churches over the issue of baptism. By 1805 Independent itinerants had planted a family of small churches around Loch Tay, and extending westwards to Rannoch and eastwards to Dunkeld. When the Haldanes embraced Baptist principles in 1808, the majority of Perthshire churches produced Baptist followings.[18] In most cases, the leaders and pastors of the Independent Churches became Baptists, leaving only a few strong Independent causes in the area, such as that in Aberfeldy which was powerfully sustained by James Kennedy.[19] The move to a Baptist position is illustrated in the remarkable career of William Tulloch, a native of Strathspey who had become the pastor of the Independent Church at Killin in 1801, and later of the church at Lawers in 1803. While at Lawers in 1808, Tulloch and his assistant, Archibald Cameron, were baptized by immersion and established a Baptist congregation. Tulloch was subsequently active in Aberfeldy (1816-19) and at Kilmavionaig, Blair Atholl, where he died in 1861.[20] Farther north, at Rothiemurchus, Lachlan Mackintosh had adopted a Baptist position by 1807, and he moved to Grantown-on-Spey to lay the foundation of the Baptist Church there. Two years earlier an Independent pastor active in the Fortrose and Avoch area of the Black Isle, David McRae, had made a similar transition and formed a Baptist Church at Fortrose.[21]

The earliest Baptist Churches were not established without considerable opposition within their communities, usually from those who occupied positions of social or ecclesiastical authority. A baptismal service being held on the day following the constitution of the Bellanoch Church was interrupted in the middle of a scripture reading by the factor of the Bellanoch landlord, Malcolm of Poltalloch, 'who said he had a general order to stop all such preaching on the estate, and would call out the Volunteers if we did not desist! We removed to another place, and got all our hearers with us.'[22] An even more dramatic and far-reaching intervention took place at a service being conducted by Donald McArthur at Colintraive Ferry on 20 October 1805. McArthur was seized violently by the local landlord, John Campbell of South Hall, and transported to Greenock where he was handed over to the press-gang. Detained for five weeks on board different warships where he suffered 'every species of indignity and hardship', McArthur was released by the Lords of the Admiralty, and in 1808 brought a case against Campbell at the Court of Session. McArthur won his case, and was awarded damages of £2,000, with a *solatium* of £105. Campbell's defence, that he was acting in his capacity as Justice of the Peace by removing a preacher of 'immoral and seditious doctrines', was of no avail.[23] Although McArthur was thus vindicated, it is said that he was not left unmolested, and that this precipitated his departure from the country a couple of years later.[24]

Missionaries on the Move

While it did not remove the threat of opposition to himself or to others, the outcome of McArthur's case in the Court of Session must have given some degree of encouragement to the various itinerant preachers who were active in the Highlands by that date. From the late eighteenth century itinerant missionaries of different persuasions had been operating in the north and west, where they supplemented the efforts already being made by the Society in Scotland for the Propagation of Christian Knowledge (SSPCK). The earliest in the field were ordained ministers of the Relief Church who were preaching throughout Kintyre by 1797. They were soon followed by the trained laymen of the Haldanes' Society for Propagating the Gospel at Home (SPGH), whose first Gaelic-speaking catechist, Hugh Ross, was appointed in 1798.[25] Specifically Baptist missionaries were few in number — no more than half-a-dozen — until 1808, and only two of these (McVicar and McLeod) are known to have had the support of societies. The existing societies were relatively informal, however, and much depended on individual resources and funds. McRae of Fortrose was assisted by the itinerant fund of the Scotch Baptists, as was his colleague farther north, Edward MacKay of Thurso.[26]

From 1808 the supply of Baptist missionaries was increased by the 'defection' of the former SPGH itinerants in Perthshire, who included such men as William Tulloch, Peter Fisher of Ardeonaig and John Anderson, the first pastor of Tullymet Baptist Church.[27] These men maintained itinerant ministries on an individual basis until 1816, when the Baptist Highland Mission was established for their support.[28] Baptist missionary activity in the Highlands was strengthened significantly when the Baptist Highland Mission and the Home Missionary Society (representing the earlier interests of Anderson and the Haldanes) merged in 1827.[29] This amalgamation produced the Baptist Home Missionary Society for Scotland (BHMS), with a total of nineteen missionaries in that year, six having come from the Baptist Highland Mission. At the time of union, the missionaries were placed in Arran, Islay, Mull, Skye, the Long Island (i.e. the Outer Hebrides), Stornoway, Gairloch, Lochcarron, Strathspey, Badenoch, Rannoch, Atholl, Tullymet, Lochgilphead, Inveraray, and Orkney and Shetland.[30] The Highland focus of the society was acknowledged in 1829 when the qualification 'Chiefly for the Highlands and Islands' was added to its title.[31]

Itinerant missionaries generally took advantage of the summer to make their most extensive tours of the Highlands. In the foundational phase of their work (until about 1830), 'long tours' were common, and their length can be gauged from the surviving journals of the men of the Baptist Highland Mission. In 1818, for instance, William Tulloch embarked on a tour lasting nine weeks and three days, in which he travelled by way of Braemar, Grantown-on-Spey, Fort William, Lismore, Mull, Iona and Oban. With William Hutchison of Kingussie he tramped the Outer Hebrides on several occasions. In winter the itinerants would operate on a more restricted circuit which often consisted of preaching stations closer to their churches. The hazards of travel were offset by the greater willingness of people to listen after dark.[32] In the later nineteenth century, as manpower increased and more churches were established, tours became shorter but itinerancy continued unabated, with missionaries stationed in the Inner Hebrides gradually gaining a more prominent role both in the islands and on the mainland. Itinerants who were active after 1850 included James Miller of Bowmore, Duncan Ferguson of the Ross of Mull, John and Duncan MacFarlane of Tiree, Alexander Grant of Tobermory, Donald MacLellan of Glenlyon, Daniel Grant of Tullymet, John Mackintosh of Lochgilphead and William Grant of Grantown-on-Spey, who succeeded his distinguished father, Peter Grant.[33]

The itinerants were essentially field-preachers who conducted their services wherever willing audiences could be found. Cottages, barns, tents and schoolhouses provided shelter initially, and continued to be used where there were no church buildings. Independent Churches would be utilized where these were available, as the baptismal question did not prevent co-operation between the Baptists and their Independent colleagues. Indeed, Dulgald Sinclair itinerated with Alexander MacKay, pastor of the Independent Church at Sannox (Arran), and William Tulloch was a close friend of James Kennedy, pastor of the Independent Church in Aberfeldy.[34] After 1843 Baptist itinerants were sometimes able to use Free Church buildings, but while relations between themselves and the Free Church were often cordial, tensions did exist, and buildings could be shut against them.[35] There is remarkably little evidence of outright condemnation of Baptists by ministers of the Established Church, even in the initial stage of their activities. The strongest opposition appears to have been that of the landlords and lairds who had a controlling interest in the local parish church, and who objected to the liberties taken in field-preaching.

Church and Community

Opposition by landlords does not appear to have hindered the work of the Baptist missionaries or to have weakened the resolve of those who formed congregations. Indeed, the location of early Baptist Churches at such places as Bellanoch and Port Bannatyne suggests that they tended to take root most firmly in areas where there was strong opposition from the landowners. The same is true of early Independent Churches, and it is possible that those who joined these small fellowships found that they were a congenial and democratic alternative to the Established Church. At the same time, it is highly likely that Baptist and other missionaries gained followings in parishes where the minister was not an Evangelical, but even where the parish minister was an Evangelical, the size of certain parishes allowed much scope for Dissenting missionaries. Generalization is, in fact, difficult, and circumstances pertaining in each locality or parish need to be considered. Missionaries were acceptable, sometimes only temporarily, in parishes where there was a dispute about an appointment, or a long vacancy or where the minister was absent for a prolonged period.[36] In the north-west Highland mainland, missionaries had to struggle against the influence of Evangelical Presbyterian laymen known as 'The Men', while in Lewis the evangelical fervour which continued from about 1823, and in which Baptist missionaries participated, was channelled towards Presbyterianism by the settlement of an Evangelical minister in 1824 and the leadership of schoolmasters of the Edinburgh Gaelic School Society.[37] This helps to explain why there are today no Baptist Churches in the north-west mainland and only one in the Outer Hebrides, whereas the Free Church has a strong following in these parts.

The groups of believers who formed the earliest Baptist Churches in the Highlands were generally strongest in Perthshire, largely as a result of earlier Independent activity. Tullymet had a membership of forty-six, with three deacons, during its first pastorate (1808-22), while Lawers had about fifty members by 1818. At Bellanoch, Argyll, only twelve members were on the roll in 1805. In Skye, Baptists numbered about twenty in 1815, and about fifty in 1822. Baptist witness in the Ross of Mull began in 1821 following the baptism of Duncan Ferguson by Dugald Sinclair, and about six others were baptized the following year. The membership of the church in Tiree was about twenty in 1838, the year of its constitution.[38]

Little is known so far about the formal creation of churches from the original fellowships of Baptist believers. The account of the constitution of the Bellanoch Church in 1805 suggests that a church was sometimes given formal recognition when its first pastor was ordained,[39] but the nucleus of any church could have existed for several years previously. Fellowships without pastors would depend on the services of itinerant missionaries, although some were led by local preachers who did not itinerate so widely. This latter arrangement appears to have pertained in Colonsay, where Malcolm Blue became the pastor after the seminal work of Dugald Sinclair in 1814-15.[40] It was, of course, normal for missionaries themselves to hold pastorates; when they were absent on tours, their pulpits might be supplied by other itinerants who were active in the area. It was also fairly common for missionaries to have local assistants who could be utilized, and who would usually have a special responsibility for the preaching stations or 'out-stations' regularly served by the church within the locality.[41] Collaboration of this kind established the churches in Islay (by 1833), Tobermory (1830), the Ross of Mull (1835) and Tiree.

It seems likely that most churches would have had some form of written constitution which would define their theological position and polity. The only written constitution known to survive for an early Highland church is that of Tullymet, drawn up at the beginning of the ministry of its third pastor, Daniel Grant, in July 1839:

> The Church of Christ, at present assembling for Divine Worship in the Baptist Chapel, Craigbea, Estate of Tullymet, acknowledges no confession of Faith, but the Bible, nor any model of Church Order but that established by God, through the agency of the Apostles, as recorded in the New Testament; hence the Faith and Order of the Church are founded upon the Word of God alone as contained in the Scriptures of the Old and New Testament, and the Church acknowledges no human Authority whatever in Religion.[42]

As they were entirely independent of one another, we need not suppose that there was uniformity of order or doctrinal understanding among the churches, but we may presume that, besides their common emphasis on believer's baptism by immersion, the churches would have acknowledged the ultimate supremacy of the Bible as their guide, and would seek to follow New Testament patterns as far as possible.

Within their communities the churches asserted their presence in various ways. The most obvious indication of the strength and permanence of any fellowship would be the construction of a meeting-house. Some churches are known to have met in upper rooms or barns originally, and to have moved to purpose-built premises at a later stage. In 1815 the church at Bellanoch removed to a site in Lochgilphead which had been purchased in the name of its pastor, Dugald Sinclair, who had succeeded Donald McVicar by that date. A new building was erected on this stance, which was conveniently situated to take advantage of the growing town, and the ground and chapel were assigned by Sinclair to the Society of Calvinistic Baptists in Lochgilphead in 1819.[43] The purchase of a site implies that the original landlord was not openly hostile to Baptists. When William Tulloch settled in Kilmavionaig, Blair Atholl, in 1819, the estate of Lude was held by an unsympathetic landlord, but it changed hands soon afterwards, and Tulloch was able to build a plain, straw-thatched house capable of holding 200 people, the cost being £34.16.8. In 1836 the old village of Kilmavionaig was demolished, and the church moved to the new village of Balentoul where another chapel was erected.[44] Much of the labour in building chapels would be supplied by the membership, as happened in Tiree in 1854-5 when the original meeting-house was replaced by a chapel with a capacity of 300. The quarrying and driving of stones were done gratis, and £40 was subscribed locally.[45] The maintenance of buildings in the Highlands, as well as their erection, was not easy, and both tasks called for support from the wider Baptist family in the Highlands and beyond. The refurbishment of the Bowmore meeting-house in 1869 was made possible by donations from friends in London, Edinburgh, Glasgow, Greenock and Rothesay. The largest contribution — £20 — came from Thomas Coats of Paisley, whose family was well known for its generosity to the churches. The opening or re-opening of a church building was often marked by some special services and a more relaxed social occasion which allowed the church to tap the considerable body of support which existed beyond its membership.[46] The strength of this support is reflected in the fact that the 1855 building in Tiree was much too small for the regular congregation, although the membership was a mere thirty-nine in that year.[47]

In addition to providing a focal point for worship, Baptist church buildings could be used sometimes for educational purposes. William Tulloch held a school in his church during the week, and it is not unlikely that other missionaries would do the same, especially as there was a close connection between religious instruction and formal education in this period. Several missionaries acted as Gaelic schoolteachers with one or other of the Gaelic school societies before they became pastors. This was the case with Alexander Grant of Tobermory and Duncan MacDougall of Tiree. MacDougall taught reading and writing in the community, and he also acted as scribe for those who were unable to write for themselves.[48]

While the erection of meeting-houses and the work of the missionaries in teaching and preaching underlined the presence of Baptists in Highland communities, no aspect of their belief or practice drew more attention than the baptism of believers by immersion, which was a prerequisite for membership of the churches. From the first, missionaries had baptized candidates in bays, lochs and streams, and this remained the normal method in the rural areas, with only a few churches, mainly in the larger villages, installing indoor baptistries after 1900.[49] The public confession of faith in this way brought many observers, some of whom were merely curious, and it provided churches with an important opportunity to demonstrate their distinctiveness. The identification of believers as Baptists ('Dippers') could bring ridicule, and this may help to explain the disparity between membership and congregational size in many churches. Candidates were frequently subjected to alternative views on baptism by Independents and Presbyterians, and tensions could flare into polemic and denunciation.[50] It could happen, however, that such occasions were the means of triggering major spiritual movements.

Revivals, Social Change and Radical Politics

Spiritual movements, generally known as 'revivals' or (perhaps more accurately) as 'awakenings', were a common feature of Highland life in the nineteenth century. The course of these movements is closely linked with the work of the itinerant missionaries of different bodies who were active in the Highlands from the late eighteenth century. An important part was also played by the schoolmasters of the Gaelic school societies who taught people to read the Gaelic Bible. Evangelical ministers of the Established Church like Lachlan MacKenzie of Lochcarron or the far-travelled John MacDonald of Ferintosh helped to prepare the ground by their fervent preaching at open-air communion services, and the work of the SSPCK was similarly influential.[51] The earliest revivals of the nineteenth century are found mainly in those areas where Independent and Baptist Churches are first attested, namely Perthshire and Argyll, together with the Clyde islands. The Independent itinerant, John Farquharson, was the human agent in a powerful awakening which affected Breadalbane in 1800-4, and in 1805 he was operating in Skye with major results. A Baptist missionary who arrived in Skye about 1806 was able to build on the new movement.[52] In the south, Bute and adjacent districts were being roused by the preaching of Donald McArthur from 1801, and by 1812 a deep spiritual movement was evident in Arran, where it was stimulated by Alexander MacKay of the Independent Church at Sannox, and Neil MacBride, minister of the parish of Kilmorie. Itinerant missionaries like Dugald Sinclair helped to transfer this enthusiasm from Arran to other islands, and soul-concern is apparent to varying degrees in most of the Inner Hebrides by 1815.[53] By the 1820s the Outer Hebrides were in the grip of revival, and by 1830 the whole Highland area had been stimulated. Thereafter it was common for revivals to occur regularly in different areas until the end of the century.[54]

The effects of periodic revivals are very clearly seen in the membership figures of Baptist Churches. A major revival affected the island and mainland churches from 1840; for the year 1843-4 the Baptist Churches in Broadford (Skye), Tiree, Bunessan (Ross of Mull), Tobermory and Lochgilphead record substantial increases in membership (Broadford, 34 to 63; Tiree, 41 to 80; Bunessan, 49 to 73; Tobermory, 40 to 61; Lochgilphead, 32 to 72).[55] Another movement, which was felt from the islands to east Perthshire, took place in the late 1850s and early 1860s. This was encouraged by an awareness of the so-called '1859 Revival', which was particularly marked in Wales and Ireland. Alexander Grant of Tobermory travelled to Ireland to observe its progress, and prayer meetings and lectures on revival were organized on his return.[56] External stimulus is also evident in the revival which broke out in Tiree in 1874. In August of that year Duncan MacFarlane, then pastor at Tobermory, came to Tiree to baptize two candidates on behalf of his brother, John. Soul-concern was aroused at the service, and the next evening MacFarlane began to give an account of the Moody and Sankey campaigns in Glasgow and Elgin. The revival continued through the autumn, and ministers and missionaries of other denominations participated. Co-operation foundered, however, when MacFarlane began to baptize candidates who had applied for baptism by immersion. Nevertheless, the Tiree Church was increased by 116, bringing its membership to 160. The Established and Independent Churches in the island gained about sixty and thirty to forty members respectively.[57] This revival stimulated the churches in Islay, Colonsay and Mull, and several further awakenings, affecting most of the island churches, are apparent throughout the 1890s.[58]

The growth of Baptist Churches through revival was counterbalanced by loss of members through migration, and especially through emigration to Canada, and (after 1836) to Australia. The social upheaval consequent upon the Potato Famine removed many who had joined the churches in the 1840s; by 1851 the Tiree Church had been reduced from its 1846 level of one hundred members to thirty-two.[59] This pattern of gain and loss is well attested throughout the century. In some parts periodic gains were not sufficient to halt a slow downward trend in membership. In Perthshire rural depopulation is particularly noticeable after 1850, and seriously affected the membership of the Tullymet Church. This reached a peak of 133 in 1842, but declined gradually to forty by 1882.[60] (See Figure 15.1). By the end of the century the churches once meeting at Glenlyon, Lawers and Killin had ceased to have an itinerant missionary of their own, and had become out-stations of Tullymet.[61] In Argyll, too, the countryside was being transformed, and by 1862 John Mackintosh was indicating his intention to concentrate on the growing town of Lochgilphead, and to preach in the country only as circumstances permitted.[62] The Lowland towns and cities were also absorbing émigré Highlanders in this period, and significant Gaelic-speaking congregations were evidently to be found in the Baptist Churches at South Portland Street, Glasgow, and Orangefield, Greenock.[63]

Emigration removed not only a substantial proportion of Baptist church members, but also several of the earliest and most influential missionaries. Donald McArthur had emigrated to North America by about 1811, Donald McVicar was active in Aldborough, Ontario, by 1818, and Dugald Sinclair had reached Lobo, Ontario, by 1831. At least three other missionaries emigrated to Breadalbane, Ontario, by 1857.[64] Those missionaries who remained frequently witnessed scenes of appalling misery and destitution among the people, many of whom were preparing for emigration. John Stewart of Oban noted the 'haggard and emaciated countenances' and the 'desponding and heart-broken looks' of the people of Strath, Skye, in 1852.[65] James MacQueen, pastor of the Broadford Church, died of smallpox in 1854 — a reminder of the prevalence of disease in this period.[66] Baptist pastors were active in the alleviation of distress, and occasionally they could assume a more overtly political role. When the Highland land agitation was at its height in the early 1880s, one of the most prominent pro-crofter speakers in the prelude to the 1885 General Election was Duncan MacGregor, the pastor of North Ashland Avenue Baptist Church, Chicago, and founder of the Scottish Land League of America. A native of Easdale, Argyll, MacGregor was much in demand as a speaker on political platforms, where he supported the candidature of Donald H. MacFarlane in Argyll. In November 1885 MacGregor returned to Scotland permanently, becoming the pastor of Dunoon Baptist Church. In 1893 he founded the Dunoon Baptist College for training evangelists and missionaries.[67] Among his students were several men who were to be of key importance in maintaining Baptist witness in the islands after 1900.

Poets and Prose-Writers

'Whenever the Lord revives his work,' wrote Daniel Grant of Tullymet in 1861, 'the people begin to sing psalms and hymns, and spiritual songs.' Many of these songs were composed in Gaelic by missionaries who were active in

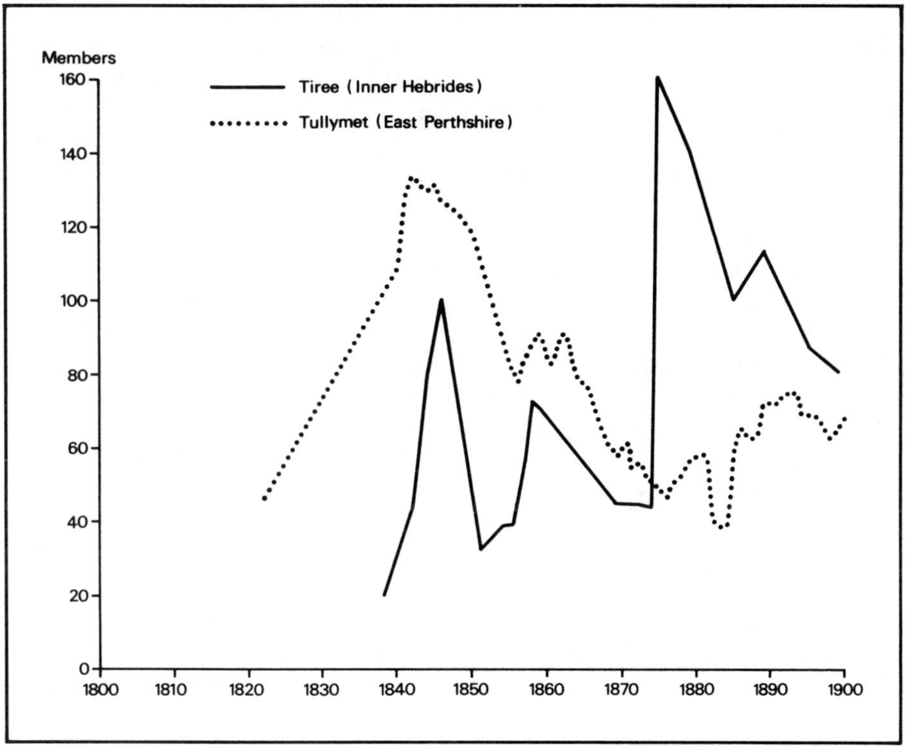

FIGURE 15.1 : MEMBERSHIP GRAPHS FOR TWO HIGHLAND BAPTIST CHUCHES, 1820-1900.

the revivals. Daniel Grant himself was the composer of numerous hymns, and he published a selection in 1842. The print-run of 1,000 was exhausted in less than a year, and a second edition followed in 1862. Grant would introduce his new hymns by singing them to the people at the end of house-meetings in the Tullymet district, and from there they would be carried to much wider audiences throughout the Highlands.[68]

As a composer of Gaelic hymns, however, Daniel Grant never achieved the popularity of his fellow-countryman and kinsman from Strathspey, Peter Grant of Grantown, whose work undoubtedly served as his model. Peter Grant's hymns were first published in 1815, and by 1842 he was writing a preface to the sixth edition. This edition was to be 'published in a cheap form, so that most of the poor Highlanders may buy copies for themselves, and that those who cannot, may be supplied gratis by their rich neighbours, who wish to see the poor rich in faith . . .'[69] By 1912 Grant's hymns had reached their twentieth edition, and a further edition appeared in 1926. In terms of published editions, Grant is second only to Dugald Buchanan, but his hymns were probably even more popular than those of Buchanan.[70]

The obvious appeal of Grant's hymns throughout the nineteenth century, and into the twentieth, reflects the extent to which the evangelical fervour of the period had permeated Gaelic society. It also indicates that Grant's hymns expressed the sentiments of those who were influenced by that fervour, and that they expressed them in a manner which was readily comprehensible. These hymns were usually set to tunes which were already well known, either through familiarity with earlier hymns, or with Gaelic and English secular songs. Music was important to Peter Grant, who had been nurtured in a rich tradition of violin-playing,[71] and this is frequently reflected in the melodious use of rhyme and assonance in his verse. In contrast to the rather more didactic hymnology of the eighteenth century, Grant's themes are concerned with Christian experience, from its beginning in personal salvation through the atonement until its end when the believer arrives at his eternal home. The wiles of the devil, the snares of the world and the coldness of earthly things are often elaborated and set against the believer's safety and satisfaction in Christ. Such themes are also found in the verse of Daniel Grant of Tullymet, and in that of several other Baptist missionaries. Duncan MacDougall of Tiree, whose sister composed the original Gaelic version of the popular carol, 'Child in a Manger', preserves a stronger doctrinal interest than is generally evident.[72] The composition of largely experiential Gaelic hymns by Baptist pastors continued well into the twentieth century, as is demonstrated by the published work of Allan MacDougall of Broadford and Archibald MacDonald of Bowmore. Lay members of congregations similarly contributed to this very substantial body of evangelical verse.[73]

While the quantity of oral prose which was delivered in Gaelic sermons by Baptist missionaries must have been immense, little has survived in written form, although it has been known for individual sermons to be remembered for a century.[74] Missionaries probably translated numerous tracts into Gaelic, but their contributions in this field are obscured by anonymity. They were also active in translating English sermons into Gaelic. Alexander MacDougall of Bowmore, a native of Bunessan, Mull, who trained at Spurgeon's Pastors' College, produced several Gaelic versions of Spurgeon's sermons, which were published between 1864 and 1882.[75] The translation of popular English hymns into Gaelic by Baptist pastors was not uncommon.

English prose writings by Baptist missionaries are well attested throughout the nineteenth and twentieth centuries. While only a few pastors like Alexander McLeod and David McRae produced important books on doctrine and church order,[76] many missionaries have left a record of their labours in their journals and their regular dispatches to the BHMS. Dugald Sinclair of Bellanoch provides an outstandingly vivid account of his foundational work in his journals for 1810-15, and the annual reports of the BHMS preserve a uniquely graphic record of Baptist activity in the Highlands until the second half of this century.[77]

New Patterns of Ministry, 1900-39

In spite of the many changes which had occurred since 1850, Baptist work in the West Highlands and Hebrides was in remarkably good heart at the beginning of the twentieth century. The period 1880-1900 had been a more stable phase of Highland history, and it provided a foundation for the next decade. New churches had developed from out-stations at Port Ellen (Islay) in 1880 and Furnace (Lochfyneside) in 1892. At Oban many years of uncertainty about the continuation of Baptist witness in the town had been resolved by the formation of the present church in 1896. A chapel was built at Oban in 1904, and another at Port Ellen in 1910.[78]

An even more significant indication of vigorous missionary activity was to be found at the village of Taynuilt in the mainland district of Lorn. Here a fresh initiative had begun in 1903, when Alexander Brown was transferred from Bunessan to continue a plan of evangelism for Lorn and Appin. In the face of opposition Brown had held initial meetings in the schools at Connel Ferry and Taynuilt, but in July 1903 the first river-side baptism took place and aroused considerable interest. By 1906 a Baptist chapel had been erected in Taynuilt, thus providing a firm base for outreach to the surrounding areas.[79] The field was particularly encouraging since the population was sustained in several localities by industrial developments of long standing, as well as by more recent enterprises. At Bonawe, across Loch Etive, granite was quarried, while the production of slate at Ballachulish had been of importance since the 1880s. Farther up Loch Leven at Kinlochleven, the British Aluminium Company opened a smelter in 1908. Around Taynuilt itself, afforestation was taking place.[80] The main difficulty was that the centres of population were widely separated, and the provision of a regular ministry at each centre was beyond the capability of a single missionary. Yet Alexander Brown worked with unflagging enthusiasm, and supplied services at Bonawe Quarries, Ballachulish and Kinlochleven as often as he could. Surmounting the purely geographical problems was a major undertaking; in 1920, for instance, Brown informed the BHMS that a motor-boat would be of great advantage for his ministry along Loch Etive. The response of the people, however, compensated for the inconveniences, and Brown's dispatches frequently give the impression that several fields could have been opened successfully if the means and the manpower had been available.[81] In Taynuilt the membership of the church had reached thirty-five by 1925 and was maintained at this level for the next ten years. Thereafter, economic uncertainty exacerbated by the Second World War led to congregational decline, and the church closed in 1945.[82]

The ministry of Alexander Brown, which terminated in 1931, was the last to resemble the large-scale itinerant ministries characteristic of the nineteenth century. The evidence indicates that by the 1890s a new pattern of ministry had developed in the west. The emphasis appears to have shifted to individual localities, self-contained districts, or islands. The islands, of course, formed natural units, and increasing dependence on steam-boat timetables may, to some extent, have determined the activities of the missionaries. Yet, as the same development is apparent on the mainland, it seems likely that it had become deliberate policy to focus evangelistic endeavour on areas within easy reach of existing churches. While pastors travelled to assist one another on special occasions, they tended to devote their attention to their immediate neighbourhoods.[83] The type of ministry which pertained in most parts until the Second World War is fairly represented in the following dispatch from Donald Bell of the Tobermory Church, written on 3 August 1903:

> Since I last reported I have been in every part of my district.I was one week in Ardnamurchan from Monday to Saturday, visiting every day and preaching every evening. I have been in all parts of my own district in Mull. One week I left home on Monday and preached in the evening in the street in Dervaig. The weather being warm and dry, the people, old and young, turned out and sat in the open air . . . On Wednesday I crossed the hill to the Kilninian side, and visited as many homes as I could before I preached in the school in the evening.[84]

Stationed at Bunessan, Archibald MacDonald was similarly engaged in the

Ross of Mull, and he conducted a special week's mission in the village in January 1910. Localized missions of this kind were now common; later, they were frequently conducted by Francis William Taylor, a native of Ardchrishnish in the Ross of Mull and a student of Dunoon Baptist College, who began his ministry in Bowmore in 1910.[85]

Planned missions, often involving a visiting preacher, were the legacy of the Moody and Sankey campaigns, and owed much to the example of the Tiree revival of 1874. A convert of that revival, Donald MacArthur, became a prominent itinerant evangelist in Lorn and elsewhere between 1893 and 1898, when he began to assist Duncan MacFarlane as pastor of the Tiree Church. Under MacArthur's ministry individual missions were encouraged, and revivals broke out in Tiree before the First World War.[86] In the other churches the work went ahead steadily with less obvious fervour than in Tiree, but with consistent results. The Port Ellen Church had a promising out-station at Lotts, the Bowmore Church was similarly active at Carnduncan, the Oban pastor was preaching from Kerrera to Strontoiller, and John Knox in Lochgilphead was sustaining a long, productive ministry.[87] Progress was abruptly checked, however, by the First World War, which accelerated the depopulation of the rural communities and deprived the churches of young blood. The Bunessan pastor reported 'a great blank in the place' when eighteen young men from the area joined the patrol boats.[88] In many districts the blanks remained after the war, and recovery was slow. The membership of most Baptist Churches continued to decline from 1918 to 1920, and the people were less responsive to evangelism. Archibald MacDonald found himself preaching alone on the street in Bowmore in 1919.[89]

Spiritual buoyancy began to return in the early 1920s, and awakenings became evident in certain communities. Faith Mission preachers were operating with success in several parts of the Highlands, and the Baptist Churches in most districts report a trickle of conversions.[90] An intense spiritual movement appeared again in Tiree in 1921 under the preaching of F.W. Taylor. When Taylor returned to Tiree in October 1922 to give temporary relief to Donald MacArthur, who was unwell, he became the principal instrument in a revival which lasted for two years. There were numerous conversions and baptisms, but the membership of the Tiree Church nevertheless fell from the figure of 129 in 1920 to ninety-seven in 1925.[91] In 1928 Taylor became the pastor in Tiree, where he ministered with remarkable power until 1939. By 1935 the membership of the Tiree Church had risen to 114.[92]

'Suitable men with a knowledge of Gaelic'

As pastors strove to raise the membership and morale of their churches in the early 1920s, the BHMS became aware of another problem. 'The main difficulty facing the Society,' states its Report for 1923, 'is to find suitable men with a knowledge of Gaelic to carry on the work in the Western Islands.'[93] Retirement and resignation had created gaps which were difficult to fill without depriving other stations of Gaelic-speaking pastors. In 1925, however, the society announced that it had acquired five Galic-speaking students.[94] Three of these — Archibald MacDonald, Neil MacArthur and Dugald Lamont — were the fruit of the recent Tiree revivals, while the fourth, Edward G. Campbell, hailed from Lotts (Islay), and the fifth, Neil D. Graham, from Bunessan. All showed considerable potential, but by 1930 three of the group were dead. Archibald MacDonald and Neil MacArthur contracted tuberculosis while studying in Edinburgh, and Neil Graham, who had been posted to Colonsay in 1926, died with tragic suddenness within weeks of moving to Bowmore in 1928.[95] Only Dugald Lamont and Edward Campbell remained, but in 1929 another Gaelic-speaking student, Hector M. Meek from Tiree, had begun training, and in 1930 he was posted to Colonsay. Campbell and Lamont were settled at Broadford and Bunessan.[96] The shortage of Gaelic-speaking pastors was increased by the sudden death of another young Tiree preacher, Alexander MacArthur, in 1931. MacArthur had only recently moved from Port Ellen to Bowmore. In 1930, two of the veteran pastors, Archibald MacDonald and Donald MacArthur, passed away.[97]

It was a critical time for the churches, and the resources of the BHMS were stretched to their limits. Much-needed help was provided by Neil MacDonald, F.W. Taylor's assistant in Tiree, who was active in pulpit-supply and missions in Mull and Skye.[98] A lady pastor also came to the aid of the churches. This was Mary Flora MacArthur, daughter of Donald MacArthur, who ministered in Tobermory from 1938 to 1941, and later in Colonsay from 1945 to 1947.[99] Inevitably and necessarily, English-only pastors came from the mainland to fill vacant charges. Albert E. Mileman came to Tobermory in 1925, Archibald MacNicol to Bowmore in 1932 and George F. Maitland to the same charge in 1937.[100] The transition to English-only pastorates had been made at Tullymet and Lochgilphead before 1900.[101]

The provision of English-only pastors for vacant charges in the islands forms part of a wider pattern of linguistic and social change which becomes particularly prominent in the life of the churches in this period. In the early nineteenth century Baptist missionaries were prepared to preach in English or Gaelic as circumstances required, but Gaelic was their principal preaching medium. By the middle of that century, preaching in English appears to have become commoner, especially in towns and villages within the Gaelic-speaking area. In Bowmore in Islay, for example, the opening of the refurbished meeting-house on Sunday 31 October 1869 was marked by two

English services and one Gaelic service. In Mull, too, the regular use of English in services is noticeable by 1900, at least in Tobermory and its neighbourhood.[102] The use of English more generally in the island churches after 1900 was stimulated by the presence of summer visitors in the services. By the 1920s and 1930s the number of summer visitors in the islands was increasing considerably, and their attendance at church services was often an encouragement to small congregations. Visiting preachers who did not speak Gaelic also gave assistance in summer time; Jane Henderson, pastor of the Lossiemouth Church from 1918 to 1921, was a popular figure in Bowmore, where she held evangelistic meetings in 1923.[103] Even in the outlying island of Tiree, English was beginning to make significant inroads by 1927, when the BHMS instructed Neil MacDonald to preach in English in the summer months in a district where he normally employed only Gaelic.[104]

As the use of Gaelic in regular worship declined, the island churches were also forging closer links with the Lowlands. These links were substantially strengthened when the BHMS became an integral part of the Baptist Union of Scotland by Deed of Incorporation in 1931.[105] This ensured regular visits from Union office-bearers, and placed the work more firmly within the denominational perspective. A special 'Highlands and Islands Sunday' was observed annually from 1938, and a leaflet describing the financial needs of the Mission was distributed.[106] The support of churches and individuals beyond the Highland area was of direct benefit to the Highland missionaries. In 1929 Edward Campbell, then in Broadford, Skye, received the gift of an Austin Seven car to aid him in his work, following the visit of the president of the Union, W. Holms Coats, to the island. Friends on the mainland also helped to supply sets of slides which pastors could use in their new-fangled 'magic lanterns'.[107] Such modern aids enlivened the mid-week meetings, and helped to hold the interest of young people when they moved from the Sunday Schools and Bible Classes which flourished in most churches.

Besides Sunday Schools and Bible Classes, some of the Highland churches maintained other organizations. The mainland churches of Oban and Lochgilphead had active branches of Christian Endeavour and the Young Worshippers' League. Several churches had Bands of Hope from at least the late 1920s. The island churches appear to have supported fewer of these organizations. The churches in Islay, however, not only sustained Bands of Hope, but also participated in Christian Endeavour.[108] Attempts were also made in this period to encourage closer fellowship between the various Baptist Churches in the Highlands, and Highland Baptist Conferences were held in Lochgilphead and Islay in 1929 and 1930.[109] Wider movements which affected British Evangelicalism between the wars are sometimes detectable in the life of the Highland churches. The Oxford Group movement, for instance, had some influence in the Port Ellen Church by the early 1940s.[110]

The inter-war years were characterized by vigorous activity on the part of Highland Baptists, and a sense of cautious optimism is communicated in the BHMS reports of the later 1920s and 1930s. Soirées and 'socials' were drawing the support of the wider community. So, too, were the sales of work which boosted fabric and repair funds, and which owed much to the industry of the women of the churches.[111] Yet there were also ominous signs of change, not least in the diminishing supply of Gaelic-speaking pastors, and optimism evaporated as the clouds of war gathered once more.

The Second World War and its Aftermath

The Second World War brought unexpected encouragements to some of the Baptist Churches within the Highland area. RAF personnel stationed in Islay helped to swell the numbers of the Bowmore Church, and two servicemen assisted with the Sunday School. The income of the church increased by 56% in 1943. In Tullymet the church was revitalized by evacuees, and attendances improved temporarily. The onset of the war evidently stimulated church attendances elsewhere: Mary Flora MacArthur reported very encouraging congregations in the Tobermory Church during 1940-1.

The benefits created by the war were, however, superficial. When service personnel and evacuees were withdrawn, the churches generally found that their memberships had declined. In Oban initial wartime uncertainty had a serious effect on summer congregational size, leading to decreased income and flagging morale, although matters had improved by 1943. The rural areas were severely disturbed by a further drain on their manpower, and in districts like the Ross of Mull depopulation intensified. In 1940 the Bunessan pastor reported 'a marked decrease' in church attendances, and noted that the work was 'growing increasingly difficult because of a declining population'. In Tiree the membership of the church had begun to decline immediately prior to the departure of F.W. Taylor, and it continued to drop sharply thereafter. Indications of imminent revival in the last years of Taylor's ministry gave way to anxiety about the war. The capitulation of France led to increased church attendances in July and August 1940, but many islanders soon preferred to remain at home and 'listen in' to the latest radio bulletins.[112]

The post-war period has seen little change in the patterns which were established during 1939-45. In spite of vigorous work among children and young people, Sunday School and membership rolls have continued to fall in most churches, and several churches have been closed since the end of the war. The Broadford Church ceased in 1944, the Taynuilt Church in 1945, the Furnace Church in 1957, the Tobermory Church in 1964 and the Tullymet Church in 1969.[113] The closures at Broadford, Taynuilt and Tobermory involved churches in villages which are still substantial by Highland standards. The evidence thus suggests that these churches declined and eventually died, not because of depopulation of the surrounding areas, but because they lost the urge and the means to evangelize a changing community. The persistent exodus of their young people to the Lowlands had a demoralizing effect.[114] In the Hebrides, the stronger churches have held missions in the 1960s and 1970s, but it is noticeable that the main responsibility for evangelism has passed to the Faith Mission, whose work in the Highlands has been of importance since its inception in 1886.[115] As the island churches have declined, the most consistent levels of membership have been maintained in the larger towns of Oban and Lochgilphead, where both churches have held steady at around twenty to thirty and thirty-six members respectively, with some recent surges of growth.[116] (See Figure 15.2.)

Falling church rolls have made it difficult to maintain ministries in all the island charges. In 1942 the charges at Bunessan and Tobermory were linked, and in 1954 both charges were placed under the care of the Oban pastor. The Colonsay Church was attached to Islay in a similar manner in 1954, but a change in ferry service has recently made it more convenient for the Oban pastor to visit the island periodically.[117] Of late, Mull has received pastoral oversight from Lochgilphead. Visiting preachers have assisted with summer services in Bunessan and Colonsay. Latterly Tullymet was served from the Pitlochry Church, which originated in 1881 as an out-station of Tullymet.[118] Since 1963 the Islay Churches at Bowmore and Port Ellen have shared a pastor. In Tiree full-time ministries have been maintained, although with English-only pastors since 1965. The last Gaelic-speaking pastor serving full-time in a Home Mission charge and preaching regularly in Gaelic was Dugald Lamont, who died in 1958 while ministering in Tiree. A Gaelic ministry was continued in Tiree on a part-time basis until 1965 by Hector Meek, who died in 1984.[119] Edward Campbell, the last survivor of the group of Gaelic-speaking students who enrolled in 1925, was latterly pastor at Bellshill, but served for many years as convener of the Home Mission Committee of the Baptist Union, until the work of the BHMS was absorbed within the wider Union programme of church extension in 1971.[120]

The dismantling of the BHMS and the transferring of its responsibilities marked the end of a distinctive unit in the evangelization of the Highlands. The BHMS served both as a means of support for individual churches, and as a cohesive force within a widely scattered family. Something of its function remains, however, in the Argyll and the Isles Baptist Association, which was reorganized in 1968.[121] The association links the churches in Oban, Lochgilphead, Mull, Islay, Colonsay and Tiree, together with Dunoon, and its annual newsletter carries reports of their continuing work for Christ.

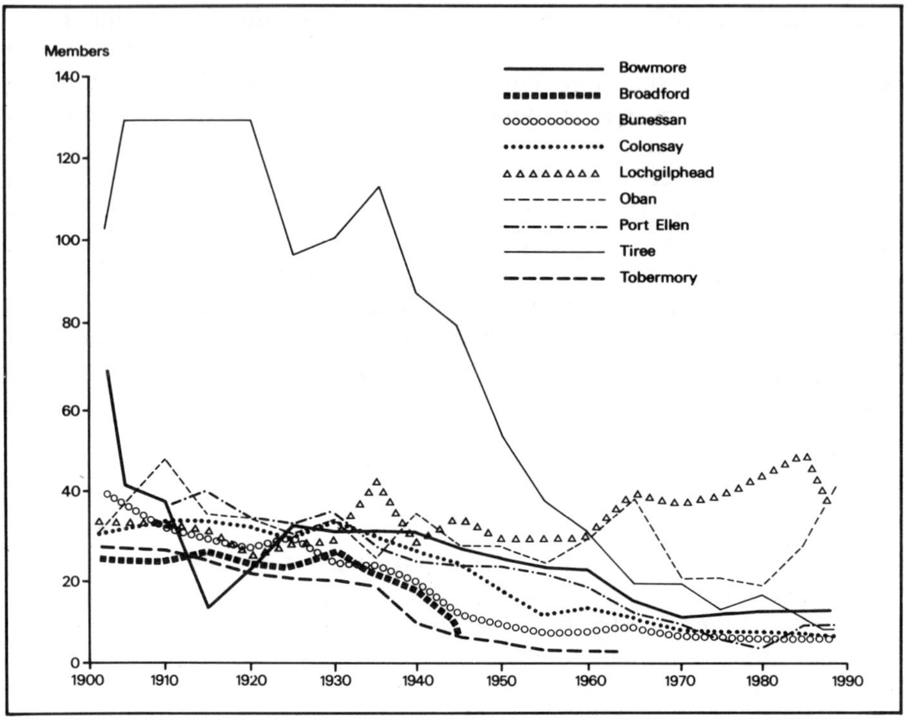

FIGURE 15.2 : MEMBERSHIP GRAPHS FOR HIGHLAND BAPTIST CHURCHES SINCE 1900.

Retrospect and Prospect

Baptist Churches in the Highlands have never experienced steady growth of their memberships. In the nineteenth century growth occurred sporadically in the context of revivals, and the increased membership was soon diminished by emigration. In the twentieth century, the churches in Oban and Lochgilphead have held their ground, but several churches in smaller villages have been closed. The rural and island churches have experienced a decline in their memberships, especially since the Second World War. In Tiree it is noticeable that Baptist membership remained high until the eve of the war, and that the leadership and revivalist ministries of Donald MacArthur and F.W. Taylor were of great significance in maintaining the impetus. Taylor's earlier ministries in Bowmore, Bunessan and Broadford, however, were not as productive as his ministry in Tiree, where revivalist preaching appears to have been particularly acceptable. MacArthur and Taylor had no successors in this tradition; the few Gaelic pastors who emerged in the 1920s evidently did not enjoy the same degree of spiritual authority as their predecessors. The absence of strong revival movements in the Inner Hebrides after 1940 may not, however, be due solely to changes in personnel and styles of preaching; it may reflect change within Highland society itself, and especially the disintegration of close-knit communities of the traditional Highland type. In the 1920s and 1930s, the Inner Hebrides became significantly more accessible to the outside world, and this is reflected in the life of the churches. The work of all Highland pastors was later made more difficult by the effect of the Second World War, which hastened rural depopulation and seriously disturbed Highland community life. Since the war, the migration of young people to the Lowlands has continued, and the Highland economy has remained unstable. The population has therefore declined in most districts, and has tended to become older. This is reflected in the membership of several Baptist Churches in the Highlands today, particularly in the islands.

Highland society at the end of the twentieth century presents many challenges for existing Baptist Churches. For the remaining island churches, the penetration of their communities is a matter of the greatest urgency, since their survival will depend partly on a fresh intake of believers. It is therefore encouraging that the Islay Churches have recently initiated a vigorous programme of district visitation and evangelism under their present pastor, Jonathan Magee, and that the fruit of this outreach is becoming apparent in a steady trickle of conversions and baptisms. In Mull, Baptists have been meeting for fellowship in Craignure, which has become an important ferry terminal for Oban.[122] In Oban itself, Baptists have participated in a co-operative programme of evangelism with the support of Baptists from the Southern Convention of the United States. This programme has helped the membership to rise above forty by 1986. The Lochgilphead Church is also experimenting with new forms of community evangelism.[123] Nevertheless, many avenues remain to be explored, both in areas where Baptists have been long established, and in areas where there has been no Baptist witness in recent years.

In at least one island which has not known Baptist activity since the 1820s, a small Baptist Church has recently emerged, although this body bears no apparent relationship to the main Scottish stream. Meeting in Benbecula, South Uist, the church hit the headlines in March 1986 when the local councillor objected to its use of Balivanich School for regular worship. The name of the church, 'The Benbecula and Uist Grace Baptist Church', suggests a Reformed emphasis, and the congregation includes military personnel from the missile range in South Uist.[124]

Baptist witness in the Highlands at the end of the twentieth century is thus maintained by vigorous churches in Oban and Lochgilphead, and by small, tenacious churches in the islands, with the exciting hope of new growth. While we may lament the passing of the traditional 'Home Mission', home mission remains a priority of the Baptist Union, and its funds have sustained the existing ministries in the churches. The future beckons — a future which demands no less vision and no less commitment than did the past.

Notes

1. Peter Brierley and Fergus Macdonald, *Prospects for Scotland: report of the 1984 census of the churches* (Bromley, Kent 1985), pp 74-5, 102-3.
2. *Report of the Baptist Home Missionary Society for Scotland (BHMS Report)*, 1921, p 14. Brierley and Macdonald, *Prospects for Scotland*, p 74.
3. For an account of the changing 'Highland/Gaelic Line', see C.W.J. Withers, *Gaelic in Scotland, 1698-1981: the geographical history of a language* (Edinburgh 1984).
4. *BHMS Report*, 1901, pp 13-14.
5. William Buchanan, *Reports of Certain Remarkable Cases in the Court of Session, and Trials in the High Court of Justiciary* (Edinburgh 1813), pp 60-72. James Brown, *The Origin and History of the Baptists in Rothesay and the West Highlands of Scotland* (Glasgow 1861), summarized in J.C. Rendall, '"The Day of Small Things": some notable personalities and events in the early days of our denomination in Scotland', *Scottish Baptist Magazine (SBM)*, May 1924, pp 57-8. James Brown, *The Religious Denominations of Glasgow* (Glasgow 1860), 1 pp 140-2. J.B., 'A Dunoon Patriarch', *SBM*, Mar. 1876, pp 58-9.
6. *An Account of the Present State of Religion throughout the Highlands of Scotland* (Edinburgh 1827), pp 90-1. The nature of McArthur's allegedly 'erroneous views' is not yet evident. He may have been an early forerunner of the movement which later emerged in the United States as the Disciples of Christ under the leadership of Alexander Campbell.
7. Buchanan, *Certain Remarkable Cases*, p 60. Rendall, ' "The Day of Small Things" ', p 58.
8. George Yuille, ed, *History of the Baptists in Scotland* (Glasgow 1926), p 63. J. McL., 'History of the Baptist Church in Greenock', *SBM*, Aug. 1877, pp 120-1.
9. All sources are adamant that McArthur discovered believer's baptism through his own study of the scriptures, but the date of his baptism suggests that he may have been part of a wider movement. For later contacts between the Orangefield Church and other 'English' Baptists, see 'History of the Baptist Church in Greenock', p 121. For the founding of the Glasgow Church, see cap 2, p 33.
10. J.W. Morris, *Memoirs of the Life and Writings of the Rev. Andrew Fuller* (London 1816), p 140.

11. ibid, pp 140-1. Yuille, ed, *Baptists in Scotland*, p 116.
12. Hugh Anderson, *The Life and Letters of Christopher Anderson* (Edinburgh 1854), pp 26-7.
13. Obituary of Dugald Sinclair by Edmund Sheppard, in *The Christian Standard* (Cincinnati, USA), 5 Nov. 1870, p 357.
14. Anderson, *Anderson*, pp 26-7; Yuille, ed, *Baptists in Scotland*, pp 60-1.
15. Anderson, *Anderson*, pp 62-3, 80.
16. ibid, pp 101-2. Dugald Sinclair, *Journal of Itinerating Exertions in Some of the More destitute parts of Scotland*, 6 vols (Edinburgh 1814-17) 1 pp 3, 7. D.E. Meek, 'Dugald Sinclair: the life and work of a Highland itinerant missionary', *Scottish Studies* (forthcoming).
17. Only in Campbeltown is there definite evidence of an Argyll Baptist Church existing alongside an Independent Church in this period, but the relationship of the one to the other is not clear. Bellanoch Church may have been a wholly Baptist foundation, even although D. McVicar was formerly in the SPGH.
18. For a study of the Perthshire churches, see D.E. Meek, 'Congregational and Baptist Activity in Highland Perthshire, 1800-1900' (forthcoming).
19. Brief biographies of Baptist and Independent missionaries active in the period c. 1797-c. 1850 can be found in D.E. Meek, 'Evangelical Missionaries in the Early Nineteenth-Century Highlands', *Scottish Studies*, 28 (1987), Appendix A.
20. Obituary of William Tulloch by his son, William Tulloch, in *BHMS Report*, 1861, pp 19-24. A.B. Thomson, *Sketches of some Baptist Pioneers in Scotland*, Fourth Series (Glasgow 1903), pp 7-18.
21. Harry Escott, *A History of Scottish Congregationalism* (Glasgow 1960), p 263. See also cap 14, p 263.
22. Anderson, *Anderson*, p 27.
23. Buchanan, *Certain Remarkable Cases*, pp 60-72.
24. Brown, *Religious Denominations*, p 142. Rendall, ' "The Day of Small Things" ', p 58.
25. See cap 2, p 31, and also Meek, 'Evangelical Missionaries'.
26. Yuille, ed, *Baptists in Scotland*, p 68.
27. John Anderson was baptized by Alexander McLeod; see Minute Book of the Church at Craigbea, Tullymet, 1839 (Baptist Union of Scotland Records 7/2).
28. Anderson, *Anderson*, p 127.
29. ibid, pp 117-18. Yuille, ed, *Baptists in Scotland*, pp 72-3.
30. *Address by the Committee of the Baptist Home Missionary Society for Scotland* (Edinburgh 1827). For Orkney and Shetland, see cap 17 and cap 18.
31. Yuille, ed, *Baptists in Scotland*, p 73.
32. Tulloch obituary, pp 22-3. Thomson, *Sketches*, pp 13-16.
33. In addition to *BHMS Reports*, the following obituaries or accounts of individual missionaries are available: *SBM*, Mar. 1875, p 62 (J. Miller); 1882, pp 140-2 (D. Ferguson); 1887, pp 16-18 (D. Grant); 1891, pp 252-3 (D. MacLellan); 1895, pp 318-20 (D. MacFarlane); Oct. 1902, pp 165-8 (W. Grant).
34. Sinclair, *Journal*, 3 p 16. Tulloch obituary, p 21. *BHMS Report*, 1858, pp 9-10.
35. Contrasting aspects of the relationship between Baptist itinerants and the Free Church are exemplified in *BHMS Reports*, 1853, p 18; 1857, pp 6-7, 13, 22; 1858, p 16.
36. Meek, 'Evangelical Missionaries' and 'Dugald Sinclair', both discuss aspects of the relationship between the Established Church and the Dissenting movement.
37. Anderson, *Anderson*, p 115. Rev. Alexander MacLeod to Mrs MacKenzie of Seaforth, 13 Aug. 1823; Rev. W. MacRae to Mrs MacKenzie of Seaforth, 23 Dec. 1823; Scottish Record Office: GD 46/17/62. V.E. Durkacz, *The Decline of the Celtic Languages* (Edinburgh 1983), pp 126-8, 130-3. Dòmhnall MacGillìosa, *An Eaglais Shaor ann an Leódhas 1843-1900* (Dùn Eideann 1981), pp 13-14.
38. Tullymet Minute Book. *Letters on the State of Religion in the Highlands of Scotland* (Glasgow 1818), p 13. *An Account of Itinerant Exertions in Different Parts of the Highlands and Islands of Scotland* (Baptist Highland Mission *Report*, 1822-3). Morris, *Fuller*, p 140. *SBM*, 1882, p 141. Letter from Donald MacLean, Cooper, Tiree, to his brother, John MacLean, in Nova Scotia, 28 Mar. 1838 (photocopy in the Archives of the School of Scottish Studies, Edinburgh).
39. Anderson, *Anderson*, pp 26-7.
40. John McNeill, *The Baptist Church in Colonsay* (Edinburgh 1914), pp 15-16. Sinclair, *Journal* 5-6.
41. *BHMS Reports*, 1856, p 19; 1859, pp 9-10; *SBM*, Oct. 1902, p 165.
42. Tullymet Minute Book.
43. *Abbreviated Register of Sasines*, Argyll 1820, item 3139.
44. Baptist Highland Mission *Report*, 1822-3, p 2. Tulloch obituary, pp 21, 23.
45. *BHMS Report*, 1855, p 12.

46. Manuscript account by Alexander MacDougall of the refurbishment of Bowmore Baptist Church in 1869, and poster for the re-opening of the church on 31 October 1869. (Originals in Bowmore Baptist Church.)
47. *BHMS Report*, 1855, pp 13-14.
48. Tulloch obituary, p 21. Yuille, ed, *Baptists in Scotland*, pp 118-19. The letter from Donald MacLean, Tiree, to his brother (see n 38) was written for MacLean by Duncan MacDougall. MacDougall's work as a teacher was remembered in Tiree until recently.
49. Churches with indoor baptistries included those built after 1900 (for example, Oban and Port Ellen) and those refurbished after that date (for example, Broadford).
50. *BHMS Report*, 1861, p 8. *SBM*, 1895, p 319. A. Farquharson, *Earrannan air an eadar-theangachadh bho Obair Iongantach Dhé ann an Eilean Thiridhe* (Glasgow 1875).
51. For general background, see John MacInnes, *The Evangelical Movement in the Highlands of Scotland* (Aberdeen 1951), and Meek, 'Evangelical Missionaries'.
52. Alexander Haldane, *Memoirs of the Lives of Robert Haldane of Airthrey and of his brother, James Alexander Haldane* (London 1852), pp 316-17. Roderick MacCowan, *The Men of Skye* (Glasgow 1902), pp 1-30.
53. Sinclair, *Journal*, 1-6. Meek, 'Dugald Sinclair'.
54. Alexander MacRae, *Revivals in the Highlands and Islands in the Nineteenth Century* (Stirling 1905). Durkacz, *Decline*, pp 126-33.
55. *The First Yearly Report of the Baptist Union of Scotland* (Cupar 1844), p 22. See *BHMS Reports*, 1840-6.
56. ibid, 1860, pp 10-11.
57. W. Tulloch, 'Sketch of the Origin and Development of the Revival in Tyree', *SBM*, Oct. 1875, pp 152-6.
58. *Scottish Baptist Year Book (SBYB)*, 1875, membership statistics. *SBM*, Mar. 1876, pp 46-7, Apr. 1876, pp 58-9, 1895, p 21. *BHMS Report*, 1898, pp 20-2. Yuille, ed, *Baptists in Scotland*, p 113.
59. *A Manual of the Baptist Denomination for the Year 1846* (London 1846), p 36. *BHMS Reports*, 1846, p 26; 1854, p 15.
60. Tullymet Minute Book.
61. *BHMS Report*, 1898, pp 16-18.
62. ibid, 1863, p 23.
63. The South Portland Street Church had a Gaelic-speaking pastor, Alexander McLeod, from 1820 to 1869; see the obituary of Mrs Dugald Sinclair by James Kilgour in *The Christian Standard*, 29 September 1888. McLeod was succeeded about 1869 by Alexander MacFarlane, who may have had Islay connections; see Bowmore MS, 1869, pp 3-4. The Orangefield Church had a Gaelic-speaking pastor, Lachlan Mackintosh of Grantown-on-Spey, from 1829 to 1832. See 'History of the Baptist Church in Greenock', p 122.
64. The three missionaries who emigrated to Breadalbane, Glengarry Co., Ontario, were William Fraser of Uig, who was pastor of Breadalbane Baptist Church from 1831 to 1850; Duncan Cameron of Lawers, who pastored the same church from 1857 to 1860; and John McEwan of Tullymet, who emigrated in 1839 and was the pastor of a church in the Indian Lands of Glengarry Co. for a brief period. For a discussion of the contribution of Highland Baptists to emigration, see D.E. Meek, 'Evangelicalism and Emigration: some aspects of the role of dissenting evangelicalism and its preachers in Highland emigration especially to Canada, c. 1800-c. 1850', in *Proceedings of the North American Congress of Celtic Studies held in Ottawa, 26-30 March 1986* (Ottawa 1988), pp 15-35.
65. *BHMS Report*, 1853, p 9.
66. ibid, 1854, pp 5-9.
67. J.D. Wood, 'Transatlantic Land Reform: America and the Crofters' Revolt', *Scottish Historical Review*, 63 (1984), pp 97-102. Yuille, ed, *Baptists in Scotland*, p 194. See, in general, James Hunter, *The Making of the Crofting Community* (Edinburgh 1976); Eric Richards, *A History of the Highland Clearances*, 2 vols (London 1982-5).
68. *BHMS Report*, 1861, pp 12-13. Mary Ferguson and Ann Matheson, *Scottish Gaelic Union Catalogue* (Edinburgh 1984), p 73. Daniel Grannd, *Laoidhean Spioradail* (Perth 1842, 2nd edn, 1862).
69. Pàdruig Grannd, *Dàin Spioradail*, Preface to the Sixth Edition, reprinted in the Nineteenth Edition (Edinburgh 1903), p vii.
70. Ferguson and Matheson, *Gaelic Catalogue*, pp 74-5.
71. Grannd, *Dàin Spioradail* (Glasgow 1926), pp 15-16.
72. Donnchadh Dùghallach, *Laoidhean Spioradail a chum cuideachadh le cràbhadh nan Gael* (Glasgow 1841); for discussion, see Eric Cregeen and D.W. Mackenzie, *Tiree Bards and their Bardachd: the poets*

in a Hebridean community (Coll 1978), pp 16-17. For some notes on MacDougall's sister. Mary, see *Tocher* 24 (1975), pp 304-123.

73. Ailein Mac Dhùghaill, *Laoidhean Molaidh* (Glasgow 1928?). A selection of hymns by Baptist and other composers, including Archibald MacDonald, is found in *Laoidhean Soisgeulach*, ed Iain Caimbeul (Glasgow 1922).

74. McNeill, *Baptist Church in Colonsay*, pp 5-6.

75. Ferguson and Matheson, *Gaelic Catalogue*, p 106

76. David McRae, *A View of the Old and New Way of Doctrine, Discipline, and Government in the Churches of Christ* (Inverness 1805). For Alexander McLeod's works, see Yuille, ed, *Baptists in Scotland*, p 304.

77. An almost complete set of *BHMS Reports* for the period 1829-46 is located in Glasgow University Library. A complete set of *BHMS Reports* for the period 1853-64 is held in the Records of the Baptist Union of Scotland. *BHMS Reports* from 1898 onwards are well preserved, and can be found in issues of *SBYB* until 1971, when the BHMS was dissolved. For Sinclair's journals, see n 16.

78. Yuille, ed, *Baptists in Scotland*, pp 117-18. Book of Records (Baptist Union of Scotland). *BHMS Report*, 1910, p 24.

79. ibid, 1903, pp 11-14; 1906, p 11.

80. C.M. MacDonald, ed, *The Third Statistical Account of Scotland: the County of Argyll*, (Edinburgh 1961 edn), pp 164, 182.

81. *BHMS Reports*, 1920, p 17; 1926, pp 19-20.

82. *SBYB*, 1925, 1935. Book of Records.

83. Beyond their districts, missionaries may have visited only those areas which were readily accessible by means of public transport. It is possible also that their districts were coming to be regarded in the same manner as parishes as the Baptists gained acceptability and respectability in the later nineteenth century.

84. *BHMS Report*, 1903, p 84. For Bell's use of steamship services when visiting Ardnamurchan, see ibid, 1898, p 23.

85. ibid, 1910, pp 8, 19, 21-3.

86. *SBM*, 1895, p 21; Oct. 1930, p 156. Yuille, ed, *Baptists in Scotland*, pp 112-13. *BHMS Reports*, 1898, pp 20-1, 26; 1900, p 15; 1902, pp 22-3; 1912, pp 29-30.

87. ibid, 1903, pp 14-15, 18; 1908, pp 191-2.

88. ibid, 1915, p 16.

89. ibid, 1919, pp 19-20.

90. For the work of the Faith Mission in this period, see A.A. Woolsey, *Channel of Revival: a biography of Duncan Campbell* (Edinburgh 1982), esp pp 62-76, and C.N. Peckham, *Heritage of Revival* Edinburgh 1986, pp 51-63. See also *BHMS Report*, 1924, p 23.

91. ibid, 1921, pp 14-15; 1923, pp 6, 15; 1924, pp 17-20. Donald Dron, 'Revival in Tiree', *SBM*, Aug. 1923, pp 101-2. *SBYB*, 1920 and 1925, membership statistics. Taylor was assisted in his work in Tiree by James Reid, Travelling Agent of the BHMS, and Donald Dron of Edinburgh.

92. *BHMS Reports*, 1929, pp 18-20; 1933, pp 218-20; 1939, pp 260-1. *SBYB*, 1935, membership statistics.

93. *BHMS Report*, 1923, p 7.

94. ibid, 1925, p 6.

95. ibid, 1926, p 6. *SBM*, Jan. 1929, p 9; Feb. 1930, p 25.

96. *BHMS Reports*, 1928, p 7; 1930, p 17.

97. ibid, 1931, p 9. *SBM*, Aug. 1930, p 124; Oct. 1930, p 156.

98. *BHMS Reports*, 1930, p 28; 1931, p 20; 1932, p 195.

99. ibid, 1938, p 241; 1939, pp 245-6; 1940, p 221; 1945, p 130; 1947, p 177. Miss MacArthur was engaged in mission work among the fisher-girls of Lerwick earlier in the 1930s, and she was also missionary at Eday and Sanday (Orkney) between 1943 and 1945.

100. *SBYB*, 1958, pp 97-8. *BHMS Reports*, 1926, p 17; 1932, p 130; 1938, p 241.

101. When John Mackintosh retired from Lochgilphead in 1869, he was succeeded by C.W. Gregory, who moved to Bacup, Lancashire, in August 1875; see *SBM*, Oct. 1875, p 123. There is no evidence that he or his successors, Finlay Forbes (1875-80) and John Knox (1881-1928), could speak Gaelic. It is unlikely that the pastors who succeeded Daniel Grant at Tullymet, namely D.G. Forbes (1884-93) and W.S. Steedman (1894-1904), would have spoken Gaelic.

102. Bowmore MS, 1869, p 2, and Bowmore poster, 1869 (see n 46). *BHMS Report*, 1902, p 23.

103. ibid, 1923, p 16; 1927, p 21; 1929, p 16; 1933, p 220.

104. ibid, 1927, p 20.

105. The terms of the Deed were published in every *BHMS Report* after 1931; see, for example, ibid, 1937, pp 7-8.
106. Highlands and Islands Sunday leaflet, 29 May 1938. The text was written by James Hair.
107. *BHMS Reports*, 1929, pp 7, 16; 1933, p 221.
108. ibid, 1926, p 19; 1929, p 21; 1933, p 220; 1935, p 233; 1937, p 28; 1938, pp 259-60.
109. ibid, 1930, p 32; *SBM*, July 1929.
110. I owe this information to my mother, Mrs H.M. Meek. For background to the Oxford Group movement, see D.W. Bebbington, 'The Oxford Group Movement between the Wars', *Voluntary Religion*, ed W.J. Sheils and Diana Wood (Oxford, 1986).
111. *BHMS Reports*, 1933, p 219; 1940, p 235.
112. ibid, 1940, pp 234-6, 237-8; 1941, pp 243-4; 1943, p 105; 1945, p 133.
113. Book of Records.
114. *BHMS Reports*, 1927, p 18; 1933, p 217.
115. In Tiree in 1936-7 Faith Mission 'Pilgrims' were able to relieve Taylor and MacDonald of 'the strain of former winter services'. See ibid, 1938, p 257.
116. See *SBYB*, 1945-85, for membership statistics.
117. *BHMS Reports*, 1943, p 103; 1954, p 165.
118. Yuille, ed, *Baptists in Scotland*, pp 167-8.
119. *BHMS Reports*, 1958, p 182; 1963, p 185.
120. *SBYB*, 1972, pp 35-6, 127.
121. The association was reorganized at a meeting in Tiree in June 1968; see *SBYB*, 1969, p 176.
122. Newsletter of the Argyll and the Isles Baptist Association, 1985.
123. ibid. *Mission Report* (Baptist Union of Scotland), Mar. 1986, p 1.
124. *The West Highland Free Press*, 14 Mar. 1986, p 8.

D.E. Meek

16. CAITHNESS

In Sir John Sinclair's First Statistical Account of Scotland (1791-9), two remarks occur relating to Caithness Baptists. In the account of Wick Parish (1794) William Sutherland claims: 'There are still about half a dozen Anabaptists on the estate of Keiss, the remains of the disciples of the late Sir William Sinclair . . . But this small exception to the general persuasion of the people is scarcely worth notice.'[1] Again, in that of Canisbay Parish (1793) Dr John Morison writes in similar vein: 'The whole inhabitants of the parish profess the religion of the established church, except a few of the Anabaptist persuasion . . . It is now greatly on the decline, and never was accompanied with any sort of outrage, wildness, or violence in its professors.'[2] It is instructive to see the scant reference to Baptist beginnings in Caithness and note the impression that this strange religious deviation is a passing phenomenon of little account. That phenomenon, however, was destined to become a living force of great account in little over a century.

In 1906, at the centenary services of Wick Baptist Church, a successor of Sutherland as parish minister complimented Baptists on their work and witness in church and community.[3] Large congregations attended morning, afternoon and evening services. At night the church was packed to capacity, and the provost, town council and magistrates occupied front seats. Town ministers and Baptist ministers from various parts of the United Kingdom were special guests.[4] A former member of the church, John Horne, who ministered at Ayr and Springburn, gave a concise history of the church from 1806 to 1906. Amongst other things, Horne highlighted the fact that the church had provided four bailies, two provosts and at least seven men for the pastoral ministry.[5] He himself was the church's first theological student.[6] From the comments of representatives present, it was evident that the fellowship was now strong, dynamic and virile. Members took their Christianity seriously, as was clear from their corporate life and community service. They had gained the respect of other churches and the town's folk in general. The biblical ideals of being 'salt' and 'light' were lived out before others.

The County: Changes and Challenges

Caithness has been described as a land with a difference. Certainly its contours contrast with other Highland counties. This remote, wind-swept and wide-open county roughly forms a 700-square mile triangular plateau with the apex at John o' Groats. It is bounded on two sides by the Pentland Firth and the North Sea. Many sea-captains, sailors and fishermen have hailed from these parts. Also Caithness has been a favourite recruiting place for

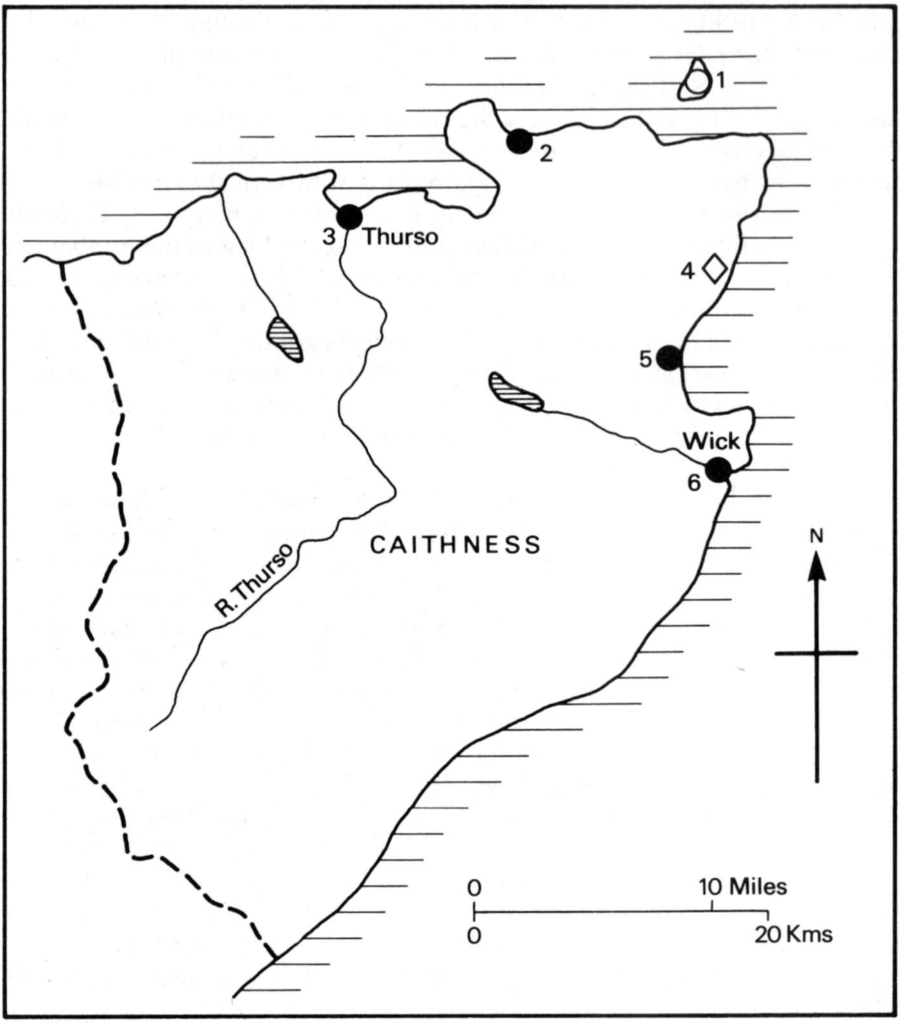

MAP 16 : CAITHNESS BAPTIST CHURCHES.

Key to Map 16

1. Stroma
2. Scarfskerry
3. Thurso
4. Freswick
5. Keiss
6. Wick

famous Highland regiments. Until the nineteenth century there were no proper roads into the county, the main links being by sea. Sir John Sinclair of Ulbster (1754-1853), MP for Caithness, did much to develop the county by road works, agricultural reform, improvements to fishing and the development of Thurso. The distinctiveness of Caithness is reinforced by remaining traces of strong Norse influences reflected in place names and settlements.

In common with most rural and fishing communities, Caithness has undergone significant changes over the last two centuries. The county experienced tremendous prosperity in the nineteenth century when the herring industry was at its height. Many town and coastal communities doubled in population. Wick was one of the largest herring ports in the United Kingdom. Its population rose from 600 in 1801 to 5,000 sixty years later.[7] Old prints show the harbour area as a thriving hive of multifarious activity. These days have long since passed, together with the life that accompanied it. The county has undergone the decline of the great herring fishing of the past, with the subsequent loss of revenue, trades, business and population. A few white fish boats still sail from local harbours, with lobster creeling from small jetties.

Caithness flagstone and slate quarries, employing over a thousand people, used to supply a very notable export trade last century. They, too, have steadily contracted during the twentieth century. There has also been a general decline in small crofting due to non-viability, expansion of larger farms, mechanization and exodus from the land. Yarn and woollen mills were once prosperous. The Blacks, long associated with Wick Baptist Church, had their wool mill at Stirkoke. But the mills have closed.

With the disappearance of employment, the population has fallen. Whereas in 1861, when Caithness recorded its highest population, there were 41,111 people in the county, by 1961 there were only 27,370.[8] Family size has contracted. Where earlier families were anything from six to twelve and fourteen, they now consist of ones, twos or threes. Many of the older church members came from large families and went to church in families. Many rural communities are no longer self-contained or self-sufficient. They used to have their own mills, quarries, shops, fisheries and schools. Today children travel considerable distances to central schools and go south for further education. There is a regular exodus of young people from the county as they seek further education, work prospects and marriage. Many never return north except for family visits and holidays. Able people of various ages and skills have been a major 'export' of the county to other parts and not least from the churches. Changes are discernible not only in population, communities and employment but also in attitudes and lifestyle. The three northernmost mainland counties of Ross and Cromarty, Sutherland and

Caithness were known as the 'Evangelical counties', being greatly influenced by 'the Ministers and Men in the Far North'.[9] These ministries produced a certain Highland character, piety and lifestyle. Today there is a general decline in sabbath observance, family worship, church attendance and strict morality. Although Caithness may compare favourably with other parts of the country, the pool of churchgoers has become smaller and the inclination to attend church has waned.

Not all, however, is declension in community and church. From the 1950s on, new developments have taken place, especially the construction of Dounreay nuclear energy plant. Its establishment brought a large influx of skilled people from the south and provided job opportunities for locals. Many new houses were built at Thurso to accommodate staff and their families. A Technical College was established in Thurso providing educational opportunities for the young. Since then other businesses have been set up, including a famous glass factory, building firms, small craft centres and firms specializing in electronic components, sub-sea pipelines, food-freezers and peat development. Thurso and Scarfskerry Churches have some skilled members from the south. Manpower Services are doing restoration and renovation work throughout the county to its benefit.

The Churches: Past and Present

Against this changing and developing background we return to consider life in the Baptist Churches of Caithness. The origins of Keiss Baptist Church go back to 1750, Wick to 1806 and Scarfskerry to 1816. Sir William Sinclair, baronet, of Dunbeath and Keiss estates, was founder and first pastor of Keiss Church. While on military service, probably in England, he adopted Baptist views on believer's baptism and the church. Returning north, Sir William commenced services on his estate and soon a small fellowship was formed under his pastoral leadership.[10] The origins of Wick Church are generally attributed to the labours of the Haldane brothers who also fostered Independency in Caithness. Scarfskerry no doubt began as an offshoot of one or other of the earlier Baptist Churches.[11]

From its earliest inception the Baptist movement was viewed with certain suspicion and sometimes strenuous opposition. The twelfth Earl of Caithness is said to have torn down with his own hands a tent erected by Baptists for worship on his estate at Mey.[12] Sir William was contemptuously dubbed 'the preaching knight'. Bishop Robert Forbes was greatly offended by Sir William's 'strolling about and preaching without commission or appointment of any man or set of men whatsoever . . .'.[13] In an orderly, traditional society Baptists suffered the major disadvantage of deviating from custom in their religious ways.

A striking feature of this early Baptist movement was lay involvement. Sir William was strictly speaking 'a layman' in clerical eyes, as were the landed gentry, James and Robert Haldane. Lay activity is seen at each of Keiss, Scarfskerry and Wick. In Keiss, following on Sir William in pastoral leadership, the names of John Budge, Donald Inrig, Andrew Rugg and Alexander Bain appear in succession. In Scarfskerry William Dunnett and Sinclair Banks performed similar service. In Wick numerous prominent people appear fulfilling leadership roles. A memorial plaque in the church vestibule lists twenty-three names of business and trades men active in the service of the church. These include Provost William Waters, banker, and Bailie Alexander Sinclair, auctioneer. Today, there are direct descendants of Banks (Scarfskerry), Inrig (Keiss) and Sinclair (Wick) in association with these churches.

The Baptist pioneers in Caithness differed from other Christian bodies not only in their use of lay leadership. Their understanding of gospel ordinances was distinctive, as was their adherence to what they saw as the New Testament principles of church practice. There was also Sir William Sinclair's innovative introduction of a hymn book containing sixty of his own hymns. Elsewhere only Psalms were sung. The early Baptists were adaptable. Before they possessed permanent church buildings or enjoyed 'settled' ministries, they functioned and witnessed. They occupied a tent on the Hill of Mey at Scarfskerry, a loft in Kirk Lane at Wick, a castle vault and later an old house at North Keiss. All the present buildings of Keiss, Scarfskerry and Wick go back only to the middle of last century.

Some remarkable ministries last century in Caithness Baptist circles are worthy of note. In Keiss, and later in Scarfskerry, the name of James Scott is outstanding. Called from missionary work in Orkney, he settled in Keiss in 1865 and continued until 1883. He was called to Scarfskerry in that same year and continued there until retirement in 1902. For thirty-seven years he laboured incessantly in Caithness and became a household name. Scott maintained the traditions of itinerant ministry, travelling on evangelistic tours round the northern part of the county. He regularly preached on the island of Stroma and at Freswick. When he left Keiss for Scarfskerry in 1883 there were a hundred members at Keiss, twenty-one at Stroma, twenty-two at Freswick and many staunch adherents.

In Scarfskerry the first settled pastor was Robert B. Wallace (1868-72). Previously he served with the North Coast Mission in Thurso. He conducted a mission in the Scarfskerry-Mey districts in 1867-8, stimulating a genuine revival with about eighty converts, many of whom linked with the Baptists. In Wick Robert G. Sowerby was called to a co-pastorate with Bailie Waters in 1848. Like Scott, Sowerby travelled all over Caithness, preaching the gospel, exercising pastoral care and giving occasional assistance at Scarfskerry and elsewhere.

Worthy of mention are two famous sets of brothers from Keiss. John Reid went to India in 1902 to serve with BMS and became its India secretary. James, his brother, became travelling agent of the Baptist Home Mission. Dr John MacBeath of Glasgow and London, an outstanding preacher, pastor and author, Scottish Baptist Union president in 1934-5, was proud of his Caithness roots. His brother Andrew served with BMS in Congo from 1925 to 1940, and later became principal of Glasgow Bible Training Institute. Another John McBeath — as the spelling shows, no relation of the previous two — was a 'Wicker' who exercised a long, fruitful ministry in Inverness. Not least was Dr Alexander B. Miller, a native of Freswick and member at Keiss, principal of the Scottish Baptist College from 1950 to 1967. The famous Jock Troup, cooper-cum-evangelist and revivalist, was married to one of the Blacks of Stirkoke, long associated with Wick Church. Jock was an instrument in the 1921 revival in Wick and elsewhere.

W.H. Millard rendered outstanding service in Wick during two ministries, in 1893-8 and again in 1919-39. He was in the forefront of the temperance cause in Caithness. He is still held in affectionate remembrance by an older generation. Other gifted pastors include W.G. Fisher (Scarfskerry), Frank Johnston (Keiss) and Archibald McNicol (Wick). Many in our churches today owe much to McNicol's faithful ministry. A strong Christian Endeavour society flourished under his leadership.

There have also been outstanding women in the churches. We know of Mrs Waters, Watten, who walked twelve miles with her husband every sabbath into Wick Church. She was blessed with a prodigious memory, great Bible knowledge and the ability to quote verbatim. She was also an able debater. Another was Mrs Babbie Brock, who was noted for 'an original and inventive mind'.[14] However, a nameless host of worthy women — pastors' wives, auxiliary office-bearers, Sunday School teachers, Christian Endeavour leaders, choir members, organists, sick visitors, church cleaners and dozens more — have rendered faithful service in the churches of Caithness.

One disturbing feature that must be mentioned is the early disagreements and secessions. In Wick a number left at intervals in the early days. Some left to join the Independents, perhaps to find greater flexibility. Others departed on doctrinal grounds. There was some controversy about the teaching of the Erskines, 'the Marrow-men' and hyper-Calvinism. Several minor losses have occurred in later years in Scarfskerry and Wick through disagreements with pastors. A number of Baptist ministers in Caithness have left the denomination for other churches and some the pastoral ministry altogether.

In this connection Caithness is not unique and such happenings have not deterred Baptist witness in the county. The work has experienced ebb and flow, gain and loss, encouragement and otherwise throughout the years. 'The good old ship has not been without her lulls and gales', Horne remarked picturesquely, 'but she holds on her way!'[15]

Modern Developments

There have been significant recent developments. At Thurso, where a Baptist cause had existed from 1805 until at least 1840,[16] there were various attempts in the 1950s to recommence the work, but they proved a failure. Dounreay workers from the south with Baptist convictions settled in existing churches of other denominations in the town. Fresh work commenced in the seventies with a house group and then services conducted in a local school. The Thurso Church was formally constituted in 1982. Richard McPhee, formerly of Scarfskerry and Canada, was called as first pastor. Since then Bryan McNeile has been called as Thurso's second pastor to his first charge.

In the 1960s Keiss and Scarfskerry Churches were linked, with A.R. Halliday as joint pastor. In the 1980s Keiss and Scarfskerry were separated and linked with the main town churches. The linking of Thurso with Scarfskerry and Wick with Keiss was felt to be a better arrangement, putting more manpower into two centres while not overlooking rural needs. Both Keiss and Scarfskerry have suffered loss in membership over the years.

The pattern of church growth and decline has reflected in large measure the economic health of the county. There was solid growth in the nineteenth century. The peak period of Baptist strength in Caithness appears to have been in 1881, at the time of the Scott and Sowerby ministries. The collective membership of the churches rose from 272 in 1879 to 301 in 1881. By 1927 the figure had fallen to 117, forty-seven below the return for the previous year. The explanation must lie in the decay of the herring fishing, though the sharpness of the fall may be an artificial result of roll revision. Membership remained rather over 100 until 1959, after which there was steady decline. By 1975 the figure was as low as sixty-six.[17]

In 1981 the total population of the county was 27,380. Thurso's population was 9,327 and that of Wick 9,830.[18] The number of Baptist members in 1986 was eighty-five.[19] There were ten baptisms in Wick during 1986 and two in Thurso. Thus since 1975 there has been some progress. The trend at present is upward. Monthly days of prayer, prayer triplets and regular prayer meetings have helped create a spiritual climate favourable to outreach.

The older work in established centres of hallowed memory needs constant review and fresh impetus. The newer work in Thurso presents opportunities for developing novel ministries. The witness and experience that gave rise to the work at Keiss are as pertinent and important as ever. Christians face an 'unfinished task' in Scotland, not least in Caithness, the birthplace of Baptist witness in this land. As inheritors of an illustrious heritage and trustees of the Great Commission of our Lord, Baptists must still 'go and make disciples'.

Notes

1. Sir John Sinclair, ed, *The Statistical Account of Scotland, 1791-1799: Caithness and Sutherland* (East Ardsley, Wakefield 1979), p 256.
2. ibid, p 21.
3. *Souvenir of Centenary Services in Wick Baptist Church on July 22, 1906* (reprinted from the *Northern Ensign*), p 14.
4. ibid, pp 3-4.
5. ibid, pp 6-7. See also John Horne, *A Short History of Wick Baptist Church* (Wick 1894), pp 1-2.
6. *Souvenir*, p 7.
7. Iain Sutherland, *Wick Harbour and the Herring Fishing* (Wick nd), pp 23, 41.
8. *Census 1961 Scotland County Report: County of Caithness* (Edinburgh 1963), p 19.
9. Alexander Auld, *Ministers and Men in the Far North* (np 1957 edn).
10. See cap 1.
11. George Yuille, ed, *History of the Baptists in Scotland* (Glasgow 1926), pp 102, 288.
12. ibid, p 102.
13. ibid, p 41.
14. ibid, p 103.
15. Horne, *Wick Baptist Church*, p 16.
16. Yuille, ed, *Baptists in Scotland*, p 289.
17. *Scottish Baptist Year Book* (SBYB).
18. *Census 1981 Report for Highland Region* (Edinburgh 1983), 2 p xxii, 4 p 3.
19. *SBYB*, 1987.

J.J. Johnston

17. ORKNEY

A Kirkwall schoolmaster describing Orkney in 1750 commented, 'The religion is presbyterianism as established in Scotland, without bigotry, enthusiasm or zeal, and without any dissenters except a very few of the episcopalian persuasion . . .'.[1] Nearly half a century later, in 1797, James Haldane, on arriving in Kirkwall, declared the islands 'as much in need of the True Gospel of Jesus Christ . . . as any of the islands of the Pacific Ocean'.[2] There was at least one possible reason why Orcadians should have differed so markedly from their Bible-loving Scots neighbours. They had an unbroken Scandinavian heritage dating from the pagan Norse settlements of the ninth and tenth centuries, which apparently brought to an end both Pictish culture and the influence of the Celtic Church. Catholic Christianity, according to the Orkneyinga Saga,[3] was forcibly thrust on the population by Olaf Tryggvason in 995, and Orkney became a Scandinavian bishopric.

The new religion was acceptable insofar as it did not interfere with existing beliefs.[4] Central to these was the distinctively Norse concept of the family as a working and fighting unit. Social practices therefore tended to reflect an adherence not to Christian morality but to the old fertility cults; while superstitious rites abounded. When Norse sea-power waned and the islands were eventually annexed to the Scottish Crown in 1471, there remained between the Orcadians and their new compatriots not only the treacherous waters of the Pentland Firth, but barriers of custom, law and language that persisted right into the eighteenth century. It is hardly surprising that a small community thus encapsulated, still deeply rooted in its pre-Christian tradition and dependent for its survival on peaceful co-existence, should remain detached from emotive issues within the Church. The turbulence of the Scottish Reformation, for example, caused scarcely a ripple in Orkney.

It was not until schooling was enforced after the Act of 1696, accelerating the disappearance of Norn as a spoken language,[5] that the general pattern began to change. Horizons widened. Bibles were read and hunger grew, culminating in the Evangelical awakening that surrounded the preaching of Haldane and other Dissenters at the close of the eighteenth century.[6] Orkney was at last responding to Christ.

Beginnings

The establishing of Baptist Churches in Orkney was the direct result of the remarkable pioneer ministry of William Tulloch of North Ronaldsay, a young catechist whose abilities had been noted by James Haldane during his first brief visit to the islands. Haldane sent him to Greville Ewing's academy

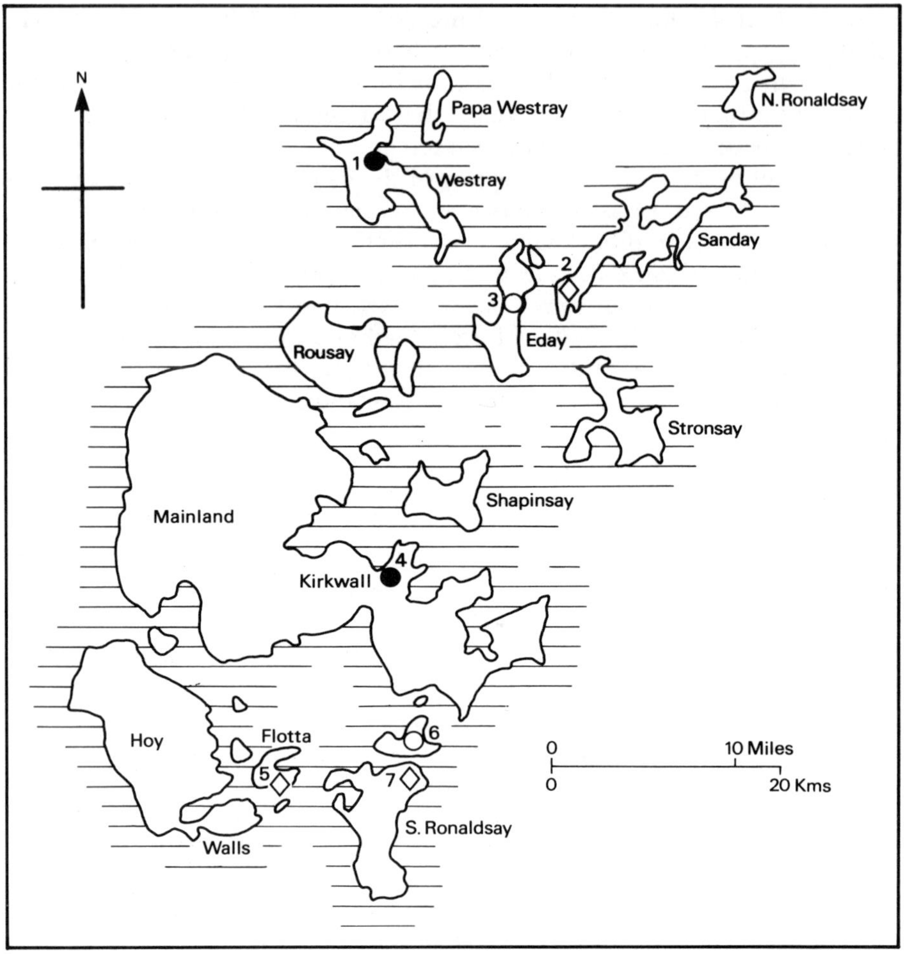

MAP 17 : ORKNEY BAPTIST CHURCHES.

Key to Map 17

1. Westray
2. Sanday
3. Eday
4. Kirkwall
5. Flotta
6. Burray
7. S. Ronaldsay

for training, and sponsored him on his return to his native Orkney as an itinerant evangelist.

Tulloch felt particularly drawn to Westray, where he gathered a group of converts for regular worship, teaching and outreach. Their parish, like others in Orkney, was then poorly served, but when it was suggested that they might form themselves into an Independent Church, certain of their number reacted violently, and not only withdrew, but barred access to the various homes and barns where they would normally have met. Undeterred, the fellowship took to the open air, and eventually to the hall of the derelict Noltland Castle, where in 1803 they were constituted as an Independent Church.[7] The following year they erected their own Tabernacle.

The first test of the new church's strength came with the news that James Haldane had embraced Baptist principles. Private argument and unrest grew until in 1810 Robert Seatter, one of Tulloch's two assistants and a spokesman for the pro-Baptist minority, openly declared his convictions. Tulloch, taking the opposite view, recognised that no congregation could contain such dissension. It was reluctantly agreed that the two groups should part company, but by the appointed date the situation was reversed, only three members remaining uncertain of the doctrine's truth. These waived their right to the building and were permitted to remain in membership when the church was formally re-constituted as a closed communion Baptist Church.[8]

The issue was perhaps more crucial than the congregation of that time realized. Baptism implied not only personal commitment to Christ but a public revoking of old allegiances and priorities, a radical step for the cautious Orcadian whose nominally Christian upbringing was subtly allied to the underlying pagan culture. The initial impact on the people of Westray was reinforced by the nature and quality of the church's leadership. William Tulloch and his team could communicate more effectively with their fellow-islanders than a Scots academic might hope to do, simply because in that small, closely inter-related community they came under constant scrutiny. Their changed lives witnessed more eloquently than mere words to the power of the gospel they preached.

Evidence of this lies in the prolonged period of growth which followed, during which William Tulloch, at the request of the Home Mission, was released for longer periods of itinerant work. Early converts from his missions to other islands were regarded as members of Westray Baptist Church, but in 1827 he organized the formation of a separate church on Eday. There the members, with regular assistance and encouragement from the Westray team, led worship, ran a Sabbath School and occasionally preached on neighbouring Sanday. By 1840, providing their own labour, they had erected a meeting-house.

Meanwhile on Burray a small fellowship had been founded by Alexander Kennedy, a native of Stroma converted through contact with Keiss Baptists. He had settled in Orkney in 1802, was baptized by a Thurso visitor in 1811, and opened his home for Sunday worship led by himself and other menfolk. Three or four times a year the Westray pastors undertook the long and frequently hazardous journey to Burray to dispense communion and preach, and in 1849 William Tulloch presided at the opening of the new chapel on the island. The following year the Westray congregation, itself in need of larger accommodation, completed its present building.

Various factors contributed to the expansion of the congregations. One was undoubtedly the consistent prayer and practical support of the parent church, and another the vision for outreach shared by William Tulloch and his successor as Home Mission evangelist, James Scott of Westray, later to become pastor of Scarfskerry, through whose ten years of itinerant ministry (1849-59) Baptist membership in the islands was increased by 175. By mid-century too, Orkney's population was approaching its highest level, having recovered from the depletion of the Napoleonic Wars when scores of young men had been press-ganged into naval service. Not least, the revival that swept Scotland in 1860 reached various parishes in Orkney, and in Westray that winter denominational barriers melted away as the islanders met nightly in each church in turn. Many lives were touched.

It was in 1868 when another wave of blessing seemed imminent that the Westray fellowship faced its second major crisis. By then the shared ministry had ended with the deaths of William Tulloch in 1858 and Robert Seatter in 1865, leaving the remaining pastor, Henry Harcus, in sole charge. The practice of exhortation had also gradually lapsed, possibly creating a degree of genuine frustration; so that when two visitors to the island introduced the new Brethren teachings on church structure, interest was immediately quickened. Whereas, however, in 1810 the divisive issue had been aired, taken to prayer and resolved in grace, here, with the personal status of the pastor at stake, discussions were clandestine and Henry Harcus was caught unawares by the rapid build-up of tension around him. Two-thirds of the membership left in a body to form their own assembly nearby. Harcus, who had served them faithfully for twenty-eight years, was utterly heartbroken. Feeling unable to cope objectively with the task of reconstruction, he resigned and took up a pastorate in Canada. Under the experienced care of Gavin Mowat of Shetland and George MacDonald of the Home Mission, who ministered consecutively over the next five years, the church recovered and settled to a new lower level of membership. The rift between the two factions, however, left a legacy of bitterness and hurt. Attitudes hardened, and no full reconciliation ever took place.[9]

The affair may well have been a critical point in Orkney's church history, for had both parties paused to take an honest look together at the question of church structure, each might have respected what the other had to offer. The Baptists after all had modified the sharp social and professional distinction between clergy and laity which in the past had stifled vital development, and half a century of dedicated teamwork on the part of their leadership had borne much fruit. It must be noted that throughout that period the actual pastorate had rested in hands other than those of William Tulloch, who had entered on the apostolic roles of evangelist, church-planter, teacher and intercessor, holding responsibility for three growing fellowships. Each fellowship was in turn producing its own crop of ministries, lending a richness and diversity that went some way to compensate for lack of formal training. This evolving pattern was not entirely rooted in the Scotch Baptist system. Rather it stemmed from Orkney's own classless society where udal law had secured equal rights of inheritance for all, and the concept of 'first among equals' was naturally inbred.[10] In reverting to one-man ministry, some of the original vigour and freshness had inevitably gone.

Into the Twentieth Century: Decline and Challenge

Of the three nineteenth-century Baptist congregations, two are now defunct. In Eday, where many had been converted through the 1860 revival, the first resident pastor, Robert Tait of Burray (1862-70), worked hard to build up a solid fellowship. However, the community itself was struggling. The island lacked the fertility of its neighbours, being covered largely in peat, and as the population began to outgrow its resources many families were forced to leave. The Baptists lost some stable members at a stage when the founding generation was dying out and the parent church in Westray was in the throes of its own problems. A new building was provided, this time through the generosity of Scottish Baptists, but morale in general was very low. In spite of the efforts of Eday's own incumbents and the pastors from Westray and Burray who helped out during several lengthy vacancies, decline had set in by the close of the century. Depopulation cannot wholly account for this. Although no actual records were kept, Albert Griffiths of Westray in a report of 1905 makes oblique reference to some serious internal hindrance to the church's recovery.[11] In 1910 Sanday was officially added to the charge with the opening of a privately erected chapel, which in fact never became more than a preaching station. It appears that from this point numbers gradually dwindled, attendance being boosted only by parish kirk members who enjoyed the less formal atmosphere of Baptist services. The last minister of Eday and Sanday, William Tregunna, closed the churches in 1954.

In Burray too depopulation took its toll, though somewhat later. With a land area of only eight square miles, fishing was the chief source of livelihood. The island prospered until the collapse of the herring industry, which was finalized by the sinking of blockships in Scapa Flow during the First World War. The church flourished likewise, appointing one of its own members, A. Sinclair of South Ronaldsay, as first paid pastor in 1863, membership reaching its peak some ten years later. Burray pastors were responsible for regular house-meetings on South Ronaldsay and, in summer only, on Flotta, but these were attended by people already in membership in the parish churches and therefore did not develop into a lasting work. After the war a steady decline set in, and the Burray pastorate came to an end when George Cowie left in 1941. The community revived to some extent, firstly with the massive influx of service personnel in the Second World War, then with the opening of road links to South Ronaldsay and East Mainland over the famous Churchill Barriers; and more recently as workers from the North Sea oil terminal on Flotta made their home there. By then, however, the church was gone. Those who remember the years prior to its final closure in 1966 have commented that its rigid conformity to the style of days gone by did nothing to attract new life or stir its sparse and ageing congregation.

Westray Baptist Church, on the other hand, served a much larger and more resilient population, which survived the period of emigration and benefited enormously from nineteenth-century reforms in agriculture and land tenancy, and from the introduction of steam navigation and road transport. Westray has achieved relative prosperity in recent years through the production of high-quality beef and the survival of a small fishing fleet. The church has succeeded in maintaining its membership level in spite of the steady annual output of youngsters who leave the island for employment or higher education. Indeed, one of the healthiest features of the Westray Church throughout its history has been the consistency and thoroughness with which its young people and children have been trained.

In comparing the three churches, one additional factor must be considered: that of timing. Westray Baptist Church came into being when congregations of the Established Church in Orkney were notoriously neglected. Shortly afterwards a wave of Evangelicalism swept the Kirk, and the official opening of the Baptist Churches in Eday and Burray in fact coincided with the formation of United Presbyterian Churches in both islands,[12] so that there the vitality of the Baptists was not distinctive. Possibly too in the revivals of 1860 and those following A.Y. McGregor's campaigns in the early 1900s, when denominational barriers broke down,[13] the issue of baptism would have been regarded as divisive. Since then, however, Orkney's spiritual climate has altered dramatically, for with the swing back into nominalism came a resurgence of the old pagan culture and values. Furthermore, in the post-war years Orkney has been flooded with incomers, mostly English, of varied background: hippies, drop-outs from urban life, businessmen, professionals, would-be farmers. Inevitably among these may be found elements of the occult, idolatry in all its modern guises, and non-Christian religions and cults. Baptism therefore has once again become a key issue, and this time it is the youngest of Westray's offspring, Kirkwall Baptist Church, that faces the implications for the rapidly changing society of the 1980s.

Kirkwall, the natural focal point of Orkney, has grown around the ancient Norse Cathedral of St Magnus. Although Scottish influence is more in evidence here, where merchants and landowners built their elegant town houses, the island capital was as spiritually barren as the rural areas until 1790, when a small Praying Society was formed.[14] This attached itself to the Anti-Burghers in 1796, just before the visit of Haldane and Aikman, while the Independent Church formed subsequently did not accept Baptist principles. There was therefore no Baptist witness in the town until the mid-twentieth century, by which time Evangelicalism was well on the wane on the Orkney Mainland.

The present Baptist congregation owes its beginnings to the population drift which is a feature of island life. Among eighty persons who left Westray in 1954 were a number of Baptist families who settled in and around Kirkwall. For a time they worshipped locally while retaining Westray membership, but it was the vision of their pastor, James Pottinger, that they would establish a Baptist fellowship in Kirkwall. This came about in 1959 with the encouragement of the late Ian MacRae (brother of Dr Andrew MacRae, subsequently General Secretary of the Baptist Union), who had also settled in Kirkwall. That year he and his wife and twelve Westray members became the founders of Kirkwall Baptist Church, acquiring their present building in 1962.

The 'transplant' operation was not altogether easy. On the one hand the townsfolk, including Evangelicals, knew little or nothing of Baptist tenets and regarded the new fellowship with wariness. On the other, the Westray nucleus, as cautious and entrenched in their own traditions, needed time to come to terms with change and to extend their influence within this very different society. With sound pastoral care and teaching ministry, the transition took place and membership grew steadily, augmented over the years by a substantial number of loyal adherents, mostly incomers of different denominations seeking Evangelical fellowship. Both Kirkwall and Westray Baptist Churches today have various flourishing activities, notably the annual Christian Endeavour camps through which many unchurched children and their families are reached.

The predictable pattern of church life, however, is being challenged on two fronts. Firstly Orkney society, although still relatively peaceful and law-abiding, is exhibiting all the symptoms of deepening spiritual need. Moral laxity and materialism are prevalent, and there is increasing awareness of alcoholism, depressive illness and marriage breakdown. Secondly, and more seriously, the Christian Church itself has been infected.

To meet the first challenge, some satisfactory attempts have been made at both leadership and congregational levels amongst Evangelicals of all persuasions to draw together in intercession and outreach, on the grounds of their fundamental unity and common concern. As this activity intensifies there are signs of a polarizing process in the community at large.

In the second area of challenge the Baptists have several lessons to share from their own history. They have seen the disastrous consequences of breakdown in communication between Christian believers. They have seen congregations perish through lack of vision and failure to let go of cherished tradition. They have also seen flexibility bring growth and fresh impetus. In the earliest days, neither worship nor evangelism was associated with church buildings, for congregations had none. They pioneered team leadership — and today this could be a vital subject for further exploration, for the needs in community and church are being recognized as so wide-ranging that no one man can adequately fill an all-purpose role.

As we near the close of the twentieth century, the ultimate vision of all believers in Orkney is revival, and an overthrow of those unseen 'principalities and powers' which might be said to have claimed the territory as their own from time immemorial. Clearly the cost of that revival is obedience: a departure from worldly attitudes, methods and values to give undivided commitment to the lordship of Christ, both individually and corporately. In principle Orkney Baptists accept this, for it is the essential meaning of believer's baptism. In practice there are testing-grounds ahead which will determine whether the vision is to be fulfilled in this generation.

Notes

1. Murdoch Mackenzie, *Orcades, or a geographical and hydrographic survey of Orkney and Lewis* (London 1750), p 2.
2. Alexander Haldane, *Memoirs of the Lives of Robert Haldane of Airthrey and of his Brother, James Alexander Haldane* (London 1852), p 169.
3. Hermann Palsson and Paul Edwards, ed, *Orkneyinga Saga: the history of the Earls of Orkney* (London 1978), p 39.
4. T.B. Willson, *History of the Church and State in Norway* (Westminster 1903), pp 18, 42.
5. J. Storer Clouston, *A History of Orkney* (Kirkwall 1932) pp 362-3.
6. B.H. Hossack, *Kirkwall in the Orkneys* (Kirkwall 1900), pp 450-2.
7. Henry Harcus, *The History of the Orkney Baptist Churches* (Ayr 1898), p 63.
8. ibid, p 73.
9. ibid, pp 92-6. Letters to the editor, *Orkney Herald*, Feb.–Apr., 1897.

10. John Gunn, *The Orkney Book* (Edinburgh 1909), p 111. 'Lord Birsay on Udal Law', *Orcadian*, 4 Sept. 1986.
11. *Scottish Baptist Year Book*, 1905, p A14.
12. Gunn, *Orkney Book*, p 111.
13. Thomas Groat, *Thirty Years a Colporteur* (Kirkwall 1939), p 40.
14. D.P. Thomson, *Orkney through the Centuries* (Perth 1956), p 17.

Katherine M. Gordon
J.W. Scott
Margaret A. Scott

18. SHETLAND

Shetland lies to the north-east of the Orkneys, roughly midway between Scotland and Norway. The capital, Lerwick, is almost equidistant from the cities of Aberdeen in Scotland and Bergen in Norway. Both island groups have a long background of prehistoric settlement and a great variety of archaeology. Both have a history of Norse occupation and colonization extending over seven centuries and in the fifteenth century both came under the rule of Scotland by the marriage of James III of Scotland to a Danish princess.

There are nevertheless many areas of contrast. The kindly red sandstone of Orkney has little counterpart in the geology of Shetland, where much of the rock is of granite and gneiss. Consequently, the soil of Shetland is less fertile and vast tracts of the landscape are covered in peat. In turn this has meant that the Orcadian is basically a farmer while the Shetlander has over many generations had to turn to the sea for a livelihood. Fishing, seafaring and whaling have been the commoner occupations. It used to be said that the Orkney man was a farmer with a boat while the Shetlander was a fisherman with a croft.

In 1471 the two island groups, which had been within the diocese of the bishop of Trondheim in Norway, were placed under the jurisdiction of St Andrews. The last Catholic bishop was Adam Bothwell, though he is also considered the first Protestant bishop; it would seem that the Reformation took a relatively peaceful path.[1] For more than a century the Church in Shetland followed an Episcopalian pattern.[2] By the end of the seventeenth century the General Assembly set up a commission to investigate. In 1700 John Brand visited the islands and reported that, 'In the matter of God and religion the people are said to be very ignorant.'[3] After this the Presbyterian system became firmly established. As the century progressed the Kirk grew stronger and in 1713 the first school was opened by the Society in Scotland for the Propagation of Christian Knowledge. The old Norse language was superseded in part because of the English taught in the schools erected by this society.

From the time of the Seven Years' War (1756-63) Britain and France were becoming locked in prolonged conflict which culminated in the Battle of Waterloo in 1815. During this period the Royal Navy required ever more seamen to crew their men-of-war and the islesmen, with their great knowledge of boats and seamanship, were a prime target for the press-gang. It has been estimated that at the time of the great naval battles of Trafalgar, Aboukir Bay, and Cape St Vincent over 3,000 Shetlanders were serving in the

Royal Navy. Since the total male population of Shetland was at that time about 11,000 the scale of impressment was tremendous.[4] Men who had struggled to make a living subject to the whims of the landlord and fish factor encountered people from all over Britain and overseas with a fresh outlook. The way was prepared for the reception of new religious ideas in Shetland.

Among those who returned from the Napoleonic Wars was John Nicolson, who had served in the Royal Artillery and for some years in the Tower of London. There he became a Wesleyan Methodist and an exhorter. On his arrival in Shetland he set about spreading the faith. So successful were Nicolson and those who joined him that by 1866 the Methodists numbered 2,015, being second only to the Established Church, as indeed they remain at present.[5]

The Methodists were not the first to break the monopoly of the Established Church. In 1799 James Haldane and William Innes had undertaken a preaching tour of the Northern Isles. Following this visit, a small group of Independents met in Lerwick. As the years passed other parts of Shetland began to join in forming Evangelical groups.

The Shetland Apostle

The story of the Shetland Baptist cause is bound up with a man of tremendous character. He has been called its unquestioned founder and organizer, truly one of the great figures in the religious life of the islands — Sinclair Thomson. Born in the parish of Sandsting, in the West Mainland of Shetland, he married and settled in the parish of Dunrossness, the southerly and most fertile area of the islands. As a young man he sailed on the whaling ships to Greenland and became noted as a fiddler.[6] On one occasion when providing music at a wedding, he narrowly escaped the clutches of the press-gang by crouching inside a large chest while several women of the company sat on the lid till the hated naval party had gone. For his musical abilities he was made precentor of Dunrossness Parish Church. He was also engaged in both smuggling and selling liquor, and was on one occasion taken to court and fined. These activities seem to have been no bar to his church duties. Rather they raised his status in the community.[7]

One Sunday in July 1809, when on his way to read banns at church, he stopped at a croft house and asked for a drink of water. The young lady of the house was reading a booklet entitled, *The Propriety of Communicating Every Lord's Day*. After making some disparaging remarks about the Independent Church of which she was a member, he asked her for a loan of the little book. This was to be a landmark in Thomson's spiritual development, and he came

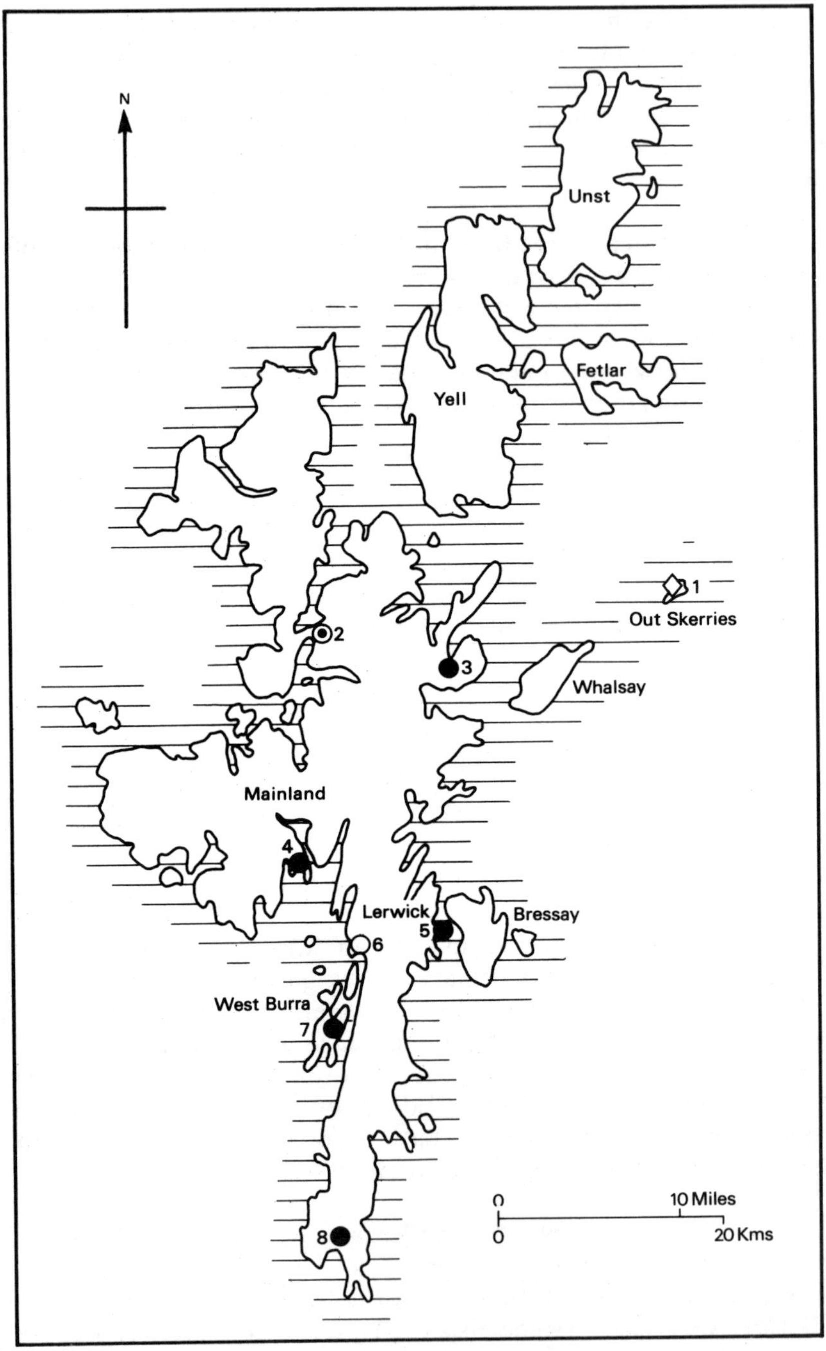

MAP 18 : SHETLAND BAPTIST CHURCHES.

Key to Map 18

1. Out Skerries
2. Brae Fellowship
3. Lunnasting
4. Sandsting
5. Lerwick
6. Scalloway
7. Burra Isle
8. Dunrossness

under conviction of his own unworthiness.[8] One day he was reading over a hymn which begins: 'Hark the voice of love and mercy, Sounds aloud from Calvary'. He now came to a personal understanding of salvation and in the freedom of a son of God set about the work of bringing others to the same experience.[9]

On one occasion he conducted a service in the absence of the parish minister, and preached to a number of local people. For this he was reprimanded by the minister and curtly dismissed from the office of precentor. He continued to attend the Established Church, but with increasing awareness of the gap between the parish church and the early church.[10] For some years he was attached to a small group of Independents who met in Lerwick and other parts of the islands; but from his intensive study of the scriptures he noted that in the practice of infant sprinkling they diverged from New Testament teaching.[11] Without knowing of the Baptists, he came to the position of believer's baptism by immersion. He was convinced that he himself should be baptized by someone qualified to administer the rite. Seeking more information, he learned that there was a group in Edinburgh named Baptists. His many efforts to journey there met with frustration and ridicule.[12]

A Shetlander, Daniel Bain, recently in the army and a member of James Haldane's church in Edinburgh, returned on a visit to his native isles, and hearing of Sinclair's desire for baptism undertook the long and difficult journey to Dunrossness to visit him. After spending the evening in discussion and prayer, Sinclair Thomson was baptized in Spiggie Loch, a few hundred yards from his own home.[13]

The following year, 1816, saw the founding of the first Baptist Church at Dunrossness. It consisted of twenty-four converts baptized since the time of Thomson's own immersion in August 1815. With the passing years other churches were founded: Burra Isle (1820, building erected 1829), Lunnasting (1836, building erected 1846), Sandsting (1843, building erected 1853), Lerwick (1840, building erected 1864), Scalloway (1850) and a preaching station in the remote Out Skerries. Each of these churches owes its inception to the pioneer work of Thomson.[14] During his lifetime he travelled the length of Shetland, on foot, on pony back, by boat, preaching, baptizing, teaching, striving to raise money for church building, and at the same time maintaining his family by working his croft land and fishing — the normal means of livelihood of the ordinary rural Shetlander.

It is estimated that he preached 6,000 times during his forty-eight years as pastor of Dunrossness Church and founder of the others.[15] His itinerant ministry is, without doubt, the fundamental factor explaining the growth of the Baptist movement during the nineteenth century. He died on 8 July 1864, almost precisely fifty-five years from that memorable day when he obtained the little book.

Education and Outreach

Another factor which contributed to growth was the high value placed by the Baptists upon education. In the case of almost every church the pastor or one of his family undertook teaching duties. In Sandsting, for example, Charles Moodie, the first pastor, described in the 1851 census returns as 'Local Baptist Preacher', was also renowned as a teacher.[16] Members of the family of his successor, Thomas Young, were also noted for their teaching abilities. In the distant Out Skerries, where for twenty years a preaching station was maintained, Sinclair Thomson helped to found a school and assisted with the payment of a teacher from his own resources.[17] With the passing of the Education Act of 1872 and the building and staffing of state schools, this aspect of the churches' work receded, but vigorous Sunday Schools were, and still are, a feature of Shetland Baptist life. Sinclair Thomson was among the first to start a Sunday School in Shetland. A recent aspect of youth work has been a summer camp of about a week's duration run by the Shetland Baptist Association during July or August, when young folk from the various Baptist congregations convene at one of Shetland's modern schools and spend time in Bible study, games, swimming and other activities under the supervision of experienced pastors and youth leaders, assisted by hard-working catering staff who prepare unending meals for amazing appetites. In 1986 there is a variety of youth work in the three larger Baptist Churches, embracing both Christian Endeavour and Boys' Brigade.

In common with Baptist Churches everywhere, the churches in Shetland have at different times had the benefit of evangelistic missions, and these have given stimulus to church growth. In 1888, 1889 and 1891 Dunrossness ran successful missions conducted by James McHendrick and his wife. Burra Isle was the venue of a fruitful mission led by the minister, John Campbell, and a Pastor Clark in 1913. During the 1930s many were led to join the

Shetland Baptist Churches as a result of meetings conducted by Faith Mission Pilgrims. Recently, in 1985, Shetland churches of all denominations have collaborated in a live-link satellite mission by Billy Graham transmitted from Sheffield. Each evening the newly built leisure centre at Clickamin was filled by more than 1,000 people from all over the islands, and the Baptist Churches have shared in receiving those who came forward. One further item which should be included in factors making for growth is the ministry of the Lerwick Baptist Male Voice Choir. For over thirty years the choir under its first leader John Pottinger, and now, for some years, Pat Jamieson, has brought the message of the gospel in a most acceptable way to the whole of Shetland, irrespective of creed.

The Twentieth Century

The twentieth century dawned with bright promises. Church buildings were extended and beautified at Lerwick (1894), Burra Isle (1904), Sandsting (1908) and Dunrossness (1912). A manse was provided in each case. Growth was evidently expected.

With the retirement of Thomas Young from the charge of Sandsting and Lunnasting in 1901, one of the last links with the pioneer days of Sinclair Thomson was severed. Thomas Young's father had been one of the early converts, baptized in Spiggie Loch by the founder, and Thomson had given the address when Thomas was baptized by Gavin Mouat, the assistant pastor at Dunrossness.[18] During the nineteenth century the majority of the pastors were native-born Shetlanders, often connected with the soil and the fishing industry, familiar with the daily lifestyle of their flock. In the succeeding century, with two or three notable exceptions,[19] the ministers were from the mainland. In many cases they were men of excellent qualities and the churches continued to grow and prosper.

Negative factors, however, were at work. Depopulation had started in Shetland in the 1870s. It continued at a modest pace until the years of the First World War, when the rate accelerated. It levelled off between 1961 and 1971. Population then started to climb, and a levelling out is again apparent. The reasons for depopulation were mainly the uncertain and changing conditions in the crofting economy. Hundreds of families emigrated to New Zealand, Canada, Australia and to the mainland of Britain. The chief victim of this movement was rural Shetland, where land holdings were amalgamated to make more viable units but with fewer people attached to the land. In 1774 there were said to be about 17,000 inhabitants. A hundred years later, in 1871, there were over 31,000. In 1971 the figures were almost the same as in 1774: just over 17,000.[20]

These changes had an impact on all aspects of rural life. The churches including the Baptists inevitably suffered. In 1850 a Baptist group had been formed in the village of Scalloway, using a shed where nets were stored as their meeting place. Their pastor was Robert Scott, a local man. Scott died in 1864, the same year as Sinclair Thomson. The small fellowship continued to meet on an occasional basis, sharing speakers with Burra Isle and other Baptist Churches. By the turn of the century its members were using an upstairs room loaned by a secular organization, but by 1924 this cause faded away. The last pastor to conduct these services was Harry Reeves, minister at Burra Isle Baptist Church.[21]

The two smaller and weaker causes, Sandsting and Lunnasting, were next to feel the impact. Their last resident pastor, William Littlewood, left in 1937. With the advent of the Second World War and difficulties arising relating to the lease of the manse, the charge was and still remains vacant. With a diminishing membership, the congregations continue to function with speakers supplied through the Shetland Baptist Association and their energetic secretary, John A. Leslie.

The large and influential Dunrossness Church had gradually built up to a membership of over 180 by 1928, with a succession of eminent ministers including William Fotheringham (1899-1916), who helped to design the beautiful church which stands as a memorial to his labours, and native-born Laurence Scollay (1923-9), who served the Shetland Baptist Churches with distinction.[22] Dunrossness is a rural community where the prevailing decline in the crofting economy has impinged heavily on the church. The membership is now under sixty. Shetland Baptists look upon Dunrossness as in some respects the 'Mother Church', the first founded and, for many years, the largest. The decline in membership has been felt with regret by all.

Two churches which have not been affected by the vagaries of depopulation are Lerwick and Burra Isle. In neither area did the problem arise. Lerwick, as an urban district, did not share the rural depopulation at all. Rather the church continued to expand both in numbers and importance as more and more crofters left their homes and opted for town residence. In 1894 the membership was ninety; it fluctuated around this figure for some years and is now over a hundred.[23] Burra Isle did not suffer the steep decline in numbers of the other country districts for the reason that its economy was based on fishing rather than crofting, and since the 1960s fishing has been relatively prosperous. In 1971 a bridge was built, linking Burra Isle to the Isle of Trondra and thence to the Mainland of Shetland. The population is rising. The present church membership is around sixty and being well maintained.[24]

It has been noted that Shetland has a long tradition of religious tolerance and a wide spectrum of belief.[25] During the 1860s, the Episcopal Church was re-established after an absence of over a hundred years, and about the same time the Roman Catholics reappeared after an absence of three hundred years. In the same decade the Brethren arrived and they too formed fellowships throughout the islands. After the Second World War the Apostolic Church (1957) and Assemblies of God (1958) both came upon the scene, successfully formed groups and obtained church buildings. Indeed over fifteen different denominations operate in the islands. A few have faded, among them the Darbyite Brethren, who were fairly widespread during the last century. It is fair to comment that all have felt the population decline and the clear shift in attitudes to a more secular and materialistic frame. For example, in 1910 there were eight Congregational Churches, with six pastors; but today there are only three churches, with a single minister. Likewise the Methodists, once the most successful denomination and almost equalling the Established Church in numbers and buildings, have declined from twelve ministers and assistants serving five circuits in 1910 to five ministers and assistants serving two circuits in 1986.[26]

In the early 1970s vast reserves of gas and oil were discovered in the North Sea, and this was to have far-reaching effects on Shetland life. The trend towards depopulation was reversed as a wave of construction workers arrived. Most of them lived in construction camps near to the oil base at Sullom Voe, but for the more permanent workforce new houses were built in various townships adjacent to the busy oil port. The small village of Brae in the North Mainland of Shetland became the most important of these growth areas, with a large school, hotels and a population of over 900 drawn from widely differing backgrounds. Here in 1982 two young people, Nelson and Mary Smith, were largely instrumental in starting a new Baptist fellowship. Regular meetings are held on Sunday, together with prayer meetings and young people's meetings. The group was begun in co-operation with Shetland Baptist Association and a small group of believers who started meeting in Brae School. So far the group has not been constituted as a church and is known as Brae Fellowship.[27] It is by far the most significant and encouraging occurrence of recent years. Shetland Baptists have found inspiration in the enthusiasm and commitment shown by this small band of earnest Christians.

Conclusion

The outlook for the different churches varies greatly from place to place. The Baptist cause has at no time from 1816 onwards been in any sense a 'popular' one. From available figures it appears that the combined membership has at no time exceeded 500, the highest recorded being 481 in 1905.[28] Dunrossness under its present pastor, David Liddle, continues as a vigorous, self-supporting church. An extension built during the pastorate of

Archibald Macmillan gives good facilities for youth work and catering needs. Burra Isle has recently settled Stanley Kelly as pastor. The lively church possesses a fine hall erected in 1964 in the main village of Hamnavoe, where services are held alternately with the church building situated at Mid-Isle. The congregation has a fine tradition of singing and strong Evangelical commitment, being heavily involved in the Scotreach programme of outreach in 1984-6. At Lerwick Kenneth C. Denman recently completed a ministry of over seven years' duration. Older members have rejoiced to see young people converted, join the church and prove to be a valuable asset. These three churches have consistently helped to provide speakers for their own and other denominations when supply was difficult.

Sandsting is one of the smaller churches in a locality of very scattered settlement. It was provided with speakers by Shetland Baptist Association for some years on a monthly basis, but since 1973 every fortnight. The half-dozen or so ageing members are very dedicated and the fabric is well maintained. Special services like harvest thanksgiving are well attended. Lunnasting, the smallest and weakest unit, has a membership of three persons, and a monthly service again supplied by Shetland Baptist Association. Attendance is mostly by adherents of the other local churches, Methodist and Church of Scotland. Its future seems doubtful, but there may still be a work for this church. Lastly there is the new fellowship at Brae, strong in young people and the most likely area for growth. Surely it will soon take its place as a constituted church, the first to be formed since the days of Sinclair Thomson.

Notes

1. J.R. Nicolson, *Shetland* (Newton Abbot 1972), p 52.
2. ibid, p 53.
3. John Brand, *A Brief Description of Orkney, Zetland, Pightland-Firth, Caithness* (Edinburgh 1701), p 102.
4. Nicolson, *Shetland*, p 172.
5. H.R. Bowes, ed, *Samuel Dunn's Shetland and Orkney Journal, 1822-25* (n.p. 1976), p iv.
6. J.A. Smith, *Sinclair Thomson: or the Shetland Apostle* (Lerwick 1969), p 9.
7. ibid, p 10.
8. ibid, pp 11-13.
9. ibid, p 16.
10. ibid, pp 19-22.
11. ibid, p 34.
12. ibid, p 35.
13. ibid, p 37.
14. ibid, pp 59-70.
15. W.P. Livingstone, *Shetland and the Shetlanders* (Edinburgh 1947), p 204.
16. *Census 1851 Scotland: Orkney and Zetland: Sandsting and Aithsting*, area 9, p 3, in Shetland Archives, Lerwick.
17. Smith, *Thomson*, p 66.
18. 'An Appreciation of the Rev. Thomas Young', *Shetland Times*, 28 Aug, 1909, p 5.
19. Laurence Scollay, Sandsting (1910-17, 1920-3), Dunrossness (1923-9) and Lerwick (1929-35). James Pottinger, Sandsting and Lunnasting (1925-35).
20. Nicolson, *Shetland*, pp 11, 89-90.

21. Information from Mrs Helen Pottinger.
22. L.H. Goudie, 'Dunrossness Baptist Church' (MS 1984).
23. William Cheyne, 'The Lerwick Baptist Church' (MS 1985).
24. Information from Mrs Helen Pottinger.
25. R.G. Cant, *Church Life in Shetland* (Lerwick 1984), p 220.
26. T. and J. Manson, *Shetland Almanac* (Lerwick 1910), pp 91-2.
27. Information from Mr Nelson Smith.
28. *Scottish Baptist Year Book.*

G.R. Deyell

APPENDIX: BAPTIST CHURCH MEMBERSHIP IN SCOTLAND

The *Reports of the Baptist Union of Scotland* (1869, 1874-98) contain the figures for the total membership of affiliated churches as they were reported each year to the assembly. In 1869 the figure was 4,215; in 1874, after which there is a complete series, the figure was 6,200. These totals are low in comparison with the previous estimated total of 5,500 Baptists given in the *First Yearly Report of the Baptist Union of Scotland* (Cupar 1844) because they exclude members of non-Union churches.

From 1893 the *Reports* also contain summaries of membership statistics for associations and their totals for the whole of Scotland. These figures are usually, though not consistently, higher than the other series because they normally include non-Union churches.

From 1899, when the *Scottish Baptist Year Book* was first published, figures reported to the assembly are no longer given. Instead there are totals drawn from the *Baptist Handbook*, issued by the Baptist Union of Great Britain and Ireland. These are normally about 1,000 higher than the totals of association statistics, which from 1906 are the only overall figures given in the *Scottish Baptist Year Book.* This series, including Union and non-Union churches in the total (but not Reformed or Bible Baptists), continues down to the present. The series in the *Baptist Handbook* continues down to 1972, when the periodical ceased publication. The *Baptist Handbook* figures remain usually, though not consistently, about 1,000 higher than those in the *Scottish Baptist Year Book.*

Consequently it is impossible to present a single sequence of total membership figures from the 1860s to the 1980s. The figures for the period down to 1900 (Table 1) are drawn from the *Baptist Handbook*, as reissued in R. Currie *et al.*, ed, *Churches and Churchgoers* (Oxford 1977). The figures for the period from 1901 (Table 2) are drawn from the *Scottish Baptist Year Book.* Statistics for a given year were published in the Handbook and Year Book of the following year. The *Year Book* notes from 1921 that the figures refer to membership in the September of each preceding year.

Table 1: Baptist Church Membership in Scotland, 1864-1900

		1882	9,875
		1883	10,096
1864	5,731	1884	10,666
		1885	10,905
		1886	11,050
		1887	11,581
1868	6,855	1888	12,120
		1889	11,773
1870	7,053	1890	12,209
1871	8,873	1891	12,304
1872	7,096	1892	12,721
1873	6,865	1893	13,208
1874	7,903	1894	12,572
1875	8,155	1895	14,907
1876	8,766	1896	15,698
1877	9,096	1897	15,901
1878	9,234	1898	16,034
1879	9,234	1899	16,905
1880	9,466	1900	16,899

Table 2: Baptist Church Membership in Scotland, 1901-86

1901	15,654	1926	22,766
1902	16,919	1927	22,654
1903	17,576	1928	22,841
1904	18,118	1929	22,699
1905	19,470	1930	22,770
1906	19,179	1931	22,520
1907	19,655	1932	22,564
1908	20,546	1933	22,900
1909	20,278	1934	23,189
1910	20,572	1935	23,310
1911	20,359	1936	23,179
1912	20,703	1937	23,112
1913	20,527	1938	22,935
1914	21,053	1939	22,962
1915	20,837	1940	23,024
1916	21,032	1941	22,249
1917	21,285	1942	21,983
1918	21,426	1943	21,528
1919	21,316	1944	21,177
1920	21,311	1945	21,121
1921	21,241	1946	20,970
1922	21,976	1947	20,602
1923	22,606	1948	20,375
1924	22,486	1949	19,963
1925	22,815	1950	19,760
1951	19,686	1971	16,552
1952	19,443	1972	16,419
1953	19,393	1973	16,475
1954	19,263	1974	19,435
1955	20,133	1975	16,138
1956	20,340	1976	15,791
1957	20,330	1977	15,874
1958	20,261	1978	16,058
1959	20,139	1979	16,271
1960	19,847	1980	16,163

1961	19,541	1981	16,489
1962	19,303	1982	16,416
1963	18,955	1983	16,471
1964	18,831	1984	16,468
1965	18,456	1985	16,548
1966	18,279	1986	16,632
1967	18,038		
1968	17,895		
1969	17,547		
1970	16,992		

INDEX

B.C. stands for Baptist Church